The New Age Dictionary

Also by Alex Jack

Poetry
Dragonbrood—An Epic of Vietnam and America

Prose
The Cancer-Prevention Diet
with Michio Kushi
Diet for a Strong Heart
with Michio Kushi
Aveline Kushi's Complete Guide to Macrobiotic Cooking
with Aveline Kushi
Macrobiotic Diet
with Michio and Aveline Kushi
The Book of Macrobiotics
with Michio Kushi
One Peaceful World
with Michio Kushi

Biography
Promenade Home:
Macrobiotics and Women's Health
with Gale Jack
Aveline:
The Life and Dream of the Woman Behind Macrobiotics Today
with Aveline Kushi

Thrillers
The Adamantine Sherlock Holmes:
The Adventures in Tibet and India
The Adventure of the Bodhisattva's Hat:
An Inspector Ginkgo Mystery

Translation and Commentary
Food Governs Your Destiny:
The Teachings of Namboku Mizuno
with Michio and Aveline Kushi
Five Trees in Paradise:
The Teachings of Jesus in the Gospel of Thomas
with Michio Kushi

THE NEW AGE DICTIONARY

A Guide to Planetary Family Consciousness

Edited by Alex Jack

Japan Publications, Inc.

"Words have an ancestor,
and affairs a sovereign . . .
Bring it about that the people
will return to the use of plain words,
Will find relish in their food
And beauty in their clothes,
Will be content in their abode,
And happy in the way they live."
—Lao Tzu

In memory of my grandparents:
Alexander Jack 1878-1943
Celelia Davis Jack Hecht 1886-1976
David Rhys Williams 1890-1970
Lucy Adams Pease Williams 1890-1969

Published by Japan Publications, Inc., Tokyo & New York

Distributors:
UNITED STATES: Kodansha International/USA, Ltd., through Farrar,
Straus & Giroux, 19 Union Square West, New York 10003. CANADA: Fit-
zhenry & Whiteside Ltd., 195 Allstate Parkway, Markham, Ontario, L3R
4T8. BRITISH ISLES AND EUROPEAN CONTINENT: Premier Book
Marketing Ltd., 1 Gower Street, London WC1E 6 HA. AUSTRALIA AND
NEW ZEALAND: Bookwise International, 54 Crittenden Road, Findon,
South Australia 5007. THE FAR EAST AND JAPAN: Japan Publications
Trading Co, Ltd., 1-2-1, Sarugaku-cho, Chiyoda-ku, Tokyo 101.

First Edition: October 1990
L.C.C.C. No. 89-63235
ISBN: 0-87040-787-2
Printed in the United States of America

How-To

biocracy   a form of society in which the
interrelation with the Earth is the context in which all social, political, and
economic decisions are made (Thomas
Berry)

main entry in bold face type

term coined by

translation in parentheses,
other languages in Italics

dhyana (jhana, *Pali*, Ch'an, *Chinese*,
Zen, *Japanese*) 'meditation', 1. one-
pointedness of mind; samadi. 2. wisdom, enlightenment (Sanskrit)

definitions in Roman type

literal meaning of term
within single quotation marks

language from which the word is derived
in parentheses at the end of the definition

Buscaglia, Leo (Dr. Love, Dr. Hug) psychologist and advocate of self-
affirmation; *Living, Loving, Learning*;
1925-

nickname or real name in parentheses
if known by a pen name or other name

major book, work of art,
or musical composition

date of birth and death

DA

Abbreviations:

A.D. Anno Domini	d. died
adj adjective	f. feminine
adv. adverb	int. interjection
b. birth	l.c. lower case letter
B.C. Before Christ	m. masculine
B.C.E. Before the Common Era	n. noun
B.P. Before the Present	pl. plural
c. century	sin. singular
ca. circa	tr. translator
cap. capital letter	v. verb
C.E. common era	? date probable or unknown

Alphabetization: entries are alphabetized according to a word-by-word method.

Arabic: There are six "throat" consonants, kh, gh, h, ' (a voiced pharyngeal fricative), h, ' (the glottal stop or as lengthener of short a), and several emphatic consonants, t, d, s, z. The three vowels, a, i, u, have both long and short varieties.

Chinese: In 1958 the National People's Congress approved the phonetic scheme of annotating Chinese characters called Hanyu pinyin, and in 1976 China officially introduced a Romanized script in Sinkiang Uighur. Ultimately, the Chinese plan to convert all written Chinese from a vocabulary of 50,000 different ideographs to the Western-style alphabet over the next several generations. Pinyin differs significantly from previous systems, such as the Wade, on which most of the Chinese words in English language books are based. The major differences are noted below and should be consulted for accurate pronunciation. The Taoist classic, *Tao Te Ching*, for example, would be spelled and pronounced *Dao De Jing* under the new method. Most Chinese words in this volume are drawn from sources using the older methods.

Peking	Wade	Peking	Wade	Peking	Wade
b	p	j	ch	t	t'
c	ts', tz'	k	k'	ue	we
ch	ch'	ong	ung	x	hs
d	t	p	p'	z	ts,tz
er	erh	q	ch'	zh	ch
g	kj	r	j		

Dates: Ancient dates are indicated by a minus (-) sign before the date, by B.C. (Before Christ), B.C.E. (Before the Common Era), or B.P. (Before the Present). Modern dates are indicated by A.D. or C.E. (Common Era). When dates are unknown the nearest century is given, except in the case of twentieth century figures where this is left blank.

Definitions: Words are recorded as generally used, although usage varies widely according to various traditions and the evolving nature of the language. When a word has been introduced by a group, or coined by an individual, the origin is noted in parentheses at the end of the word.

Etymology: The language of origin (if other than English) is indicated at the end of the entry in parentheses. The literal meaning of an entry is indicated at the beginning of a definition with single quotation marks.

Hebrew: In various Romanization systems, b and v are often interchanged, as are h and ch, v and w, y and j and i, k and kh, and p and f.

Inflections: Alternative spellings are indicated at the beginning of a definition in parentheses. Inflections of major entries are indicated in bold face type within the definition by part of speech and generally are not defined further.

Japanese: The major Romanization system is pronounced phonetically as in English. In general, however, vowels are much shorter than English, especially u and i after voiceless consonants, although there are long vowels as well. Words are spoken with even stress and rhythm.

Names and Nationalities: People are indexed according to surname, pen name, spiritual name, or other name generally observed or recognized by. Honorary titles, such as Pir, Venerable, Thich, Guru, and the like, should be disregarded in looking up an entry. However, in the event that the entire name is an adopted one, look up the initial word, e.g., Ram Dass is located under R. Chinese, Japanese, Korean, Vietnamese, and Arabic surnames precede the given names in ordinary usage. In Arabic, *al* and *ya* before an entry are generally ignored in alphabetizing, and *ibn* and *el* (son and daughter of) are heeded. Original names, nicknames, and diminutives are noted in parentheses at the beginning of a biographical entry. Land or region of birth is noted whenever possible, except for Americans.

Pronunciation: Except in rare instances and for a few general guidelines noted in this section under individual languages, pronunciation is beyond the scope of this work.

Sanskrit: Words are generally unaccented or spoken with a slight stress on the penultimate syllable. Consonants with an h after them (aspirants) are stressed more heavily than in English. S and sh are commonly interchanged in various Romanization methods (e.g., Siva or Shiva), as are v and w, o and au.

Spanish: Pronounce j as h, e.g., Navajo.

Spelling: There are many difficulties in transliterating words of foreign origin into English. Some languages have nearly twice as many letters as the Roman alphabet and express sounds not found in English. Scholars generally employ diacritical marks to approximate sounds in the original, but do not always agree on which Romanization method to follow. For daily practice and usage, many Far Eastern, South Asian, and Middle Eastern words relating to meditation, healing, and the spiritual sciences are passing directly into Engish, however Procrustian its twenty-six letters, just as many Greek and Latin terms relating to medicine, law, and the physical sciences passed into English at an earlier era. It is beyond the scope of this volume to pass judgment on which Romanization method is preferable or present a uniform listing. General spelling variations are noted in the how-to section under the individual languages.

Tibetan: There are many Romanization systems in use. In current Lhasa dialect, q is pronounced g, qh as k, k as g, pa as b, c as j, ts as dds, and t as d.

Typeface. Entries are indicated in bold face type; definitions in Roman; and works of art, music, literature, and film in italics. Inflections are indicated by bold face within definitions.

The Song of the Earth
Introduction to the New Age Dictionary
Second Edition

There have been many changes in the fifteen years since *The New Age Dictionary* first appeared. Just in the last few months, there has been a mental and spiritual axis shift in planetary consciousness as we entered the last decade of the century. The Berlin Wall has tumbled down, authoritarian regimes on the left and right have crumbled, and Earth Day has become the biggest holiday on the planet. The explosion of interest in the New Age has reached into the White House and Kremlin—the proverbial last to know. In a recent speech, George Bush proclaimed "a New Age of Freedom" between East and West. Hare Krishnas, among other beneficiaries of *glasnost*, danced before Soviet President Gorbachev at this spring's May Day parade in Moscow.

Whether the euphoria over the thawing of the Cold War lasts, it is clear that the New Age is less an event than a process. Post-industrialist Alvin Toffler calls it the Third Wave; futurist Hazel Henderson, the Solar Age. John Naisbitt and Yoneji Masuda speak of the Information Age; physicist Fritjof Capra, the Turning Point. Pierre Teilhard de Chardin described it as the Noosphere— or envelope of widening cosmic consciousness surrounding the Earth. Scientist James Locklock terms the current epoch in which the planet is viewed as a living entity as the Age of Gaia after the ancient Greek Goddess of the Earth. With his usual clarity and simplicity, macrobiotic educator Michio Kushi speaks of the coming Era of Humanity. The New Age, however it is described, is not so much a time as a state of mind. It would appear that modern civilization, after the adolescent binges of the last three or four centuries, finally has grown up and decided to settle down and live peacefully with other species of life as inhabitants of a common planet.

In preparing the new edition, I gradually came to realize that this chronicle is not an English but a planetary dictionary. True, the *lingua franca* of the modern world rests on a scaffold of English—the language of international travel and business. But increasingly, thousands of spiritual, psychological, and ecological terms are entering the common vocabulary drawn from Sanskrit, Chinese, Tibetan, Japanese, Arabic, and dozens of bioregional tongues such as Sioux, Yoruba, and Gaelic.

In centuries past, Greek and Latin dominated English and other European languages. An estimated 40 percent of ordinary dictionary entries are made up of scientific, medical, and technical terms drawn primarily from classical roots. *The New Age Dictionary* is unique in that it presents thousands of Oriental, Middle Eastern, African, Latin American, and Native American concepts, expressions, and references that are moving into planetary discourse. The language that will emerge from this global data bank in the next century will be a true marriage of East and West, North and South, as the techno-scientific babble of the present century is balanced by the eco-spiritual terminology of the past/future.

In the last decade and a half, my own work as a writer and teacher have taken me back/forward toward the discovery/rediscovery of the ancient/future spiritual One World in which a common language may have unified/may reunify the Earth. Much of this material has been developed and presented by Michio Kushi in his Spiritual Development Seminars at the Kushi Institute of the Berkshires, where I have been teaching the last several years. In that age of Lost Paradise, the form and content of words were one. Sounds conveyed a universal meaning grounded in natural order. Words carried a quantum of healing energy and vibration accessible to all. Whether living on the equator or the arctic, the savannah or the mountains, people could intuitively understand each other because they were living and eating in harmony with their environment and receiving more ki, or natural electromagnetic energy, of the Milky Way, which was directly overhead at that time owing to the precessional change. Let's look at several examples:

• *A* is the most yin (open, expanded) sound, signifying God, One Infinity, spirit, energy as wave. *M* is the most yang (closed, contracted) sound, signifying physicalization, matter, energy as particle. *U* is inbetween, more balanced. AUM (aka OM) the traditional Sanskrit chant composed of these three sounds, represents the journey from the infinite to the phenomenal world, from *A* to

M. By chanting this sound, we activate all parts of our mind/body (the spiritual channel, chakras, meridians, organs, tissues and cells) and harmonize with the universe as a whole.

• Another basic sound is MA. This sound signifies the journey from the world of manifestation back to the world of the unmanifest. It is the universal sound that babies make when they are born. As Michio says, mothers around the world think their infants are calling them when they cry MA MA. Actually, they are proclaiming the desire to return to their eternal spiritual home. (Most of us lose this memory by age two or three after being exposed to 28 flavors of ice cream, 35 cable TV channels, and 52 running shoes.)

• In the world of sound, L represents the spiral, the comprehensive pattern of life that underlies everything from galaxies to atoms, from the structure of the human body to the unfolding pattern of history. The traditional Islamic name of God—ALLAH—represents a descent from the unlimited world of spirit (A) to the spirallic world of manifestation (L) and then an ascent back to the absolute world (A).

• Tens of thousands of years ago, when the world was one, human beings built large mountains and buildings to collect, store, and transmit ki from Heaven and Earth for agriculture, transportation, and healing. These places were known by the ancient words PI (High), RA (Energy), MI (Storage), TO (Place)—or pyramids.

The healing power of sound is intuitively felt by most people today in that other common tongue—the kingdom of music. Around the world, rock bands reign supreme over billions of subjects worshipping CDs and Walkmans, stereos and boom boxes. Musicians serve as cultural arbiters for everything from endorsing soda pop to ending world hunger, from merchandizing designer jeans to saving the rain forests. Once in awhile, a consummate artist such as John Lennon, John Denver, or Kitaro comes along whose music mirrors natural order and begins to ground and awaken everyone who hears it. But chaos and disorder are still the general rule, within ungrounded New Age music especially. As we return to a more balanced way of life and rediscover our common dream of a healthy, peaceful planet, a new form of goverance will emerge. The politics of the future will not be the electronic town meeting (computerized ballot box) but planetary family councils (similar to the Councils of All Beings envisioned by deep ecologist John Seed) in which wise children, adults, and elders meet, representing not only human beings, but also voicing the concerns of the ozone layer, mountains, forests, watersheds, spotted owls, red squirrels, humpbacked whales, Hopi blue corn, and other plant and animal life. In form, these councils may resemble the ancient Celtic perpetual choirs and Chinese dynasties which ruled by musical ceremonies and pageants based on harmonizing earthly music and discourse with celestial order, seasonal change, and cycles of planting and harvest.

At a personal level, this enchantment begins with living in balance with our environment. By eating simply and harmonizing with the stars overhead and the flowers and seeds below, we discover our true dream in life. We find that our originality—the unique individual melody of our life—is actually the Song of the Earth being sung through us. It is the flute of Krishna and Kokopelli, the Circle of the Dance depicted on Achilles's Shield, the Music of the Spheres lifting Dante and Beatrice in Paradise.

Many of the new entries in this edition of *The New Age Dictionary* have been derived from the teachings and writings of the planet's deepest contemporary thinkers: Michio and Aveline Kushi, George Ohsawa, Carl Jung, Pierre Teilhard de Chardin, Robert Bly, Gary Snyder, Riane Eisler, Joseph Campbell, Marija Gumbutas, Krishnamurti, Starhawk, the Dalai Lama, James Lovelock, Frances Moore Lappe, Thomas Berry, Hazel Henderson, Wendell Berry, and Charlene Spretnak, to name a few. As editor of the *East West Journal* in the late 70s and early 80s, I was privileged to meet, interview, and edit some of these luminaries. Other entries come from holistic publications including *New Age Journal, Whole Earth Review, Yoga Journal, Utne Reader, New Frontier, Gnosis, ReVision, Critique, Mother Earth News, Not Man Apart, Greenpeace, In Context, Vegetarian Times, Solstice, Body/Mind/Spirit, Earth Star, Many Hands, Spectrum, New Realities, Chrysalis, Parabola, Shaman's Drum, E,* and *Noetic Sciences Review.* Other entries were obtained from questionnaires sent out to scores of intentional communities, New Age publishers, record companies, and other organizations.

Altogether between three and four thousand new or updated entries were collected and integrated with the ten thousand terms in the first edition. Thanks to computer technology, the original listings could be scanned and put on disk without retyping and the new references inputed and merged on a Macintosh SE. From Microsoft Word, the entries were then flowed into pages and columns formatted by Ready/Set/Go, a desktop publishing program. After some minor adjustments for ASCII, the universal computer text file language, the references were sorted, edited, revised, and otherwise massaged several times. As in most dictionaries, the entries far exceeded the publisher's allotted space. Ultimately about 2500 (mainly more esoteric) terms were deleted—but not lost in electronic hyperspace. They were saved on disk and will be made available as part of an Unabridged New Age Data Base to anyone who wishes to have access to them. (See the Resource section at the end of the book for details.) The net result is that this edition contains about fifty percent new material.

The editor is grateful to his family, friends, and associates for their help in this project. Mr. Iwao Yoshizaki and Mr. Yoshiro Fujiwara, president and vice president of Japan Publications, originally suggested that a new edition of the dictionary be prepared for the 1990s, and for their encouragement and support I am thankful. My mother, Esther, a librarian at Brookline High School, assisted in updating hundreds of biographical entries. Without her help, I would still be minding the P's and Q's. My wife, Gale, an excellent writer and editor as well as cook and nurturer, proofread the end result and helped me withdraw emotionally from many obscure items. Unlike Dr. Strong, the eccentric dictionary-maker in *David Copperfield* who went around with citation slips sticking out of his hat and who proceeded at a pace that would enable him to finish his work by the next millennium, the revision of *The New Age Dictionary* proceeded relatively quickly (less than a year). I am grateful to Michio and Aveline Kushi, my associates on the faculty of the Kushi Institute, and my students for their inspiration, insights, and clarity of expression in our common pursuit of the truths of life. As the *I Ching* observes, learning in a community of congenial friends is a refreshing and vitalizing force.

Finally, to the reader I would be grateful for your reflections on this work. Ultimately, as Samuel Johnson noted, the test of any dictionary is whether it is useful—simple, clear, and practical. I would appreciate hearing from you and receiving your comments and suggestions for new entries and listings in the next edition. By then, let us hope that planetary family consciousness (seeing everyone as brothers and sisters of one healthy, peaceful world) will have taken further root and that the Song of the Earth will have begun to form in every heart and tongue.

Alex Jack
One Peaceful World Village
Becket, Massachusetts
May, 1990

Language and the New Age
Introduction to the New Age Dictionary
First Edition

Between the Atlantic and Pacific is rising an invisible continent of millions of people who do not look to the White House, the public schools, the medical profession, or the armed forces for any guidance whatsoever in their lives. It is a generation that looks to the wisdom of the North American Indian past rather than the Revolution of 1776. In fact, as members of this generation learn to grow their own food, heal their own bodies, and become their own spiritual guides, the geographic space that they occupy is frequently referred to by its traditional Indian name: Turtle Island; and the historical current with which it most identifies is commonly called, in the words of Gary Snyder, the Great Subculture, whose roots stretch back to the Paleolithic.

The New Age is not exclusively a North American development. The Soviet Union—the heartland of dialectical materialism—is on the planetary forefront of psychotronics, cosmobiology, telepathy, and extraterrestrial communication. To the East, China is rediscovering her roots. Acupuncture, Tai-Chi, and herbal medicine are now actively promoted by the state.

The developing noospheric consciousness is attributed by some to the cuspal juncture of Pisces and Aquarius. The mandalized cultures of the just ending 2,160-year cycle—in Mesoamerica, Africa, Asia, the Pacific Island, North America, and, most recently, Tibet — have been shattered and scattered. In turn, the unknown invaders from across the waters, beyond the mountains, or out of the skies have fashioned psychic structures and boundaries to their technological cosmoses, which are dissolving at the end of the precessional epoch also.

The interface of the Old and New Ages manifests itself in unprecedented planetary strife, as well as worldwide sightings of UFOs, prophecies of rising continents and sinking coastlines, miracle drugs, pop religions, and instant panaceas of all kinds. The cultic, occult, and cataclysmic movements associated with the Warring States in ancient China, Hellenistic Rome, and Dark Ages Europe represented a similar stirring up of the planetary unconscious prior to the dawn of a new, conscious order.

Concomitant with the apocalyptic theme felt so widely at present is a yearning for the Golden Ages of the past. In a scientific culture increasingly growing aware of its imbalance, there is a natural yearning for the traditional cultures displaced by modern civilization and for the renaissance epochs of the past: ancient Egypt; Stonehenge; the high Inca, Maya, and Tibetan cosmologies; T'ang Dynasty China; Puranic and Gupta India; the Arabian Nights realm of Haran al-Rashid; the Heinan and Kamakura periods in Japan; Meroe and other black African cultures; Thomas More's *Utopia* and the communal movements of the eighteenth and nineteenth centuries. There are also many exponents of the projected future science-fiction paradises of our own cinematic and comic book era.

> *The call from the Cosmic Heart is vibrating*
> *throughout the Earth, the New Age is here, and*
> *the Spiritual vibrations are refreshing the earth*
> *and all living things.* — Elizabeth Delvine King,
> The Higher Metaphysics (1918)

In the constellation of Golden Ages, the New Age is still only a luminous speck. Yet like all star systems, the New Age manifests a triple form: 1) a distant outer halo, 2) an intermediate disk, and 3) an inner nucleus. On the outermost level of our sunseed, that of the halo, like far-distant planets and comets, orbit the Hopi; the Iroquois Five Nations; pilgrim dissidents; the Shakers, Quakers, and Mormons; Afro-American culture bearers; the Plains Indians; the abolitionists; the utopian, anarchist, and socialist experimentors; feminists; unionists; pacifists; and natural foods pioneers.

Further in, at the disk of the sunseed, the major planets of East West synthesis include the Transcendentalists Thoreau and Emerson, the arrival of Vedanta and Zen in the West at the World Parliament of Religions in Chicago in 1893 through the remarkable pilgrimages of Swami Vivekenanda and Abbot Soyen Shaku, and a myriad of cross-pollinating movements in the twentieth century from Eyptology to Baha'i, from Rosicrucianism to macrobiotics, from Gurdjieff's teachings to Dane Rudhyar's, from Paramahansa Yogananda to Alan Watts, from the Beats to the Flower Generation, from the Findhorn community to Naropa Institute.

At the innermost level, the nucleus of the sunseed, a feminine consciousness patiently works to bring a holistic era into fruition. Three remarkable women, Helena Blavatsky, Annie Besant, and Alice Bailey, recognized themselves as midwives of the New Age. Together with other far-seeing women—Corinee Heline, Joan Grant, Maria Corelli, Diane Fortune, Mabel Collins, to name just a few—they broke the ground for the creation of a new order based on total equality of the sexes within a framework of group consciousness and enlightened cooperation. These women are truly the soul of the New Age, and their teachings are becoming rediscovered after decades of relative obscurity. With the rise of the women's movement, the Mother Goddess is reawakening in the West after a Piscean age of slumber.

> It's good for a young person to work at McDonald's. It makes you an efficient person. If you make the wrong size hamburger, you get fired. It's a smooth-running machine that the Army should emulate. — General Creighton Abrams, U.S. Supreme Commander in Vietnam (1975)

> South Vietnam's revolutionary government is seeking economic independence through a healthy and simple way of life and in Saigon recently opened a public-operated restaurant based upon macrobiotic principles which serves grains and vegetables....The female chairperson of the People's Revolutionary Committee . . . said, "The purpose of this restaurant is to further the peoples' health through the most simple and reasonable method." — Mainichi Shinbun (Dec. 17, 1975)

Despite rich antecedents, the counterculture remains largely unaware of its heritage. At the popular level, the New Age is perceived as the organic successor to the Vietnam peace movement of the 1960s. Though largely superficial, the connections merit reflection, as many persons, young and old, measure their own growth and self-development around events of this period. The analogy between attitudes toward food and toward warfare became readily apparent at this time as many young men facing the draft and those in the military began to feel like "cattle led to the slaughter," "raw meat on the hoof," or "cannon fodder." At the most elemental level, it was a time of eat or be eaten. The direct connection between the quality of a nation's diet and its aggressiveness was not widely recognized here. The Zen monks and nuns of Vietnam, however when asked by reporters (such as myself) "When will the war end?", replied, "When people stop eating animal food."

As the Southeast Asian war ended, it was a brief quantum leap from concern over the quantity of bodies drafted to the quality and health of those bodies in peacetime. Who had control over the foods and medicines on the market? The villain of Act I, the military-industrial complex, was replaced in Act II by agribusiness. In the early 1970s, as people took stock of their lives and reflected on the turmoil of the 1960s, they began to analyse the relationship between food and foreign policy. They discovered how America imports oil from the Third World to fuel its industrial economy and a chemicalized, high-technology agricultural system, and, in return, exports famine and illness.

The successful effort of tiny Vietnam to survive computerized bombs and chemical defoliants inspired many Westerners to study Oriental philosophy and medicine. They discovered that a deep relationship to food was the foundation of traditional South Asian and Far Eastern cultures. The central theme of the *Vedas*, the *Upanishads*, and the *Bhagavad Gita* (from which comes the aphorism "You are what you eat") is eating simply, appreciating the continual sacrifice of life on all levels of the food chain, and understanding the intimate connection between physical and spiritual nourishment. From China's Shang Dynasty, celebrated for its incomparable bronze ritual cooking vessels, comes the *I Ching*, which chronicles the correspondences between human thoughts and the seasons, unconscious impulses and the underlying rhythms of the cosmos.

The *I Ching*, originally an oracle based on the manipulation of fifty yarrow stalks, symbolized the transition from a divinatory system based on meat eating and animal sacrifice to one of a vegetable and grain quality. Yet even among the Paleolithic hunting cultures, shamanistic ritual focused on the voluntary sacrifice of the animal for the welfare of the tribe. Whether on the North American plains or the North Indian vale, nomadic people entered into deep relationships with the souls of the animals they hunted; meditation and yoga are believed to have evolved from these relationships.

Food's mystical ramifications include not only quiet, motionless sitting (to woo the spirit of the animal into sacrificing itself) but also the scope and power of language (to communicate with the heavenly creator and celebrate the hunt or harvest). For in addition to being the vehicle of ingestion, the mouth is also the vehicle of speech. It is essential that we keep this fundamental connection in mind when learning any language or using any dictionary.

Mythologically, the spiritual quest has often been symbolized by special foods: the apple of the Garden of Eden, the Golden Apples of the Hesperides, manna in the *Bible*, soma in the *Vedas*, mangoes in Indian folklore, the Peaches of Immortality among the Chinese. Interestingly, several of these key words for the Absolute are also sacred foods. For example, in Hindi, *Aum* (Om) means mango as well as the mystical sound, and in Chinese *tao* means peace as well as the ineffable way. *Siddartha*, the given name of the Buddha, is usually translated by moderns scholars as "he who attains his undertakings" although the word also means mustard seed, an herb that figures prominently in the wisdom literature of both East and West.

Curiously, if not synchronistically, the close connection between language and food was demonstrated when unforeseen difficulties arose in typesetting this book. In the heat and humidity of the summer [1976], the entire end of the alphabet, from U-Z, and parts of several other letters had to be entirely reset as the galleys began to fade in the absence of thorough air-conditioning and dehumidification. The dilemma was finally resolved by storing the remaining galleys in the refrigerator between the tofu and the mango chutney.

The general debasement of language during the 20th century—from Hitler's "final solution" to Lyndon Johnson's "pacification" of Vietnam—coincides with the widespread introduction of processed and artificial food over the same period.

> The New Age is not going to be built out of bailing wire and string. It's going to take a lot of very clear thinking. — John Todd, New Alchemy Institute

On the road to taking control over their lives after the war in Southeast Asia, many people (whatever their path) discovered that eating well was square one. In just a few short years, a natural foods movement developed around a tasty, simple, complete, and inextensive diet based on whole grains, seasonal fruits and vegetables, and unsweetened beverages and deserts that required no exotic imports or esoteric cooking skills. The results were evident, joyful, and long-lasting. Applying this empirical approach to other areas of life, these New Age pioneers developed housing communes, food coops, crafts collaboratives, free schools, holistic clinics, movement and dance centers, small presses—the list is endless.

Whenever the Aquarian Age actually commences—and calculations span from A.D. 1600 to 2300—astrologers generally agree that it will reach a peak about one thousand years from now. While the ultimate social, political, and technological contours of that day remain as misty as Venus's surface atmosphere, seed projects and communities such as the New Alchemy Institute, Arcosanti, Auroville, the Farm, Findhorn, Lima, Lindisfarne, Taize, and Twin Oaks indicate that after decades of consumerism and alienation, people can relearn how to live cooperatively and prosper.

Language is perhaps one of the simplest ways to measure the current levels of whole earth consciousness. Three key words that can be used to distinguish the New Age from the Old are *food*, *peace*, and *cancer*.

1. Are we conscious of food? Do we see a connection between the quality of our daily food and our way of life? Do we act on a connection between our diet and the pattern of global hunger and oppression of the animals? Do we see ourselves as part of nature or separate from it?

2. Are we at peace? Do we see peace as something more than the cessation of hostilities or absence of conflict? Do we see peace as the harmonious, natural state of human beings joyfully sharing their lives with one another? Do we experience peace as inner calm, the stillness of heart and mind toward which all things flow?

3. Do we see cancer as a dreadful scourge that must be wiped out by scientific holy war? Or do we see cancer as the natural, healthy reaction of the body to localize toxins after years of dietary or environmental abuse? Do we agree with Ivan Illich that "American Cancer Society proclamations that cancer is curable and progress has been made are reminiscent of Vietnam optimism prior to the deluge" (*East West Journal*, March, 1976)? Can we prevent or recover from cancer by simple methods of self-healing, or will we submit ourselves to the surgical altars of high technology?

The New Age Dictionary strives to focus on the three levels of consciousness, inner peace, and unity of mind, body, and spirit. And since our generation is but a leaf on the great tree of life, it is not surprising that the vast majority of words in this book stretch back centuries, to the traditional cultures whose periods of harmonious living are enshrined in our dreams and myths. However far out on a limb certain disciplines today might seem, chances are they ultimately connect with the main branches of the great tree, which include Shamanism, Taoism, Shinto, Buddhism, Hinduism, Judeo-Christianity (including Marxism and psychoanalysis), and Islam. Among the tens of thousands of words employed in these traditions, *The New Age Dictionary* includes several thousand of those frequently encountered in traditional literature, history, and scripture. Definitions are as concise as possible, to allow the reader or writer to place a given word in general context. There are many fine specialized reference works already available, but most of us do not need nine-tenths of the information found in these tomes. *The Buddhist Encyclopedia*, published by the government of Sri Lanka, for example, includes 1272 pages just for words beginning with the letter A! On the other hand, this book is only a beginning in the direction of unifying humanity's rich and rewarding heritage. Areas of spelling standardization, pronunciation, etymology, and general comprehensiveness leave much to be desired. Yet until something better like a *Sitter's Guide to Kalpic Literature* comes along, it is hoped that this volume will prove a reliable guide to many of the key concepts of East and West. It would require substantial study and reflection to intuit the inner meaning of many of the words listed here, of course. Defining *dharma*, for instance, may justly be said to be the central theme of the *Mahabharata*, the great India epic of twenty five hundred years ago (eighteen volumes in English translation) of which the *Bhagavad Gita* is a small episode.

Although a mandala includes both positive and negative energies, mythological, fictional, and biographical entries in this edition have been limited largely to peacemakers, visionaries, and teachers. A wide selection of comic book and science-fiction characters has been included, as these art forms are truly a New Age phenomenon, whose roots can be found in the origins of tribal culture—that far distant time when human beings first became conscious of themselves as storytellers on this planet.

> Dictionaries are like watches: the worst is better than none, and the best cannot be expected to go quite true. — Samuel Johnson, <u>Words and Dictionaries</u>

Despite—and because of—the wide spectrum of entries, there are undoubtedly errors of fact and judgment in this books, as well as gaps. Scribes and lexicographers are known for perpetuating errors and transmitting prejudiced cultural values down through the centuries. One of the most glaring examples of this was pointed out in a recent issue of *Vegetarian World*:

"The Brotherhood of Buddha, an international vegetarian religious order, is calling American scholars to task for repeatedly lending currency to the erroneous story about the death of the founder of Buddhism.

"The latest offense, according to the Brotherhood, is in the *Funk & Wagnall's New Encyclopedia*, a 27-volume low-priced book set recently sold widely through American supermarkets. The article asserts that Buddha died from the effects of eating contaminated pork.

"A spokesman for the order says 'Gautama Buddha' was a scrupulous vegetarian. The pork story started with a bad translation of the original Pali language in which Buddha's thoughts were first written. The word 'truffle', a mushroom gathered by trained pigs, was incorrectly rendered 'pig flesh' instead of 'pig-found flesh'. Choking on or eating poisoned mushrooms, accordingly, was what really led to Buddha's tragic death in about his 80th year."

Curiously, another well-known transcribing error concerns the Buddha. In the Middle Ages, tales of a saintly Eastern monarch named King Josapahat reached Europe. After determining that this altruistic Christian sovereign of a far-distant Asian land merited renown, the Vatican formally canonized him in the 14th century. Many centuries later, with the development of modern linguistics, it was discovered that *Josaphat* was none other than a corrupt translation of *Bodhisattva*. One of the great ironies of East-West history is that the Buddha is a recognized saint of the Roman Catholic Church.

The presence of errors such as these in contemporary reference books was one of the impetuses behind creating the current volume. Another was the difficulty of finding many contemporary words in standard dictionaries. With the rise of the counterculture, reference publishers have included a sprinkling of New Age terms in their offering. *6000 Words*, the 1961-76 supplement to *Webster's Third International*—the platinum meter rod of the English language, American style—includes a variety of terms from Eastern and Western wisdom traditions and from the counterculture, but these entries invariably sound stale and undigested. In some cases there are totally incorrect, and when it comes to food, a false defintion is dangerous to your health:

> *macrobiotics adj: of, relating to, or being an extremely*
> *restricted diet (as one containing cheifly whole*
> *grains) that is usually undertaken by its advocates*
> *to promote health and well-being although it may*
> *actually be deficient in essential nutrients (as*
> *fats).* — Webster's 6000 Words (1976)

Webster's 1976 edition, it might be noted, refers to all black people in its listings as *Negroes*, all definitions are written exclusively with masculine pronouns, and there is a surfeit of terms from professional sports, pornography, and warfare; so to single out its treatment of natural foods is to do an injustice to the book as a whole.

In volumes such as this, New Age and traditional entries, if any, appear as after-thoughts, like the natural lines many agribusiness corporations and food processors add to their regular artificial markets to capture a share of the alternative community. The generally lamentable state of English language dictionaries has been described succinctly by Swami Rama: "If we ask any teachers or any university professors to tell us the meaning of 'meditation,' they will have to go to consult their dictionaries. And do you know what is the definition of meditation there? The definition of meditation is contemplation, and the definition of contemplation is meditation, so there is no explanation at all. . . . The meaning of the word meditation has not been explained anywhere in the English language."

In this void, clearly what has been needed is a single-volume reference, a simple, practical, and comprehensive guide to the words, people, places, and historical roots of the New Age—a volume that the Sufi poets of old would have termed the *Glossary of Glossaries*.

The *I Ching* speaks of the Ten Thousand Things to symbolize the universe, the phenomenal world of endless forms and ideas that delight the mind and senses. There is a danger that the nearly ten thousand entries in this volume may add to our knowledge, but substract from our wisdom. As Robert Bly pointed out in *East West Journal* (August, 1976), it is important to create one's own language, rather than just accept "received language." The example he used was Jung's phrase the "collective unconscious." "When you talk about Jung's ideas, it's important never to say the phrase 'collective unconscious'. That's his phrase. You must make up one for the same experience. Call it 'the great lake.' If you're an earth type, call it the 'granite magma layer'. If you're an air type, call it 'the beehive of thoughts'. Ask your own psyche to rise, and slowly eat the phrase, and change it as it wishes."

The ultimate dictionary—and language—is one that transcends itself. The American Indians, people of few words and much silence, have no word for *religion*, because they do not see it as something different from their daily life. Traditional vocabularies are often extremely limited and written alphabets nonexistent, yet they reflect a culture in harmony with nature to an extent only dreamed of by literate societies. In editing this volume, the flood of so many occult terms prompted me to want to abandon the whole project and to redefine common, simple everyday things in a new light. In fact, one of the examples I was thinking of, *tree*, was singled out in an identical manner in an inspiring article "Evolving a New Language" by Francois Duquesne in *One Earth*, the new journal of the Findhorn community in Scotland: "The major change will be in the depth of meaning we give to the words we use as symbols to clothe our thoughts and perceptions. The word 'tree', for instance, is just a symbol for a living being the intensity of whose aliveness is revealed according to the depth of our own perceptions. It may appear to us only as an object which can be quantified and categorized according to its height, colour, shape, age and species; or it may burst into life full of sentience, intelligence, beauty and language. The tree has not changed, nor has the symbol, only our consciousness and the depth of our perception."

What turns language will take in the New Age are not clear. Creation of, or return to, a universal tongue with a simpler vocabulary is one possibility. The development of a rich metalinguistic Glass Bead Game is another. Telepathic communication, learning the language of birds, animals, and plants, and the applications of mantras to psychotronic energy systems are further possibilities.

I shall conclude these reflections on language and the New Age by describing a dream I had this spring while working on this volume. Dream symbols are the language of the psyche and often express more clearly realities which words can only point to. Indeed, ths dream dealt directly with themes of reconciling spirit and matter, individual freedom and group consciousness, and the difference between esoteric, abstract pursuits and common, everyday events in a way that written or spoken words could never do.

In the dream, I was attending a dance exhibition in a large tent with numerous people. A Sufi or yogi of radiant disposition was performing a whirling dance, casting off sheaths of his body to display ever more subtle veils of the soul. Many in the audience seemed hypnotized by this performance, but I felt generally turned off and resolved to leave. Suddenly, everyone fell prostrate to the ground, which vexed me all the more. Curious, I looked up to see what had interrupted this gathering and, in awe, beheld God Almighty watching over us from on high.

He had a long white beard, a crown on his head, long flowing robes, and was sitting on a bejeweled throne—a figure right out of the Bible, Blake's engravings, and a thousand and one evangelical broadcasts on the far end of the radio dial. I, too, instinctively fell immobile to the floor, as waves of blissful energy emanated from His presence to fill every corner of the tabernacle. In this hushed setting, God proceeded to narrate a wonderful history of the universe, taking special care to enumerate the plagues and pestilences regularly sent to humanity over the centuries as compensation for living inharmoniously with the rest of nature.

At each word God spoke (in a deep, resounding voice, of course), we were transported back in time to experience particular scourges: "And I send sandstorms . . . " and in a flash I was in the desert, sand blowing so thickly around me I couldn't breathe.

At length God explained that He was also the God of mercy, compassion, and forgiveness, and he bid us to get up off our knees, cooperate with one another, and celebrate life. Soon everyone had forgotten his or her earlier individualistic, highly esoteric preoccupations; all linked arms and formed a traditional circle dance. As we danced, waves of bliss from the throne intensified, and soon we were lost in pure ecstasy, the distinction between self and other melting away in radiant light.

Sometime during this dance, I woke up back on the earth plane, rooted to my bed by oceanic feelings of love from head to toe. It was several days before the visionary energy subsided, and I gravitated back to ordinary consciousness.

May you enjoy this book, and may it enjoy you.
May harmony flow from its use.
May the divine word resonate within all beings.
Save the whale.

Alex Jack
Marblehead, Massachusetts
August, 1976

Acknowledgments

The editor is grateful to the scribes of old who have bequeathed to us the vocabulary of their wisdom and to the lexicographers of the future who will pass along our own. For this project, I especially wish to thank Rev. Jitsudo Baran of the Zen Mission Society at Shasta Abbey for permission to reprint many Zen terms from *Zen Is Eternal Life* by Roshi Jiyu Kennett, Fritjof Capra, author of *The Tao of Physics*, for contributing terms relating to the new physics, Kit Kitterman and Jack Albert for materials relating to Alice Bailey, Lucy Stone and Simon Grimes of the Pansophic Institute for valuable African entries, Jeremiah Liebermann and Claude Stark for numerous books and suggestions.

Other individuals whose help I appreciate are Roshi Robert Aitken, David Blair, Jon E. Boys, Daniel Curzon, Samuel Bercholz, Larry Gara, Martha Honey, Richard Johnson, Karen Kaye, Bruce Kitchen, James Lampkin, Jay and Ricki Linksmar, Fran Macy, John B. Miller, Heid Morgan, Just Natural, Swami Savitri Priya, Noel Peattie, Audrey Royer, Russian Samarin, June Singer, Jane Storck, Frank V. Tiso, and Ann Fawcett.

I am grateful to all of the groups which contributed original entries for this volume: Alcheringa • Amidst the Paradox • Ananda Marga • Ananda Meditation Retreat and Cooperative Village • Archaeus Project • Association for the Understanding of Man • Atmaniketan Ashram • AUM Esoteric Study Center • Center for Hypnosis Training and Consultation • Church of Scientology • Claymont Society for Continuous Education • CSA • Dena Foundation • Dialogue House and Associates • Eckankar • Esalen Institute • est • Fransisters and Brothers • Gay Sunshine • General Psionics Triad • Health Research • Heartsong Review • Hering Family Health Clinic • Himalayan Institute • International Buddhist Meditation Center • International Community of Christ • International Society for Krsna Consciousness • Institute for the Study of Nonviolence • Institute of Mentalphysics • Integral Yoga Institute • Intuitus • Jain Meditation International Center • Khaneghah and Maktab of Malekma Naseralishah • Koinonia Foundation • Kripalu Yoga Ashram • Kundalini Research Foundation • Kushi Institute • Le Centre du Silence • Lucis Trust • Mark-Age • Matagiri • New Age Press • Omega Institute • Pansophic Institute • Paruas Rajneesh Meditation Center • Polarity Health Institute • Psychosynthesis Institute of Palo Alto • Rainbow Family Tribe • Rosicrucian Fellowship • San Francisco Zen Center • Sikh Dharma Brotherhood • Sipapu • Sri Chinmoy Centers • Storefront Classroom Collective • Sufism Reoriented • Sufi Order • Survival Research Foundation • Synergos • Taoist Sanctuary • Twin Oaks • Universal White Brotherhood • White Lotus Study Center • Womanspirit Collective • Women's History Research Center • World Conference on Religion and Peace • Zen Mission Society

The editor is especially indebted to the many teachers, writers, and planetary thinkers whose work has enriched his own life and many of whose concepts and terms have been included in this volume.

He would also like to thank his associates at the *East West Journal*, especially Sherman Goldman, Leonard Jacobs, and Sandy MacDonald, for advice and encouragement; his landlady Mildred England who took an abiding interest in this project; and Rev. Robert Hill in whose refrigerator the galleys were kept during the summer to prevent fading.

Alas, it was not possible to include in the text every New Age organization, group, center, or individual who contributed entries to this project. For any errors of omission or commission, the editor alone is responsible and will strive to remedy them in future editions. — A.J.

Aa

A 1. the first letter; primary sound; a symbol of ultimate reality or inner nature. 2. sound that vibrates with One Infinity (Michio Kushi)

A Course in Miracles teachings of Jesus growing out of material psychically received by Helen Schucman from 1965-1972

A-frame cabin with a triangular front and back and a roof sloping to the ground like a capital A

A Land Ethic essay by Aldo Leopold in *A Sand County Almanac* that laid out the ethical principles governing human-Earth relations, 1949

aargh comic book exclamation of surprise or disgust

Aaron 'Exalted', Hebrew high priest, older brother of Moses (Hebrew)

Aaru heavenly fields (Egyptian)

ab heart (Egyptian)

Abbasids caliphate with capital at Baghdad, 750-1258

Abbey, Edward naturalist of the desert country of Utah and Arizona; *Down the River;* 1927-89

abductee someone taken aboard an UFO

Abehsera, Michel Morrocan-born Jewish and macrobiotic teacher; *Zen Macrobiotic Cooking*

abhidharma 'higher teaching', one of the three Baskets consisting of extensive expositions of Buddhist philosophy (Sanskrit)

abhimukhi facing directly the Buddha Mind; sixth stage of the bodhisattva path (Sanskrit)

abhisara defiance of custom and environment for the sake of the beloved (Sanskrit)

Abkhasians long-lived people in the Caucuses region, U.S.S.R.

Abnaki confederacy of Indian tribes in Maine, including the Malacites, Passamaquoddys, Penobscots

abosom 'children of Nyame', higher gods, tutelary spirits (Yoruba)

Abou ben Adhem prayerful hero of Leigh Hunt's poem of that name who finds his name in the book of those who love God

Abrams, Albert pioneer radiesthesiologist, inventor of the Abrams Box; d. 1922

abreaction the release of psychic tension through therapeutic resolution of a repressed experience

Absolute that which exists in and by itself, beyond name and form, without relation to anything else. 2. infinity. 3. the beyond, void out of which the material and spiritual worlds precede and return

Adi-Buddha.........Mahayana Buddhism
Brahman................................. Hinduism
Ceugant...................................... Welsh
Eyn Sof.................................. Kabbalah
Sunyata............... Mahayana Buddhism
Tao.........................Chinese philosophy

abu stone platform on Easter Island

Abu-Bakr friend, father-in-law, and first Caliph of Muhammad; 7th c.

Abul Abbas Kasim ibn Firnas Andalusian inventor who designed a flying machine; 9th c.

Abul Simbal Egyptian cliffside site of two temples by Pharoah Ramses II

Abulafia, Abraham Kabbalist and poet; *Alphabets and Music;* 1240-92

Abundant Life Seed Foundation seed bank, Port Townsend, Wash.

aburage deep-fried tofu (Japanese)

Abydos ancient town in Upper Egypt, site of pilgrimage to Osiris's grave

Abzug, Bella Congresswoman, feminist, peace activist; 1920-

acala immovable; eighth stage of the bodhisattva path (Sanskrit)

access opportunity, resources of knowledge, tools, education

acharya spiritual teacher or master; honorific title (Sanskrit)

Achilles's Shield shield made by Hephaestus for Achilles depicting Heaven and Earth and the four Ages of Humanity: 1) the Circle of Vintage and Harvest. 2) the Circle of Hunting. 3) the Circle of the Cities of War and Peace. 4) the Circle of the Dance (Homer)

acid LSD. **acid head** LSD user

acid rain acidic rainfall that causes damage to forests and fresh water lakes as the result of massive burning of nonrenewable fossil fuels, especially from driving automobiles, creating electricity, and industrial manufacturing

acid rock psychedelic music inspired by,

or similar to, an LSD trip

acidophilus (acidophilic) adj. affinity for an acid environment, e.g. yogurt

Acoma 'Sky City', pueblo of the Acoma Indians in New Mexico

acronychal adj. occurring at sunset

Acropolis sacred area in the center of a city-state reserved for the Gods

acrostic-telestic message conveyed simultaneously by reading down the letters at the beginning and end of the lines of a composition

actinism burns or other apparent changes on the skin after exposure to a UFO encounter

action contract agreement or personal affirmation based on a future act of power and beauty

Action for Children's Television militant mothers opposed to cereal and candy advertising on kids' TV programs

activate v. to energize, charge, make ki flow more active

active imagination symbols arising in dreams or fantasies from the unconscious depths (Jung)

actualization power social organization associated with gylany or a Goddess-centered culture (Riane Eisler)

acupoint point on the body treated by acupuncture or acupressure

acupressure (shiatsu, *Japanese*) healing art based on massage, stimulating the flow of life energy through the body

acupuncture healing art developed in China based on inserting needles in various parts of the body to relieve pain and release blocked life energy

Adam first man in Genesis

Adam Qadmon primordial man in the Kabbalah (Hebrew)

Adams, Henry historian who saw history as play of two forces: the Virgin and Dynamo; 1838-1918

Adams, Jane pacifist, founder of Hill House; 1860-1935

Adams, Richard English novelist; *Watership Down*; 1920-

Adamu the Babylonian-Sumerian designation for human species

adept spiritual master

adi first, primeval, the highest plane (Sanskrit)

Adi-Buddha first Buddha, primordial source of all beings (Sanskrit)

Adirondacks 'eaters of bark', peoples of the St. Lawrence River area who flavored their food with bark like porcu-

pines

Adler, Irene operatic contralto, Bohemian sweetheart of Sherlock Holmes

Adliparmiut Innuit afterlife realm of snow and ice, peace, and hunting

Admetos sixth Uranian planet ruling the womb, metamorphosis, development

adrenal glands endocrine glands located above the kidneys; physical counterpart of the third chakra

aduki (azuki) hard red bean from northern Japan (Japanese)

adult someone who can exist in the physical world without a lot of supportive devices (Jonas and Kline)

Advaita Vedanta nondualistic school of Hindu philosophy (Sanskrit)

Advaitin follower of Advaita Vedanta

adversity difficulties and obstacles that should be accepted with an open heart and without complaint of injustice and that enable one to enter the Path (Bodhidharma)

Adyar South Indian city, headquarters of the Theosophical Society

adytum inner shrine (Greek)

Aeoliah German-born New Age musician, *Crystal Illumination*

aeon eternal force that emanates from the first principle and inhabits the spiritual world in gnostic cosmology

Aerial Phenomena Research Organization file of reported UFO landings and aerial sightings maintained in Tucson, Arizona

aeroform organism living in outer space made of a subtle substance and having a strange form or shape

aerator device that attaches to the showerhead to reduce water flow and save energy

Affa 1. emptiness (Enochian). 2. UFO intelligence living on the planet Uranus who communicated with US armed forces investigators in 1959

affect-image archetype; the self-personification of an emotional complex

affectional adj. sexually oriented toward

affinities two beings who have shared many lifetimes (Rudolf Steiner)

affinity group social unit organized around something in common

affinity zone social unit of people whose philosophies are compatible and who get together socially or vocationally

affirmation a positive statement of being affirming or asserting something in order to help manifest it in the physical world

affliction unfavorable aspect in a horoscope that can be overcome with diligence

aflatoxin one of various mycotoxins that affect grains and other food adversely (from *Aspergillus flavus* toxin)

Africanus, Leo Granada-born explorer in the Sudan and author about Africa; 16th c.

Afro 1. natural curly black hairstyle. 2. prefix denoting black

Afro-Asiatic (Hamito-Semitic) language family of the Semitic, Berber, Chushitic, Egyptian, Chadic tongues

AFSC American Friends Service Committee; international Quaker relief and social action agency, 1917-

Aganippe fountain near Mt. Helicon sacred to the Muses (Greek)

Agape 1. Christian love. 2. fairy in Spenser's *Faerie Queene* (Greek)

Agapemone 'Abode of Love', English utopian community founded by Henry Prince, 1849

agar-agar a white gelatin processed from a sea vegetable into bars, flakes, or powder, and used in macrobiotic cooking to make kanten and vegetable aspics

agaric magic mushroom

age an astrological epoch, one-twelfth of the Sun cycle or precession of the equinoxes lasting 2160 years

Age of Perfect Virtue Taoist Golden Age

Age of the Yellow Ancestor mythical Golden Age in China

age regression recalling under hypnosis or in meditation events from one's present or past life

ageism discrimination or stereotyping based on age, especially old age

agent sender in telepathy tests

Ages of Humanity Golden Age followed by the Ages of Silver, Brass, Heroes, and Iron in Greek mythology (Hesiod)

Agharta subterranean world in Buddhist mythology (Sanskrit)

Agpaoa, Tony Phillipine healer and psychic surgeon

Agra North Indian city, site of the Taj Mahal

agribusiness network of monopolistic food processors, large chemicalized farms, and government regulatory agencies

agriculture (from 'to revolve' and 'to dwell') cultivation of land; to live and produce food and nourishment, taking care of the soil and the environment

Agrippa von Nettlesheim, Heinrich Cologne theologian and magus; *De Occulta philosophia*; 1486-1535

agroforestry using trees for agriculture and crop production

agrogeology 'growing from rocks', science of remineralizing the Earth from rock dust and other organic minerals

AH (anno Hegirae) after Muhammad's flight from Mecca to Medina in 622; start of the Islamic era (Latin)

Ahab captain of the *Pequod* in Melville's *Moby Dick*

aham I, ego (Sanskrit)

ahimsa noninjury, nonviolence, active love (Sanskrit)

Ahmadiyya Pakistani followers of the Mahdi who taught that Jesus survived the cross and went to Kashmir

Ahura Mazda Zoroastrian Creator

Aiaia Mediterranean isle of Circe the Sorceress in *The Odyssey*

AIDS (Acquired Immuno-Deficiency Syndrome) disease characterized by chronic lack of natural immunity to disease resulting from a long-time imbalance in the way of life, especially an unnatural modern way of eating high in saturated fat and cholesterol, animal protein, and sugar and low in whole grains and other complex carbohydrates; other risk factors include lack of breastfeeding, overmedication, abuse of drugs and alcohol, exposure to artificial electromagnetic radiation, use of electricity or microwave for cooking, promiscuous sexual behavior, and other lifestyle and environmental influences that cause a weakening in the blood and lymphatic system and lower the body's natural immunity to the AIDS virus

Aihara, Cornelia (Chiko Yokota) Japanese-born macrobiotic teacher; *Macrobiotic Kitchen*

Aihara, Herman Japanese-born macrobiotic teacher; *Learning from Salmon*

Aikido 'the way of unifying ki', martial art based on graceful spherical motion developed by Ueshiba, 1925-

AIM American Indian Movement founded by Russell Means, 1972-

Aim 1. 16th Hebrew letter: hearing, E, 70. 2. (l.c.) mantric seed syllable denoting Agni's consort (Sanskrit)

Ainu prehistoric light-featured people living in Hokkaido, Japan, who live by hunting, fishing, and bear worship

Aiolio Mediterranean island in *The Odyssey* where winds are kept in ox-skin sacks

air signs Gemini, Libra, Aquarius associated with mental energy

Airola, Paavo biochemist, nutritionist, naturopathic physician; *Are You Confused?*; 1915-87

Aitken, Robert Zen roshi, founder of the Diamond Sangha in Hawaii; 1917-

Aivanhov, Omraam Mikhael Bulgarian-born spiritual master; *The Second Birth*; 1900-86

Ajainin Indian priest from Lahore who became Jesus's disciple in Benares (*Aquarian Gospel*)

Ajanta Buddhist cave complex in West India, ca.-2-7th c.

ajapa mantra *soham* (I Am He); natural mantra produced by the breath, inhaling *so*, exhaling *ham* (Sanskrit)

ajari Shugendo Buddhist teacher (Japanese)

Ajita 'unconquered', personal name of Maitreya (Sanskrit)

ajna point between the eyebrows, Third Eye, sixth chakra (Sanskrit)

aka cord between the physical and astral bodies (Hawaiian)

Akamba Kenyan people noted for storytelling

akara fundamental sound symbolized by the first letter of the alphabet (Sanskrit)

akasha ether, subtlest, all-pervasive material manifestation (Sanskrit)

Akashic Record celestial medium on which every thought and action of the material world is available to psychic observation (from Sanskrit)

akhfa deeply hidden; one of the five lata'ifs (Arabic)

Akhilananda, Swami Indian Vedantist, founder of the Boston Ramakrishna Vedanta Society; *Hindu View of Christ*; 1894-1962

Akizuki, Tatsuichiro, M.D. director of St. Francis's Hospital in Nagasaki who saved all his patients after the atomic bombing by putting them on a macrobiotic diet; *Nagasaki, 1945*; 1916-

Akpallus mythical fisherfolk of the Near East

Aksakov, Alexander Russian spiritualist, Swedenborgian, pioneer psychic researcher; 1832-1903

Akshobhya Unshakable Buddha in the Vajrayana (Sanskrit)

aku-aku spirit, immaterial double (Easter Island)

Akupara tortoise upon which the Earth rests (Sanskrit)

Akwesasne 'People of the Longhouse', Mohawk Nation

al hadiar alaswad black stone in the Kaaba (Arabic)

al-Firdaws Paradise (Arabic)

al-Ianna 'the garden', abode of the blessed (Arabic)

al-Qahira 'victorious', Cairo; Fatimid capital, 10th c. (Arabic)

Ala Ibo Mother Goddess

Aladdin hero with a wonderful lamp

alayavijnana store-consciousness, collective unconsciousness (Sanskrit)

albedo light, brightness; alchemical term for consciousness (Latin)

Albert alligator in *Pogo*

Albigenses heretical Christian sect from Albi, France, which believed in reincarnation, 11th-14th c.

Albors (Alburz) sacred mountain peak where Mithras lived (Persian)

Alcabitius 1. astrological house system based on trisection of the diurnal arc of the declination circle of the ascendant projected by hour circles onto the ecliptic. 2. trisection of the ascendant arcs by vertical circles

alchemy quest for the secrets of life by the transmutation of base metals into gold in the West; by discovering the formula of the life elixir in the East. n. **alchemist**. adj. **alchemical**. v. **alchemize**

alcheringa n. and v. 'eternal dream time', inspiration, contacting the mystery between dreaming and here-and-now, logos (Arunta of Australia)

Alcott, (Amos) Bronson radical educator, Transcendentalist; *Unfolding the Doctrine and Discipline of Human Culture*; 1799-1888

Alcott, Louisa May novelist, suffragist; *Little Women*; 1832-88

Aldebaran Bull's Eye; fixed star in 15 degrees of Taurus

Aldermaston site in England of ban-the-bomb marches, 1950s-

alembic alchemical still

Aleofane island of the Riatlaro Archipelago in which language is tonal and opposites are often signified by the same word (Godfrey Sweven, 1901)

Aleph 1. first letter of the Hebrew alphabet: unity, A, 1. 2. shining sphere an inch across containing the sum total of the spatial universe (Borges). 3. number equal to all its parts, higher than infinity

alerce a soaring cedar in the south of Chile; southern relative of the giant sequoia, oldest of which is 4,200 years

Aletheia personal growth center in Ashland, Oregon, led by Jack Schwartz, 1958-

Alexander meditation master in Hesse's *Glass Bead Game*

Alexander, Franz Gabriel physician and a father of psychosomatic medicine; 1891-1964

Alexander, Matthias actor who developed a radical system of body dynamics, especially in respect to incorrect alignment of head, neck, shoulders; early 20th c.

Alexander Technique structural integration method developed by F. M. Alexander

Alexandria Egyptian city founded by Alexander the Great; spiritual center for Jews, Gnostics, and alchemists until the Arab Conquest, -332-

Alf laila wa-laila 'The Arabian Nights', Persian romance of *1001 Nights*

Alfheim realm of the elves in Scandinavian mythology

Alfonso X (the Wise) Christian monarch of Castillo and Leon, patron of Moslem culture, encyclopedic author; *Cantigas de Santa Maria*; 1221-84

algeny changing the essense of a living thing by transforming it from one state to another; biotechnology (Joshua Lederberg)

Algonquian largest Indian family on the East Coast, including Wampanoags, Pequots, Narragansets, Shanees, Delawares

Ali son-in-law of Muhammad, fourth Caliph, revered by the Shi'ites, husband of Fatima; ca. 600-61

Ali Baba poor woodcutter in the Arabian Nights

Alianza militant Hispanic movement in the Southwest, 1967-

Alice's Restaurant natural foods restaurant in Stockbridge, Mass., operated by Alice Brock where 'you can get anything you want', as immortalized in Arlo Guthrie's song

'alim (pt. 'ulama') one trained in spiritual sciences (Arabic)

alkahest universal solvent in alchemy (Arabic)

Allah 'the god', Supreme Being of Islam (Arabic)

Allen, Woody film actor and director; *Annie Hall*; 1935-

allopathy method of treating disease by use of agents, producing effects different from those of the malady; conventional medicine

Allport, Gordon analyst; *Becoming*; 1897-1967

ally source of power of a warrior, capable of assuming a variety of forms; that which is outside the realm of reason (don Juan)

allyu basic cooperative unit of the Incas

Alma Queen of Body Castle in Spencer's *Faerie Queene*

Almohads first united Islamic empire of North Africa and Spain, capital Seville, 12th c.

Almoravids North African Islamic empire, capital Marrakech, 11th c.

almuten most friendly or well-disposed planet in the horoscope

aloha love, affection, hello, goodbye (Hawaiian)

Alpha Centauri triple star of which Proxima is the nearest to our Sun, ca. 4.3 light years distant

alpha and omega 1. first and last letters of the Greek alphabet signifying eternity and time. 2. Jesus

alpha particle composite of two protons and two neutrons emanating from certain radioactive substances

alpha wave brain wave associated with a relaxed, alert, zenic consciousness

alphabet of human thought universal language sought by Leibniz that would function as a type of calculus

alphagenics science of detection, measurement, and mental control of brain waves

Alsirat (Al Sirat) bridge to Paradise (Arabic)

Alta Atlantean city on Poseidia (Cayce)

Altaic language family of the Turkic, Mongolian, and Tungusic tongues

altered states of consciousness general term for sleep, dreams, trances, hallucinogenic experiences, satori

alternative 1. unconventional or unorthodox approach, treatment, remedy, medicine, or practice designed to promote physical, mental, psychological, or spiritual health, happiness, and well-being. 2. small and underfinanced

alternative trade organizations (ATO) group that assists the Third World's poorest producers to market their crafts and commodities directly to First World consumers

Altimira Paleolithic caves near Santillana del Mar, Spain, renowned for a drawing of a person harvesting wild honey

Altruria 'Land of Altruism', Mediterranean vegetarian island utopia in William Dean Howell's *A Traveler from Altruria*, 1894

Alvar collective name of twelve Vaishnava poets of Tamil, ca. 6th-9th c.

Ama heavenly paradise formerly linked to Earth by a bridge which collapsed into the ocean and became the isthmus west of Kyoto (Japanese)

Amal Islamic painter at the court of Akbar; *Poet in the Garden*; 17th c.

amalgam common mercury-silver fillings in teeth believed to be hazardous

Amana Germanic utopian Community of True Inspiration in Iowa led by Christian Metz, 1843-1933

amani peace (Swahili)

amaranth small grain, staple of the ancient Aztecs

Amaravati Indra's heaven (Sanskrit)

Amarnath Kashmiri cave on a 16,000-foot mountain where Shiva taught Parvati the tantra

amargi 1. freedom. 2. return to the mother (Sumerian)

amasake (amazake) a sweet, creamy beverage made from fermented sweet rice and popular in macrobiotic cooking (Japanese)

Amaterasu (Amaterasu-omi-kami) Heavenly Shining Great Graceful Spirit; Shinto Sun Goddess

Amaurot 'shadowy town', capital of More's *Utopia* (Greek)

Amazon 'without breast', 1. one of the fabled female warriors living near Scythia. 2. long river in Latin America flowing from the Andes across Brazil to the Atlantic. 3. strong independent woman (Greek)

Ambedkar, Bhimrao Ramji Indian statesman, leader of the Buddhist revival in India which saw one-half million harijans convert to Buddhism; 1892-1956

Ambrosius childhood name of Merlin

Amenophis IV Ikhnaton

Amenti Egyptian Underworld

amerdeen apricot sheet, sun-dried and pressed from the Near East

American Holistic Medical Association group of holistic health practitioners, 1970s-

American Society for Psychical Research ESP society, 1885-

Amerind American Indian (Major J. W. Powell, 1899)

Amfortas (Anfortas) custodian of the Holy Grail; the Fisher-King

Amharic language of Ethiopia

Amida (Amitabha, *Sanskrit*) Buddha of Boundless Light (Japanese)

amino acid organic compound of carbon, hydrogen, oxygen, and nitrogen that combines in molecules to form protein

Amish Christian sect founded by Jacob Amman, a Swiss Mennonite, which came to America in the 18th c., now living principally in Lancaster County, Pa., noted for a traditional, nontechnological lifestyle

Amitabha (Amida, *Japanese*, A'mi-to, *Chinese*) Buddha of Boundless Light who resides in the Pure Land in the Western Heaven; historically he was a king who renounced everything and after meditating five kalpas made vows for saving all beings, the 18th of which is the basis of Pure Land Buddhism (Sanskrit)

Amlodhi (Hamlet) 'simpleton', owner in Norse myth of a fabled mill which ground out peace and plenty but in decaying times ground out salt and later rock and sand, creating a vast whirlpool leading to the land of the dead; described in an account by Saxo Grammaticus, 12th c.

Amma 1. Dogon Supreme Being. 2. (l.c.) ancient Oriental massage

Amnesty International human rights and political prisoners organization with headquarters in London, 1961-

Amoghasiddhi Buddha of Infallible Realization

AMORC Ancient and Mystical Order Rosae Crucis

Amos first Hebrew literary prophet; ca. -8th c.

amplication elaboration and clarification of a dream-image by means of directed association and of parallels from myth and legend (Jung)

amrita nectar, ambrosia (Sanskrit)

Amritsar capital of the Punjab in India,

sacred city of the Sikhs

amshavatara partial incarnation of the Lord (Sanskrit)

amulet object that naturally produces certain effects, e.g., ruby

Amundsen, Roald latter-day Viking, explorer of the Northwest Passage and South Pole; 1872-?1928

amurakh frightening, numinous onset of the sacred vocation of a Shaman (Siberian)

An Quang Pagoda Buddhist temple in Cholon, headquarters of the Vietnamese peace movement

Ana'l Haqq Sufi saying 'I am God' (Arabic)

Anabaptist 'to baptise again', member of a European Protestant sect practicing communal living and nonresistance; known today in America and Russia as Mennonites, 16th c.

anabolic adj. natural healing force (Paracelsus)

Anael Hebrew Angel of Love

anagamin 'nonreturner', third stage of Theravada Buddhism (Pali)

anagogic adj. magical evocation, calling forth the gods in oneself (Jung)

anagogical adj. leading the senses through contemplation to a state beyond the senses (Abbot Suger of Notre Dame, 12th c.)

anahata heart chakra, symbolized by a 12-petal lotus (Sanskrit)

anahata nada soundless sound (Sanskrit)

Anahuac 'place at the center in the midst of the circle', pilgrimage spot sought by Quetzalcoatl (Nahuatl)

analytical psychology Jungian therapy

anamnesis 1. ecstasy-causing reminders, e.g., music of the spheres (Greek). 2. recovery of buried memory, both individual and collective (Jung)

Ananda 1. divine bliss. 2. a chief disciple of the Buddha, who, because of his clinging to erudition, was not enlightened until twenty years after Buddha's death, under Makakashyo; second Zen patriarch and transmitter of the original scriptures (Sanskrit)

Ananda Cooperative Village spiritual community founded by Swami Kriyananda near Nevada City, Calif., 1968-

Ananda Marga 'Path of Bliss', international yoga society founded by Shrii Shrii Anandamaurti, 1955-

Anandamoyi Ma, Sri Bengali woman saint who lived in Benares and started ashrams throughout India; 1896-1982

Anansi spider hero and trickster of West Africa

Ananta 'infinite', King of the Serpent World (Sanskrit)

anarchism doctrine or practice of voluntary, cooperative social, economic, and political organization and opposition to all forms of government or coercion

Anasazi 1. 'Ancient Ones', pre-Navajo people of the Southwest. 2. (l.c.) bean

anatma (anatta, *Pali*) nonego (Sanskrit)

anatomy destiny (Freud)

Anaximander Greek philosopher who held the ultimate substance was infinite, formless matter; -6th c.

Anaximenes of Miletus Greek philosopher who held the ultimate substance was air; -6th c.

Ancestral Land Taoist term for Third Eye

Ancestress Goddess as old Grandmother or Wise Woman

anchorite (f. anchoress) 'withdrawer', ascetic, desert hermit, pillar saint, especially one confined to a cell (Greek)

Ancient and Mystical Order Rosae Crucis occult organization with headquarters in San Jose, Calif.

ancient forest movement environmentalist network to save the old-growth forests of the Pacific northwest, Canada and Alaska including Friends of Clayoquot Sound, the Cathedral Forest Action Group and other citizens' groups

Ancient Future New Age world fusion group; *Visions of a Peaceful Planet*

Ancient Spiritual and Scientific World Community era during which the world was unified in peace and harmony, ca. -23,000-11,000 (Michio Kushi)

anda cosmic or golden egg (Sanskrit)

Andal 'she who dives deep into the ocean of divine love', South Indian saint; *Sacred Utterance*; 7th c.

Andreae, Johann Valentin German social reformer, utopian; *Christianopolis*; 1586-1654

Andrews, Lynn author, shaman, and New Age teacher, *Medicine Woman*

androcentric male-centered

Androcles Roman who befriended a lion and was spared in the arena

androcracy a social system ruled through force or the threat of force (Riane Eisler)

androgeny conscious awareness of the

coexistence of the masculine principle
and the feminine principle within each
person, irrespective of physiological
sex

Anduin great river in Middle-earth

Anfortas (Amfortas) Parzival's maternal
uncle; Grail King until succeeded by
Parzival; the Fisher-King

anga 'limb', one of eight steps in Raja
Yoga (Sanskrit)

angakok (pl. angakut) Innuit shaman

Angas Jain scriptures (Sanskrit)

angel 1. messenger, heavenly envoy
(Greek). 2. someone who understands
and manifests the Order of the Universe
in daily life (Michio Kushi)

Angel of Humility being who struck
Dante's forehead with his wings and
the first P on his head, symbolizing
pride, instantly disappeared

Angela of Foligno, Blessed Franciscan
mystic; *The Book of Divine Consola-
tions*; 1248-1309

Angelico, Fra Florentine artist, monk;
Madonna dei Linaiuoli; 1387-1455

Angell, George T. Boston attorney, animal welfare activist; 1823-1909

Angkor Thom third Angkor built by Jay-
avarman VII, including the Bayon with
fifty towers each bearing four faces of
the Buddha

Angkor Wat 'Temple of the Capital',
masterpiece of Khmer Hindu architecture, funerary temple of King Suryavar-
man II, near present-day Siem Riep,
Cambodia, 1113-50

angular on or close to the first, fourth,
seventh, or tenth house cusps

Anguta Central Innuit Supreme Being

angya pilgrimage in quest of a spiritual
teacher (Japanese)

anibue 'opening of the eyes', enlightenment (Yoruba)

anicca (anitya, *Sanskrit*) impermanence;
Buddhist teaching that all things are
subject to change (Pali)

Anider 'waterless', main river of More's
Utopia (Greek)

anima personification of the feminine nature of a man's unconsciousness (Jung)

anima mundi world soul (Latin)

animal kingdom the seventh stage of
creation, developing out of the vegetable world as a more highly charged and
activated order of life, with human beings, the most conscious and physically
active species, at the apex

animal liberation movement for more

humane treatment of animals, especially recognition of their consciousness as
sentient beings and fellow inhabitants
of the planet, 1971-

Animal Liberation Front (ALF) militant
animal rights group that has disrupted
research labs, 1979-

Animal Republic a vast island whose
birds and beasts rid themselves of human tyranny in Jean Jacobe de Fremont
d'Ablancourt's *Suppllement de
l'Historie Veritable de Lucien*, 1654

Animula microscopic heroines in Fitz-
James O'Brien's *The Diamond Lens*,
1858

animus personification of the masculine
nature of a woman's unconscious
(Jung)

Aniruddha cousin of Buddha and one of
his chief disciples

anjali mudra palms held together in
prayer (Sanskrit)

Ann 'grace', mother of Mary (Hebrew)

anna-kshetra free kitchen (Sanskrit)

Annapurna 'Rich in Food', Divine
Mother, consort of Shiva, presiding deity of Benares

**Annual Conference on the Great Moth-
er and the New Father** yearly gathering to look at relationships, sex and role
models, and community hosted by Robert Bly

annual ring formation of two concentric
layers of new growth each ring of
which provides a basis for determining
the age of trees

annuit coeptis 'He Smiles on Our Undertakings', adapted from Virgil's *Aeneid*
on the Geat Seal of the United States
with a picture of a pyramid and an eye
in the capstone

Annunciation announcement by the archangel Gabriel to Mary that she would
give birth to Jesus

Annuvin 'not the world', magical northern land in the *Mabinogion* (Welsh)

Anokye, Okomfo Ashanti spiritual leader; 17th c.

anomoly thing or alleged thing that
doesn't fit science or the conventional
view of reality

anpsi animal psi

Anschauung n. intuition (German)

ant being who guided Solomon across the
desert

antahkarana mind vehicle: mind, intellect, ego, subconscious; bridge between the higher and lower mind (San-

skrit)

Antares Scorpion's Heart; fixed star in 15 degrees of Scorpio

antediluvian adj. before the Flood, e.g., Atlantean civilization (from Latin)

Anthony, Susan B. feminist; *History of Women Suffrage*; 1820-1906

anthropic principles four parts of a theory, held by some nuclear physicists, that the universe is intrinsically a perpetually self-creating whole

anthropogenesis process of human evolution (Teilhard)

anthropos original man; an archetypal figure in myth and religion such as Adam or P'an Ku

Anthroposophical Society spiritual movement founded by Rudolf Steiner, emphasizing eurythmy, biodynamic gardening and farming, and Christian Theosophy, 1912-

anti-Stratfordian n. or adj. one who believes the Shakespearean canon was written by someone else or a committee

Antichthon 'counter-Earth', 1. hypothetical continent in the southern hemisphere. 2. imaginary planet invented by the Pythagoreans to bring the heavenly bodies to ten (Greek)

antigravity overcoming gravity by increased rate of spin or levitation

Antikythera amphora metallic object raised from the sea near the Greek island of Antikythera in 1901, identified in 1960 by Derek de Solla Price as a bronze machine for calculating the planets, ca. 1st c.

Antilia (Island of the Seven Cities) mythical Atlantic island of happiness (Portuguese)

antimadeha stage of entering one's last body prior to nirvana (Sanskrit)

antimatter matter that is composed of antiparticles instead of particles and may exist in other parts of the universe

antiparticle counterpart existing for each subatomic particle with the same mass but opposite electric charge, and which mutually annihilates with a particle upon meeting

antipathy disharmony between two planets that rule or are exalted in opposite signs in astrology

antipodes places on opposite sides of the globe (Greek)

antipsychiatry radical mental health movement associated with R. D. Laing questioning the usefulness of psychoa-

nalysis, cultural definitions of sickness and mental health, and the counseling of patients to adjust to society's norms, 1960s-

antiscion reflex position of a planet's birth position in Uranian astrology

antiseptic healing agent that inhibits growth of microorganisms on living tissue

antitime hypothesized reverse particle of time

antivertex point directly opposite the vertex in astrology

Antony, St. Egyptian hermit; ca. 251-356

Anubis Egyptian jackel-headed God of the Underworld and Opener of the Ways

anugraha release, salvation, grace; fifth dance step of Shiva (Sanskrit)

Anuradhapura ancient capital of Ceylon until the 10th c.

Anyang capital of the Shang Dynasty in China

Aoukar medieval name for Ghana

Apache (from Zuni *Apachu*, 'the enemy') Athapascan tribe which first came to the Southwest ca. 1000 and call themselves Tinneh, 'The People'

aperature of Brahma (brahmarandhra, *Sanskrit*) spot on top of the head where the consciousness departs from the body at death (Sanskrit)

Aphrodite 'from foam', Greek Goddess of Beauty and Love

Apis bull-headed Egyptian deity

Apocatastasis 1. the great return to the Pleroma (fullness of heaven) in Gnosticism. 2. Christian doctrine that all beings will be saved; taught by Origen, Clement of Alexandria, and Gregory of Nyssa and condemned by the Council of Constantinople in 543 (Greek)

Apocrypha 'hidden', noncanonical section of the Hebrew Bible

Apollo 1. Greek Sun God, chief physician of life, and father of the Muses. 2. Greek sage who welcomed Jesus in Athens (*Aquarian Gospel*)

Apollo 8 spacecraft that beamed back the first televised picture of Earth in December, 1969

Apollon fifth Uranian planet ruling science, commerce, industry

Apollonius of Tyana neopythagorean philosopher, ascetic, magus; 1st c.

apotropaic relating to an action that neutralizes or counters negative vibrations such as knocking on wood

appam deep-fried pancake made of rice and lentil-flour (Hindi)

applied kinesiology technique using body muscles to test and evaluate the body's different nerve and energy patterns developed during the 1960s by George Goodheart, D.C.

applying aspect approach of a planet to a degree where it will be in aspect with another

apport an object or being that appears to manifest spontaneously from the air

Apsu abyss filled with fresh water surrounding Earth in Sumerian myth

Apuleius Roman author, devotee of Isis; *The Metamorphoses of Lucius or The Golden Ass*; ca. 124-70

aquaculture sea or pond-farming

Aquarian Age era of coming peace, wisdom, and group effort, ca. 2000-4100

Aquarian Conspiracy 1. New Age book by Marilyn Ferguson, 1980. 2. naturally spreading leaderless but powerful network of individuals and communities that sees life with a healthier set of assumptions

Aquarian Gospel story of Jesus, especially the eighteen lost years, when he traveled to India, Tibet, Egypt, Persia, and Greece; transcribed via automatic typewriting by Levi, 1907

Aquarius 'Waterbearer', 11th sign of the zodiac; ruler Uranus; of the airy element; keywords: consecration, originality, eccentric innovative energy (Greek)

aquavideo science of locating water underground (Vernon Cameron)

arabesque Arabic or Moresque rhythmic decoration consisting of light scroll work and foliage

Arabian points solar chart planet positions marked on a natal chart

Arachne 'the Spider', reputed 13th sign of the zodiac, between Taurus and Gemini, governing intuition (Greek)

Aragon first ruler of the Reunited Kingdom of Middle Earth

arahant 'worthy', fourth and final stage of Theravada Buddhism (Pali)

Aramaic Persian language spoken by Jews and others during Inter- and New Testament times

arame a thin, wiry black sea vegetable similar to hiziki (Japanese)

Ararat, Mount site in eastern Turkey where Noah's Ark is thought to have docked after the Flood

Araucanians a people of Chile and the Argentine pampas

Arbofilia the Association for the Protection of Trees in Costa Rica, 1980-

Arbor Day national tree-planting day, observed the last Friday in April

arbor vitae tree of life (Latin)

ARC Affinity, Reality, and Communication; prerequisites to knowledge (Scientology)

Arcadia mountainous region of southern Greece; home of Pan, shepherds, and poets

Arcane School esoteric school and correspondence course founded by Alice and Foster Bailey

archaeus adj. referring to the soul-like or psychoid ordering principle of life (Paracelsus, *Latin*)

archai terrestrial powers above archangels

archangel chief or principal angel

arche first principle source (Aristotle, Greek)

Archean the age when the only organisms on Earth were bacteria and when the atmosphere was dominated by methane and oxygen was only a trace gas

archeomythology a field that includes archeology, comparative mythology, and folklore (Marija Gimbutas)

archeosophy philosophic archeology through the medium of symbols (Szekely)

archetype 'basic type for form', 1. an ideal pattern or form to which all things of a cerain type conform (Plato). 2. unrepresentable, unconcious, preexistent form in the psyche that can nevertheless express itself personally or collectively in forms conditioned by the times (Jung, from Greek)

archy cockroach who was the reincarnation of a free-verse poet in *Archy & Mehitabel*

arcismati full of flames; fourth stage of the bodhisattva path (Sanskrit)

arcology science of architecture and ecology perceived as a 3-D landscape or topography (Soleri)

Arcosanti Paolo Soleri's utopian city under construction in the Arizona desert

Arcturan astrological house system based on equal division of the horizon from the east point by longitude circles

Arcturus 'bear guard', golden star in Bootes; fourth brightest in the sky; a favorite in science fiction (Greek)

Areal, Antonio Jose (To Ze) Portuguese-bank robber and terrorist who changed his way of eating in prison and became a macrobiotic teacher and counselor

arepa an oval-shaped corn ball or cake made from whole corn dough and baked or pan-fried (Spanish)

Arete of Cyrene ancient Greek female ethicist and natural philosopher

Argo Jason's ship

Argos Odysseus's dog

Arguelles, Jose artist and historian who theorized the Harmonic Convergence; *The Mayan Factor*, 1939-

arhat (arahant, *Japanese,* lohan, *Chinese*) worthy, adept in Theravada Buddhism (Sanskrit)

Arica 'open', spiritual movement founded by Oscar Ichazo in Arica, Chile

Ariel 1. poetic name for Jerusalem. 2. airy spirit in *The Tempest*

Aries the Ram; first zodiac sign; ruler Mars; of the firery element; keywords: activity, intellectual energy

'arif (pl. 'irfan, 'urafa) initiate, gnostic, master of a craft (Arabic)

Arignote ancient Greek female philosopher; *Sacred Discourse*

Arigo (Jose Pedro de Freitas) Brazilian healer; 1918-71

Aristophanes Greek playwright; *Lysistrata*; -448-385

Aristotle Greek philosopher; *Metaphysics*; -384-22

Arjan, Guru fifth Sikh Guru from India, compiler of the *Adi Granth* and builder of the Golden Temple; 1563-1606

Arjuna 'white', archer, seeker, and friend dear to Krishna in the *Bhagavad Gita* and *Mahabharata* (Sanskrit)

Ark Gandhian community founded by Lanza del Vasta in La Borie Novele, France

Arkeology search for Noah's ark

Armageddon site of the final battle between light and darkness

armor ingrained patterns, attitudes, beliefs, moods, or postures that block and restrict (Wilhelm Reich)

Arnold, Edwin English Orientalist; *The Light of Asia*; 1832-1904

Arnold, Kenneth sighter of first UFO over Mt. Rainier on June 24, 1947

Arowhena heroine in Butler's *Erewhon*

arrowroot a starch flour processed from the root of an American plant, used as a thickening agent for sauces, stews, gravies, or desserts

arrogance 1. material or spiritual attachment that impedes or blocks the free flow of energy. 2. mistaking the part for the whole. 3. improper balance between self and nature leading to taking more or less than we need

art 1. that which holds a mirror up to nature (Shakespeare). 2. the grandchild of creation (Dante). 3. a harmony parallel to nature (Cezanne). 4. the human disposition of sensible or intelligible matter for an esthetic end (James Joyce). 5. that which creates forms so the radiance of the divine can be revealed; the clothing of God's grace (Joseph Campbell). 6. the way of beauty which melts the mind, enchants the heart, and casts a spell of esthetic arrest (Campbell). 7. the way of expression that heals or gives appreciation of the Order of the Universe (Aveline Kushi). 8. national parks of the mind (Levi-Strauss). 9. an aid to healing the spirit which talks about the Order of the Universe expressed in the seasons and growth of our spirit through stages of darkness and light, differentiation and integration (Sherman Goldman). 10. a samurai sword that punches a hole through your solar plexus so that the universe can start to flow through you again; that which opens up your crown chakra and sends you soaring into the seventh heaven (Sherman Goldman). 11. creating a dream world we enter to discover life is a dream (Sherman Goldman). 12. that which breaks the familiar molds

Artemis 1. Greek Goddess of the Forest. 2. symbol of wildness in women which is not to be lost (Robert Bly)

artha wealth, worldly success (Sanskrit)

Arthur (from *Arth Vawr*, 'Great Bear', *Welsh and Celtic*) British king and sovereign about whose Round Table the Knights of the Holy Grail gathered

Arthurian Stream literature of the Holy Grail, King Arthur, Parzival

artifex 1. maker, master, expert (Latin). 2. in alchemy, the alchemist, who is not the master of the Philosopher's Stone [the Self], but rather its minister (Jung)

artificial reincarnation assuming the identity of someone else under hypnosis

artist 1. a master of metaphorical language who reawakens the heart and eye to wonder (Joseph Campbell). 2. the true seer and prophet of his or her century, the justifier of life, and a revolutionary far more fundamental than an idealist or activist (Joseph Campbell). 3. one who works with rhythms or patterns of energy. 4. one who masters and goes beyond all of the conditions, techniques, technologies, practices, transmissions, histories, traditions, teachers, lineages, and gets back to the creative base (Gary Snyder). 6. one who pays attention to his or her life, does not try too much, goes step by step, avoids shortcuts, does the work well, and sticks with or builds community (Gary Snyder)

Arundale, George Sydney English-born Indian educator and Theosophist; *The Lotus Fire*; 1878-1945

Arya Deva Indian disciple of Nagarjuna who furthered the Madhyamika School of Buddhism; ca. 2nd c.

asana posture, yogic position (Sanskrit)

Asanga Indian Buddhist, brother of Vasubandhu, founder of the Yogachara school; 310-90

Asasa Ya 'Earth Thursday', Ashanti Goddess of the Earth

Ascalon St. George's magical sword

ascendant zodiacal degree on the eastern horizon at the minute of birth, signifying the personality self, especially as viewed by others

Ascended Masters realized souls not on the earthplane in many esoteric traditions

asceticism 'exercise, training', science of self-knowledge through discipline of mind and body (Greek)

ascorbic acid Vitamin C

Asgard realm of the Scandinavian divinities

asha 'truth', principle of goodness in Zoroastrianism (Persian)

Ashanti 1. Earth Goddess (Yoruba). 2. historic region and people of West Africa (present-day Ghana) whose kingdom, capital Kumasi, reached its height from the 17th-19th c.

Ashoka Maurya Indian ruler who converted to Buddhism after a series of bloody conquests, propagated vegetarianism, and erected many stupas and stone pillars inscribed with edicts proclaiming the Dharma; -273-32

ashram (ashrama) 1. spiritual commune, household, or hermitage. 2. four stages of life: *brahmacharya* (student), *grhastha* (householder), *vanaprasta* (forest-

dweller), *sanyasa* (wanderer) (Sanskrit)

ashramite ashram member or dweller

Ashtoreth the Hebrew Mother Goddess whose worship continued in Old Testament times despite efforts at suppression

Ashvaghosha Indian Buddhist master; *The Awakening of Faith*; 2nd c.

Asita Indian ascetic who visited Siddhartha at the time of his birth and foresaw his destiny

Aska ancient name for the Earth when the planet was last unified about fifteen thousand years ago, preserved in fragments of geographical places names such as *Asuka*, the old name for Japan, *Naska* (Peruvian plain), *Madagaskar*, *Saskatchewan, Nebraska, Alaska,* the *Basque* country; symbolized by a flying bird (Michio Kushi)

Aslan creator of Narnia, who usually appears to visitors in the guise of a lion or lamb (C.S. Lewis, 1952)

asomatic adj. out of the body, bodiless

aspect measured relationship between planets, or planets and the ascendant or midheaven

Assagioli, Roberto Italian founder of psychosynthesis; 1888-1974

assiah world of function in the Kabbalah (Hebrew)

association spontaneous linking of thoughts, feelings, and perceptions

Association for Research and Enlightenment Edgar Cayce Foundation in Virginia Beach, Va.

Association for the Understanding of Man research organization working with psychic Ray Stanford in Austin, Texas

Association of Space Explorers society of astronauts and cosmonauts promoting peaceful space exploration, founded by astronaut Rusty Schweickart

astanga eight-fold yogic path (Sanskrit)

Asterix gnome from Gaul in French comics

Asteroid B 612 home of the prince in Saint-Exupery's *Little Prince*

asteroids belt of particles in orbit between Jupiter and Mars

astral adj. 1. star. 2. subtle realm beyond the physical (from Greek)

astral body subtle or dream body that disengages during sleep or through consciousness techniques; exact replica of the physical body with a higher frequency of vibration

astral light auric or nonphysical light perceived as vibrations surrounding beings or objects

astral projection leaving the physical body and traveling to another location or reality

astroarchaeology science studying the relation between ancient ruins and visitors from outer space

astrodiagnosis health or medical evaluation through use of a horoscope

Astroeth Atlantean city of light

astrokinetics dynamics of planetary influences (Edward Whitman)

astrologer one who teaches astrology or reads charts

astrological birth control method developed in Czechoslovakia to determine a woman's fertile period according to birth data and sun and moon phases

astrologist one who believes in astrology

astrology 1. science of mapping and interpreting stars, planets, and other heavenly influences on life on Earth. 2. the study of celestial order based on the cosmic tones or celestial music

astrometerology astrological study of weather forecasting

astromythological adj. relating to the stars and mythology

Astronomicon oldest known treatise on astrology by the Roman Manilius, ca.10

astronumerology science synthesizing astrology and numerology

astropsychiatry science relating mental and emotional therapy to a horoscope

astrosome astral element; voluntary conscious leaving of the physical body

astrotwins two people born on the same day, not necessarily related or known to each other

asura 'without wine', 1. Titan; occupant of the world of fighting, anger, and dissension. 2. angry state of mind (Sanskrit)

at-Tariqa (pl. at-Turq) 'path', wandering company of Sufis (Arabic)

Ata 1. people on a peaceful, utopian island who used dream interpretation to guide their lives in *The Kin of Ata Are Waiting for You*, a novel by Dorothy Bryant. 2. (l.c.) father, dervish, holy man; a title (Turkish)

atef crown of Upper Egypt

Athapaskan (Athabaskan) 1. family of languages spoken by Native people in Northwest Canada, Alaska, the Pacific

Northwest, California, Arizona, and the Rio Grande basis, including Navajo, Apache. 2. member of one of these tribes

athelas healing herb in *Lord of the Rings*

Athena (Athene) 1. Greek Goddess of Wisdom who held back the dawn for Odysseus and Penelope. 2. a feminine archetype expressed by a woman interested in a kind of male power, philosophy, and consciousness (Robert Bly)

Atlantean n. or adj. 1. native of Atlantis or pertaining to Atlantis. 2. fourth root race (Theosophy). 3. fourth age in Max Heindel's teaching in which the union of polar ice and volcanic fire led to further human physicality and which saw the emergence of seven races: the Rmoahals, Tlavatlis, Toltecs, Turanians, Semites, Akkadians, and Mongolians

Atlantes (Atarantes, Atlantioi) tribes in northwest Africa described by classical Greek writers

Atlantides (sin. Atlantis) 'daughters of Atlas', seven daughters of Atlas and Pleione who eventually became the stars of the Pleiades: Alkyone, Merope, Kelaino, Elektra, Sterope, Taygete, Maia (Greek)

Atlantis sunken continent of myth and legend, generally located in the Atlantic Ocean, believed to have self-destructed through misuse of a high technology ca. -10,000-12,000; originally based on Plato's account in the *Timeas* and *Crito*; contemporary accounts are based on psychic sources and visions, as the search for material evidence continues

Atlantism field or study of Atlantis

Atlantist n. or adj. devotee or believer in Atlantis

Atlas elder twin of Kleito and Poseidon, chief king of the confederacy of Atlantis, which was named after him (Plato)

atman 1. imperishable, that which holds everything, inmost self. 2. divine spark within identical to Brahman (Sanskrit)

atom 1. tiny spiral that emits a musical note. 2. smallest constituent of an element capable of retaining the element's chemical properties, composed of a nucleus and electrons whirling around it

Atomic Chart Walter Russell's Periodic Table of the Elements composed of nine octaves, including three 'inaudible' octaves beyond physical measurement and before hydrogen, with carbon, in the center of the fourth octave, as the balance of stability for the entire spectrum of organic life

Atomic Dome skeletal remains of the former Industrial Hall in Hiroshima kept standing as a peace memorial

Attar (Farid al-Din) Persian Sufi mystic and poet; *The Conference of the Birds*; 1150-1230

attractor event that governs the dynamics of systems; subdivided into *point* or *static* attractors that govern equilibrium; *periodic* attractors that govern cyclical or oscillatory movements; and *chaotic* or *strange* attractors that are characteristic of far-from-equilibrium or disequilibrium states

attune to get in harmony, alignment, synchronization

attunement aligning the individual with the natural energy in the environment

atua 1. physical body (Arunta of Australia). 2. Maori gods

Atvan sacred island in Earthsea

A.U. astronomical unit; mean distance of the Earth from the Sun, ca. 93 million miles

Au Co legendary founder of Vietnam who bore Sir Dragon 100 children

Aubrey holes diggings at Stonehenge that provided a system for counting the years and predicting movements of the Moon

Aubrey, John English explorer of Stonehenge; *Miscellanies*; 1626-97.

Audbumia celestial cow of Norse myth

Audible Life Stream divine ray both audible and visible composing life and all elemental substances; Eck (Eckankar)

auditing application of Scientology procedures to someone by a Scientologist (Scientology)

auditor trained listener in Scientology training

Audubon, John James artist and ornithologist; *Birds of America*; 1785-1851

Augustine, St. Christian mystic; *Confessions*; 354-430

aUI (pronounced ah-oo-ee) the Language of Space; a tongue with thirty-one symbols given by a small plant-like being with wings to John Weilgart as a boy

aulos reed instrument used in ecstatic cults (Greek)

Aum (OM) a sound that vibrates the whole spiritual channel, charges all the chakras, and harmonizes mind and body; traditional chant (Sanskrit)

Austin, Mary writer, naturalist, and feminist; *Land of Little Rain*; 1868-1934

australopithecus (australopithines) earliest known species of fully bipedal primates, represented by *Australopithecus afarensis*, found in Ethiopia and Tanzania, and *A. africanus* and *A. robustus* of South Africa and *A. boisei* of Tanzania; earliest forebear of human beings from about 3.8 million years ago in Africa

aura subtle light surrounding a person or object. adj. **auric**

aura balancing technique for clearing, smoothing, or harmonizing the auric field around a person's head or body

Aurobindo Ghose, Sri Indian philosopher; *The Life Divine*; 1872-1950

Aurora 1. Roman Goddess of the Dawn. 2. root or mother of philosophy (Boehme). 3. Christian communal community in Oregon led by Dr. William Keil, 1855-80

Auroville concentric city of 400 persons devoted to the teachings of Sri Aurobindo and the Mother near Pondicherry, India, 1968-

autogenic training (AT) various methods of meditation, visualization, or biofeedback training used to modify behavior and consciousness

automatic writing writing produced when a person goes into an altered state and a spirit entity takes over the person's writing arm and hand to communicate

autoscopy 1. vision of one's image outside the body. 2. vision of one's own double in a dying state. 3. vision of one's internal organs. adj. **autoscopic**

autosuggestion sending mental messages to the unconscious, self-programming

Avalokiteshvara (Kuan Yin, *Chinese*, Chenresigs, *Tibetan*) Bodhisattva of Compassion (Sanskrit)

Avalon 'Land of Apples', 1. beautiful lake and rock island where Arthur received the sword Excalibur. 2. ballroom in San Francisco and site of psychedelic gatherings in late 1960s and early 1970s

Avatamsaka Sutra (Hua-yen-ching, *Chinese*, Kegon-kyo, *Japanese*) 'Garland Scripture', teaching of the Buddha during the three weeks immediately after his enlightenment while he was still in a deep state of meditation (Sanskrit)

avatar (avatara) incarnation of the supreme deity in human form, e.g., Krishna, Rama, Zoroaster, Jesus (Sanskrit)

Avatars of Vishnu forms Vishnu took to incarnate and save the world:

Matsya... Fish
Kurma....................................... Tortoise
Varaha... Boar
Narasimha............................ Man-Lion
Vamana...................................... Dwarf
Parashurama........... Rama with the Axe
Rama............... Hero of the *Ramayana*
Krishna.......... hero of the *Mahabharata*
Buddha........................ Enlightened One
Kalki................................. White Horse

Avesta Zoroastrian scriptures (Persian)

Avicebron Kabbalistic scholar and student of Taoism; 11th c.

avidhya primordial ignorance, delusion (Sanskrit)

Avila home town in Spain of St.Teresa

Avvaiyar Tamil female saint and ethicist; *Atti Chudi;* ca. -2nd c.

Awahoksu Abode of all Spiritual Power (Pawnee)

awake v. 1. to be conscious in essence, to be conscious of one's existence and of one's actions at the same time (Bennett). 2. to maintain a consciousness of heaven while living on the Earth

award-burd control of the breath; Sufi exercise (Persian)

awareness 1. spiritual or higher consciousness. 2. not using the mind to look for reality (Bodhidharma)

Awareness Techniques methods to visualize past reincarnations while fully conscious

Awonawilona Zuni Supreme Being

axis mundi center of the world (Latin)

ayahuasca (yage) hallucinogenic drug

Ayar four brothers and four sisters who were ancestors of the Incas

Ayers Rock center of the universe in Australian mythology

Ayesha second wife of Muhammad, daughter of Abu-Bakr; 7th c.

Aymara 1. ancient people in pre-Incan South America who lived on quinoa. 2. Indian language of Bolivia and Peru

Ayodhya 'that which cannot be beaten', land ruled by Rama (Sanskrit)

Ayurveda traditional Indian medicine relying on herbs, diet, and folk remedies (Sanskrit)

Azania 1. ancient iron-age culture in southern Africa which left many mysterious cultural remains. 2. ancient name for the African coast around the

Horn. 3. name used for their country by South African Liberation movements today (Greek)

azilut world of emanation in the Kabbalah (Hebrew)

azim, ya 'O Most High', Sufi greeting (Arabic)

Azrael angel who separates the soul from the body at death in certain Hebrew and Arabic traditions

Aztlan island containing seven cities and a sacred mountain with seven caves from which the Aztecs originated

azuki (aduki) a small, dark red bean popular in macrobiotic cooking (Japanese)

Azuma New Age visionary composer from Japan; *Asian Wind*

Bb

B-values virtues derived from being (Maslow)

ba 'animation', after-death bird-soul (Egyptian)

Baal Shem Tov (the Besht) 'Master of the Good Name', Israel ben Eliezer, Ukrainian-born founder of Hasidism; 1700-60

Baalbek terrace north of Damascus with 2000-ton stone blocks of mysterious origin

Bab (Mirza Ali Muhammad) 'Gate', proclaimed Mahdi in Persia; 1819-50

baba 1. father (Sanskrit). 2. missionary, folk preacher, shaikh (Turkish)

baba ganoosh Near Eastern-style smoked eggplant

Babaji deathless Himalayan saint, guru of Lahiri Mahasaya; ca. 8th c.-

Babar 1. founder of the Moghul Dynasty in India; 1483-1530. 2. little elephant hero of Jean de Brunhoff

Babbitt, Edwin scientist and artist; *The Healing Power of Color*; 19th c.

Babe Paul Bunyan's wonderful blue ox

baby boomers generation born between 1946 and 1964 noted for countercultural and social activist tendencies

Bach, Edward English homeopath; 1886-1936

Bach Flower Remedies homeopathic treatment developed by Edward Bach while wandering the forest and licking the dew from wildflowers

Bach, Johann Sebastian divine German composer; *Mass in B Minor*; 1685-1750

back invisible, hidden, negative, downside (macrobiotics)

back country rural or wilderness environment

backbeat background rock rhythm (Afro-American)

backcrack realigning the back during massage

Backster, Clive scientist who published research in 1967 showing the sensitivity of plants to human

backward displacement ESP responses preceding the intended targets

Bacon, Francis English mind; *Advancement of Learning*; 1561-1626

Bacon, Roger English scientist and philosopher; ca. 1214-94

Bactriana medieval Central Asian state, originally Persian, later Greek

bad trip negative experience resulting from taking a hallucinogenic drug, involving a sense of separation, fragmentation, or loss of self and reality

Badger messenger of the Hopi

baectyl cone-shaped stone associated with the Mother Goddess in Minoan art

Baer, Steve pioneer dome builder

Baez, Joan folksinger and satyagrahini; *Any Day Now*; 1941-

bag 1. n. state of mind, lifestyle, occupation, interest (Afro-American). 2. v. to sack your own natural foods

Baggins, Bilbo hobbit who took the One Ring from Gollum; b. Third Age 2890

Baggins, Frodo hobbit who carried the One Ring of Power to the Cracks of Doom in *Lord of the Rings;* b. Third Age 2968

Baha'i way of life of Persian origin stressing radical monotheism, prophets, and scriptures, 19th c.-

Baha'u'llah (Mirza Husayn Ali) founder of Baha'i; 1817-92

Bahir 'brightness' or 'illumination', a book of the Kabbalah that appeared in Provence in 1176

Bailey, Alice English-born occultist and New Age prophet, founder of Arcana, School of Esoteric Studies, Full Moon Meditation; *The Reappearance of the Christ*; 1880-1949

Baja lower California

Baker, Richard Zen roshi, teacher of the San Francisco Zen Center

Baker Street Irregulars 1. London urchins who helped Sherlock Holmes. 2. Holmesian devotees

Bakin Japanese utopian author; *Musobyoe, the Tale of a Wanderer*; 1767-1848

baklava almond and honey pastry (Turkish)

Baksei Chamkrong first Khmer temple mountain built in stone, 947

baktun period of 400 years (Mayan)

Bakunin, Mikhail Russian anarchist; *God and the State*; 1814-76

balam 1. jaguar. 2. high priest (Mayan)

Balanced Rock megalithic dolmen in North Salem, N.Y.

Balarama Krishna's older brother

Balder (Baldr) 'bright, shining', Scandinavian mythological hero

Balfour, Eve organic researcher; *The Living Soil*

Balfour, Gerald English psychical researcher; *Ear of Dionysius*; 1853-1945

Bali beautiful Indonesian island renowned for Hindu epic dances

Ballard, Edna I AM leader; 1886-1971

Ballard, Guy W. leader of the I AM Religious Activity and co-founder of the Saint Germain Foundation, 1878-1939

Ballentine, Rudolph, M.D., holistic physician and educator, president of Himalayan International Institute, *Diet and Nutrition*

Ballou, Adin Unitarian clergyman, founder of Hopedale, 1803-90

Balthazar one of the three Magi

Bamboo Grove monastic park frequented by Buddha near Rajagriha

Bamiyan Buddhist art complex in a high cliff in Afghanistan

Ban Chiang northeast Thai village, excavation site of an ancient Bronze Age civilization that may have supplied tin to Mesopotamia, and appears to have had no warfare or violence for thousands of years; ca. -3600-250; discovered in 1976

Bana (Banabhatta) Indian poet; *Harshacharita*; 7th c.

bancha tea the twigs, stems, and leaves from mature tea bushes; main beverage in macrobiotic cooking; also known as kukicha (Japanese)

Band folk rock group (Robbie Robertson, Richard Manuel, Garth Hudson, Rick Danko, Levon Helm); *Cripple Creek*; 1960s

Bandersnatch fruminous being in

Through the Looking Glass

Banteay Srei Women's Citadel near Angkor

Bantu 1. people originally from the Cameroon who migrated south and west about 2000 years ago. 2. their language spoken throughout central and southern Africa

Banyacya, Thomas Hopi tribal leader

baptism 1. ceremony dedicated to spiritual development. 2. day to day making one's spirit higher (Michio Kushi)

bapu 1. father (Sanskrit). 2. (cap.) nickname for Gandhi

Barabbas 'Son of Abbas', prisoner released instead of Jesus

baraka 'blessing', power bestowed by Allah (Arabic)

Barbelo Lower Sophia, Mother Goddess aspect; the gnostic second principle in the image of the archetypal parent, mother-father God, the eternal aeon

bardo 'between two', state between death and rebirth, or any state of consciousness (Tibetan)

skyes-gnas............................ earth plane
rmi-lam.............................. dream plane
ting-nge-'dzin.............. one-pointedness
'chi'i kha.................... facing death
chos-nyid............ postmortem existence
srid-pa... rebirth

Bardo Thodol (Bardo Thosgrol) Tibetan Book of the Dead

Barefoot Shiatsu macrobiotic massage developed as a response to the Western condition requiring a more rigorous style of treatment (Shizuko Yamamoto)

barefooting walking or hiking without shoes or boots; based on Tarahumara Indians; popularized by Boy Scoutmaster Jim Haskins, 1986-

Bark Paintings mythical scenes depicted on trees by Australian aborigines

barley a whole cereal grain; the traditional staple of Southern Europe, the Middle East, and North Africa

barley malt a natural sweetener made from concentrated barley that has a rich, roasted taste

barrel root cellar underground organic garden storage device

Barrett, Sir William British physicist and founder of the Society for Psychical Research; 1844-1925

Barritt, Elihu peace organizer, founder of the League of Universal Brotherhood; 1810-79

Barry St. Bernard who saved forty persons in the Swiss Alps; d. 1814

base n. or adj. lowest chakra

Basho Japanese Zen master and haiku poet; *The Narrow Road to the Deep North*; 1644-94

basilisk fabled animal of the Egyptian desert whose glance was lethal and which could be subdued only with a mirror

Basque region of 700,000 people along the Spanish-French border noted for a pre-Indo-European tongue unlike any other in Europe

Bast 1. (Bastet) Egyptian Cat Goddess. 2. (l.c.) spiritual expansion (Arabic)

basumati (basmati) thin, long-grain brown rice (Hindi)

Bat Creek Inscription Hebrew text dating to 2nd c. found on a stone in Tennessee in 1823

Bateleur, Le Magician in the Tarot (French)

Bates, William natural therapist; *Better Eyesight Without Glasses*; 1860-1931

Bateson, Gregory psychiatrist, consciousness researcher; *Steps to an Ecology of Mind*; 1904-80

baubiologie 'biological architecture', natural home movement (German)

Bauersfeld, Walter German inventor of the geodesic dome in 1922

Bauhaus art school founded by Walter Gropius with noted expressionists Klee, Faininger, Kandinsky, 1919

Bauls 'mad', Bengali sect founded by Chaitanya, which worships Krishna and Radha (Bengali)

Baum, L. Frank author; *Wonderful Wizard of Oz*; 1856-1919

Bawa, Guru Sufi teacher from Sri Lanka

Bayard fabled magical horse of Charlemagne

Bayeux tapestry 231-foot linen in the French town of Bayeux depicting the Norman conquest, 12th c.

Bayon temple of Angkor Thom in Cambodia

Bayside site in New York associated with visions and messages from the Virgin Mary, 1970-

Be-In outdoors gathering where people come, relax, sing, and do whatever moves them; first held in San Francisco, Jan. 14, 1967

beadwork 1. the craft of working with beads. 2. the beads

Beagle Brothers perennial adversaries of Scrooge McDuck

17

beamship type of UFO

Bear Butte sacred mountain in Black Hills of South Dakota, known to Sioux as Mato Pah, 'Sleeping Bear Mountain'

Bear Tribe community led by Sun Bear, 1970-

Beat (Beatific Generation) avant-garde literary movement and way of life popularized by Ginsberg, Kerouac, Cassady, Curso, Snyder, 1950s

beatific vision 1. Christian mystical experience. 2. visions of Dante in the *Divine Comedy* where the Griffon reveals its human and godly nature and when Beatrice removes her veil and Dante beholds the radiance of Divine Love

Beatles (Paul McCartney, John Lennon, George Harrison, Ringo Starr) British rock group whose music and lyrics reflected and inspired the 1960s generation; *Let It Be*; 1962-69

Beatnik follower of the Beat poets

Beatrice (Beatrice dei Portinari) the bride of Dante's spirit who guides him to Paradise in the *Divine Comedy* and whose smile confers the bliss of faith, grace, and divine love; 1266-90

Beauraing community in Belgium in which the Virgin Mary appeared 33 times to five young children in 1932-33

beauty the quality that unites wholeness, harmony, and radiance (Aquinas)

Beauty Unknown book depicting 27 New Age guides from the solar system and various galaxies, received through Daphne and Nelson, 1974

Bedouin member of one of the wandering tribes of the Sahara, Arabia, Syria

beefsteak (shiso, *Japanese*) hearty plant in whose leaves umeboshi are aged

Beelzebub 'Lord of the Flies', 1. Philistine God. 2. visitor from another planet who narrates Gurdjieff's *Meetings with Remarkable Men*

Beep Beep the Roadrunner

Beethoven, Ludwig von German composer; *Ninth Symphony*; 1770-1827

Befana good fairy of Italian children, female counterpart of Santa Claus

Beghard member of a communal Christian movement of medieval Germany and the Netherlands

being miracle of miracles; manifesting from the Father (Jesus, *Gospel of Thomas*)

Bellamy, Edward utopian novelist; *Looking Backward*; 1850-98

Beloved Disciple (John the Priest) follower of Jesus at whose house the Last Supper transpired; traditionally identified with St. John

Beltane Celtic spring festival May 1

Bely, Andrey Russian symbolist poet and disciple of Steiner; *The Silver Dove*; 1880-1934

Benedict, Dirk (Dirk Niewoehner) actor and film star who healed himself of prostate cancer with macrobiotics; *Confessions of a Kamikaze Cowboy*; 1945-

benefic favorable or fortunate planet

beneficials friendly insects and birds which contribute to organic farming

Bengali 1. native of Bengal, India or East Bengal, Bangladesh. 2. Indic language spoken in Bengal with a variety of the Devanagari script

Benin West African city renowned for bronze terra cotta and naturalistic heads, 13-18th c.

Benjamin youngest son of Jacob and Rachel, brother of Joseph in the Bible

Bennett, John Godolphin English spiritual teacher, student of Gurdieff, musician; *The Long Pilgrimage*; 1897-1974

Benneville, George de founder of Universalism; 1703-93,

bennu heron, sacred bird of Osiris (Egyptian)

Bensalem utopian South Pacific Island in Francis Bacon's *New Atlantis*, 1627

Benson, Herbert, M.D. holistic physician and meditator; *The Relaxation Response*; 1935-

Benten Japanese Goddess of Music, Arts, and Beauty

Bento box lacquerware Japanese food box

Beowulf hero of an Anglo-Saxon epic of the same name

Berber North African nomad

Berdiaeff, Nikolai Russian mystic; The *Beginning and the End*; 1874-1948

Berenger, Sauniere French priest who discovered parchments in a church in Renne-le-Chateau pertaining to the Holy Grail, 1852-1917

Berger, Arthur S. American author, attorney, thanatologist; *Evidence of Life after Death*; 1920-

Bergh, Henry founder of the American Society for the Prevention of Cruelty to Animals; 1813-88

Bergier, Jacques French physicist and alchemical researcher; *The Morning of the Magicians*; 1912-

Bergman, Ingmar Swedish film director;

The Seventh Seal; 1918-

Berkeley, Bishop George Irish subjective idealist philosopher; *Three Dialogues between Hylas and Philonous*; 1685-1753

Berkeley Zen Center Buddhist community established by Shunryu Suzuki-Roshi, 1967-

Bermoothes Bermuda, island of *The Tempest*

Bernard, Claude French physiologist; 1813-78

Bernard, Raymond (Walter Sigmeister) author on natural diet and living; *From Chrishna to Christ*; ca. 1900-66

Bernard, St. 1. French mystic and abbot of Clairvaux; *De Diligendo Deo*; 1090-1153. 2. large bodhisattva rescue dog of Switzerland descended from the Tibetan mastiff

Berrigan, Daniel Jesuit poet, peace activist; *America Is Hard to Find*; 1921-

Berrigan, Phillip Catholic priest, peace activist; 1923-

Berry, Chuck rock and roll singer; *Go Johnny Go*; 1926-

Berry, Thomas Catholic eco-theologian; *The Dream of the Earth*; 1914-

Berry, Wendell poet, novelist, and Kentucky farmer; *The Unsettling of America*; 1934-

Bertalonffy, Ludwig Von father of General Systems Theory; 1901-72

Berylune the fairy in *The Blue Bird*

Besant, Annie English-born Theosophist, Indian educator, social reformer; *Autobiography*; 1847-1933

besoul v. infusion of a soul into

beta second letter of the Greek alphabet

beta body astral body

beta particle elementary particle emitted from a nucleus during radioactive decay with a single electrical charge and a mass 1/1837 of a proton; an electron if negatively charged, positron if positively

beta waves brain waves indicating normal waking state with consciousness directed to the external environment

Beth second Hebrew letter: speech, locomotion, B, 2

Bethany site where Jesus raised Lazarus

Bethel Christian communal community in Missouri led by Dr. William Keil, 1844-77

Beulah Israel when she shall be married, land of rest in *Pilgrim's Progress*

beyond within mystical awareness (Sidney Cohen)

Bhadrapala Bodhisattva who attained enlightenment while bathing

Bhagavad Gita 'Divine Song', song sung by Lord Krishna to Arjuna revealing the mystical union of the soul with the Absolute; part of the *Mahabharata* (Sanskrit)

Bhagavata Purana story of the avatars of Vishnu and of Krishna's childhood adventures

Bhaishajyaguru Bodhisattva of Healing

bhajan devotional music, singing holy songs (Sanskrit)

Bhajan, Yogi (S.S.S. Harbhajan Singh) Indian-born Sikh teacher, founder of 3HO; 1929-

bhakta devotional singer (Sanskrit)

bhakti devotion (Sanskrit)

Bhakti Yoga skillful practice of devotion and worship, e.g., Hare Krishna movement (Sanskrit)

Bhaktivedanta, A. C. (Swami Prabupada, Abhay Charan De) Bengali-born businessman and founder of the international Hare Krishna movement; *Bhagavad Gita As It Is*; 1895-1966

bhang hemp, usually mixed into little balls with sweets and swallowed one by one (Hindi)

Bharat Natya Hindu temple dancing (Sanskrit)

Bharata India (Sanskrit)

Bharata Yuddha Javanese epic dealing with the last stage of the *Mahabharata* war, 12th c.

Bharati, Swami Agehananda Austrian-born Hindu monk and teacher; *The Tantric Tradition*; 1923-

bhargo divine light, effulgence, glorious form (Sanskrit)

Bhartrhari Sanskrit lyric poet who abandoned asceticism seven times for married life; 7th c.

bhava becoming; a link in the Buddhist chain (Pali)

bhavachakra wheel of life (Sanskrit)

bhavan house, garden pavilion, commune (Sanskrit)

Bhave, Vinoba Indian leader of the Bhudan and Gramdan movements, disciple of Gandhi; *Commentary on the Gita*; 1895-1982

bhikkhu (bhikshu, *Sanskrit*) Buddhist monk, mendicant, or priest (Pali)

Bhopal site in India of the Union Carbide chemical explosion that killed and injured thousands, December 4, 1984

Bhudan (Bhoodan) 'land gift', voluntary land redistribution movement organized by Vinoba Bhave on his walks across India (Hindi)

bhuh Earth plane (Sanskrit)

bhujiya deep-fried vegetables dipped in a batter of chick-pea flour (Hindi)

Bhumi Earth deity who requested Brahma to send Krishna to Earth to settle strife

Bhutan small Himalayan kingdom

bhuvah astral world, higher etheric plane (Sanskrit)

bi-quintile planets 144 degrees apart; minor favorable aspect

Bible Christian Church first vegetarian religious group in America, which arrived in Philadelphia from England, 1817

bibliomancy divination by reading the first words when a page of a book falls open at random containing the reply to a question

bicorporeal signs double-bodied astrology signs: Gemini, Pisces, Sagittarius

Bifrost rainbow bridge in Scandinavian mythology

bifurcation point or evolutionary branch in a whole system which can lead to the choice between or among more than one possible future (Prigogine and Stengers)

Big Bopper (J. P. Richardson) rock and roll singer; *Chantilly Lace*; 1930-59

Bighorn Medicine Wheel stone circle in Wyoming

Bihari Indic language of Bihar, including Bhojpuri, Maithili, Magah

Bihzad Persian artist and calligrapher; *Shahnama*; ca. 1440-1527

bija syllable or seed corresponding to a particular psychic force from which a visualization springs (Sanskrit)

bike-user friendly receptive to bicyclists

bilocate to be in two or more places at once through the use of higher consciousness techniques

Bimbisara ruler of Magadha during Buddha's life and a supporter of Buddhism

Bimini legendary island of the fountain of youth searched for by Ponce de Leon (Spanish)

Binah sephiroth of mind in the Kabbalah (Hebrew)

binary system number system that has two as its base; basis of modern computers and the *I Ching*

binary triplet configuration the univer-

sal resonant mechanism governing whole systems; a whole number code and visual construct (Jose Arguelles)

bindu 1. drop, globule, dot. 2. mystical mark of the anusvara. 3. semen (Sanskrit)

Bingham, Hiram farmer, soldier, and professor who rediscovered Machu Picchu in 1911; 1875-1956

bio-electricity life energy

bio-electromagnetic adj. relating to fields that may emanate from living tissue in one person and are capable of producing demonstrable clinical improvements in another

bioacidic adj. relating to fast foods, heavily processed foods, irradiated foods, microwaved foods, etc. that adversely affect the health of the person (Szekely)

bioactive adj. living; relating especially to raw foods (Szekely)

bioautomation hypnotic programming of biological self-development (Peter Mutke)

biocentric adj. viewing the Earth rather than humanity as center of the planet; not one species on top but rather a web of which we are one strand interconnected with all other strands

Biochemic healing system of W. H. Schuessler utilizing tissue salts

biocide the death of the Earth through chemical pollution or nuclear annihilation (George Ohsawa, 1963)

biocircuit a device that is placed near or against the body at two or more points, connecting them to form a circuit, thereby enhancing the movement of natural energy in the body

bioclimatology the study of atmospheric and environmental influences on the human organism

bioclock internal mechanism regulating biological rhythms and their influences on plants, animals, or humans

biocommunication 1. modern Soviet term for telepathy. 2. conscious or unconscious exchange of energy between two living organisms

biocomputer human consciousness principle; the brain or conscious mind or the unconscious or subconscious mind operating like a computer to process, program, and categorize information from the environment (Lilly)

biocracy a form of society in which the interrelation with the Earth is the context in which all social, political, and economic decisions are made (Thomas Berry)

biocybernetics 1. discipline of applying feedback models of analysis to living systems. 2. Soviet term for psychical research

biodegradable n. or adj. organic substance that decomposes naturally; environmentally safe

biodiversity extent of the variety of animal and plant life in a given ecosystem

biodynamics organic gardening and farming method developed by Rudolf Steiner utilizing raised platforms, composting, and special soil preparations

bioelectrode the emission of energy from living things that appears in Kirlian photography

Bioenergetic Analysis therapeutic method developed by Alexander Lowen emphasizing expressive mobility and easy flow of energy in body-breathing, sound, and postures

bioenergetic station chakra (Joseph Campbell)

bioenergetics 1. modern Soviet term for psychokinesis. 2. theory that every cell in the body registers emotional or energetic reactions that can be used for healing or development of consciousness

biofeedback a science or learned technique for consciously controlling biological processes such as listening to amplified brain waves through the use of a monitoring instrument that feeds back information to the user (Barbara Brown)

bioflavonoid (Vitamin P) substance found in the pulp and tissue of citrus fruits that builds resistance

bioform living organism of varying size and shape that appears to exist in outer space (ufology)

biogas gasoline from manure, farm waste, vegetable waste, excreta

biogenesis production of living organisms from other living organisms

biogenetics theory that individual development is replicated in the development of the species as a whole

biogenic adj. living; relating to foods that are highest in life force and enzymes (Szekely)

bioinformation 1. study of the brain and its functioning. 2. modern Soviet term for extrasensory perception

biointroscopy Soviet term for reading colors with the fingers

biological clock natural compass within an organism subtly attuned to environmental and cosmic influences regardless of external stimuli

biological contact Soviet term for sympathetic measurable interaction during telepathy

biological degeneration decline of modern civilization through cancer, heart disease, AIDS, and other degenerative diseases (Michio Kushi)

biological plasma the electrical discharge or field of energy that appears around objects in Kirlian photography

biological plasma body Soviet term for the astral body

biological regeneration recovery of health and happiness by modern society according to natural order (Michio Kushi)

biological revolution reversing the decline of modern civilization through return to natural order; macrobiotics (Michio Kushi)

biological transmutation the theory that atoms, elements, and particles can change into one another under certain ordinary environmental conditions without being smashed in a nuclear accelerator

biologogram wave structure that is created by the oscillation of bioplasma

bioluminescence invisible rays that surround an object or individual that can be picked up by Kirlian photography

biomagnetics the science dealing with magnetic fields and their effects on living organisms and the environment

biomass actual quantity of living beings in a particular environment

biome a region that shares essentially the same geographical features and conditions, e.g, central Texas is part of the Temperate Grasslands Biome that also occurs in Argentina, Uruguay, Australia, and parts of Asia and Europe; thirteen others classified by M. D. F. Udvardy for the International Union for the Conservation of Nature

biomimetic complex of mechanistic ideas and devices that becomes a substrate for the incarnation of psychic forces

bion basic unit of orgone energy (Reich)

bionization the trend toward increasing artificialization of human life, including organ transplants, artificial organs, test tube births, and other practices that separate us from millions of years of biological evolution (Michio Kushi)

biophysical effect method (BPE) Soviet term for dowsing

biophysics the study of the relation of energy, matter, and their effects on living organisms and the environment

bioplasma Soviet term for life energy or psychic energy

bioplasmic force field aura

biopsychic relating to the biological, psychic, and spiritual field influencing or governing human beings and the environment

biorapport Soviet term for the influence of one person in a group on the others

bioregion 1. geographical territory defined by watersheds, river valleys, coastal plains, or other physical feature; by range of species of plants and animals; by climatic zones; by human language groups; or other natural environmental or cultural unit as opposed to political boundaries. 2. geographic zone that is both self-governing and self-sufficient

bioregional movement trend toward living on the Earth according to natural ecological boundaries and regions rather than political or economic zones

biorelativity the interaction of people with their physical environment via psychic or mind energy (Jeffrey Goodman)

bioresonance theory that every living thing resonates at its own unique frequency like a musical chord

biorhythm 1. science studying changes in the individual's physical, emotional, and mental states on the basis of 23-, 28-, and 33-day cycles calculated from the date of birth; founded by Hermann Swoboda and Wilhelm Fleiss, early 20th c. adj. **biorhythmic**

bioshelter area to test out ecological systems (New Alchemy Institute)

biosignal extraterrestrial communication received electronically

biosociation creative act, thinking or operating on more than one plane (Koestler)

biosphere (Edward Seuss, 1875) 1. the envelope of life, i.e., the area of living matter on the Earth's crust occupied by transformers which convert cosmic radiations into effective terrestrial energy: electrical, chemical, mechanical, thermal, etc. (Vernadsky). 2. Earth as a living organism (Teilhard). 3. an integrated planet containing a single culture

Biosphere II a self-sustaining 3-acre glass-enclosed environment independent of the outside world except for electricity and information in Oracle, Arizona, 1990-

biota the collection of all individual living organisms

biotechnological age the era from 1980 to about 2030 A.D. which is characterized by increasing artificialization of human beings and their environment (Michio Kushi)

biotectonic adj. living technology, fusion of the vegetal and technological

biotecture house made of plant material

biotelecommunication 1. study or tuning into relations between living systems, especially the subtle effects of electromagnetic fields. 2. Soviet term for psychical research

biotelepathy supportive relation between two or more living organisms at a distance, e.g., resonance of twins

biotic n. or adj. living, ecological

biotin (Vitamin H) bacterial growth factor found in certain animal and plant foods

biotonic therapy color and spectrobiological healing developed by Maryla de Chrapowick

Bip Marcel Marceau's Everyperson character in mime

bipolar relating to something having two complementary/antagonistic functions or structures

Bird Goddess Neolithic Goddess appearing with wings, a beak, or a bird's body

Birmingham Innocents four girls killed in a bomb blast by segregationists in Alabama on Sept. 15, 1963: Addie Mae Collins, 14: Denise McNair, 11; Carole Robertson, 14; Cynthia Wesley, 14

birth opening into a new situation (Trungpa)

birth path number number in numerology derived from month, date, and year of birth

birth time exact moment of birth

Biruni, al Persian physician, astrologer, scientist; *A History of India*; 973-1048

biryani spiced saffron rice (Hindi)

Bjarni Heriolfsson Viking who sailed to the North American continent in 986 according to Norse sagas

Black Crown Ceremony (Vajra Mukut,

Sanskrit) Tibetan Buddhist ceremony transmitting the energy and intelligence of the awakened state of mind; performed by the Karmapa

Black Elk (Sapa Hehaka) Oglala Souix medicine man; *The Sacred Pipe*; Moon of the Popping Trees in the Winter When the Four Crows Were Killed (1863)-1950

black hole collapsed star, postulated by the general theory of relativity, but not observed so far, whose force of gravity is so strong that nothing, not, can escape from its surface

Black Knight withdrawn, meditative figure of medieval European romance

Black Mesa great ridge in Arizona from which jut three mesas where Hopis live

Black Stone of Pessinus aniconic image of the Phrygian Great Mother taken to Rome during the last of the Punic wars

Blackfeet people of Montana and Alberta who speak Blackfoot

blade symbol of the dominator model of society, especially that governed by men (Riane Eisler)

Blake, William English poet, mystic, artist; *Book of Job*; 1757-1827

Blarney Stone Irish rock that gives power of easy speech when kissed

Blavatsky, Helena Petrovna Russian born co-founder of the Theosophical Society; *The Secret Doctrine*; 1836-91

Blessing Way Navaho healing ceremony and path of peace, harmony, and prosperity

blind spring place where ley lines cross (Guy Underwood)

bliss out v. to briefly feel whole and joyous; opposite of freak out

block idea, feeling, physical disorder, etc. that impedes health, happiness, and unlimited development of consciousness

blocking the prevention of the smooth energy flow through the body by physical, mental, or spiritual stagnation

Blofeld, John English authority on Buddhism; *The Wheel of Life*; 1913-

Bloom, Leopold and Molly central characters in Joyce's *Ulysses*

Bloom, Marshall radical journalist, New Age pioneer; 1944-69

blow one's mind v. 1. to lose self-control. 2. to get high, experience intensely. 3. to surprise (Afro-American)

Bloy, Leon French novelist; *Woman as Holy Spirit*; 1846-1917

Blue Bird dove symbolizing happiness

and the great secret of things in a fairy play by the same name by Maurice Maeterlinck, 1907

blue-green algae freshwater algae harvested from Upper Klamath Lake in Oregon, high in vitamins and minerals

Blue Meanies heavies in the *Yellow Submarine* who tried to turn the inhabitants blue and grey until driven off by the Beatles and their colorful selves were restored

blueprint life pattern imprinted in the psyche, which an individual follows out on the earthplane

Bly, Robert poet and bard; *Sleepers Holding Hands*; 1926-

bo (gathering point) point on the front of the body where energy that has flowed through the organs comes out and gathers to go toward the arm and leg meridians (Japanese)

Boat of Millions of Years solar barque of Ra in Egyptian mythology

Boaz pillar of Solomon's temple symbolizing good

Bobbie sheepdog who traveled from Indiana to Oregon to find its family

Boccaccio, Giovanni Italian writer; *Decameron*; 1313-75

Bode's Law law describing the orbits of the planets increasing in distance from the sun by a 1:2 ratio or octave (Johann D. Titius and Johann Bode)

Bodhgaya site in Bihar, India, where Buddha received enlightenment meditating under a tree

bodhi enlightenment, wisdom (Sanskrit)

bodhicitta (bodaishin, *Japanese*) will to supreme enlightenment (Sanskrit)

Bodhidharma (Tamo, *Chinese*, Daruma, *Japanese*) incredibly fierce-looking South Indian Buddhist who traveled to China and founded Ch'an Buddhism after meditating for nine years in front of a wall at Shaolin; first Zen Patriarch; 440-528

bodhisattva (pu-sa, *Chinese*, bosatu, *Japanese*) 'enlightenment being', 1. one who seeks enlightenment for all living beings, postponing his or her own happiness and final nirvana to assist others. 2. parents (Dalai Lama). 3. laborers, farmers, and others who perform hard labor for society (Mizuno) (Sanskrit)

body 1. the multi-spiraled constitution of humans and other living beings serving as the placenta for consciousness in this life and that to come (Michio Kushi). 2.

moving particles of the Earth (Wendell Berry). 3. a vehicle of consciousness; in the *Upanishads* the bodies, or sheaths, of the soul are (Sanskrit):

karana sharira..................... causal body
shukshuma sharira.............. subtle body
linga sharira......................... astral body
sthula sharira....................... gross body

body-awareness techniques sensory methods employed in Gestalt and other therapies

body cleansing a program of fasting and elimination of toxins to maintain body health

body language emotional and attitudinal communication transmitted by posture, behavior

bodywork the use of a number of therapies for healing that employ physical techniques or methods such as massage

Boehme, Jakob German mystic; *Mysterium Magnum*; 1575-1624

Boericke, William homeopath; *Materia Medica with Repertory*

boffing long foam sword combat invented by Jack Nottingham

Bogomiles mystical Christian sect in Bulgaria and Thrace, 12th c.

Bohemian n. or adj. artistic, offbeat individual (from the Jewish quarter of Prague, Bohemia)

Bohm, David theoretical physicist; *Wholeness and the Implicate Order*; 1918-

Bohmian adj. holonomic or holistic; after physicist David Bohm

Bohr, Niels Danish physicist whose theories came to him in a dream; 1885-1962

Boibel Loth secret alphabet calendar mysteries of the Druids

boiled salad a salad whose ingredients are lightly boiled or dipped in hot water before serving

Bois-Guilbert, Brian de misguided Knight Templar in Scott's *Ivanhoe*

boji a stone used to take away pain by closing holes in the energy field of the human body

bok choy a leafy green and white vegetable popular in Chinese-style cooking

bokuseki 'ink traces', Zen calligraphy (Japanese)

Bolen, Jean Shinoda psychiatrist, Jungian analyst and author; *The Tao of Psychology*

bollos polones boiled corn balls made from whole corn dough (Spanish)

Bolongongo, Shamba Bushongo king

who abolished his army, introduced raffia weaving and the arts of peace; ca. 1600

Bon-pa pre-Buddhist shamanistic way of life in Tibet (Tibetan)

Bonito 1. Pueblo in Chaco Canyon, N.M. built ca. 900. 2. (l.c.) flakes shaved from dried bonito fish used in soup stocks or as a garnish (Japanese)

bonsai dwarf tree (Japanese)

bonze (bozu) head of a Buddhist monastery (Japanese)

boogie v. to be alive, flow with it, be energetic, get it on (Afro-American)

Book of Thoth Tarot cards

Book of Truth, or the Voice of Osiris Aquarian testament received through El Eros, 1956

Bookchin, Murray social activist and cultural critic; *The Ecology of Freedom*

boomer member of the baby boom generation

Boone, Allen interspecies communicator; *Kinship with All Life*

boot up v. to start up

Booth, William founder of the Salvation Army; 1829-90

bootstrap hypothesis idea that nature cannot be reduced to fundamental entities, such as elementary particles but has to be understood entirely through its self-consistency

bop rock and roll. n. **bopper, bopster** devotee of bop (Afro-American)

border adj. phenomena of an ambiguous nature

Borobudur giant Buddhist pyramid of mystical design in Java, 8th c.

borscht beet or cabbage soup (Russian)

Borysenko, Joan medical scientist and psychologist; *Minding the Body, Mending the Mind*

bosatsu bodhisattva (Japanese)

Bosch, Hieronymus Dutch artist noted for astral images; *Garden of Earthly Delights*; 1450-1516

Boscovitch, Roger Yugoslavian-born genius who prefigured the unitary theory of the universe, quantum theory, wave mechanics, and atoms formed of nucleons; *Theory of Natural Philosophy*; 1711-87

Bose, Jagadis Chandra Indian scientist, pioneer plant researcher; *Plant Autographs and Their Revelations*; 1858-1937

Boston Women's Health Collective feminist collective that challenged medical male-practice and published *Our Bodies, Our Selves,* 1971

botane ancient Hellenic term relating to the consciousness of plants and their ability to react subtly to humans, animals, or the environment around them

bottom line first or lowest line of an *I Ching* hexagram

Bouvet, Joachim (Po Chi) one of the first French Jesuits to enter China and leader of the Figurists who held a common origin for Chinese and Western culture; 1656-1730

Bovis, Andre French inventor, discoverer of pyramidal energy

Bowman, Dave surviving crew member of the *Discovery* in *2001*

BPE Biophysical Effects Method; Soviet term for dowsing

Bragi Scandinavian God of Poetry

Brahe, Tycho Danish astronomer who developed a system from Arabic and Chinese sources; 1546-1601

Braheny, Kevin New Age musician, synthesist; *The Way Home* (*Perelandra*)

Brahma Hindu God of Creation

Brahma-randhra opening in the crown of the head (Sanskrit)

Brahma-Vihara divine state of a bodhisattva (Sanskrit)

karuna................................. compassion
maitra.. love
upeksha.............................. equanimity
mudita.............................. joy in others

brahmachari male celibate, student (Sanskrit)

brahmacharini female celibate, student (Sanskrit)

brahmacharya celibacy (Sanskrit)

Brahmaloka Brahma's heaven

Brahman World Soul, absolute (Sanskrit)

Brahmi Sanskrit script of Semitic origin used until the 7th c.

brain 1. physical organ of consciousness. 2. the enchanted loom (Alan Watts)

brain building use of machines to tune up brains and enhance creativity and intelligence,

Bran 1. 'raven', mythical British King. 2. Celtic God of the Underworld. 3. (l.c.) the outer coating of the whole grain removed together with the germ during refining to produce white flour or white rice; may be used in pickling or as a garnish

branches of time science-fiction theme of rewinding the reel of life and playing it out again

Brand, Stewart publisher, editor, and author; *The Whole-Earth Catalogue*; 1938-

Brandywine river in Middle Earth

Brautigan, Richard Oregon writer; *Trout Fishing in America*; 1935-

Brave New World Aldous Huxley's utopian novel of a society ruled by science and pleasure-giving devices and drugs, 1932 (from *The Tempest*)

Bread and Puppet Theatre avant-garde drama group, 1962-

Bread and Roses 1. demands of textile workers during the Lawrence, Mass. strike organized by Emma Goldman, 1912. 2. symbol of the women's liberation movement

Bread for the World national citizens' movement devoted to getting government to act on root causes of hunger and poverty, Washington, D.C.

bread of angels knowledge of God

Breasil legendary lost island discovered by Irish monks in medieval times

breatharian dietary practice of receiving nourishment via the air

breathwork working with breath inhalation and exhalation patterns to achieve physical, emotional, and spiritual change

Brenden, St. Irish monk reputed to have found a lost utopian island in the north Atlantic; 484-577

Brer Rabbit resilient hero of African fables

Brethren Christian peace church, which began in Germany, 18th c.-

Breuil, Abbe Henri French cataloguer who sketched thousands of underground paleolithic caves; 1877-1961

brewer's yeast concentrated source of high-quality protein and many B vitamins

Briarpatch network of over 300 alternative organizations and businesses in San Francisco which sought to survive in the cracks of modern civilization, 1973- . **Briars**, members of Briarpatch

Brico, Antonio conductor, disciple of Yogananda, founder of the New York Women's Symphony; 1902-89

Brigid Celtic Goddess of Rivers and Waters

Bristlecone Pine oldest known planetary being, resident of California, ca.-2600-

b'riyah world of formation in the Kabbalah (Hebrew)

Broceliande Elfin kingdom in Tennyson's *The Idylls of the King*

Brock, Alice restaurateur; 1940-

Bronte, Emily English novelist; *Wuthering Heights*; 1818-48

Brook Farm Transcendentalist utopian community in West Roxbury, Mass., founded by George Ripley, 1841-47

Brosse, Therese performer of the first electrocardiographic study of yoga in 1935

Brother Sun, Sister Moon canticle acknowledging the equality of all God's creation by St. Francis

Brotherhood of the Spirit Christian commune in western Massachusetts

Brower, David (the Archdruid) environmentalist and founder of Friends of the Earth; *Gentle Wisdom*; 1912-

Brown, Edward Espe Zen priest, poet, and cook; *The Tassajara Bread Book*

Brown, Frank A. researcher in biological rhythms of plants and animals; *Biological Clocks*; 1908-

Brown, Jerry former California governor, Jesuit, and Zen student, 1938-

brown rice 1. whole unpolished rice; available in short, medium, and long grain, containing an ideal balance of nutrients. 2. the principal staple in macrobiotic cooking. 3. the icon of anti-modernity (Warren Belasco)

Brown, Rosemary English psychic composer, who has channeled 400 new works of Beethoven, Chopin, Grieg, Schubert, Bach, and Liszt since 1964; *Unfinished Symphonies*; 1917-

Brown, Virginia registered nurse and mother who recovered from terminal malignant melanoma with macrobiotics; *Macrobiotic Miracle*; 1916-

Bruderhof German Christian movement founded by Eberhard Arnold, now chiefly in America and England, 1920s-

Brueghel the Elder, Pieter Flemish artist; *Adoration of the Magi*; 1525-69

Bruin bear in *Reynard the Fox*

brujo sorcerer, healer of Mexico and the American Southwest

Bruno, Giordano Italian Dominican philosopher, astronomer, poet, Egyptian mystery cultist, believer in a multiplicity of inhabited worlds; *Del infinito*; ca. 1548-1600

Brynhild estranged lover of Sigurd, Valkyrie in *Volsunga*

BT Basic Technique; practice by which each card in an ESP test is laid aside by the experimenter as it is called by the subject and a check is made at the end

Bubba Free John (Franklin Jones) spiritual teacher, retired head of the Dawn Horse Communion; 1939-

bubble of perception closed world of ordinary reality, cluster of personality (don Juan)

Buber, Martin German-born Jewish philosopher, mystic, peace advocate; *I and Thou*; 1878-1965

Bucephalus horse of Alexander the Great

buckwheat a hardy cereal grass eaten in the form of kasha or soba noodles

buckwheat plaster plaster made from buckwheat flour used in macrobiotic home care to draw out liquid and reduce swelling

Buddha 'awakened one', 1. Siddartha Gautama, chief personage of historical Buddhism, also known as Sakyamuni, or sage of the Sakya tribe; -623-543 (Theravada), -566-486 or -563-483 (Mahayana). 2. principle of enlightenment. 3. any enlighted beings, in any of the realms. 4. any of countless past or future turners of the Wheel of the Law in the Mahayana. 5. one who has attained universal understanding and spirit (Michio Kushi). 6. rice (Japanese proverb) (Sanskrit)

Buddha Nature (buddhata, *Sanskrit*, bussho, *Japanese*) 1. one's own true nature, true self. 2. miraculous awareness; responding, perceiving, and arching your brows, blinking your eyes, moving your hands and feet (Bodhidharma)

Buddha Purnima Indian celebration of Buddha's birthday, full moon in May

Buddha Realms planes and orders of consciousness that can be brought to awareness through meditation on appropriate mythological forms

Buddhadharma the Dharma as taught by a line of enlightened human beings (Sanskrit)

buddhafield subtle energy field of awareness and compassion

Buddhaghosa Theravada monk of Ceylon; *Visuddhi Magga*; 4th or 5th c.

buddhata Buddha Nature, awakening mind (Sanskrit)

buddhi faculty of discimination and discernment, higher than the mind (Sanskrit)

Buddhism 1. religion based on the teachings of the historical Buddha that came out in India, spread to Sri Lanka, Tibet, China, Southeast Asia, and Japan and more recently to America, Europe, and elsewhere. 2. a way of life that holds that the universe and all creatures in it are intrinsically in a state of complete widom, love, and compassion, acting in natural response and mutual interdependence; realized by giving the self up and away (Gary Snyder)

Buddhist Economics a Middle Way between materialist heedlessness and traditionalist immobility proposed by E. F. Schumacher in *Small Is Beautiful*

Buddhist Ray first Buddhist periodical in America near Santa Cruz, 1887

Buddhist Society of America group founded by Shigetsu Sasaki, later renamed First Zen Institute of America, 1930-

Budge, Ernest Alfred British Egyptologist; tr. *The Egyptian Book of the Dead*; 1857-1934

budo martial arts (Japanese)

Buffalo great being who stands at the western gate of the universe and holds back the waters that periodically inundate the Earth in the Lakota system of ages; every year the buffalo loses a hair on one of its legs; every age it loses a leg; when all legs are lost, the world is flooded and renewed

Bugs Bunny anarchistic comic strip hare

Builders of the Adytum hermetic group founded by Paul F. Case

bulghur a form of whole wheat originally from the Near East that has been cracked, partially boiled, and dried

bummer 1. any negative experience. 2. unpleasant psychedelic trip

Bunraku puppet theater with extra large dolls and black-hooded operators (Japanese)

Bunyan, John English preacher; *Pilgrim's Progress*; 1628-88

Bunyan, Paul legendary North American logger and lumber-jack

Buraq 'lightning', fabulous winged mare with a woman's head and peacock's tail on which Muhammad flew to Jerusalem and Heaven on his Night Journey (Arabic)

Burbank, Luther botanist; *The Training of the Human Plant;* 1849-1926

burdock a hardy wild plant with a long, dark root that is valued in cooking for its strengthening qualities

Burkitt, Denis P. British surgeon who

linked cancer in Africa with the rise of the modern diet and who popularized fiber; *Eat Right — To Stay Healthy and Enjoy Life More*, 1979

Burmese principle language of Burma written in a distinctive alphabet of circles or portions of circles: originally written on palm leaves where straight lines would cause leaves to split

Burmese position form of cross-legged sitting in which the feet are not placed over the thighs, but are both resting on the sitting surface

burn v. to extinguish karma, to make conscious the consequences of past action without shame, fear, anger, or censoring

burning ghat riverbank steps on which cremations are made in India

Burritt, Elihu blacksmith, pacifist, organizer of the League of Universal Brotherhood; 1810-79

Buryat 1. Soviet Republic, capital Ulan-Ude. 2. people around Lake Baikal in southern Siberia. 3. Mongolian-style language spoken there

Buscaglia, Leo (Dr. Love, Dr. Hug) psychologist and advocate of self-affirmation; *Living, Loving, Learning*; 1925-

bushido 'way of the flower of manhood', samurai code (Japanese)

Bushman language of the Bushmen of the Kalahari Desert

Bushongo medieval African people in the region of the Sankuru River whose high culture dated back fifteen centuries

Butsu Buddha (Japanese)

butsuden Buddha hall in a Zen monastery (Japanese)

byo-ki 'disturbed energy', sickness (Japanese)

Cc

C-3PO human-shaped bronze droid in *Star Wars*

Caacal Tablets texts revealed to James Churchward by a Hindu priest concerning two sunken continents

Cabala spelling usually employed when discussing the spread of kabbalistic teachings and symbols into Christian circles during the Renaissance

Cabet, Etienne French utopian; *Journey to Icaria*; 1788-1856

cactese modulated sound language of cacti

Caddy, Eileen co-founder of Findhorn; *Footprints on the Path*; 1908-

Caddy, Peter co-founder of Findhorn

cadent houses third, sixth, ninth, and twelfth houses in astrology representing compromise

caduceus wand of Hermes

Caer Sidi 'Revolving Castle', Welsh otherworld of treasure and revelry (Celtic)

Cage, John zenic composer; *Imaginary Landscape No. 5*; 1912-

Cagliostro, Alessandro di (Giuseppe Balsamo) Italian adventurer and magus; 1743-95

Cahokia largest ceremonial center of Mississippian culture, near East St. Louis, Ill., containing a mound 100-feet high and covering 16 acres, A.D. 800-1500

Cainnic, St. Irish solitary who read from a book in the antlers of a friendly stag

Cairbre chief bard of Celtic legend

cairn heap of stones set up as a landmark. monument, or tombstone

Calchas Greek soothsayer at Troy

calcination cooking, initial stage of alchemy

calcium mineral essential for bone development, blood clotting, muscle tone, and nerve functioning; found in abundance in leafy green vegetables and sea vegetables

Calcutta 'Kali Ghat', capital of Bengal, India

Caldicott, Helen Australian-born pediatrcian and founder of Physicians for Social Responsibility; *What You Can Do About Nuclear War*; 1938-

Caliban native islander in *The Tempest*

caliphate 'successor', temporal and spiritual ruler of Islam (Arabic)

call subject's guess in trying to identify the target in an ESP test

Callanish megalithic stone circle in Scotland

Calliope Greek muse of epic poetry

Callistris Patriarch of Constantinople who taught breathing exercises and repetition of the Lord's Prayer for 'entering the heart by means of attention'; 14th c.

calumet ceremonial wand of the North American Indians

Calvino, Italo Italian metaphysical novelist; *Invisible Cities*; 1923-85

Calypso nymph who detained Odysseus for seven years on Ogygia island

Camara, Dom Helder Pessoa Archbishop of Olinda and Recife, Brazil; Latin American social revolutionary; 1909-

Camelot seat of King Arthur's court and the Round Table

Camerarius, Rudolf Jakob German botanist who discovered that plants have sex; 1665-1721

Campanella, Giovan Domenico Italian friar, poet, philosopher, astrologer, utopian novelist; *The City of the Sun*; 1568-1639

Campanus astrological system based on equal division of the prime vertical from the east point by house circles

Campbell, Joseph mythologist; *The Masks of God*; 1904-87

Camus, Albert French novelist; *The Stranger*; 1913-60

Cana site where Jesus healed a nobleman's child

Cancer (*karkinos*, 'crab', *Greek*) 1. the crab, fourth zodiac sign; ruler, the Moon; of the watery element; keywords: tenacity, nurturing energy. 2. (l.c.) a disease of the whole body in which mucus and toxins accumulated over years following a disorderly way of life and imbalanced eating are localized as tumors or a degenerating blood or lymph condition and which, if diagnosed early, can often be relieved by a macrobiotic diet (Michio Kushi)

Candace one of a matrilineal line of rulers in Meroe

Candida Albicans a yeast that under normal circumstances lives healthfully inside the body but through temporary overgrowth can result in symptoms of oral thrush in children or vaginitis in women

candlemagic burning candles of special colors, shapes, and aromas to achieve magical ends

Candomble Afro-Caribbean or Brazilian ceremony

Cannon, Walter Bradford neurologist and physiologist; *The Wisdom of the Body*; 1871-1945

Canopus star and cosmic source of order and control in *Shikasta*

Canterbury pilgrimage city in Kent, England; site of Becket's shrine; subject of Chaucer's *Canterbury Tales*

Canyon de Chelly sacred site in Arizona populated with Anasazi ruins, A.D. 300-

Cao-Dai Vietnamese way of life combining Taoism, Buddhism, and Christianity, whose prophets include Mark Twain and Victor Hugo; the Supreme Being symbolized by an eye surrounded by clouds; headquarters in Tay Ninh

Cape Cormorin (Kanya Kumari) resplendent city and beach at the tip of South India

Capernaum site where Jesus chose the twelve apostles

Capra, Fritjof Austrian-born physicist; *The Tao of Physics*; 1939-

Capricorn sea-goat, tenth zodiac sign; ruler Saturn; of the earthy element; keywords: duty, concentrating energy

capstone top of the Great Pyramid

Caracol, El 'the Snail', Mayan observatory in Chichen Itza (Spanish)

Caraka Samhita India's chief medical text on Ayurvedic principles

caravan group of traders, travelers, merchants, or pilgrims traveling together

carbohydrate substance containing carbon, hydrogen, and oxygen, such as starch or sugar

carbon steel iron with carbon and other elements added used for quality knives and cooking utensils

cardinal directions East, South, West, North

cardinal signs Aries, Cancer, Libra, Capricorn signifying pioneers, activists, initiatory energy

Carib only surviving pre-Columbian Indians in the Caribbean

caritas love of God (Latin)

Carlson, Chester inventor of Xeroxing who received instructions clairaudially; 1906-68

carob (St. John's bread) chocolate-like natural sweetener; product of the carob tree

carole dance circle in which participants hold hands and concentrate on linking with all humanity and raising human consciousness

carotene yellow compound of carbon and hydrogen in plants that forms Vitamin A

Carpenter, Edward English socialist, mystic, crafts organizer; *Civilization: Its Cause and Cure*; 1844-1929

Carrington, Hereward English psychi-

cal researcher; *Your Psychic Powers and How to Develop Them*; 1881-1959

carrying capacity the ability of an environment to sustain a given population of a species

Carson, Rachel ecologist; *Silent Spring*; 1907-64

Carter, Jimmy president; founder of the Carter Center in Atlanta; carpenter; world hunger and human rights activist; 1924-

Carthusians order of monks founded by St. Bruno at La Chartreux, France, 1086-

Carton, Sidney hero of Dickens's *A Tale of Two Cities* who took Charles Darnay's place on the guillotine

Carus, Paul German-born philosopher of Buddhism; 1852-1919

Carver, George Washington scientist who developed 300 products from peanuts; 1864-1943

Casbah residential area with lush gardens in Marrakech

cashew kidney-shaped nut native to Brazil and the West Indies

Cassady, Neal archetypal Beat; *The First Third and Other Writings*; 1926-68

Cassandra Greek prophetess whose predictions were never believed

Cassian, John monk, pilgrim, Egyptian anchorite; *Dialogues*; ca. 350-435

cast-iron a hard, brittle, nonmalleable iron-carbon alloy used for making heavy cookware

Castagno, Andrea del Florentine artist; *Last Supper*; 1423-57

Castalia 1. spring on Mt. Parnassus sacred to the Muses; source of visionary inspiration. 2. country in Hesse's *Glass Bead Game*

Castaneda, Carlos anthropologist, apprentice sorcerer; *The Teachings of Don Juan*; 1935-

castile fine, hard, bland, odorless soap made either partly or completely with olive oil and sodium hydroxide

Castle of the Grail site of the Holy Grail and dwelling of Amfortas

Castle of the Maidens site where the seven Knights of Darkness imprisoned the seven Maidens of Virtue in the Grail legend

Castle, Irene dancer and animal rescue worker; 1893-1969

Catal Huyuk Anatolian excavation site of the largest neolithic settlement in the Near East, ca. -7th c.

catastrophism field or study of natural disasters, especially as related to prophecy, mythology, world ages, millennialism. n. or adj. **catastrophist**

Caterpiller philosophical being in *Alice in Wonderland*

Cathari 'pure', Albigenses (Greek)

Catherine of Genoa, St. Italian mystic; *The Treatise on Purgatory*; 1447-1510

Catherine of Siena, St. Italian mystic; *Divine Dialogue*; 1347-80

Catholic Workers radical back-to-the land social movement founded by Dorothy Day and Peter Maurin with headquarters in Tivoli, N.Y., 1933-

Catlin, George explorer-artist of Indian America; 1796-1873

Catonsville Nine peace activists who napalmed Selective Service files in Catonsville, Md., May 17, 1968: Dan and Phil Berrigan, David Darst, John Hogan, Tom Lewis, Mari and Tom Melville, Mary Maylan, George Mische

Catt, Cary Chapman feminist; *Woman Suffrage and Politics*; 1859-1947

Caucasus region between the Black and Caspian Seas where some forty Caucasian languages are spoken

Caulfield, Holden 17-year-old adventurer in Salinger's *The Catcher in the Rye*

Cauwenberghe, Marc Van Belgium-born macrobiotic physician and educator; *Macrobiotic Home Remedies;* 1944-

Caves of the Thousand Buddhas art complex at Tun-Huang, China

Cayce, Edgar (the Sleeping Prophet) trance therapist, philosopher, healer; *A Search for God*; 1877-1945

Cayuga people of Cayuga Lake region, Great Pipe people

Ce Acatl 'One Reed', 1. epithet of the morning star (Nahuatl). 2. Topiltzin legendary founder of Tula and the Toltec empire

celebration partner person who celebrates life and guides others; teacher (Margo Anand)

celestial city 1. ideal pattern set in the heavens, where those who want to see it can do so, and establish it in their own hearts (Plato). 2. (cap.) city with the Tree of Life and goal in Bunyan's *The Pilgrim's Progress*

Celestial River Chinese and Japanese term for the Milky Way

Celestial Seasonings natural herbal tea company founded in Boulder, 1970-

celestial sphere sphere of infinite radius with its center at the point of the observer

Cellini, Benvenuto Florentine sculptor; *Perseus with the Head of Medusa*; 1500-71

cellophane noodles thin, transparent Chinese mung bean noodles

cells tiny spirallic structures analogous to leaves of a tree formed by the meridians and which carry blood, ki, and consciousness to all parts of the body (Michio Kushi)

cellular consciousness theory that cells possess awareness

Celtic Cross Tarot reading in which cards are laid out in the form of a cross

center 1. physical, emotional, mental, psychic, or spiritual region of the body or energy space, e.g. a chakra. 2. spiritual home. 3. an educational, learning, or healing center. 4. v. to find a calm and comfortable space within oneself

Center for Defense Information peace group led by former high Pentagon officials, based in Washington, D.C.

Center for Spiritual Awareness meditation, yoga, publishing center founded by Ed and Lois O'Neal in Lakemont, Ga., 1962-

center of silence neutral space in absolute silence from which clarity of seeing can be manifested on all planes (Le Centre du Silence)

Central Premonitions Registry clearinghouse for psychic predictions in New York City

centration cosmic consciousness, personalization (Teilhard)

Centre du Silence, Le mime center founded by Samuel Avital in Boulder, Colo., 1971-

centrifugal adj. 1. force moving or directed away from the center or axis (Christian Hugyens). 2. yin force spiralling upwards and outward (macrobiotics)

centripetal adj. 1. force moving or directed toward the center or axis (Issac Newton). 2. yang force spiralling downwards and inwards (macrobiotics)

centro-complexity condition of high evolutionary development (Teilhard)

cereal n. or adj. any edible grain or grass

cerealian n. or adj.cereal-eater

cerebralization evolutionary thrust toward more sensitive and elaborate nervous systems (Teilhard)

ceremonial magic occult magic, witchcraft

Ceres 1. Eleusinian Goddess of Grain. 2. a planetoid between Mars and Jupiter

Ceridwen Celtic Goddess, symbol of the aspiring soul

Cervantes, Miguel de Spanish novelist; *Don Quixote*; 1547-1616

cetacean member of Earth's most highly developed species: whales, porpoises, dolphins

ceugant absolute, infinite (Welsh)

Cezanne, Paul French post-Impressionist artist; *Card Players*; 1839-1906

CFC (chlorofluorocarbons, freon) chemicals that circulate in refrigerators and air conditioners that destroy the ozone in the upper atmosphere

CFS chronic fatigue syndrome

Ch'a' Ching Tea Classic written by Lu Yu, 9th c. (Chinese)

Chaa, Achaan Thai forest bhikkhu and vipassana master

Chabad largest Hasidic sect (from an acronym of the Hebrew words for wisdom, understanding, knowledge)

Chac human form of the Maya creator Itzamna, son of the Sun

Chac Mool figure of the Maya God of Rain in a resting position with knees drawn up, symbolic of a floating cloud

Chaco Canyon site in New Mexico with the remains of a great Anasazi city complex

chado (cha-no-yu) 'hot water for tea', the way of tea (Japanese)

Chagall, Marc Russian-born surrealist noted for rooftop violinists and floating brides; *Snowing*; 1887-1985

chain-grammar stylistic mode of Joyce's *Finnegans Wake*

Chain of Dependent Origination (pratiyda-samupada, *Sanskrit*) karmic cycle in Buddhism

avidya..................................... ignorance
samskara................ karmic impressions
vijnana........................... consciousness
namarupa...................... name and form
shadayatana...................... sense organs
sparsha............................ sense contact
vedana.................................... feelings
trishna...................................... craving
upadana.................................. clinging
bhava.................... becoming, existence
jati... birth
jaramavana............... old age and death

chaitanya absolute consciousness (Sanskrit)

Chaitanya Mahaprabhu Bengali saint

and incarnation of Krishna-Radha; 1486-1533

chakin shibori chestnut or squash twists (Japanese)

chakra (cakra) 'wheel', spiritual energy center (Sanskrit)
1. Muladhara.....................base of spine
2. Svadhisthana.............lower abdomen
3. Manipura...................................navel
4. Anahata...................................heart
5. Visuddii..................................throat
6. Ajna...............................third eye
7. Sahasrara...................crown of head

Chaldean Oracles a collection of Greek oracular verses, mostly in hexameters, which were preserved in fragments by various Neoplatonic writers

chalice symbol of partnership society, especially the unstratified, equalitarian era of the Goddess (Riane Eisler)

Chamonix French alpine city, site of a Sufi camp

Champa medieval Hindu kingdom in central Vietnam

Ch'an (dhyana, *Sanskrit*) meditative school of Buddhism brought to China by Bodhidharma in the 6th c. and which became Zen in Japan in the 12th c. (Chinese)

Chan Chan pre-Incan city of walls and superhighways

Chandana, Arya first woman disciple of Mahavira and head of the Jain order of nuns

Chaney, James civil rights organizer; 1943-64

chang Tibetan barley beer

Chang Caine wandering Shaolin priest played by David Carradine in *Kung Fu*, 19th c.

Chang-an ancient capital of China during the Han, Sui, and T'ang Dynasties; start of the Silk Road; modern Xian

Chang-Kuo one of the Chinese Eight Immortals, depicted riding backwards on a white paper mule; patron of artists and scribes

Chang Ling Chinese Taoist healer and alchemist; 157-78

Chang Lu Chinese artist; *Two Hermits Listening to a Crane*; 1368-1444

Chang Tsai Chinese adminstrative official who had an inscription on his wall 'All people are my brothers and sisters and all things are my companions'; 11th c.

Chang Tsao Chinese artist of pine trees, noted for using both hands; 8th c.

change 1. universal law of flux. 2. profound, difficult, or challenging experience (Afro-American). v. **to go through changes** to experience major transitions in life

channel person who is used to transmit communications, energies, thoughts, or deeds from a discarnate soul or entity

channel, clear one who does not interfere with transmissions

channel, communications one who is able to relay messages from this and higher planes

channel, open one who is able to receive communications but is not attuned to their source

channel, pure one who receives transmissions without interference

channeling 1. process in which a person communicates messages from a discarnate source. 2. communicating with the higher self or spirit guardians

Channing, William Ellery Unitarian clergyman and abolitionist; 1780-1842

chanting rhythmic repetition of sound, such as a mantra, in which vibrational energy is received and discharged

chantways traditional Navaho practices involving chanting and prayer

chanunpa sacred pipe (Lakota)

Chao-chou Chinese Ch'an student who put his straw sandals on his head and walked away in response to his teacher P'u-yuan of Nan-ch'uan's cat-killing koan; 8th c.

Chao Pu-yu Chinese acupuncturist, pioneer in curing deaf mute children with pressure on the ya-men point

chaos theory science that focuses on sudden and fundamental change

Chaotic Meditation meditative technique of Bhagwan Shree Rajneesh utilizing deep breathing, physical movement, and catharsis

chapati thin flat wheat bread (Hindi)

Chaplin, Charlie mime, silent film comedian; *Modern Times*; 1889-1977

Chapman, John (Johnny Appleseed) long-haired wanderer, planter, and Swedenborgian mystic; 1774-1845

character armor sum total of typical character attributes which an individual develops as a blocking against emotional excitation, resulting in rigidity of the body, lack of emotional contact, deadness (Reich)

Charcot, Jean Martin French physician, teacher of Freud, first to treat mental disorders with hypnosis; 1825-93

charge v. to impart psychic energy to

charging one of the basic processes of change in the universe (Walter Russell)

Chariot 1. symbol of the Church Triumphant in the *Divine Comedy*, drawn by the Griffon. 2. Tarot #7: triumph, divine protection

Chariot of God vision of Ezekiel

Chariot of the Gods 1. lofty volcano in the Cameroons. 2. controversial book about extraterrestrial contact by von Daniken

charism extraordinary phenomenon, either mental or physical, that may accompany a life of prayer, meditation, or religious passion in Catholicism

Charlotte bodhisattva spider in White's *Charlotte's Web*

charmed particle heavy, long-lived subatomic particle

Charon ferryman of departed souls in Greek mythology

Chartres 1. city in northern France. 2. gothic cathedral there of mystical design, 13th c.

Chaturbhuj temple with a beautiful four-armed Vishnu at Khajuraho, India

Chaucer, Geoffrey English poet; *Canterbury Tales*; 1344-1400

Chaudhuri, Haridas Indian-born educator, founder of the California Institute of Asian Studies; 1913-75

Chavez, Ceasar farmworkers organizer; 1927-

check TM technique to evaluate whether one is meditating correctly

chedi spire pagoda (Thai)

Cheiro (Count Louis Hamon) Irish occultist; *Language of the Hand*; 1866-1939

chela disciple (Sanskrit)

Chelcicky, Peter leader of the Bohemian Brethren; ca. 1390-1460

Chelm Jewish town in Poland noted for zany reasoning and behavior

chemicalize v. to ingest, inject, or take great amounts of chemicals in food or medicine

chemosphere atmospheric zone with a high ozone concentration, 20-60 miles above Earth's surface

chen 1. thunder, the arousing; one of eight trigrams in the *I Ching*. 2. firm perseverance, fourth and final cyclical movement of Heaven (Chinese)

Chen Jung Chinese artist noted for dragon paintings; *Nine Dragons*; 13th c.

cheng inner sincerity (Chinese)

Cheng Ho Chinese admiral who made seven voyages to the West, including Africa; 5th c.

Chenoboskion site in Egypt of recent discoveries of Gnostic manuscripts

Chenresigs (Avalokiteshvara, *Sanskrit*) Bodhisattva of Compassion; patron deity of Tibet incarnated as the Dalai Lama (Tibetan)

Cheops (Khufu) Egyptian pharoah, builder of the Great Pyramid at Gizeh; ca. -3000

Cheops' Boat 146-foot boat made of Lebanon cedar discovered in a chamber at the foot of the Great Pyramid in 1954

cheou chao yang Triple Heater; meridian going from the extremities of the fingers to the face (Chinese)

cheou tsiue yin Heart Governor; meridian from the chest to the extremities of the fingers (Chinese)

Chernobyl site in the U.S.S.R. of a nuclear accident in which dozens were killed and thousands injured, April 26, 1986

cherubim cosmic powers governing harmony

Chesed sephiroth of grace, clemency, and will in the Kabbalah (Hebrew)

Cheshire Cat levitating, grinning being in *Alice in Wonderland*

Cheth eighth Hebrew letter: aspiration, Ch, 8

Chewbacca 7-foot Wookie pirate and companion to Luke Skywalker in *Star Wars*

chewing thorough mastication of food in the mouth to achieve oneness, silence, emptiness; charging of Heaven and Earth's forces

chewing table eating area reserved for quiet, thorough chewing

ch'i 1. universal life energy (Chinese). 2. an inherent oxygen in the body which gives stamina and vitality and ultimately brings one to the pliability of an infant (Master T. T. Liang). 3. breath of nature which accumulates in mountains and rivers of the Earth producing a peaceful and harmonious atmosphere for healing, meditation, and contemplating destiny. 4. the spirit of desire and understanding that enters the foetus from the influence of the environment, the mother, and the place of birth (Japanese)

ch'i kung (ch'i gung, ch'i gong, qui-

gong) 'mastery of ch'i', martial arts exercises derived from animal forms and postures (Chinese)

chi-lin unicorn (Chinese)

Ch'i Po physician adviser in *The Yellow Emperor's Classic of Internal Medicine*

Chi Rho monogram for Christ composed of the first two letters of the Greek word for *Christ* (Greek)

ch'i-t'iao 'spirit branch', blossomless branch in a Zen painting (Japanese)

chiaotze vegetables wrapped in thin dough (Chinese)

chiaroscuro science of light and shade (Leonardo da Vinci, *Italian*)

Chibchas highly advanced people on the mountain plateau of Colombia at the time of the Incas

Chicago, Judy artist and feminist; *The Dinner Party*

Chicana adj. Mexican feminine culture

Chicano one of Mexican descent

Chichen Itza 'People of the Well', Maya capital in the Yucatan

Chickasaw 1. people from Mississippi forced to move to Oklahoma. 2. their language

Chiengmai 'Rose of the North', serene Thai hill station

chigo ancient house with extended gables and a long pole inside to collect and generate Heaven and Earth's energy (Michio Kushi)

Chih-i (Chih-K'ai) Chinese founder of the Tien T'ai school of Buddhism; 538-97

Chijevsky, A. L. Soviet cosmobiologist; *The Sun and Us*

Chikamatsu, Monzaemon Japanese dramatist; *The Battles of Coxinga*; ca. 1653-1725

Chikhai Bardo first after-death plane, transitional state at the moment of death (Tibetan)

Chilam Balam of Chumayel sacred collection of Maya books

chilane Maya diviner

Chimu ancient Peruvian empire

Chin Nung one of the Eight Strange Artistic Masters of Yangchou, China; 1687-?1774

chin-tan elixir of life (Chinese)

Chinese n. or adj. 1. (sin. or pl.) inhabitant or descendents of China. 2. world's most widely spoken language, written in ideographs and spoken in four tones, including Mandarin, Cantonese, Fukienese, Hakka, Hsiang

Chinese New Year New Moon in Aquarius

Chinese Wand Exercise series of movements designed to circulate the blood properly with the use of a 50-inch bamboo stick

Ching 1. (Manchu) Chinese Dynasty 1644-1912. 2. (l.c.) book, text (Chinese)

ching tso quiet sitting, meditation (Chinese)

chinking plugging the spaces between logs in a log cabin

Chinmoy, Sri (Kumar Ghose) Bengal-born spiritual master, founder of the U.N. Meditation Center, artist, poet; 1931-

chinso Zen portrait (Japanese)

Chios legendary Greek island home of Homer

Chipko 'cling', movement in India to preserve trees from developers by hugging them, 1975- (Hindi)

chirality handedness; characteristic of nuclear particles

Chirico, Giorgio de Italian founder of metaphysical painting; *Enigma of the Oracle*; 1888-1978

chirimen iriko very small dried fish (Japanese)

chirognomy (chiromancy, chirognosy, chirosophy) scientific or psychic study of the hand and fingers (from Greek)

Chiron (Cheiron) Greek centaur and healer who taught Aesculapius, Achilles, and Hercules; identified with Sagittarius (Latin)

chiropractic n. or adj. 'hand practice', science of manipulation of the body's joints, especially spinal adjustment. n. **chiropractor** (Daniel Palmer, from Greek)

Chishti Sufi order emphasizing music founded by Abu Kshaq Shami Chishti, who migrated from Asia Minor and settled at Chishti in Khurasan; 10th c.

chit mind, pure consciousness (Sanskrit)

Chitrabhanu, Munishree Indian Jain teacher, founder of the Jain Meditation International Center; *Ten Days Journey into the Self*; 1922-

Chladni, Ernest German physicist, discoverer of the relationship between sand patterns and violin music; 18th c.

Chladni figures shifting harmonic patterns of sand, shells, metal filings, plastics, liquids, etc. in organic, mandala-like shapes

chlorella type of green algae

Chocmah sephiroth of wisdom in the Kabbalah (Hebrew)

Choctaw 1. people from southern Mississippi forced to move to Oklahoma. 2. their language

Chohan one of the directors of the seven rays working under the archangels in Theosophy and other esoteric traditions including El Morya, Lanto, Paul the Venetian, Serapis Bey, Hilarion, Nada, Saint Germain

cholesterol a waxy constituent of all animal fats and oils which can contribute to heart disease, cancer, and other sicknesses; the liver naturally produces all the serum cholesterol needed by the body.

Cholulu site of a Mexican pyramid with ground area bigger than Egypt's Great Pyramid

Chomo Lhari Goddess and 24,000-foot mountain peak in Bhutan

Chomolongma Mt. Everest (Tibetan)

Chonyid Bardo second after-death stage, glimpsing reality (Tibetan)

Chopra, Deepak Indian-born holistic medical doctor; *Quantum Healing*

chorten (choten) 'support for worship', reliquary statue (Tibetan)

Chou, the Duke of (Tan, son of King Wen) founder of the Chou Dynasty in China and originator of the Yao, or explanations of the *I Ching's* individual lines; d. -1105

Chowka, Peter Barry journalist and holistic cancer researcher

chowrie whisk to brush away insects during meditation

Chretien de Troyes French poet, earliest transcriber of the Holy Grail legends; *Le Conte del Graal*; 12th c.

Christ 'Messiah, Annointed One', 1. Jesus of Nazareth's divine manifestation. 2. any fully realized person (Greek)

Christic Institute legal educational center monitoring covert action in Latin America, based in Washington, D.C.

Christian hero of *Pilgrim's Progress*

Christiana heroine of *Pilgrim's Progress*

Christianapolis title and ideal commonwealth of Valentin Andreas, based on Rosicrucian principles and science, 1619

Christensen, Alice yoga teacher; *Light of Yoga*; 1928-

Christine de Pian French medieval feminist scholar; *Book of the City of Ladies*;

14th c.

Christogenesis evolution of Christ Consciousness (Teilhard)

Christopher, St. patron saint of travelers, depicted as a giant crossing a river with the Christ child on his shoulders

Christos Solar Logos (Steiner)

chromosome threadlike body, vehicle of genes

chromotherapy art of healing with colored lights

chronocrator 'ruler of time', various methods of the division of life into periods of time under successive planetary rulers (from Greek)

Chronos Greek God of Time

Chrysomallus winged ram who became the Golden Fleece (Greek)

chthonian adj. dwelling in the Earth, Underworld deities (from Greek)

Chu-Chu Chinese excavation site noted for an ancient belt made partly of aluminum

Chuang largest ethnic minority in China, about 8 million people living in Kwangsi Chuang Autonomous Region bordering Vietnam

Chuang-tzu Chinese Taoist sage who dreamt he was a butterfly, or vice versa; *Chuang-tzu*; -4th c.

Chukchi 1. Soviet district in northeasternmost Siberia, capital Anadyr. 2. people there. 3. language there

Chukwu Ibo heavenly creator

Chung-li Ch'uan one of the Chinese Eight Immortals, represented with a long beard and peach; patron of alchemists

Church of All Worlds 1. group founded by Michael Smith in Heinlein's *Stranger in a Strange Land*. 2. group based on the novel founded in Missouri, 1961-

Church of General Psionics group founded by Henry D. Frazier and Yogi Yukteswar Sri Babajhan in Palos Verdes, Calif., 1958-

Church of Latter-Day Saints Mormons

Church of Light astrological church founded by C. C. Zain, 1932-

Church of the Holy Sepulchure Jerusalem temple over the spot where Jesus died; holiest spot in Christendom

Church of the New Jerusalem Swedenborg Church

Church of World Messianity Japanese healing community founded by Mokichi Okada, 1933-

Church Universal and Triumphant re-ligious community headed by Elizabeth Clare Prophet near Yellowstone Park

Churchward, Colonel James esoteric author; *The Lost Continent of Mu*; 1852-1936

Churchy La Femme turtle in *Pogo*

chursashi sushi rice and cut-up vegetables served salad-style (Japanese)

chutney seasoned or pickled fruits and vegetables served with curry (Hindi)

Cibola legendary site of seven golden cities in ancient Mexico

Cid Spanish epic and ballad hero

cinnabar principal ore of mercury, alchemical ingredient

Cipactonal first woman in Nahuatl mythology

Circe enchantress who turned Odysseus's men into swine

circle 1. symbol of the cosmos and heaven (Plato). 2. witches' coven. 3. mediumistic or healing group

Circle of Life sacred harmony of the natural world shared by all living beings (Native American)

circumflexion consciousness coiling about the closed convexity of Earth (Teilhard)

Cistercians Roman Catholic order of monks founded by Robert de Molesmes in Citeaux, France, 1098-

citizen diplomacy individual, universities, unions, day-care centers, churches, and cities that reach out across political, geographical, ideological, and governmental barriers to form people-to-people relationships that promote peace, harmony, and cooperation. **citizen diplomat**

citta mind, pure consciousness (Pali)

City of Destruction home left behind by Christian in *Pilgrim's Progress*

City of Nine Gates the human body with nine orifices

City of the Golden Gate capital of Atlantis (Theosophy)

City of the Sun title and ideal commonwealth of Campanella, noted for a community of goods, free love, and astrology, 1602

City of Willows Eastern Heaven in Chinese mythology

City on a Hill Pilgrim vision of the universal human community

Civilian Conservation Corps (C.C.C.) Depression Era environmental brigades, 1930s

clairaudience extrasensory data perceived as sound (French)

clairsentience extrasensory data perceived as heightened feeling or awareness (French)

clairvoyance extrasensory data perceived as heightened sight, especially of future events (French)

Clamshell Alliance citizens' group to stop nuclear power in Seabrook, N.H.

Clarion paradisical planet among some UFO cults

Clark, Walter Houston psychologist, consciousness researcher; *Chemical Ecstasy*; 1902-

Clarke, Arthur C. science-fiction author; *2001: A Space Odyssey*; 1917-

Clavicle Tarot's Major Arcana (Eliphas Levi)

Claymont Society for Continuous Education Fourth Way school in Charlestown, W.V., 1975-

clean adj. 1. tidy and spotless. 2. healthy, giving out strong energy, good vibrations. 3. drug-free

Cleansing purification or Earth changes

clear 1. v. to remove blocks or complexes in the unconscious or subconscious mind. 2. v. to purify a crystal or other object used in healing or meditation. 3. n. practitioner who functions at a high level and has mastered the survival of self (Scientology). 4. adj. not attached or divided, embracing everything (Michio Kushi)

clear-cut n. or adj. forest that has been systematically leveled

Clear Light 1. the Dharmakaya, or absolute core of being in Buddhism. 2. the subtle, sparkling, bright, dazzling, glorious and radiantly awesome light experienced after death in *The Tibetan Book of the Dead*. 3. the radiance of one's own true nature which should not be daunting, terrifying, or awesome

clearinghouse information center

Cleghorn, Sarah Vermont pacifist, socialist, suffragist, antivivisectionist; 1876-1957

Cleophas cousin of Jesus, one of two witnesses to the resurrection along the road to Emmaus

Clergy & Laity Concerned national antiwar group, 1965-

cliche astral image indicative of future events (French)

click turning point, usually spontaneous

click consonants feature of the Khoisan languages produced by drawing air into the mouth and clicking the tongue

Cliff Palace largest Anasazi cliff dwelling in America, four stories high with 23 kivas and 220 rooms

Climachus, John Greek Christian hermit and mystic; *The Ladder*; 7th c.

climacteric every seventh and ninth year of life when the Moon repeats its squares and triunes

climax an optimum condition of diversity and stability whether in a forest, culture, or ecosystem where half of the energy flows in the system does not come from annual growth but from recycling of dead growth

Clinical Theology an active form of psychotherapy to resolve traumas that occurred during birth (Frank Lake)

clivus multrum Swedish-designed composting toilet (Latin)

close-encounter UFO experience 1. **-of-the-first-kind** a close-range sighting of a UFO. 2. **-of-the-second-kind** a UFO encounter that leaves effects on the viewer or environment. 3. **-of-the-third-kind** direct contact with occupants of a UFO, usually involving abduction and being taken aboard the spacecraft. 4. **-of-the-fourth-kind** sexual encounter with a UFO occupant

closed loop adj. sustainable ecosystem

closet n. or adj. secret homosexual behavior. v. **to come out of the closet** to proclaim or be open about one's gayness

Clotho Greek Fate who spun the thread of life

Cloud Cuckoo Land city built on air governed by the birds in Aristophanes's *The Birds*, -414

Cloud of Unknowing anonymous mystical classic, 14th c.

Club of Rome an economic association dedicated to rational planning for the future publicizing Jay Forrester's world model, 1970s

Clubb, Henry S. British-born organizer of the Vegetarian Society of America; *The Vegetarian*; 1827-1921

CNVA Committee for Non-Violent Action, pacifist direct-action group at Voluntown, Conn.

CO conscientious objector to war

co indefinite third person singular pronoun used to represent a person when sex is unknown, e.g. 'Everyone knows co is immortal'; possessive form **cos**. n. **coself** (co is never used as a noun, or when the sex of the referent is known,

Twin Oaks, 1960s)

co-adaptation cooperation within species

co-counseling type of therapy involving two people

co-creation the act of creating from a state of full awareness in partnership with humankind, the living Earth, or God

co-creator intentional thoughts, mental activity, and other use of consciousness that help influence, shape, or govern reality

co-evolution seeing species and their environment as part of a single system

CoEvolution Quarterly whole systems journal edited by Stewart Brand, 1970s

co-evolve v. to pool our strengths and help each other learn, cooperate, and commit ourselves to each other

co-extensive adj. equal or coincident in space, time, or scope

co-housing (bofaellesskaber, 'living communities', *Danish*), community practice of people owning their own homes but sharing other communally owned amenities such as gardens, a library, laundry, workshops, or dining hall

co-inherence exchanged life at work in the Godhead, mutuality (Charles Williams)

co-learning cooperation within lifetimes

co-marital adj. having sexual relations as a couple with at least one other person

co-preneur member of an entrepreneurial couple; visionary partnership

co-significator natural ruler of a house in the horoscope, e.g., Aries in the first house

coagulation solidification of a new state in alchemy

Coatlicue Nahuatl Earth Mother

Cochise Human vegetarian who ground seeds and nuts on flat millingstones in Arizona, ca. -20,000

Cock's Foot Mountain peak in Bihar, India where Kasyapa is waiting in ecstatic meditation for Maitreya

codependency being affected by someone else's behavior or addiction and determined to control it

Codex Borgia text describing the Aztec calendar and pantheon

codon one of 64 six-line structures in the DNA genetic code

Coffin, William Sloane Presbyterian minister, social activist; *Civil Disobedience*; 1924-

cognicentrism adj. relating to narrow-

conscious experience (Harner, 1980)

coincidentia oppositorum the union of opposites; alchemical term representing the archetype of balance and compensation, often associated with the Self (Jung, *Latin*)

Colbin, Annemarie natural foods cooking teacher; *The Book of Whole Meals*

Colchis legendary land of Medea and the Golden Fleece

cold dark matter hypothesis that most of the mass in the universe, between 90 and 99 percent, is an invisible and as-yet-unidentified form; hidden or missing mass that may play a major role in forming stars and universes, 1990

cold fusion process of achieving a room temperature nuclear reaction yielding more energy than put in; reported by University of Utah researchers Stanley Pons and Martin Fleischmann, 1989

cold-pressed pertaining to oils processed at low temperatures to preserve their natural qualities

Coleridge, Samuel Taylor English poet; *Rime of the Ancient Mariner*; 1772-1834

collective group organized around a common purpose

collective unconsciousness universal storehouse of knowledge within everyone (Jung)

College of Unreason center of higher education in Erewhon staffed by professors of inconsistency and evasion

Colomche 'dance of the reeds', sacred dance of the Maya

colonic enema

colonic irrigation cleansing of the intestines by juice fasts, enemas, and other methods to flush out toxins

Columba, St. Irish monk, ascetic, and founder of the monastery of Iona; 6th c.

Columbine daughter of Pantaloon, sweetheart of Harlequin in the Commedia dell' Arte

Columbus, Christopher rediscoverer of America, who Zen-like went West to get East; probably of Spanish Jewish ancestry; *Book of Prophecies; 1451-1506*

comeback science-fiction theme of future beings who return to the earthly present

Comenius, John Amos Czech mystic; *The Angel of Peace;* 1592-1672

comet heavenly body with a solid nucleus and a luminous, gaseous tail, that revolves around the Sun in an eccentric orbit

coming out 1. process of forming homosexual identity. 2. publicly acknowledging or proclaiming one's homosexuality

comix underground comic books

Commedia dell' Arte Italian Pantomime, 17th c.

Common Cause grassroots citizens' organization lobbying on Capitol Hill, 1970-

Commoner, Barry urban ecologist; *The Closing Circle: Nature, Man, and Technology*; 1917-

commune group living together cooperatively, usually united around work, politics, spiritual path, sexual preference, therapy, or some other lifestyle. adj. **communal. communalist, communard** member of a commune

community 1. people defining a unity of being together, making a commitment to stay together as a whole, correcting their use of energy, and finding a way to be mutually employed; sharing a commitment to place; coming into right relation to nature; the natural unit of play (Gary Snyder). 2. weaving the mantle of the Goddess (Starhawk)

Community Development Credit Unions (CDCUs) financial cooperatives that service and are owned by the residents of low-income communities whose goal is to revitalize poor neighborhoods

community land trust incorporated, quasi-public nonprofit body holding land in stewardship for protection from exploitation and speculation and for promotion of ethical distribution and rational consumption of resources among residents of land holdings in trust

compact fluorescent type of energy-efficient lighting

compassion (mahakaruna, *Sanskrit,* daiji, *Japanese*) loving kindness toward all living things, which arises naturally out of meditation; recognition of shared humanity

complementarity quantum physics notion that there are pairs of quantities or concepts which represent mutually exclusive descriptions of the same reality (Niels Bohr)

complex psychic fragments that have split off owing to traumatic influences or incompatible tendencies (Jung)

complexification nature's process of ever finer specialization (Teilhard)

computronium a flexible computer-generated 'element' capable of mimicking all other elements and particles, real or imagined; programmable matter (Tommaso Toffoli and Norman Margolus, 1990)

Con-Tici Viracocha ruler of the original Viracochas who brought culture to the Inca

Conan Cimmerian hero of Robert E. Howard's post-Atlantean novels

concavation tunnel effect experienced leaving the body during an astral projection

Concordist English Transcendentalist and vegetarian movement that published *New Age* monthly, 19th c.

condition an individual's day-to-day or year-to-year state of health in contrast to constitution or characteristics acquired at birth (Michio Kushi)

Condwiramurs wife of Parzival

configuration picture or pattern formed in a horoscope

Confucius (Kung Fu-tsu) Chinese sage; *Analects*; -551-479

coniunctio marriage of opposites in alchemy (Latin)

conjunction coincidence of two planets in the same zodiacal degree by longitude, usually within 7 degrees; generally a favorable major aspect

conscience the balancing point; One Infinity evaluating and judging our day-to-day behavior; an awareness lost if we forget our eternal; source, if sick or blocked, or eating poor quality food (Michio Kushi)

conscientious objection refusing to serve in the armed forces for reasons of conscience or religious belief

conscientization development of a critical understanding of society and an awareness of students' ability to change it (Paulo Freire)

conscious adj. awareness of the path

consciousness 1. the created changing image and vibrational exchange moving between the poles of One Infinity and the infinitessimal one; received in the form of waves given to all cells of the body like a TV station and interpreted into images including intention, will, desire, thought; the capacity of all things, galaxies, people, animals, and plants, to interpret according to their quality, capacity, and structure; changing according to yin and yang and governed by our environment and way of living, especially way of eating (Michio Kushi). 2. awareness, wakefulness. 3. totality of one's perceptions, thoughts, and feelings. 4. state of illumination. 5. spectrum of mindfulness ranging from unconsciousness to dream consciousness to waking consciousness to enlightened consciousness. 6. one of the skandhas in Buddhism. 7. divine attribute manifesting with truth and bliss in Hindusim. 8. one of 89 mental states in Buddhism including the trances of the realm of the infinity of space, the infinity of consciousness, nothingness, neither perception nor yet nonperception. 9. one of four types of awareness described in the *Upanishads* (Sanskrit):

jagrat................................. waking state
svapna........... sleep, dream, after-death
shushupti...................... dreamless sleep
turiya.................. at-one-ment with God

consciousness-raising n. or adj. inspiring radical, ecological, women's, gay, or spiritual awareness in self or others

consecrate v. 1. make holy. 2. imbuing sacred symbols with the power of the four elements in ceremonial magic

Conselheiro, Antonio Brazilian mystic, communalist; 19th c.

conspiracy (from *conspirare*, 'to breathe together', *Latin*) 1. process of harmonizing or working together. 2. a food coop

constellation cluster of stars or people

constitution an individual's characteristics determined before birth by the health and vitality of the parents, grandparents, and ancestors, especially by the food eaten by the mother during pregnancy (Michio Kushi)

construct 1. stable pattern of consciousness. 2. intelligently fashioned vehicle manifesting to human vision or as a UFO

contact connection with someone else on this or another plane of existence

contact high elevated feeling from someone else's vibrations

contactee recepient of a UFO visit or message

contrasexual adj. masculinity of a woman or the femininity of a man

control discarnate spirit that seems to take physical control of a medium. Some celebrated psychic controls and the mediums through whom they com-

municate are:

Chiang........................ Douglas Johnson
Emmanuel.........................Pat Rodegast
Dr. Fisher.................. Elwood Babbitt
Fletcher............................... Arthur Ford
Dr. Fritz.. Arigo
John King............ Eusapia Palladino
Lazaris................................. Jach Pursel
Ramtha................................J. Z. Knight
Seth................................... Jane Roberts
Uvani, Abdul Latif......... Eileen Garrett
Walter.................. Margery Crandon
Patience Worth.................. Mrs. Curran
Yada di Shi'ite, E............ Mark Probert

conventicle small group organized to surmount the apocalypse

Convention on International Trade in Endangered Species (CITES) international treaty signed by over 100 nations prohibiting transport or sale of endangered species and materials across borders

convivial catharctic three-day therapeutic retreat developed by Mexican psychiatrist Salvador Roquet, M.D.

Conway, Hugh English hero of *Lost Horizon* who is groomed as the successor to the High Lama of Shangri-La, leaves, and then seeks to return to Paradise; 1893-

Conze, Edward Oriental scholar; *Buddhist Mind*; 1904-

Cook, Theodore Andrea British investigator of spirals; *The Curves of Life*

cooking the supreme art that humanity has invented, serving to maintain life's basic functions, both mental and physical, and elevating human consciousness toward endless spiritual realization; the art dealing with the essence of all environmental factors, including water, fire, pressure, atmosphere, various species of plant and animal life, salt and other mineral compounds, seasonal and climatic changes, and celestial and astronomical cycles and affecting the stages of individual development from embryonic life to childhood, maturity, and old age; the comprehensive art that creates life itself, bringing either health, happiness, and peace or sickness, misery, and destruction (Michio and Aveline Kushi)

cool adj. 1. self-assured, knowledgeable, aware, not easily angered or excited. 2. exciting, agreeable, invigorating

cool medium multisensory, participatory medium like TV (McLuhan)

cooperative gardening garden on city land, by a church, or in an abandoned lot that is used individually or collectively

Cordoba Spanish Andalusian city of Moorish heritage

Cordova-Rios, Manuel Peruvian captured by an Amazonian tribe who became their chief and returned to civilization to practice healing as told in Lamb's *Wizard of the Upper Amazon*

CORE Congress of Racial Equality, race relations group that conducted the first Freedom Rides, 1942-

Corelli, Marie English novelist and mystic; *Adath: A Story of Reincarnation*; 1855-1924

Cornaro, Luigi Venetian architect and health reformer; *The Art of Living Long*; 1464-1566

Cornarvon Range mountains west of Brisbane, Australia, noted for ochre rock paintings

corona aura

corona-discharge photography Kirlian photography

corporate responsibility movement including churches, public and private pension funds, and private citizens to divest from aparthied, defense, and other investments to more socially responsible ends

correspondences 1. doctrine of relations between visible and invisible words (Swedenborg). 2. transference of the data of one sense perception into the language of another (Baudelaire)

corresponding lines lines in identical positions in both upper and lower trigrams in the *I Ching*

Corso, Gregory Beat author and poet; Gasoline; *Elegiac Feelings American*; 1930-

cos pronoun indicating his/hers, e.g., 'to each cos own' (Twin Oaks)

Cosanti Foundation Paolo Soleri's arcology center in the Arizona desert

coself him/herself, e.g., 'let your child perform it coself' (Twin Oaks)

Cosme experimental settlement in Paraguay founded by William Lane, 1893-98

cosmecology study of cosmic ecology and energy forces

cosmic n. or adj. universe as a whole (from Greek)

cosmic coiling evolution (Teilhard)

cosmic computer universal consciousness (Lilly)

Cosmic Consciousness attunement to the infinite; title of a book by Canadian psychiatrist R. M. Bucke, 1905

cosmic cross two planets in opposition, each squared by a third one making a T-square or T-cross

cosmic humanism theory of the eight-dimensional cosmos based on integrative principles from science, religion, art, and humanities (Oliver Reiser)

cosmic mind collective mind of a community in Stapledon's fiction

cosmic ray highly energetic particle entering the Earth's atmosphere from outer space, colliding with the atmosphere's air molecules, and producing a great variety of secondary particles

cosmic tones celestial notes of perfect harmony and the source of all audible, earthly sounds; twelve in number emanating from the primal sound in Chinese cosmology

cosmical adj. star or planet rising with the Sun

cosmobiology 1. Soviet and Eastern European term for astrology. 2. (cap.) system of astrology developed by Ebertin emphasizing the developmental tension factors (the midpoint of the squares as the base for all aspects) within the process of becoming; no reference to houses; 1930s-

cosmodyne steller dynamics, kind of astral energy available at a given time

cosmogenesis process of universal evolution (Teilhard)

cosmogony narrative of cosmic origins

Cosmogram 90-degree circular diagram used in Cosmobiology

cosmology science of the universe's origin, functioning, and ultimate purpose and direction

Cosolargy religious science taught by the International Community of Christ utilizing cosmic solar energy

Cottrell, Martha macrobiotic physician and teacher; *AIDS and Natural Immunity*

Council of All Beings community event in which participants take the part of plant and animal species and speak to the humans who endanger them (John Seed, 1980s)

countercuisine organic, natural foods movement that took on the food establishment, 1966- (Warren Belasco)

counterculture underground, alternative

subculture, 1960s-

countergravity force that repels objects instead of attracting them

counterprogram life-affirming unconscious behavior pattern that works against a more deadly one (Lilly)

couscous partially refined cracked wheat

Cousins, Norman author, editor, and investigator of holistic healing methods; *Anatomy of an Illness*; 1915-

coven witchcraft circle

covenant (from 'to eat together', *Hebrew*) compact, agreement, declaration of community principles

Cowardly lion timid being in the *Wizard of Oz*

Cowherd, William founder of the Bible-Christian church, vegetarian church in England; 1763-1816

Cox, Harvey Baptist theologian, social activist; *The Secular City*; 1929-

Coyote creator, culture-bearer, and trickster of numerous North American peoples

CR Critical Ratio; method of determining whether the observed deviation in ESP testing is significantly above chance

crack event an ontologically ambiguous experience whose nature exists somewhere between the axis dividing the world of the everyday from the world of the apparently impossible (Peter Rojcewicz)

cracked wheat whole wheat berries that have been processed and cut into small pieces

Craftsman God the god who fashions the world; the divine smith who governs metallurgy and the sacred sciences

Demiurge	Greek
Hephaistos	Greek
Vulcan	Roman
Wayland the Smith	English
Ptah, Khnun	Egyptian
Enki, Ea	Sumerian

craftsmanship honesty and integrity in one's work, identifying with the person who will use one's craft (Gary Snyder)

Crandon, Nina (Margery) trance medium; 1888-1941

crane bird that symbolizes longevity and wisdom in Taoism

CraniaoSacral Therapy holistic technique that evolved out of osteopathy and focuses on the neck and back

crash v. 1. to sleep, go to bed. 2. to come down suddenly from a psychedelic trip. n. **crashpad** temporary sleeping place

Craske, Margaret English-born ballet teacher and associate of Meher Baba; *The Dance of Love*; 1892-1990

Crazy Dance mystical ceremony of the Omaha and Arapaho

Crazy Wisdom unorthodox, inscrutable, or outrageously humorous antics and spiritual practice of Tibetan spiritual masters

creation generation of multiple electric wave units from the Universal One (Walter Russell)

creation myths myths about the origin of the world, often falling into one of four types: 1. creation from nothing in which God fashions Heaven and Earth from a sound, word, or thought. 2. creation from a cosmic egg in which the universe arises from complementary-opposite principles. 3. an Earth diver story in which an emissary from the heavenly realm plunges into the chaos below and brings up clay or mud to fashion the Earth. 4. an emergence myth in which the First People emerge into the world of light from the underworld below

creation spirituality movement associated with Father Matthew Fox blending catholic mysticism, feminism, and environmentalism, 1980s-

Creatrix the Mother Goddess

Cree major Indian language of Ontario, Manitoba, Saskatchewan

Creek 1. people originally from Georgia and Alabama forced to move to Oklahoma. 2. their language

Creme, Benjamin messianic teacher, founder of Tara Center, London

creode a pathway of developmental activity; a habit (C.H. Waddington, 1961)

crepusculum 'twilight, dusk', Arcanum XVIII in the Tarot (Latin)

crescent Goddess symbol of becoming, symbol of the start of the lunar cycle

crescograph device invented by Jagadis Chandra Bose to measure pain experienced by trees and other plants

Critias dialogue by Plato containing the legend of Atlantis

critical day day in which a biorhythmic cycle crosses the zero, or midpoint, of the graph from positive to negative or negative to positive, signifying a period of greater stress and anxiety

critical path paradigm or model for getting from here to there (Buckminster Fuller)

Croagh Partick Irish mountain where St. Patrick fasted forty days

Croatan 1. Raleigh's Lost Colony. 2. people in Robeson County, N.C., believed to be descended therefrom

cromlech structure of three or more upright stones with a flat, unhewn table stone resting on them

Crookes, Sir William English physicist and pioneer psychical investigator; 1832-1919

cross 1. Christian symbol for the unity of the material and spiritual, the self and the ego, spirit and matter, male and female, East and West. 2. cross-like mark on the hand in palmistry

cross-modal perception ability to some primates to translate visual images into tactile ones

crossing the water metaphor for taking a voyage, determination, or a large undertaking in the *I Ching*

Crow Siouan people who live in Montana and Wyoming and call themselves Absarokee, 'Children of the Large-Beaked Bird'

Crow Dog, Leonard Sioux medicine man; *The Eye of the Heart of Crow Dog*

Crowley, Aleister English magus; *The Book of Thoth*; 1875-1947

crown n. or adj. highest chakra

Crowne, Lenina soma-addicted young woman in Huxley's *Brave New World*

CRP critical rotation position; postulated radionic orientation (De La Warr)

Crucitarian Age present age at the cusp of Aquarius and Pisces (Cayce)

cruelty-free adj. cosmetics that don't require animal testing

Crumb, R. underground cartoonist; *Felix the Cat*; 1943-

cryptomnesia hidden memory, referring to thoughts and ideas that seem new and original but which are actually memories of things forgotten

cryptozoology the science of hidden or unknown animals (Bernard Heuvelmans)

crystal a mineral capable of receiving, storing, transmitting, or amplifying vibrational energy and often used as a tool for healing, prophecy, or communication

cubit traditional English measure 1.5 feet

Cuceb 'that which revolves', Maya ritual epic of prophecy, part of the *Chilam Balum*

Cuernavaca Mexican city noted for social activist centers, such as Illich's Inter-Cultural Documentation Center

cultural coding educational process of handing on from one generating to another similar to genetic coding; differentiated in a wide variety of patterns that characterize the various societies (Thomas Berry)

Cultural Survival network to support traditional societies around the world, based in Cambridge, Mass.

Cultural Transformation theory that the original direction of human cultural evolution was toward partnership but following a period of chaos and cultural disruption a shift toward a dominator model occurred (Riane Eisler)

cummings, e. e. imaginative and unconventional poet; *Is 5*; 1894-1962

cun acupuncture unit of measure derived from the distance between the second and third joints of the middle finger of the subject when forming a ring with the thumb (Chinese)

Cundrie 'La Surziere', messenger of the Holy Grail

cuneiform Sumerian wedge-shaped writing

cup-marks worldwide strings of cuplike impressions in rocks of unknown origin

Cupid Roman God of Love

Cupido first Uranian planet ruling culture, art, society, immediate family, marriage

cupping Oriental healing technique of placing glass cups on specific meridians and points to cleanse, tonify, or reduce tension

Cups Tarot suit associated with love and wisdom

curandero (f. curandera) Central American shaman

Curie, Maria Sklodowska Polish-born scientist and spiritualist; 1867-1934

curl one of a Buddha's thirty-two auspicious signs between the brows that emits rays of light

Curtis, Edward S. ethnologist, photographer; *North America Indians*; 1868-1952

Curve of Life intersecting movement of time and the quantity of nervous tissue at each geological stage (Teilhard)

Cusanus, Nicolaus German humanist, theologian; *On Learned Ignorance*; 1401-64

cusp line or interface between two houses

of a horoscope. adj. **cuspal** exhibiting some qualities of both signs

Cuzco Incan capital

cyberbiology (from *kybernan*, 'to steer'; *kybernet(es)*, 'the helmsman', *Greek*) the consciousness-directed aspects of our relationship to ourselves and our environment (Earl Bakken)

cyberphysiology the conscious self-regulation of normally autonomous physiological functions including techniques such as psychoneuroimmunology, depth psychology, and biofeedback (Earl Bakken)

cyberspace artificial reality (William Gibson)

cyclocosmic adj. universal rhythms (Rudhyar)

Cylons supremely logical metal-cased alien humanoids in *Battlestar Galactica* who seek to obliterate human beings

cymatics science of creating form with sound and studying the interrelationships of wave forms to matter

Cymru Wales. n. **Cymry** the Welsh

Cynegetic Human a hunter and a gatherer (Paul Shepard)

Cynthia (Artemis) Roman Goddess of the Moon

Cyrano de Bergerac 1. French poet, science-fiction author; *A Voyage to the Moon*; 1619-55. 2. play by Edmond Rostand, 1897

Dd

D the Deuteronomist historian in the Hebrew Bible

da dynamic energy filling creation in Dahomean tradition

da-cha prayer-flag inscribed with mantras (Tibetan)

Da Liu Chinese-born Tai Chi and *I Ching* teacher; *I Ching Numerology*; 1910-

Da Love-Ananda (Da Free John) spiritual teacher; 1939-

dabar word, logos in the Kabbalah (Hebrew)

Dacca capital of Bangladesh, city of a thousand mosques, muslin, silk

dactyl soothsayer from Phrygia, associated with the discovery of the musical scale

Dada 'hobby-horse', anarchistic art movement formed in Zurich by Tzara, Arp, and Ball, 1916-

Dadaji (Swami Pranavanandji) deathless grandfather guru of Yogi Amrit Desai

Daedalus architect of the Cretan labyrinth

daemon 1. supernatural power. 2. demigod who inspired Socrates (Greek). 3. the moving part of our lives (Joseph Campbell)

dagoba stupa or pagoda (Singhalese)

Dagon chief pagoda of Rangoon, noted for relics of Buddha and 320-foot bell

dahl lentil sauce or soup (Hindi)

Dai Bosatsu lay Zen monastery in the Catskills, 1976-

dai-funshun Great Perseverence, one of the three essentials in Zen practice (Japanese)

dai-gidan Great Doubt, one of the three essentials of Zen practice (Japanese)

dai-shinkon Great Faith, one of the three essentials of Zen practice (Japanese)

Daibutsu 'Great Buddha', colossal statue of the Buddha Vairochana in the J'odai temple in Nara, Japan (Japanese)

daikon 'great root', a long white radish that helps in digestion of oily foods or fish and shellfish and helps the body dissolve stored deposits of saturated fat (Japanese)

daimoku the chant *nam myoho renge kyo* (Japanese)

Dainichi Bodhisattva Vairochana (Japanese)

daishi 'great master', Buddhist title, usually conferred posthumously (Japanese)

Daitya smaller, southern island of Atlantis, which resulted from a cataclysm 200,000 years ago (Steiner)

dakbungalow Indian government guest lodge or travel stop

dakini female deity of meditation, bestower of secret knowledge (Sanskrit)

Dalada Maligawa Temple of the Tooth in Kandy, Sri Lanka

Dalai Lama 'Exalted Ocean', spiritual leader of Tibetan Buddhism, now in exile in Dharmsala, India; 14th and current Dalai is Gejong Tenzin Gyatsho, 1935- (Tibetan and Mongolian)

dalang story-teller, puppet-master of Bali (Indonesian)

Daleth fourth Hebrew letter: breast, D, 4

Daly, Mary feminist theologian; *Beyond God the Father*; 1928-

damaru magic Tibetan drum (Sanskrit)

Damayanti epic love story of Damayanti and Nala (Sanskrit)

Damiano, Peter ascetic whose spinning soul appeared to Dante in the Seventh Heaven and who expounded to him the mysteries of predestination and karma

dan chu acupoint on the sternum, near the heart chakra (Japanese)

Dan George, Chief Squamish Indian leader; 1899-

dancing diaphram action that occurs during laughing as tension is released (Le Centre du Silence)

Daniel Jewish prophet and sage who refused the meat of the King's table and survived the lion's den, -6th c.

Daniels, Jonathan Episcopal seminarian, civil rights activist; 1939-65

Daniken, Erich von Danish author, popularizer of the theory that space visitors brought civilization to the ancients; *Chariots of the Gods*

Dante Alighieri Florentine poet and mystic; *The Divine Comedy*; 1265-1321

Danu mother of the Tuatha DeDanaan, Supreme Being of the Druids

Daphne the daughter of Tiresias; name by which the Sibyl was known

Dar Es Salaam 'Abode of Peace', capital of Tanzania

dargah court, Sufi convent, shrine, or tomb (Persian)

daridra narayana God who assumes the role of the poor (Sanskrit)

Darjeeling 'Place of Thunderbolts', 7000-foot hill station in northeast India (from Tibetan)

Dark Lord wrathful adversary in *Lord of the Rings*

Dark Pass Taoist term for the Third Eye

Dark Wood the forest of error where Dante strayed from the True Way and which opens the *Divine Comedy*

darood mental repetition of Toward the One (Arabic)

Darrow, Clarence maverick lawyer; *The Story of My Life*; 1857-1938

darshana 1. 'philosophy', six systems of orthodox Hindu thought: Nyaya, Vaisheshika, Sankhya, Purva Mimamsa, Vedanta. 2. 'showing', audience or being in the presence of a sage (Sanskrit)

Daruma Bodhidharma (Japanese)

Darwin, Charles evolutionist who played a bassoon for his plants; *The Origin of Species*; 1809-82

Das, Bhagavan 'Servant of God', 1. Indian educator and Theosophist; *The Es-*

sential Unity of All Religions. 2. teacher of Ram Dass, musician

dasabhumika '10 stages' of a bodhisattva's training from the *Kegon Sutra* (Sanskrit)
1. pramudita.......................... joyous life
2. vimala............................ pure conduct
3. prabhakari...................... illumination
4 archismati............................. radiance
5 sudurjaya .... mastering difficulties
6. abhimukhi........ facing Buddha Mind
7. surangama................... all-embracing
8 acala............ immovable, Iron Human
9. sadhumati............ true understanding
10. dharmamegha............... consecration

dashi soup stock made from kombu broth (Japanese)

dashiki loose brightly colored pull-over shirt (from Yoruba)

Dass, Baba Hari Indian yogi and founder of the Hanuman Fellowship and Mount Madonna Center

daughter-right the need of women and girls to bond with mothers

David king of Judah and Israel, musician, poet; *Psalms*; ca. -10th c.

David-Neel, Alexandra French adventuress; *Initiations & Initiates in Tibet*; 1868-1969

Davis, Adelle nutritionist; *Let's Eat Right*; 1904-75

Davis, Andrew Jackson (Poughkeepsie Seer) spiritualist; *The Principles of Nature, Her Divine Role*; 1826-1910

Davis, Rennie peace activist and Divine Light Mission organizer; 1941-

Davis, Roy Eugene disciple of Yogananda, director of the Center for Spiritual Awareness; *Darshan: the Vision of Light*; 1931-

Dawa-Samdup, Lama Kazi Sikkimese translator of the *Tibetan Book of the Dead*; 1868-1922

Dawn Horse Communion community in Middletown, Calif., formerly led by Bubba Free John

day care center place providing daily care for preschool children for working parents

Day, Dorothy co-founder of the Catholic Worker movement; 1897-1980

Day-Glo bright psychedelic colors

Day of Brahma (kalpa) 4,320,000,000 years or 1000 cycles of four yugas

daya mercy, compassion (Sanskrit)

Dazu site of Buddhist stone carvings in Sichuan Province, China

D.C. Doctor of Chiropractic

De La Warr, George English radionics researcher; *Biomagnetism*; 1904-

De Quincey, Thomas English writer; *Confessions of an English Opium Eater*; 1785-1859

de Rubruquis Central Asian traveler, who led a French embassy to China; 13th c.

de Wohl, Louis Austrian astrologer who escaped Hitler's service; *Secret Service of the Sky*; 1902-61

de-develop v. to reduce from an overeducated or developed state

de-educate v. to relearn naturally by experience

Dead Sea Scrolls manuscripts containing Jewish texts and Essene-style commentaries found in Qumran caves in 1947, ca. -100-70 C.E.

Deaf Smith Texas panhandle county noted for organic farming

death 1. life's other side, afterlife, discarnate realm of existence. 2. end of this life, cessation of the vital functions. 3. (cap.) great yogi, speaker of the *Katha Upanishad*. 4. (Dharma-Raja or Yama, *Sanskrit*) Lord of Karma and King of Dharma in Hinduism. 5. Tarot #13: transformation, 6. sleep; field of service and learning; entrance into fuller life; freedom from the handicaps of the fleshly vehicle; continuance of the living process in consciousness and carrying forward of the interests and tendencies of this life (Bailey). 7. spiritual teacher, constant companion of the warrior an arm's distance away (don Juan). 8. that which is fixed, petrified, attached (Joseph Campbell). 9. process of dissolving ourselves to become more harmonious on another level (Michio Kushi). 10. state that arises when any individual fails to get energy and food, to maintain its identity (Lovelock)

Death Wielder (Death Mother) the Goddess as taker of life (Marija Gimbutus)

deautomatization reduction of the normal selectivity of input, e.g., during meditation (Arthur Deikman)

debility detriment or fall of a planet

Debs, Eugene V. locomotive fireman, socialist; *Walls and Bars*; 1855-1926

Debussy, Claude French composer; *Pelleas and Melisande;* 1862-1918

decan (decanate) one of three 10-degree segments of an astrology sign

Deccan South India

decentralized adj. empowering, participatory, unstructured, free

decile planets 36 degrees apart; minor favorable aspect

Declaration of Sentiments feminist document drafted by Elizabeth Cady Stanton and signed by 100 women and men at the first women's rights convention in Seneca Falls, N.Y., 1848

declination distance north or south of the celestial equator

decoction liquid preparation made by boiling a medicinal plant with water

Dedalus, Stephen Young teacher in Joyce's *Ulysses*

Dee, John English alchemist and astrologer; 1527-1608

Dee, Judge Chinese magistrate and detective popularized in Robert Van Gulik's mystery novels; T'ang Dynasty

deep ecology the deeper, more spiritual approach to nature by asking penetrating questions about life, society, and nature (Arne Naess, 1973)

deep fry v. to saute in a lot of oil; tempura-style cooking

deepening reclaiming the dark: the fertile Earth where the hidden seed lies unfolding, the unseen power that rises within us, reclaiming all the lost parts of ourselves; as opposed to enlightenment (Starhawk)

Deer Park Meditation Center site in Madison, Wisconsin, where the Dalai Lama gave the Kalachakra Tantra Ceremony in 1981

Defoe, Daniel English writer and dissenter; *Robinson Crusoe*; 1660-1731

Deganawida (Dekanawida) 'the Peacemaker,' Huron founder of the Iroquois League of Five Nations who developed the Great Law of Peace; 16th c.

deground v. to artificialize, to take away spiritual energy (Robert Bly)

Deguchi Nao foundress of Omoto, visionary farm girl from Japan; 1836-1918

Deguchi Onisaburo Japanese shaman, messiah of Omoto, peace activist; 1871-1948

deja entendu 'already heard', feeling that sounds or voices have been heard in the past (French)

deja vu 'already seen', state of having seen or experienced something before (French)

Delaware 1. people inhabiting the Delaware Valley driven to Oklahoma by Iroquois and colonists. 2. their language

Delectable Mountains topographical feature of *Pilgrim's Progress*

Delhi pillar ancient iron pillar in Delhi, India, impervious to rust

Della Porta, Giovanni Italian Renaissance physiognomist

Dellinger, David editor, pacifist, member of the Chicago 7; *Revolutionory Nonviolence*; 1915-

Deloria, Vine Siouan author and lawyer; *Custer Died for Your Sins*; 1933-

Delos holiest of ancient Greek islands, birthplace of Apollo

Delphi Greek city, oracular site, and location of the Pythian Games

Delphic Injunction Know Thyself

Delphic Oracle oracle spoken by Apollo from a laurel tree and later an open air temple through the Pythia

delta wave slowest of the brain's waves, associated with deep sleep

delusion cloudy thinking or belief such as 'I am right and others are wrong'

dematerialize v. to change the rate of frequency vibration so as to disappear from third dimensional range of Earth plane sensing

Demby, Constance New Age musician; *Sacred Space Vol. 1*

Demeter 1. Greek Grain Goddess. 2. archetype of the woman firmly rooted in feeding, in Earth mysteries, in nutrition (Robert Bly)

demiurge 1. artificer in Platonism. 2. creator of the material world in Gnosticism (Greek). 3. the molder who forms the small self and leads its steps through life, who repairs the body when sick and makes a new body for another reincarnation, who speaks when we do self-reflection (Sherman Goldman)

Demning, Barbara social activist, satyagrahini

demythologize v. to deny that divinity and spirit are immanent in nature and separate from one's body, work, and home (Joseph Campbell)

Denck, Hans German mystic; *On the Law of God*; 1495-1527

Denderah site of an ancient circular zodiac in Egypt

dentie a black tooth powder made from seasalt and charred eggplant (Japanese)

Denver, John singer and environmental, peace, and macrobiotic activist; *Country Roads*; 1943-

deoxyribonucleic acid (DNA) constituent of the nucleus of cells that functions in the transfer of genetic characteristics and in the synthesis of protein

depotentiation the release or redirection of built-up libido stored in a complex, usually implying its reallocation for healthier use (Jung)

Depth Psychology study of the unconscious, including Freudian and Jungian analysis

dereflection logotherapeutic technique used to combat a compulsive tendency to constantly observe oneself (Frankl)

derma vision seeing with the skin or by touch

dermatone area of skin served by the same spinal nerve group

dermography appearance of writing on the skin

dervish Sufi dancer (from Persian)

Desai, Yogi Amrit Indian-born yoga teacher and founder of the Kripalu Yoga Ashram; 1942-

descendent seventh house cusp

Desert Intaglios figures in the California desert of a man, an animal, and a spiral

desert saint Copic ascetic, 4th c.-

Deskaheh (Hi-Whi-Iss, Levi General) Iroquois statesman who sought independence for his people from the League of Nations; 1873-1925

destiny life course; the point of collision between energy coming in and out (Michio Kushi)

destiny number number in numerology derived from adding the name and birth numbers

detriment low energy point of a planet

Deuter, (Georg) Chaitanya Hari East West musician, *Tea from an Empty Cup*

Deutero-Isaiah (Second Isaiah) author of *Isaiah*, chapters 40-55, the Suffering Servant; -6th c.

deva 1. (f. devi) gods, heavenly beings. 2. heaven. 3. great people who know and lead others (Sanskrit)

devachan god region (Tibetan)

Devadatta cousin of the Buddha who tried to kill him with a mad elephant, which was overcome with love

Devaki Krishna's mother

devanagari 'divine city', Sanskrit and Indic alphabet derived from Gupta, consisting of 48 signs and cross bars, 7th c.

devi goddess (Sanskrit)

Devi, Indra Russian-born yoga teacher, now based in Argentina; 1899-

deviation amount an observed number of hits or an average score in an ESP test varies from chance expectation

devic adj. nature kingdom

Devil Tarot #15: disease, great strength

Devil's Tower (Mato Tipila, 'Bear Lodge') spectatular butte in Wyoming

Devotio moderna spiritual movement begun in the Netherlands that produced the Brothers and Sisters of the Common Life, 15th c.

Dewi Sri Balinese Goddess of Rice

dhakir mentioner, recollector, or commemorator, one engaged in dhikr (Arabic)

dhamma (dharma, *Sanskrit*) teaching of the Buddha (Pali)

Dhammapada 'Path of Teaching', Buddhist scripture containing the Four Noble Truths and Eightfold Path, accepted by the Council of Ashoka, -240 (Pali)

dhanurasana bow posture in yoga (Sanskrit)

Dhanwantari Hindu God of Medicine who emerged from the Ocean of Milk

dharana concentration; sixth step in yoga (Sanskrit)

dharani mantra in written form, usually visualized as a series of shining syllables revolving in a circle (Sanskrit)

dharma (fa, *Chinese*, ho, *Japanese*) 1. law, truth, way, right in Hinduism. 2. teachings of the Buddha and Patriarchs in Buddhism. 3. second of the three refuges in Buddhism. 4. thing, e.g., 'All dharmas are empty' in Buddhism (Sanskrit). 5. the grain of things in the larger picture, living close to Earth, living more simply, living more responsibly (Gary Snyder)

dharma combat (hossen, *Japanese*) verbal joust or battle of wits between realized beings

dharma door avenue for cultivating the way

dharma hall Zen meditation hall

dharma heir senior Zen priest who has been named by a master as a master in his or her own right with permission to teach

dharmachakra (horin, *Japanese*) 'wheel', 1. an eight-spoked wheel symbolizing the eightfold path and the flow of the teaching. 2. group meditation in Ananda Marga (Sanskrit)

dharmadhatu 1. seed or potentiality of truth, aggregate of matter. 2. local chapter of Trungpa's Vajradhata movement (Sanskrit)

Dharmakara monk who vowed to become a Buddha as told in the *Sukhavati-vyuha*

dharmakaya (hosshin, *Japanese*) 'law body', highest of the three bodies of the Buddha, representing absolute truth, Buddha Mind (Sanskrit)

dharma-megha 'clouds of dharma', tenth and final stage of the Bodhisattva path (Sanskrit)

Dharmapala, Anagarika (David Hewivitarie), a Ceylonese born founder of Buddhism in the U.S. and Europe; 1864-1933

Dharma-Raja 'King of Truth', Lord of death who judges karma (Sanskrit)

dharma-trail by-path of wisdom

dharmi substratum, that which possesses dharma (Sanskrit)

Dharmsala (McLeod) Indian hill station, Tibetan refugee center, residence of the Dalai Lama

dharna fasting on a doorstep; Gandhian sit-in (Hindi)

dhawq taste, tasting with various mystical senses (Arabic)

dhikr 'remembrance', repetition of God's names (Arabic)

dhoti flowing garment of Hindu males (Hindi)

Dhu'n-Nun Nasri Egyptian Sufi mystic who emphasized ecstasy and theory of gnosis; 10th c.

dhupa incense sticks (Sanskrit)

dhyana (jhana, *Pali*, Ch'an, *Chinese*, Zen, *Japanese*) 'meditation', 1. one-pointedness of mind; samadhi. 2. wisdom, enlightenment (Sanskrit)

Dhyani Buddhas five Buddhas of Tibetan tantric meditation (Sanskrit)

Akshobya	East
Ratnasambhava	South
Amitabha	West
Amoghasiddha	North
Vairocana	Center

Di Prima, Diane Beat poet; *Earthsong, Memoirs of a Beatnik*; 1934-

Diacecht Irish God of Healing

Diagram of Fou-Hsi circular arrangement of the eight trigrams of the *I Ching*

diakonic socially aware; dialectical imagination creative, mystical mode of consciousness (Norman Brown, from Greek)

dialogical interrogation of single ways of seeing; multiple consciousness (Bakhtim)

Dialogue House personal growth and spiritual development center founded by Ira Progoff in New York City, 1966-

Diamond Ether female counterpart to Manjusri

Diamond Rule Christian communal love as practiced by Aurora and Bethel communities

Diamond Sangha Hawaiian Zen center founded by Robert Aitken, 1959-

Diamond State realization that all is mind in Buddhism

Diamond Sutra (Vajraccedika Prajna Paramita, *Sanskrit*) Mahayanist Perfection of Wisdom text introducing the Bodhisattva vow, the Pure Land and final Nirvana, 4th c.; one copy is the world's oldest extant printed book, commissioned by Chinese Wang Chieh for his parents in 868, on display in the British Museum

Diamond Vehicle (Vajrayana, *Sanskrit*) teachings of Tibetan Buddhism

Diana Roman Goddess of the Moon

Dianetics (from *dia* 'through' and *nous* 'soul', *Greek*) spiritual healing technology; what the soul is doing to the body; a way of handling the energy of which life is made in such a way as to bring about a greater efficiency in the organism and in the spiritual life of the individual (L. Ron Hubbard, 1948)

diatonic scale Western musical scale with seven major tones

Dickinson, Emily brooding New England poet; *Poems*;1830-86

didache 'teaching', Christian doctrine (Greek)

Diderot, Denis French encyclopediest, utopian; *Supplement to Bougainvilla's Voyage of Ideal Life in Tahiti*; 1713-84

didjeridu ancient hollow tubed instrument of aboriginal Australians with a drone sound

Diemma el F'na 'Meeting Place of the Dead', outdoors art and street theatre area in Marrakech

Dienne renowned medieval Mali city

diet (from *diata*, Hippocrates, *Greek*) one's usual form of nourishment, sustenance, food or drink; often chosen consciously, though sometimes not; the major dietary practices include the following:

fast food.............................. precooked
junk food............. processed, artificial
omnivorous............. all and everything
carnivorous.............. meat and potatoes
semi-vegetarian............... fish, no meat
macrobiotic......... grains and vegetables
vegetarian...................... no meat or fish
vegan............... no meat, fish, or dairy
vitarian................................. raw foods
fruitarian...................................... fruits
fastarian...................................... fasting
breatharian.. air
helioarian................................. sunlight

diet #7 all brown rice diet; a healing regimen recommended for up to ten days (George Ohsawa)

Dietary Goals for the United States (McGovern Report) historic report of the Senate Select Committee on Nutrition and Human Needs associating six major degenerative diseases with the modern diet, 1976

dietetics nutritional practice applied to individuals or groups

differential effect significant difference in ESP tests when two variables are compared

diffusionist n. or adj. one who believes in pre-Columbian contacts between Mesoamerica, Africa, Asia, or Europe

dig v. to enjoy, fully understand, empathize, affirm, intuit (Afro-American). **can you dig it?** understand

Diggers 1. English land reform movement, 17th c. 2. San Francisco communalist and free store movement, 1960s

digging in to put down roots

Dike Goddess of Justice in Virgil's *Fourth Eclogue*

diksha initiation (Sanskrit)

Dilasani stories of the Pit River people

Dillard, Annie naturalist, poet, and essayist; *Pilgrim at Tinker's Creek*; 1945-

Dilmun Sumerian paradise where Utunipishtim dwelt

dimension 1. plane or realm of manifestation. 2. range of frequency vibration expression

Dine 'People', Navajo name for themselves

dinergy 'across, through, opposite + energy', the universal pattern-making process; logarithmic spiral (Gyorgy Doczi)

Diogenes the Cynic Greek philosopher who lived in a tub and searched for an honest person with a lamp by daylight; ca. -412-323

Dionysis Greek God of Wine. adj. **Dionysian** chaotic, emotional

Dionysius the Areopagite neoplatonic philosopher; *The Divine Names and*

Mystical Theology; 6th c.

Diop, Sheikh Anta historian who traced Egyptian culture to a black civilization; *The African Origin of Civilization*; 1923-

Dioscorides Greek healer, pharmacologist; *De Materia Medica*; 1st c.

Diotema a priestess of Mantinea who taught Socrates

Dipankara first Buddha in the current world cycle and 24th before Sakyamuni

Diravamsa Thai-born meditation master in the U.S. since 1977

direct voice speaking by a spirit without using the vocal cords of a medium

disaccharide a type of simple sugar such as sucrose that enters the bloodstream rapidly and may cause imbalance

discharge n. or v. the body's elimination of mucus, toxins, and other accumulations through normal or abnormal mechanisms ranging from urination and bowel movement to coughing and sneezing to cysts and tumors (Michio Kushi)

discipline dispassion, discrimination, self-control; spritual practice on oneself

disease 'dis-ease', body's natural effort to heal itself from misuse or abuse, improper diet, or lack of exercise

diseconomies of scale overdevelopment (Leopold Kohr)

disempower v. to limit or reduce participation or involvement

dishtam link between karma and its fruit, destiny (Sanskrit)

displacement ESP responses to targets other than those for which the calls were intended

dissipative structures phenomena that have structure but not the permanency of solids and which dissipate when the supply of energy is turned off; e.g., living organisms, refrigerators, flames, whirlpools, and certain chemical reactions (Prigogine)

distance healing healing someone from afar via meditation or prayer

diuretic agent that increases the volume and flow of urine

diurnal arc 'day path', upper half of a horoscope

Divali (Diwali) Hindu festival of lights celebrated in the autumn in honor of Lakshmi and Parvati (Sanskrit)

divided consciousness ability or state of performing two or more tasks simultaneously

divine analogy doctrine of correspondences (Blake)

Divine Comedy epic poem of Dante's climb to grace and the Mystic Rose, guided by Virgil and Beatrice, 1300

Divine Life Society yoga network founded by Sivananda with 400 branches worldwide, 1939-

Divine Light celestial radiance perceived by the Third Eye; eternal effulgence within all beings brighter than the Sun, realized by turning away from the physical senses and looking within, and whose mystical union confers truth, consciousness, and bliss

bhargo... Hindus
Inner Light............................... Quakers
Noor-e-Ilahi................................. Sufis

Divine Light Mission (Divya Sandesh Parishad, *Hindi*) spiritual organization founded by Param Sant Satgurudev Shri Hans Ji Maharaj in Badrinath, India, and continued by his son Maharaj Ji, 1960-

Divine Sound (shabd, *Sanskrit*) eternal vibration within all beings that is realized by chanting or focusing the breath; activating the Inner Ear

divya divine, celestial, heavenly, luminous (Sanskrit)

divyabhava state of the enlightened; third and final stage of tantra (Sanskrit)

Dix, Dorothea prison reformer; *Conversations About Common Things*; 1802-87

Djambu Baros Batak tree of life with a word for the soul on each leaf, indicative of earthly lessons (Indonesian)

D.K. (Djwhal Khul) the Tibetan who psychically dictated books to Alice Bailey

DMT dimethyltryptamine; psychotropic chemical

DNA deoxyribonuceic acid

do 'way' (tao, *Chinese*), 1. spiritual path. 2. suffix for an art emphasizing spiritual discipline (Japanese)

Do'a New Age world music group; *Companions of the Crimson Colored Ark*

Do-in a form of Oriental self-massage based on harmonizing the energy flowing through the meridians (Japanese)

Doctrine of Signatures theory that flowers, herbs, plants, and other living things have a unique quality, vibration, or signature; e.g., love for a rose

Doczi, Gyorgy Hungarian-born architect and student of the Golden Section; *The Power of Limits*; 1909-

Dodge, David L. merchant and founder of America's first peace society; *The Mediator's Kingdom Not of This World*; 1774-1852

Dodgson, Charles Lutwidge (Lewis Carroll) English mathematician; *Alice's Adventures in Wonderland*; 1832-98

Dogen Kigen Japanese founder of the Soto Zen school; *Shobogenzo*; 1200-53

Dogon people of Timbuktu

Dogu 23,000-year-old statues found in Japan resembling astronauts in spacesuits

doha mystical song (Sanskrit)

doing nothing conscious reversal of subject and ground (don Juan)

dojo 'place of do', a place where very disciplined, severe teaching is offered such as a judo or Aikido hall, monastery, meditation center (Japanese)

dokusan private conference with a Zen master (Japanese)

Dolci, Danilo Italian architect, social reformer, nonviolent activist; *Outlaws*; 1924-

dolma saviouress (Tibetan)

dolmen a huge megalithic stone balanced on several small stone supports

domal dignity planet occupying its own sign in astrology

Domdaniel underground seminary for wayward magicians off the coast of Tunis in the *Arabian Nights*

Dome of the Rock (Qubbat al-Sakhra', *Arabic*) Islamic shrine in Jerusalem

domination power social organization associated with hierarchic and authoritarian society; androcracy (Riane Eisler)

Dominic, St. founder of the Dominican order noted for doctrine and learning; 1170-1221

dominion planetary power governing movement

Domino, Fats rock and roll performer; *Blueberry Hill*; 1928-

don Juan Matus Yaqui sorcerer, teacher of Carlos Castaneda in the Mexican desert; 1900-

Don Quixote anachronistic knight and novel by Cervantes

Donden, Yeshe Tibetan physician and director of the Tibetan Medical Center in Dharamsala, India

Donne, John English metaphysical poet; *Death, Be Not Proud*; ca. 1571-1631

Donnelly, Ignatius populist Congressman, occultist, Baconian; *Atlantis: The Antediluvian World*; 1831-1901

Donovan (Donovan P. Leitch) Scottish singer; *Celia of the Seals*; 1946-

Doom, Dr. Tibetan-educated villain of *The Fantastic Four*

Doonesbury, Michael comic strip by Gary Trudeau

Doors mystical rock group (James Morrison, Raymond Manzarek, Robert Krieger, John Densmore); *Absolutely Live, 13*; 1960s

dope (drugs) doing something without actually working; enjoying the fruits without actually doing the labor with your own body (Robert Bly)

doppelganger 'double-goer' astral body of a living person (German)

DOR (Deadly ORgone) a negative form of energy that can adversely affect living things (Reich)

Dorian adj. *mi*-musical mode; severe, pathetic, or martial music (Greek)

Dorin (Tao-lin, *Chinese*) Chinese Ch'an master known as Bird's Nest for meditating among the branches of trees; T'ang era (Japanese)

dorje scepter (Tibetan)

Dorje Chang Celestial Buddha, usually depicted dark blue in color, holding a scepter and bell (Tibetan)

Dornach Swiss town, site of Steiner's Goetheanum, 1913-

Dorothy Gale heroine of *The Wizard of Oz*

dosa 1. 'depravity', confusion of mind due to anger, malevolence, or hatred (Pali). 2. highly seasoned pancake style bread made of rice and lentils (Hindi)

Dossey, Larry holistic physician and biofeedback researcher; *Space, Time, and Medicine*; 1940-

Dostoevski, Feodor Russian mystical novelist; *The Brothers Karamazov*; 1821-81

double astral projection of inconceivable power (don Juan)

double blind experimental technique in which neither the subject nor the experimentor knows whether a particular condition is part of the control or the test group

double-helix intertwined configuration of the DNA molecules similar to kundalini

Doubleday, Abner popularizer of baseball, Theosophist; 1819-93

Doubting Castle abode of Giant Despair in *Pilgrim's Progress*

Doucet, Suzanne New Age musician and

singer, songwriter; *Reflecting Light II*

Douglass, Frederick abolitionist; *The Life and Times*; ca. 1817-95

Doukhobours 'Spirit Wrestlers', Russian Christian pacifist community now chiefly in Canada, 18th c.-

down v. to go down within in hypnosis

down home adj. funky, mellow, country, like home used to be

download transfer articles from a computer network to an individual monitor

dowsing practice of locating water, minerals, or other objects through the use of a rod, pendulum, or other object

Doyle, Sir Arthur Conan Dr. Watson's literary agent, spiritualist; *The Adventures of Sherlock Holmes*; 1859-1930

dragon (lung, *Chinese*, rong, *Vietnamese*, ryu, *Japanese*, naga, *Sanskrit*) 1. great beneficent being in Far Eastern mythology which guards hidden treasures and heavenly mansions, presides over the weather, and bestows rewards on deserving persons; traditionally represented with the horns of a deer, the head of a camel or horse, the eyes of a prawn or devil, the neck of a snake, the belly of a giant clam, the scales of a fish, the claws of an eagle, the feet of a tiger, and the ears of a cow; symbol of Heaven, yang energy, fortune, the Tao, virtue. 2. symbol of the defender of the Dharma in Buddhism. 3. one of a superhuman race of serpents in Hinduism. 4. dreadful beastie in Western mythology, which is forever carrying off maidens or laying waste the countryside, as in the tales of St. George, Perseus, Jason, Siegfried. 5. symbol of wisdom in the hermetic tradition and alchemy. 6. symbol of that which encloses and turns the psyche in on itself (Joseph Campbell)

Dragon's Head (Caput Draconis, *Latin*) Moon's northern node

Dragon's Tail (Cauda Draconis, *Latin*) Moon's southern node

Dragonwagon, Crescent natural foods author; *The Commune Cookbook*

Draper catalog system for classifying stars according to their observable characteristics, such as color

Draupadi wife of the five Pandu princes in the *Mahabharata*

Dravidian n. or adj. 1. pre-Aryan people of southern India and Ceylon. 2. contemporary South Indian language and people

dream 1. view, goal, or purpose in life. 2. sleeping consciousness. 3. a private myth (Joseph Campbell). 4. v. to awaken to the numinous powers ever present in the phenomenal world about us and whose powers possess us in our high creative moments (Thomas Berry)

Dream Dance mystical dance of the Potawatomi, Menominee, Chippewa

dream glossary notebook to jot down dreams and symbols

dream journal diary in which dreams are recorded or analysed

Dreamers mystical movement led by Chief Joseph, 18th c.

dreaming true possession of control and consciousness in the dream state

dreamscape archetypal space or landscape encountered in dreaming

dreamwork systematic inquiry into or therapeutic use of dreams for growth and self-development

Drepung 'Rice Heap', large Tibetan Buddhist monastery in Lhasa, center of the Gelugpas

Drop City first dome community, located on the outskirts of Trinidad, Colo., 1967

Drown, Ruth radionics researcher; *The Science and Philosophy of the Drown Radio Therapy*; 1891-?40s

Drsh (Darash) intuitional level of text interpretation in the Kabbalah (Hebrew)

Druid 'oakwise', member of an order of Celtic priests, poets, healers, and judges in pre-Christian Britain, Ireland, and France

Druid New Moon first day in the Moon's second quarter

Druze Near Eastern follower of al-Hakim, al-Darazi, and Hamza ben 'Ali; Islamic offshoot that believes in reincarnation

dry-roast v. to toast grains, seeds, or flour in an unoiled frying pan

dryad wood nymph

DT (Down Through) clairvoyant technique of naming the cards of a deck before any are removed or checked

Du Bois, William Edward Burghardt pan-African scholar; *Encyclopedia Africana*; 1868-1963

du'a 'blessing', prayer said of the first chapter of the *Qur'an* (Arabic)

dualism separation, absence of love; seeing oneself as different from the sacred universe

dualistic monism philosophy or view of

life in which the One appears as two or polarity

Dubois, Mark ecoactivist who chained himself in a section of the Stanislaus River of California to prevent flooding and development

Dubos, Rene French scientist and ecologist; *The Dreams of Reason*; 1901-82

Duccio di Buoninsegna founder of the Sienese school of art; *Rucellai Madonna*; 1255-1319

Duce, Ivy Oneita murshida of Sufism Reoriented; *How a Master Works*; 1895-

Dufty, Bill journalist, screen writer, macrobiotic luminary; *Sugar Blues;* 1916-

dukkha suffering; first of the Four Noble Truths (Pali)

dulcimer trapezoidal zither (French)

Dulcinea del Toboso Don Quixote's lady

dulse a red-purple sea vegetable used in soups, salads, vegetable dishes, or as a garnish

Dunbar, Helen Flanders psychiatrist and pioneer psychosomatic physician; *Emotions and Bodily Changes*; 1902-59

Dumezil, G. French scientist who established mythology as an independent branch of the social sciences; 1898-1986

Duncan, Isadora dancer, free spirit; *My Life*; 1878-1927

Dunedain 'Men of the West', men befriended by elves in *Lord of the Rings*

Dunne, John William mathematician, engineer, psychic; *The Serial Universe*; 1875-1949

durangama going far away; seventh stage of the Bodhisattva path (Sanskrit)

Durbar central square in Katmandu

Durer, Albrecht German artist, engraver, woodcutter; *The Dream of the Doctor*; 1471-1528

Durga Benares Monkey Temple, 17th c.

durum a wheat, the grain of which yields flour used in making spaghetti and pasta

durva grass three-pointed sacred grass used in Hindu ritual by separating outer from inner blades (as the body from the Atman)

Duryodhana head of the Kauravas, chief adversary in the *Mahabharata*

Dvapara Yuga third Hindu world age in which righteousness began to fall and Krishna appeared

Dvaraka 'City of Many Gates', Indian holy city in Gujarat; legendary capital of Krishna

dwarf custodian of gems and metals in Norse and Germanic legend

dweller on the threshold an initiate facing his or her past karma and advancing to higher consciousness

dyad twin objects, energies, or beings

dyadic eye fixation meditation technique of mutually gazing into one another's eyes

Dyer, Mary Quaker martyred by the Mass Bay colony in 1660

Dylan Celtic Sea God

Dylan, Bob (Robert Zimmerman) poet laureate of the 1960s; *Blowin' in the Wind*; 1941-

dymaxion yielding maximum performance from available technology (Buckminster Fuller)

dynadran power unit driven with psi energies within flying saucers (One World Family)

dynamic urge, thrust, and purpose of life in eight manifestations (Scientology)

Dynamo historical force of rampant dehumanizing technology (Henry Adams)

dzogchen Great Perfection (Tibetan)

Ee

E 1. author or tradition in the Hebrew Bible associated with a merciful outlook and the Shiloh priesthood. 2. (l.c.) symbol of the logarithmic spiral which increases with each turn about three times; expressed in modern mathematics by the number 2.71828....

E-Meter electronic instrument that measures the mental state or change of state in an individual (Scientology)

Ea (Enki) Sumerian culture bearer

Earth 1. the nest of humanity (Dante). 2. third planet from the Sun, generally represented in world mythology as a feminine being of high consciousness, though a masculine being in Egyptian tradition. 3. Grandmother or Mother of all beings (Sioux and other traditional peoples) 4. Gaia (the Greek Goddess of the Earth), a living self-regulating organism. 5. planet for our training; our playground in preparation for the next life in the vibrational world (Michio Kushi). 6. the primary model in architecture, the primary scientist, the primary educator, healer, and technologist, the primary manifestation of the ultimate mystery of things (Thomas Berry)

Earth Deities

Asasaya	Ashanti
Bhumi	Sanskrit
Coatlicue	Nahuatl
Estanatlehi	Navajo
Gaia	Greek
Geb	Egypt
Geo	Greek
Jord	Norse
Nu Wa	Chinese
Tara	Tibetan

Earth Spheres

geosphere	core, rock
hydrosphere	water
atmosphere	air
biosphere	life
noosphere	mind, consciousness

earth changes anticipated climatic events of coming decades, often catastrophic

Earth Day environmental awareness day, April 22; celebrated from 1970-

Earth Diver type of creation myth in which a representative from heaven dives into the unformed chaos to bring forth the first seed of order and life

Earth First! environmental organization whose activist members sit in front of logging trucks, hike into nuclear test sites, and dress in bear costumes to block development in national parks, based in Tucson, Arizona, 1980s-

Earth Island Institute environmental organization founded by David Brower in San Francisco, 1982-

earth link event or happening linking ecological or spiritual consciousness of the planet as a whole

Earth Mother 1. the Goddess in a form symbolizing the fecundity of women and the Earth. 2. a woman who nourishes and cares for others

Earth Observation System a NASA project to pool Earth data; a 15-year effort involving U.S., European, and Japanese satellites to begin in 1997

Earth-Peace Room place to bring together innovative people, programs, and projects that can contribute to building a sustainable world (Barbara Marx Hubbard)

Earth signs Taurus, Virgo, Capricorn

Earth's Force the centrifugal energy generated from the rotation of the Earth on its axis that goes upward and outward; yin energy (Michio Kushi)

earthbound adj. 1. within the Earth's confines. 2. ordinary consciousness

earthling inhabitant of Earth

Earthly Paradise perfected human community atop Mount Purgatory in the *Divine Comedy* surrounded by a wall of flames

earthmanship wise stewardship of the Earth and its resources

earthplane material existence, state of incarnation on Earth

Earthsea utopian archipelago ruled by magic in Ursula K. LeGuin's epics

earthsong song or spirit of the Earth

earthsteward ecologist or wise guardian of the natural world

earthwright geomancer or one versed in the natural energy of the Earth

Earwicker, H. C. dreamer in Joyce's *Finnegans Wake*

east place where one receives guidance in the *I Ching*

East-point nodal axis of the Earth; point where the Earth's equator conjoins the ecliptic, symbolizing self-expression in social terms in Uranian astrology

East West (East-West, East/West) adj. 1. whole earth, wholistic, transnational, synthesizing the Orient and Occident. 2. apparent path of the Sun. 3. descriptive adjective often used for Sri Aurobindo or macrobiotic centers

East West Foundation macrobiotic educational group founded by Michio Kushi, 1973-

Eatherly, Claude Hiroshima A-bomb pilot, peace activist, and political/ mental health prisoner; *Burning Conscience*; 1918-

eating taking in various energies, particles, and elements and organic chemical compounds absorbed and arranged in the form of vegetables, including the digestion and absorption of food and liquid through our digestive vessels, air and electromagnetic energy through our respiratory system, and waves and vibrations through our nervous system and higher consciousness centers (Michio Kushi)

Eawahtah prehistoric people known as the Mound Builders (Oahaspe)

Ebertin, Rheinhold German astrologer and developer of Cosmobiology; *The*

Combination of Stellar Influences; 1901-

ECaP Exceptional Cancer Patient; holistic cancer support network developed by Bernie Siegel

Ecclesia, Mt. 'Church', 40 acres headquarters of the Rosicrucian Fellowship in Oceanside, Calif.

echinacea purple cornflower, North American herb used for healing by the Plains Indians

echo communications system of dolphins and bats

Eck Audible Life Current; eternal truth and eternal paradox within all; science of total awareness that grows out of soul travel

Eckankar 'Co-worker with God', ancient science of soul travel brought out in the West by Sri Paul Twitchell, 1965- . n. **Eckist** student of Eckankar

Eckhart, Maister German philosopher, Dominican scholar; *Sermons*; 1260-1327

eclectic n. or adj. believer in the truth of opposing schools, a synthesizer

ecliptic Sun's path or apparent motion

ecoactivist environmental activist

ecoaware adj. environmentally concerned

ecocatastrophe environmental disaster

ecocommunity environmentally designed and harmoniously functioning community

ecoculture subsistence culture

ecofarming environmentally aware agriculture

ecofeminist 1. environmentally aware feminist. 2. the period characterized by spontaneities and nurturing qualities (Thomas Berry)

ecofreak ecology activist

ecofriendly adj. biodegradable, recyclable

ecojustice righting environmental wrongs

ecological consciousness cultivating the insight that everything is connected; appreciating nature and solitude; a vision of nonexploitive science and technology (Bill Devall and George Sessions)

ecological resistance civil disobedience or activism on behalf of the environment

ecologo logo attesting to environmental safety or recyclability of products and services

ecology 1. study of organisms in relation to their environment. 2. movement to conserve nature and create a natural, nonpolluting environment. adj. **ecological**

ecolution ecology plus evolution plus revolution plus revelation (Rainbow Family Tribe)

Economy third and final Rappist utopian community in Beaver County, Pa., 1824-1904

ecophilosophy one's theory or approach to the environment

ecopolitical adj. relating to political activity that is environmentally aware

ecosophy (from *sophia*, 'wisdom') Earth wisdom; deep ecology, a shift in perspective and cultural values from science to wisdom (Arne Naess)

ecosphere 1. total environment of life-supporting systems. 2. system formed by the interaction of a group of organisms and their environment 3. part of the atmosphere in which it is possible to breathe naturally

ecotactic technique to preserve the environment (Sierra Club, 1970)

ecotechnology small unit, environmentally concerned industry directly controlled and managed by the people

eco-theologian theologian who holds that the Biblical tradition calling us to subjugate nature and emphasizing humanity as distinct from the rest of creation has contributed to the current environmental crisis (Thomas Berry)

Ecotopia 'home place', 1. novel by Ernest Callenbach about an independent Northwest in 1980, 1975. 2. ecological utopia or community. adj. **ecotopian**

ecotourism travel that is mindful of the environment and traditional culture

Ecover company that introduced biodegradable liquid laundry detergent and other environmentally safe products

eco-yoga yoga that extends balance into our relations with the environment

Ecstatic Mother (Dancing Mother) a feminine archetype that tends to intensify mental and spiritual life until it reaches ecstasy; traditionally sculpted dancing, in her teens or twenties, out of doors or in the fields; e.g., the Muse Artemis, Sophia (Robert Bly)

ecstasy 'put out of one's senses', pure delight (from Greek)

ectenic adj. physical force postulated to explain paranormal events (Count Agenor de Gasparin)

ectoplasm subtle living matter present in the body materialized by a medium

ecumene (oecumene) inhabited world, cultural continuum (from Greek). adj. **ecumenical**

Edda Scandinavian and Icelandic mythological literature

Eddy, Mary Baker founder of Christian Science; *Science and Health;* 1824-1910

Eden original earthly paradise in *Genesis;* possibly located by Juris Zarins, an archaeologist who in 1980 evaluated satellite survey images showing that the Tigris and Euphrates were once met by two other rivers, one of which is now dammed, the other a dry bed, in a valley once rich in bdellium and gold, in a small area south of the spot where the four rivers met, a region now covered by the tip of the Persian Gulf (Hebrew). adj. **edenic**

Edison, Thomas Alva inventor and psychotronic theorizer; 1847-1931

Edo Japanese period 1615-1868

ego 1. self; feeling of I, me, mine. 2. subjective mode of consciousness that differentiates itself from the objective world. 3. identity maker, giver of names and forms. 4. architect who identifies, creates, and experiences existence. 5. experiencer who mediates between the primitive impulses of the id and the demands of society (Freud). 6. Higher Self, individuality, soul; that which bends every effort to quicken vibration and to force the oft-rebelling lower vehicle of personality to respond and measure up to rapidly increasing force (Bailey). 7. futile effort to secure happiness and maintain itself in relation to something else; watcher of egolessness (Trungpa). 8. veil between the self and God in Hinduism. 9. succession of confusions producing an illusory sense of self in Buddhism. 10. the evaluating and judging principle (Joseph Campbell)

ego boundary visualized location in space beyond which the perception of self ceases to extend

ego program barrier to movement from one space to another (Lilly)

egolessness 1. absence of any preconceptions, philosophy, reference points, landmarks, and sense of identity of what is and what should be. 2. recognition that ego is impermanent and the absence of the concept of egolessness (Trungpa)

Egypt 'House of the Soul of Ptah', land of Memphis, divided between Upper and Lower Kingdoms in ancient times; home of pyramids, the Nile, alchemy, magic, beekeeping, writing, papyrus, and beer

Egyptian royal cubit sacred measure used in building the pyramids and other construction; about 1.728 feet

E.I. environmental illness

eidetic adj. images seen when the eyes are closed

eidolon (pl. eidola) 'image', astral image, shadow (Greek)

Eight Glorious Emblems Mahayana Buddhist symbols: Golden Fish, Royal Umbrella, Conch of Victory, Lucky Diagram, Banner of Victory, Vase, Lotus, Wheel of the Law

Eight Immortals (pa hsien, *Chinese*) band of merry souls in Taoist tradition who attained enlightenment and periodically return to Earth to instruct and guide:

Chung-li Ch'uan... patron of alchemists
Lu Tung-pin............ spirits and seances
Chang-Kuo.............. artists and scribes
Lan Ts'ai-ho............................... florists
Han Hsiang-Tzu................. musicians
Ts'ao Kuo-chiu.......................... theatre
Ho Hsien-ku................ shops and home
Li T'ieh-kuai............................. healing

Eight Postures T'ai Chi basic exercises: Ward Off, Roll Back, Press, Push, Pull, Split, Elbow-Stroke, Shoulder-Stroke

eightfold way unified theory of subatomic particles

eighth house segment of a horoscope ruling inheritances, death, sex, the occult

Einstein, Albert German-born physicist, philosopher, and peace promoter; *The Meaning of Relativity;* 1879-1955

Eirik the Red Norse discoverer of Greenland; 10th c.

Eisai, Myoan conveyor of Rinzai Zen and tea cultivation from China to Japan; 1141-1215

Eisler, Riane Austrian-born scholar, futurist, and activist; *The Chalice and the Blade;* 1931-

Eka (Hui-ku, *Chinese*) student of Bodhidharma who severed his arm (Japanese). 2. (l.c.) one (Sanskrit)

El-ahrairah 'The Prince with a Thousand Enemies', Rabbit folk hero in *Watership Down*

El Dorado legendary Golden Land in Mexico, 16th c.

El Eros (H.C. Randall-Stevens) British psychic whose visions were presented by Master Oneferu, an Atlanto-Egyptian spirit

El Mas'udi Arabian traveler, historian, geographer; *Meadows of Gold Mines of Gems*; 10th c.

El Santuario de Chimayo healing site in New Mexico combining Catholic and Native American influence

Elaine mother of Lancelot and half-sister of Arthur

elan vital vital energy (Bergson, *French*)

Elder Brother 1. heavenly mediator who has elected to stay on Earth. 2. master of Chinese philosophy in Hesse's *The Glass Bead Game*

eldil (pl. eldila) entity of higher intelligence mediating between human and cosmic consciousness (C.S. Lewis)

Eleanor of Aquitaine Queen and patron of musicians and poets in France and England; ca. 1122-1204

electional astrology science of choosing an auspicious time for an undertaking

electrodiagnosis technique using instruments to test impulse resistances along the meridians

electrography Kirlian photography

electromagnetic radiation (electromagnetic spectrum) radiation of different wavelengths extending from radio waves to gamma rays and including visible light; often divided between natural (including ki or universal life energy) and artificial such as electrical or microwave

electrons 1. a current or stream of energy which flows from the eternal source and comes to a stop in the form called a proton and in between appears to rest at various stops called subatomic particles (George Ohsawa). 2. subatomic particles with negative electric charge belonging to the lepton category

electronic town meeting computer networking

elektrosmog electromagnetic indoor pollution (German)

elemental fairy or sprite

elementary idea archetype (Bastian)

elements 1. fundamental constituents of the material world: earth, air, fire, water, and sometimes ether. 2. substance that cannot be separated into different substances except by nuclear disintegration. 3. frequencies of energy found in all living things. 4. atoms and compounds; the orderly manifestation of subatomic particles into spirallic atomic structures (Michio Kushi)

Elendil crown placed on Aragorn in the *Lord of the Rings*

elevation distance of a planet above the horizon

eleventh house segment of the horoscope ruling friendships, hopes, desires, social relations

El Fayum neolithic settlement in Asia Minor, ca. -4500

elf wee person of myth and legend. adj. **elfin**

Elf-stone a green gem in *Lord of the Rings*

elfindom realm of elfs and dwarves

Eliade, Mircea comparative mythologist; *Cosmos and History*; 1907-86

Elihu prophet who taught Jesus in Zoan (*Aquarian Gospel*)

Elijah Biblical prophet, messenger of God; spiritual overlord of Earth in many esoteric teachings; -9th c.

Eliot, George (Mary Ann Evans) incomparable English novelist; Middlemarch; 1819-80

Elixir Vitae 'elixir of life', the Philosopher's Stone (Latin)

Elizabeth of Bohemia (Princess Palatine) spiritual friend of Descartes, George Fox, and William Penn; 1618-80

Elizabeth of Schonau German Benedictine contemplative; 1138-65

Ellora (Elura) cave complex in western India with thirty-four Buddhist, Hindu, and Jain temples

Elohim one or more of the seven servants in the Godhead, heading the seven rays of life and the primary tones (Hebrew)

Eloi exquisite future people in Wells's *The Time Machine*

eloptic energy postulated for radionic treatment of crops by Hieronymous

Elrond Lord of Rivendell, keeper of the Last Homely House east of the East, sage in the *Lord of the Rings*

Elsa sweetheart of Lohengrin

Elyot, Sir Thomas English dietary authority; *The Castle of Health;* 16th c.

Emerald City capital of Oz

emergence the appearance of new characteristics in wholes

emergentist a biologist who believes that life, sensation, or mind emerges at unique successive levels of organization and is not reducible to the laws of elementary particles

Emerson, Ralph Waldo nature poet, essayist, Transcendental philosopher; *Brahma*; 1803-82

Emmanuel an entity channeled by Pat Rodegast; *Emmanuel's Book: A Manual for Living Comfortably in the Cosmos*

Emmaus road along which the returned Jesus appeared

empanada a deep-fried tortilla filled with beans or vegetables (Spanish)

emparadise v. to empower spiritually

Empedocles Greek philosopher and mystic who viewed the universe as a conflict of Love and Strife; *On Nature*; ca. -493-433

Emre, Yunus Turkish dervish poet; *The Drop That Became the Sea*; 13th c.

Emperor Tarot #4: will

empower v. to energize, liberate, free, activate, charge. n. **empowerment**

Empress Tarot #3: initiative, action

emptiness (nothingness) 1. that which serves for effectiveness, like the hub of a wheel, the hollow of a clay pot, the open doors and windows of a house, the flutelike space between Heaven and Earth (Lao Tzu). 2. condition of opening oneself and receiving energy and vibration; attracting things when void (Michio Kushi)

empty circle Zen diagram that symbolizes wholeness, immaculacy, emptiness, Buddha Mind, nirvana, the source; it appears in the eighth diagram of the Ox-herding Pictures

empyrean 1. realm of light enclosing the nine heavenly spheres and illuminated souls in medieval Christian philosophy. 2. the heaven of pure light and love unending (Beatrice)

En-gedi Dead Sea oasis, archaeological site, and kibbutz in southeast Israel, ca. -4000

enactment finding one's voice and living on behalf of the planet; connotes movement, action, change

encounter group sensitivity training and experience movement devoted to interpersonal relationships, contact and sharing with others, direct experience of feelings

endocrine system system of glands that through their secretions control many vital physiological processes; physical counterparts to the chakras

endogenous rhythms internal source of biological clocks

endogeny growth from within

endopsychic adj. potentialities inherent within the mind (Roszak)

endorphins secretions activated by the brain that have pain-killing capabilities

endosomatic adj. inside the body (P.D. Medawar)

endosperm starchy inner part of the whole grain or seed surrounding the germ or embryo

enemy illusory antagonist; the phantom of an angel who appears to test and make you stronger and develop your understanding and consciousness (Michio Kushi)

energetics branch of physics that deals with energy

energy 1. eternal delight (William Blake). 2. life force, cosmic ether, healing medium, vitalizing force, primal juice, cosmic electricity (see listing under *life energy*). 3. mc^2: mass times the square of the speed of light (Einstein). 4. that which is always conserved. 5. vim, vigor, health, growth. 6. quantity that can take a great variety of forms and constitutes a measure of the capacity to overcome inertia. 7. electromagnetic fields consisting of positive, negative, and neutral charges which build and sustain the human body and all other matter. 8. forces of nature harnassed for human use including: coal, petroleum, natural gas, nuclear fission, nuclear fusion, hydroelectric, geothermal, organic waste and refuse, algae bacteria agriculture, wind, tides, ocean waves, ocean currents, temperature differential, solar terrestrial and extraterrestrial, gravity, electrostatic, hydrogen, water salination, osmotic pumps. n. **energizer**. adj. **energetic**. adv. **energetically**. v. **energize**

energy beam light or laser emitted by a UFO

energy body aura seen in Kirlian photography

energy flow something directed positively

engaged adj. committed, active politically or socially

Engaruka ancient stone city in the hills of Kenya and Tanganyika with 6000 houses, discovered in 1935

Engels, Friedrich German philosopher and Communist saint; *Origins of the Family*; 1820-95

engram a disturbing memory or impression caused by shocks recorded in the reactive mind (Scientology)

ENIAC first electronic computer, assembled at the University of Pennsylvania, 1946

Enitharmon personification of the Eternal Virgin, stony and wrathful mother in Blake's poetry

Enkidu Babylonian giant friend of Gilgamesh

enlightenment (bodhi, *Sanskrit*) 1. universal consciousness; traditionally compared to a mind full of light like the moon in a cloudless sky or a mirror without any dust on it. 2. awareness that you are a manifestation of one Infinity, always moving according to yin and yang and the Order of the Universe (Michio Kushi). 3. seeing not an alienated world to be gotten out of but a realized world in which we know that all plays a part (Gary Snyder). 4. enlightenment experiences are described as: aha experience, awareness, born-again, conversion, cosmic consciousness, convictional event, deep knowing, divine intervention, Eureka, felt shift, flash point, gestalt formation, getting it, gift of the guru, gnosis, grace, greater reality, illumination, inner feeling, inner voice, insight, awareness, left-right brain shift, miracle, moment-of-clarity, moment-of-truth, mystical experience, peak experience, quantum leap, religious experience, satori, spiritual awakening, sudden decision, surrender, transformation, turning point, vision

enneagram an ancient psychological topology that describes nine personality types and their interrelationships

Eno (Hui-Neng, *Chinese*) Sixth Patriarch of Zen (Japanese)

Enoch Biblical patriarch who walked with God in *Genesis*, and whose mystical journeys to heaven and hell are described in the *Book of Enoch*, the largest book of the Pseudepigrapha, ca. 2nd c., and the *Book of the Secrets of Enoch*, Slavonic version of a Greek manuscript, ca. 1st c.

Enochian 1. occult language revealed to John Dee by an angel, 1581. 2. branch of magic founded by Dee and Edward Kelly and practiced by Aleister Crowley and the Hermetic Order of the Golden Dawn

ent one of the oldest inhabitants of Middle Earth, resembling different species

of trees. f. **entmaiden, entwife**

entelechy vital force urging the organism toward fulfillment (from Greek)

entencephalic adj. sensory image that carries an association of images from another sense, e.g. a sound suggesting a certain color

Enterprise, U.S.S. a Constellation Class starship in the Star Fleet in *Star Trek*, with a crew of 430

entity reincarnated personality (Cayce)

entropy measure of disorder and unavailable or unusable energy; the tendency to run down, to burn out

Enuma elish Babylonian creation myth

environment that which creates and nourishes living beings

environmentalist ecology activist; one concerned with preserving or restoring nature

enzyme biochemical substance formed in living cells, which speeds up chemical reactions

ephemeralization doing more with less (Buckminster Fuller)

ephemeris (pl. ephemerides) 'calendar', 1. table showing the daily places of a planet. 2. almanac of such tables (Greek)

Ephrata vegetarian and pacifist monastic settlement founded by Johann Beissel in Lancaster County, Pa., 1728-1900

Epimetheus brother of Prometheus who opened Pandora's box (Greek)

E.P.O. evening primrose oil

epoptic direct vision, third and highest grade of initiation in the Eleusinian Mysteries (Greek)

Equal House system astrological system of house division whereby the ascendent serves as the cusp of the first house and the other houses are all 30 degrees away

equator 1. line imagined dividing the Earth into northern and southern hemispheres. 2. celestial line extended into space

equinox 'equal night', first day of spring or autumn when day and night are of equal length (Greek)

Er character who regained consciousness on his funeral pyre and related his experiences in Hades in Plato's *Republic*

Era of Humanity coming age of health and peace (Michio Kushi)

Erasmus, Desiderius Dutch-born priest and Renaissance humanist; *Complaint of Peace*; ca. 1466-1536

Erewhon (*nowhere* spelled backwards) 1. utopian novel by Samuel Butler in which the sick are jailed and the immoral are put in the hospital, 1872. 2. pioneer macrobiotic and natural foods company founded by Michio and Aveline Kushi in Boston, 1966-

ergonomic adj. designed taking into account human health and safety

Erhard, Werner (John Paul Rosenberg) educator, founder of est; 1935-

Ericksonian hypnotherapy therapy pioneered by Milton H. Erickson, M.D.

Ericson, Leif Greenlander who explored the coast of Labrador; 10th c.

Ericsson, John Swedish-born engineer and solar energy pioneer; *The Use of Solar Heat for Mechanical Power*; 1803-89

Eridu walled city visited by Gilgamesh

Erishkegal Sumerian Queen of the Underworld

Eros Greek God of Love

Erskine, Thomas Lord Chancellor of England who introduced the first bill against cruelty to animals; 1750-1823

Eru (Iluvatar), source of all creation who created the world by his music in Tolkien's sagas

Esalen Institute human potential center founded by Michael Murphy and Dick Price in Big Sur, Calif., 1961-

escort international volunteer who joins a team that accompanies members of local human rights commissions in Central America

Esko, Edward macrobiotic teacher and counselor; *Macrobiotic Cooking for Everybody*; 1950-

Esko, Wendy macrobiotic cooking teacher; *Introduction to Macrobiotic Cooking*; 1949-

esoteric adj. hidden from view, occult

ESP 1. extra-sensory perception; knowledge beyond the five senses. 2. elementary spiritual powers (Mark-Age)

Esperanto 'one who hopes', language invented by L. L. Zamenhof with simplified grammar and logically constructed vocabulary, 1887

Espiritista 1. a Philippines religion involving psychic surgery and other spiritual healing. 2. Philippino medium (Spanish)

Essene 'pious one', member of a mystical Jewish sect that lived by the Dead Sea; ca. -2nd-2nd c. C.E.

Essene Gospel of Peace Aramaic manuscript reportedly found and translated by Szekely, 1937

est 60-hour educational experience developed by Werner Erhard that transforms one's ability to experience living so that the situations that one has been putting up with clear up just in the process of life itself, 1971-84 . adj. **estian**.

Estanatlehi 'Changing Woman', Navajo Earth Goddess

ET 1. extraterrestrial. 2. visitor to Earth in a movie by William Kotzwinkle of the same name who wanted to go home

ETC Extra-Terrestrial Civilization

Eternal Breath God's breath that quickened the dust to life; ki, vibration

etheric adj. ethereal, astral

etheric body astral or dream body

etheric formative force creative force of the living world raising matter upward, streaming in from the universe's periphery counter to physical forces (Steiner)

ethical investing making investments based on social or ethical criteria, especially helping community-based projects, low-income housing, land trusts, alternative-energy companies

ethnoastronomy art of mapping archaeological sites geometrized by the heavens (Grossinger)

ethnomedicine medicine of traditional society based on respect for the environment and psychological and spiritual states

ethnopharmacology science of plants and spiritual transformation

ethnopoetics traditional or folk poetry derived from the sense of center; songs, prayers, chants, dreams, sacred-fictional narratives, proverbs, riddles, sermons, etc.

ETI Extraterrestrial Intelligence, hypothesis that ancient astronauts contacted Earth

Etteilla Grand Tarot deck with Egyptian and Kabbalistic symbols interpreted by M. Alliette, 17th c.

Euchronia realizable utopia in a beautiful time to come, 19th c. ideal (from Greek)

eudaimonia union with the divine daimon in oneself (Greek)

Eudoxus of Cnidus Greek astronomer who constructed the first known celestial globe; ca. -4th c.

Euenor and Leukippe couple from whom the population of Atlantis sprang

(Plato)

Euphonia musical utopia of Hector Berlioz, 1852

eupsychia utopia that is neither here nor there, but within us (Greek)

eupsychian adj. therapies of health and growth (Maslow, from Greek)

eurhythmy plays and dances developed by Steiner. adj. **eurhythmic**

Eurydice wife of Orpheus who was lost when he looked back on his return from the Underworld

Euterpe Greek Muse of music and joy

eutonics art and practice of personality readjustment through basic body movements (Rudhyar)

Eve first woman in Genesis

Evenki (Tungus) 1. a Siberian people 2. their language

event horizon boundary where space and time interchange

Everard, William English digger; 17th c.

Evers, Medgar Mississippi civil rights activist; 1926-63

Everyman 1. allegorical title and hero of an English morality play, 15th c. 2. one of three ketches that embarked for Pacific nuclear testing zones, 1960s

Evliya Chelebi Ottoman traveler; *Book of Travels*; 1614-83

exaltation high energy point of a planet

Excalibur King Arthur's magical sword

Exceptional Cancer Patients (ECaP) holistic therapy program founded by Bernie Siegel, 1978-

exchanger part of the solar energy unit that releases stored up heat

exobiology science exploring extraterrestrial life

exogenous rhythms external source of biological clocks, imposed outside by the environment

exosomatic adj. outside the body (P. B. Medawar)

exosphere highest region of the atmosphere

exoteric adj. open for all to see, public

experiential matrix archetype (Grof)

Expo New Age, holistic health, or countercultural exposition, 1970s-

expressive media use of various art materials and modes of artistic expression, dance, sculpture, drawing, and vocalization as avenues of self-discovery

extended family family group consisting of a fundamental social group and near relatives, e.g. cousins, grandparents, aunts, uncles

External System category of martial arts that emphasizes outer qualities such as eye, fist, or foot development

extraterrestrial (ET) n. or adj. being from a planet other than Earth

eyephone virtual-reality goggle

eyn sof absolute in the Kabbalah (Hebrew)

Ezekiel Biblical prophet and visionary who beheld the Chariot of God; -6th c.

Ezra Jewish scribe who may have joined the four strands of the Bible into a continuous narrative; -5th or 4th c.

Ff

F transneptunian planet ruling racial stocks, East West contact

Fa-Yuan Zen temple in Peking dating to the 7th century; site of macrobiotic banquet for Chinese religious leaders, 1980

Fabulous Furry Freak Brothers comic strip by Gilbert Shelton, 1960s

fadic number destiny number in numerology

Fafnir dragon in the *Volusunga* saga

Fagunwa, Daniel Nigerian novelist; *The Skillful Hunter in the Forest of Spirits*; ca. 1910-63

faith 1. understanding that moves mountains and renders nothing impossible (Jesus). 2. deep confidence in the Order of the Universe and accepting everything humbly and unconditionally (George Ohsawa). 3. acting egolessly, without calculation or convenience, living life unconditionally (Michio Kushi)

Faithism way of Oahaspe

fakir (faqir) needy person, either physically or spiritually (Arabic)

Fakreddon Valley beautiful meetingplace for wandering holy men from around the world in William Beckford's *Vathek*, 1787

falafel deep-fried cecil bean balls or patties (Arabic)

Falasha Ethiopian descendent of Jews who celebrates Jewish festivals and worships in a mosque

fall 1. the loss of innocence, loss of the sense of the sacred dimension in life. 2. detriment of a planet, opposite its exaltation

fallah (pl. fallahun) cultivator, peasant (Arabic)

Fallopius, Gabriel Renaissance anatomist after whom the Fallopian tubes are named who associated cancer with imbalanced diet; 1523-62

false father identification with a corporation or corporate image such as IBM, AT&T, the Pentagon (Robert Bly)

Fama Fraternitatis earliest document to mention the Rosicrucian order, 1614

Fame-Seeker disciple of the Bodhisattva Mystic-Light who read and recited many sutras but forgot and lost them all; Maitreya in a previous lifetime

Familist 'Family of Love', English heretical movement led by Henry Niclaes which interpreted the Bible allegorically, 16th c.

family 1. the Earth or humanity as a whole. 2. a spiritual community. 3. a biological unit consisting of parents, children, and other relatives. 4. the spirit that comes from eating together and developing a similar quality and dream (Michio Kushi). 5. the Practice Hall for achieving dharma or enlightenment (Gary Snyder)

Famine Early Warning System U.S. AID program that identifies areas of world hunger from satellite data and photos, 1985-

Fan K'uan Chinese landscape artist and recluse; *Traveling Amid Mountains and Gorges*; 11th c.

fana' 'passing away', annihilating consciousness before the will of God (Arabic)

Fang Shih Taoist healers and alchemists (Chinese)

Fantasia animated movie by Walt Disney featuring dancing hippos, warring dinosaurs, and the classical music of Bach, Beethoven, and Mussorgsky, 1940

Fantastic Four comic strip of hulks, things, and four superpeople by Stan Lee and Jack Kibby, 1960s

fantasy 1. literary genre in which an imaginary dream world is portrayed not necessarily consistent with any known or imagined scientific laws. 2. various techniques of tapping into the unconsciousness for insights and personal development

far out inter. or adv. amazing, incredible, profound, beyond unconventional norms (like the stars, the ebb tide, or on a tree limb)

Faraday Cage copper cage that blocks out electromagnetic signals, used in ESP tests

Farm vegetarian spiritual community in Summertown, Tenn., led by Stephen Gaskin, 1970-

farmer 1. husbandman and husband, the begetter and conserver of the Earth's bounty, midwife and mother, nurturer of life (Wendell Berry). 2. one involved in a dance with the land in which the partners are always at opposite sexual poles and the lead keeps changing with the farmer as seed-bearer, causing growth, the land, as seed-bearer, causing harvest (Wendell Berry)

farmers' market direct outlet for farmers who sell their produce to the public, often organic

Farnaby, Will protagonist of Huxley's *Island*

fast n. or v. to purify mind and body, especially by reducing food and drink

fastarian one who fasts regularly

fastarianism dietary practice of nourishing the body by eating only when truly hungry

Fatehpur Sikri Akbar's abandoned capital in northwest India

Father-Mother God bipolar manifestation of Spirit

Fatima 1. daughter of Muhammad. 2. enchantress in the *Arabian Nights*. 3. seventh and last wife who foiled Bluebeard. 4. Portuguese community near which Mary appeared six times to three young shepherd children in 1917

Fatimids Islamic rulers of North Africa, Arabia, and Syria, 10-11th c.

Faust, Johannes German scholar and magician whose life inspired plays by Marlowe and Goethe; 1480-1540. adj. **Faustian** spirit of self-worship

Fawcett, Col. Perry H. explorer in the Amazon; *Lost Trails, Lost Cities*; 1867-?1925

Feast of Fools yearly inversion of the social order in the Middle Ages

Feathered Pipe Ranch holistic education center in the Rocky Mountains near Helena, Montana

Feathered Serpent Quetzalcoatl

Fechner, Gustav Theodor psychologist; *Nana, or the Soul Life of Plants*; 1801-87

Fedallah Parsee magician in Melville's *Moby Dick*

Federation the United Federation of Planets in *Star Trek*, a peaceful conglomerate, principally opposed by the Klingons

Feldenkrais method structural integration method developed by Moshe Feldenkrais

Fellowship of Reconciliation international pacifist organization, 1914-

femality woman's uniqueness (Margaret Fuller, 1848)

feminine n. or adj. more yin qualities characteristic of females but found in both sexes: being more receptive, cooperative, introspective, gentle, nourishing, spatial, seasonal, spontaneous

feminine signs Taurus, Cancer, Virgo, Scorpio, Capricorn, Pisces

feminism movement to achieve women's rights and transform society toward more harmony between the sexes; the ideology of the women's liberation movement

Fenelon, Francois French archbishop and utopian; *Telemaque*; 1651-1715

Feng-kan companion of Kanzan and Jittoku who kept a pet tiger (Japanese)

feng shui 'wind-water', geomancy; art of selecting fortunate sites for landscaping, buildings, and household arrangement (Chinese)

Fenollosa, Ernest Francisco museum curator and Orientalist; tr. *The Book of Tea*; 1853-1908

Feraferia 'nature celebration', Los Angeles witchcraft group devoted to the Magic Maiden of the Aquarian Age, 1967-

Ferdinand 'bold in peace', 1. lover in *The Tempest*. 2. peaceful bull

Fere, Maud Tresillian New Zealand physician who healed herself of colon cancer on a whole foods diet; *Does Diet Cure Cancer?*, 1971

Ferfiz (Feirefiz) Parzival's Muslim brother with whom he is reconciled at the end of the Grail quest

Ferguson, Marilyn brain-mind researcher; *The Aquarian Conspiracy*; 1938-

Ferho Gnostic term for life energy

Ferlinghetti, Lawrence San Francisco Beat poet; *Coney Island of the Mind*; 1919-

fermion particle having a half-odd integer number of quantum units of spin

Ferrer progressive anarchist school and community in Stelton, N.J., 1910-40s

Festival of Salvation celebration at which King Harsha gave away all the wealth of the kingdom every five years in 7th c. India

Feuilletonistic Age pre-Utopian age in Hesse's *Magister Ludi*

fey adj. elfin, occult

Fez Moroccan city, capital of the first Shi'a dynasty

fiber (fibre) the part of whole grains, vegetables, and fruits that is not broken down in digestion and gives bulk to wastes

Fibonnaci Series a series of numbers in a ratio that approximates the Golden Section and is found in spiral patterns in nature such as flower petals, pine cone scales, and sunflower florets: 1, 3, 5, 8, 13, 21, . . . ; the sum of any two consequent terms equals the next term (after the 13th c. Italian mathemetician)

field 1. realm of consciousness. 2. condition in space that will produce a force on a body in that space

field-line path (psychosynthesis)

field particle quantum

fifth (perfect fifth) the 3:2 ratio between two pitches

Fifth Dimension rock band; *The Age of Aquarius*

fifth house segment of the horoscope ruling love, children, speculation

Fifth Sun current era in Maya and Nahua myth in which creatures are tested by the gods

Figurists Christian missionaries in China who held the view that Fu Hsi was not a Chinese but the original lawgiver of all humanity; same as Hermes Trismegistus, Enoch, and Zoroaster

Finch, Jack North Carolinian who saved the vanishing bluebird in Appalachia

Findhorn spiritual community in northern Scotland noted for fabulous gardens, 1963-

Finn, Huck homeless, ragged immortal in Mark Twain's novels

Finney, Charles evangelist, abolitionist, Oberlin president; 1792-1875

Fionn, Finn mythical hero of Ireland and Scotland

firaq homesickness for the divine (Arabic)

firasat wisdom of things at a distance (Arabic)

Firdausi (Abul Kasim Mansur) Persian poet; *Shahnamah*; ca. 941-1020

fire symbol of consciousness, truth, spirit, passion to seek, and truth spreading people to people, disciple to disciple (Jesus, *Gospel of Thomas*)

fire signs Aries, Leo, Sagittarius

firewalking walking on hot coals

first house segment of the horoscope ruling the personality

First Mesa Hopi mesa, including village of Walpi, built in 1600

first mind mind of the sincere beginner in Zen: open, naive, determined, and willing to bow

First Parents Izanami and Izagami; Adam and Eve; and other pairs of humanity's original ancestors

First People Earth's original inhabitants who were in harmony and communicated with the animals and followed a vegetarian diet

First Point of Aries beginning degree of the zodiac

First Ring of Power mastering the ability to impart order to the perception of one's daily world (don Juan)

First Time time of the creation and first people; a perfect era of magical beginnings where animals and humans could understand each other's speech, when there was no unnatural death or disease, and people could commune with God directly

First Wave 1. agrarian revolution (Alvin Toffler). 2. the women's suffrage movement and early feminism from 1890-1920s

fish gate the chakra at the base of the spine

Fisher King the inauthentic custodian of the Holy Grail

Five Buddhas nonhistorical Buddhas often depicted in mandalas; Mahavairocana, Akshobhyha, Ratnasambhava, Amitabha, Amoghasiddhi

Five Dynasties Chinese era 907-60

Five Nations Iroquois league of the Cayuga, Mohawk, Onondaga, Oneida, Seneca, ca. 1590

Five Transformations (five elements, five phases) the stages that the process of change goes through as electromatic energy or vibration is generated between poles of centripetal and centrifugal force

tree.................................upward energy
fire...................................active energy
soil.............................downward energy
metal..........................gathering energy
water..............................floating energy

Five Trees in Paradise the universal process of change, the knowledge of which conveys eternal life (Jesus, *Gospel of Thomas*)

fixed signs Taurus, Leo, Scorpio, and Aquarius signifying conserving energy; symbolized by the four Gospels of the *New Testament* and by the Sphinx

Flame comic book hero whose superpowers came from Tibetan lamas when he was a child, 1939

Flammarion, Camille French astronomer and psychic investigator; *Death and Its Mystery*; 1842-1925

flare pattern the bright part of the aura in a Kirlian photograph unique to a particular species

Flatey Book chief Norse literary source for Bjarni's discovery of America

Fletcher, Horace nutritionist who advocated chewing; *The ABC of Nutrition*; 1849-1919

Fleur-de-lis heraldic flower of illumination (French)

Fliess, Wilhelm German doctor and co-discoverer of biorhythms; *The Course of Life*; 1859-1928

Flinders, Carol natural foods cook and author; *Laurel's Kitchen*

Flood ancient deluge recalled in the story of Noah, the destruction of Atlantis, the flood of Deucalion and Pyrrha and the flood of Ogyges in Greek myth, the Babylonian story of Utnapishtim, the Hindu story of Manu who is warned by a great fish, and other accounts

Flore and Blanchfleur alchemical poem, 8th c.

Flores, Fernando founder of Logonet; *Understanding Computers and Cognition*

floromancy art or belief in the consciousness of plants

flotation tank water chamber isolated from all outside distractions, often containing epsom salts

flower child young person who wore flowers, bells, and beads, especially during the Summer of Love, 1967

flower clock flower garden that told time by the opening and closing of different flowers, devised by Linnaeus

flower essence therapy the use of extracts from flowering plants as a healing method

flower power hippie ideal of changing society through love and peace

Fludd, Robert English doctor, mystic, Rosicrucian; *Apology*; 1574-1637

fluid adj. flowing, spontaneous, flexible, alive

fluidic body astral body

fly agaric (amanita muscaria) magic mushroom

focusing technique for self-knowledge developed by Eugene T. Gendlin

fog an aura of anonymity cultivated by erasing one's personal history (don Juan)

Fogg, Phineas hero of Verne's *Round the World in 80 Days*

fohat vital force (Tibetan)

folacin (folic acid) water-soluble vitamin that aids in red-blood cell formation; found in leafy green vegetables and sea vegetables, especially nori and hiziki; one of the Vitamin B complexes

Folan, Lilias host of PBS yoga series, *Lilias, Yoga and You*; 1935-

folk art nonprofessional art in a traditional pattern

folk rock folk music with a rock background

folkie devotee of folk music

Fonda, Jane actress, peace activist, and fitness instructor; 1937-

food 1. the stream of nourishment that is taken in the form of physicalized food, ki energy, and waves and vibrations and that creates our physical health, mental outlook, and spiritual dream (Michio Kushi). 2. that which creates and forms all things; Brahman; the wisdom of the wise (*Taittiriya Upanishad*). 3. a sacrament by which we share our oneness with the creation. 4. a medium of communication, a symbol of a whole way of life, an edible dynamic (Warren Belasco)

food bank organization that collects excess food and distributes it to soup kitchens, drug-rehabilitation centers, homeless people, and other programs for the hungry

food chain cycle of dependency of one type of life on another

food conspiracy cooperative buying club

food coop cooperative buying and distributing food to its members who contribute several hours a month to purchasing, bookkeeping, delivery

Food First (Institute for Food and Development Policy) world hunger and nutritional/agricultural information center founded by Francis Moore Lappe and Joseph Collins in San Francisco

food mill a small handmill operated by a crank to make purees, sauces, and dips

Fool 1. Tarot #0 or unnumbered signifying folly, inspiration, enlightenment, the beginning and end of the path. 2. companion of Lear

Fools Crow, Frank Lakota medicine man; 1890-1989

Foont, Flakey New Age seeker in R. Crumb's comix

FOR Fellowship of Reconciliation

forage v. to search for wild food

Forbidden City area enclosing the former imperial palaces in Peking and Hue

Force the energy that is generated by and binds all living things in *Star Wars*

force field Soviet term for electrical aura

Ford, Arthur trance medium; 1896-1971

Ford, Frank Deaf Smith farmer and organic organizer

Forest Academy Yoga Vedanta yoga training center in Rishikesh, India, founded by Sivananda, 1948-

Forest of Laughter collection of traditional Vietnamese folk poems, stories

forget v. 1. to intentionally drop desires, ideas, conceptual forms, sensations, imagery (Meister Eckhart). 2. to lose memory of one's eternal source and origin and purpose in life

Fort, Charles Hoy cataloguer of the strange and unexplained; *Book of the Damned*; 1874-1932. adj. **fortean** phenomena or facts inexplicable to science. n. **forteana** strange phenomena

Fort Hood Three first group of U.S. soldiers to refuse to go to Vietnam: James Johnson, David Samas, Dennis Mora, 1966

Fortunate Islands isles in Greek and Roman myth beyond the Mediterrarean inhabited by happy spirits where life is easy and the soil is fertile

Fortunatus medieval hero with an inexhaustible purse and wishing cup

Fortune, Dion (Violet Mary Worth) occult writer; *Sea Priestess*; 1891-1946

Fortune, part of (pars fortunae, *Latin*) solar chart Moon marked on a natal horoscope

Forum transformation seminar founded by Werner Erhard, 1984-

Foundation for Inner Peace association associated with A Course in Miracles

Foundation for Research on the Nature of Man ESP institute in Durham, N.C., formerly the Parapsychology Laboratory at Duke

Foundation on Economic Trends group monitoring biotechnology headed by Jeremy Rifkin in Washington, D.C.

Fountain of Youth elixir of Indian and Semitic legend sought for by Ponce de Leon in Florida

Four Beasts four winged animals described in Ezekiel and which later came to symbolize the four gospels

four continents lands surrounding Mt. Sumeru in Indian tradition: Jambudvipa (South), Purvavideha (East), Aparagodaniya (West), Uttarakuru (North) (Sanskrit)

Four Corners region from southern Utah and southwestern Colorado and covering the northern halves of Arizona and New Mexico

four-leggeds Native American term for animals

Four Noble Truths summary of the Dharma taught by Buddha soon after his enlightenment: 1. all existence is filled with suffering. 2. suffering is caused by clinging to things, spiritual or material. 3. suffering can be transcended and nirvana realized here and now. 4. the way to end suffering is by daily practice of the Eightfold Path

four pillars Greens' platform of ecology, social responsibility, democracy and nonviolence, 1980s

four things that can't be understood the way of an eagle in the sky, the way of a serpent on a rock, the way of a ship on the high seas, the way of a man with a woman (*Proverbs* 18-19)

Four Vows Mahayana Buddhist vows to: 1. save all beings. 2. uproot all passions. 3. pass through all gates of the Dharma. 4. realize the way of perfection

Fourier, Charles French social scientist, reformer; 1772-1837

fourth dimension next higher frequency vibration range into which Earth is being transmuted

Fourth Force transpersonal psychology

fourth house segment of the horoscope ruling home and parents, property, and savings

Fourth Way 1. path of transformation while in the world (Bennett). 2. schools associated with the teachings of Gurdjieff or Bennett

Fox 1. Indian people living in eastern Iowa. 2. their Algonquian language

Fox, George English mystic, founder of the Society of Friends; *Journal*; 1624-90

Fox, Matthew holistic Dominican priest; *The Coming of the Cosmic Christ*

Fox Sisters Leah, Kate, and Margaret; sisters in Hydesville, N.Y. who started spiritualism in 1848

Francesco di Giorgio Martini Florentine master, architect of the Siena cathedral; 1439-1502

Francis of Assisi, St. Italian friar, hermit; *The Mirror of Perfection*; 1182-1226

Franciscans 1. order of monks founded by St. Francis, 13th c. 2. order of nuns founded by St. Clare, 13th c.

Francois de Sales, St. French mystic, founder of the Order of the Visitation; *Introduction to the Devout Life*; 1567-1622

Frank, Ann Jewish refugee in Amsterdam; *The Diary of a Young Girl*; 1929-1945

Frankl, Viktor German-born analyst; *Man's Search for Meaning*; 1905-

Franklin, Ben printer, inventor, vegetarian, statesman; *Poor Richard's Almanac*; 1706-90

Fransisters and Franbrothers silent retreat center in Denver founded by Laurel Elizabeth Keyes, 1963-

Frazer, James George British anthropologist; *Golden Bough*; 1854-1941

freak 1. individual, unique one-of-a kind person, 2. enthusiast. 3. long-haired hippie. adj. **freaky** strange, psychedelic

freak out n. or v. to lose one's center, become upset, angry, excited, shocked, especially after a bad psychedelic trip

free association technique of evoking spontaneous references or ideas to words or symbols, especially in dream interpretation (Freud)

free beach seashore where people are free to swim without a bathing suit

free school school offering an alternative curriculum or style of teaching

free space (wild space) feminist commune where women can explore and develop themselves

free store hippie store where everything is free; everyone is owner, manager, clerk, and customer

Freedom for Health right to choice of health care, diet, and nutrition

Freedom Rides efforts by civil rights activists to integrate buses and other public transportation, 1943, 1961-63

Freeland communtarian utopia in East Africa in Theodor Hertzka's *Freiland*, 1890

Freemasonry fraternal and occult movement originating in England, 18th c.-

Freeze moratorium on nuclear weapons manufacture and testing

Freire, Paulo Brazilian educator; *Pedagogy of the Oppressed*, 1970

frequency vibration range of energy expressing as matter

Freud, Sigmund founder of psychoanalysis; *The Interpretation of Dreams*; 1856-1939

Freya 'lady', Scandinavian Goddess of Love

Freytag-Loringhoven, Else von Dadaist poetess; *Love-Chemical Relationship*; 1874-1927

Friedan, Betty feminist, founder of N.O.W.; *The Feminine Mystique*; 1921-

Friends of God mystical movement led by John Tauler which started in Strassburg and spread to Switzerland and Bavaria, 14th c.

Friends of the Earth (FOE) activist environmental organization, based in Washington, D.C., 1969-

Friends, Society of (Quakers) spiritual movement founded by George Fox in England based on the doctrine of the Inner Light, silent meditation, peace, 1668-

Friesland legendary island in the north Atlantic, 16th c.

Frigg Scandinavian Goddess of Love after whom Friday is named

Frimutel Parzival's maternal grandfather and a Grail King

frisbee plastic or rubber discus, beloved by college students, children, and dogs, mid-20th c.

Frisch, Karl von German zoologist who demonstrated bees communicate by dancing; *Bees: Their Vision, Chemical Senses and Language*; 1886-1982

Fritz the Cat truckin' feline of R. Crumb's comix

Fromm, Erich German-born psychoanalyst; *The Art of Loving*; 1900-80

front n. the visible, immediate, or positive side of any phenomena (macrobiotics)

fruitarian one who eats principally fruits and juices n. **fruitarianism**

fu 1. happiness (Chinese). 2. wheat gluten that is dried into sheets or cakes (Japa-

nese

Fu Hsi (Fou Hi, Fu Xi) legendary Chinese ruler who copied the Eight Trigrams from the back of a dragon-horse in the Yellow River and discovered the philosophy of yin and yang; ca. -2852

Fubi Kwanz master of the Katsupari Monastery in the Gobi Desert (Eckankar)

Fudayl b. 'Iyad bandit turned Sufi saint, founder of the first Islamic monastic order; d. 801

Fudd, Elmer balding adversary of Bugs Bunny

Fudesaki 'Writings', psychically received teachings of Nao Deguchi

Fudo 'Immovable One', a King of Light depicted on a rock surrounded by flames representing the fires of hate, greed, and delusion; his lasso captures delusions and his vajra cuts through delusions (Japanese)

Fugen (Samantabhadra, *Sanskrit*) 'Full of Virtue', bodhisattva personifying active love, diligent training; usually seated on a white elephant on Sakyamuni's right (Japanese)

Fuji, Mt. (Fuji-yama) Japan's sacred mountain, abode of the Goddess Konohana-sakuya-hime

Fukuoka, Masanobu Japanese natural farmer; *The One-Straw Revolution*; 1914-

Fulcanelli nom de plume of a mysterious French alchemist; *The Mystery of the Cathedrals*; early 20th c.

Full Moon Meditation movement inspired by Alice Bailey

full-spectrum adj. natural lighting

Fuller, Margaret Transcendentalist author and teacher; *Woman in the Nineteenth Century*; 1810-50

Fuller, R. Buckminster (Bucky) ecologist, designer, futurist; *Spaceship Earth*; 1895-1983. adj. **Fullerian**

funky 'musty, foul smelling', adj. earthy, quaint; a collage of styles, flavors, and gestures. n. **funk, funkiness**

furaha joy, happiness, bliss (Swahili)

further shore 1. Buddhist image for Nirvana. 2. that which is beyond the opposites (Joseph Campbell)

fusion style of contemporary music characterized by a blending of musical styles from all over the world, usually jazzy, fast-paced, rhythmic

futon cotton mattress or padded quilt (Japanese)

Gg

G transneptunian planet related to the precession of the equinox

Gabirol, Solomon Ibn Spanish Jewish philosopher and neoplatonist; *The Fountain of Life*; ca. 1021-58

Gabriel 'God Is Mighty', archangel who appeared to Mary at the Annunciation, transmitted the *Qur'an* to Muhammad, and will blow the trumpet on Judgment Day

Gabriel de Foigny French monk and utopian author; *Terra Incognito Australis*; 17th c.

Gaden paradise presided over by Maitreya (Tibetan)

Gadong Oracle monk consulted by the Tibetan heads of state

Gaelic language of Ireland and Scotland

Gagarin, Yuri Soviet cosmonaut and the first human in space; 1934-68

Gaia 1. the Greek Goddess of the Earth. 2. seeing the Earth as one giant self-regulating organism of which we are an inextricable part; hypothesis that treats the planet as a living being (James Lovelock and Lynn Margolis, 1972). adj. **Gaian** of humanity as one body

Gaiwiyo 'code', message brought by the Four Beings to the Seneca prophet Handsome Lake in the 1790s

Galactic Spiral the 200-million-year orbit of the solar system around the center of the galaxy divided into four seasons of 50 million years (Michio Kushi)

galactic autumn the evolutionary period when more modern plants and mammals and tree fruits appeared (Michio Kushi)

galactic center point in the Milky Way around which the Sun moves in a period of 200 million years; currently in the first degree of Capricorn, 30,000 light years distant

galactic spring the evolutionary period when ancient plants and reptiles and birds appeared (Michio Kushi)

galactic summer the evolutionary period when biological life become more expanded and cooler giving rise to dinosaurs and other life forms (Michio Kushi)

galactic winter the evolutionary period when more contracted and warmer (warm-blooded) animals came out on Earth (Michio Kushi)

Galactica a space-going battlestar featured in *Battlestar Galactica*, flagship of the Twelve Worlds' Warfleet

Galahad, Sir noblest and purest knight of the Round Table

galaxy 1. large star cluster, nebulae, and interstellar matter catalogued as a spiral, elliptic, irregular, peculiar, radio, exploding, or Seyfret. 2. a vast spiral of energy that is created and substantially held in balance by a more yang centripetal force generated by the periphery of space and a more yin centrifugal expanding force generated outward from the center of the spiral (Michio Kushi)

Galileo Galilei Italian astronomer; 1564-1642

Galloway, Donald English medium; *Incredible Journey*

gamma ray highly energetic photon or quantum of electromagnetic radiation

Gampopa, Je Tibetan Buddhist, disciple of Milarepa, teacher of the first Karmapa; 1079-1135

Gandalf the Grey wizard in *Lord of the Rings*

Gandhara northwest region of India and Afghanistan notable for the development of Mahayanist art along Greek lines

Gandharva celestial denizen of the heavenly world noted for beautiful singing (Sanskrit)

Gandhi, M. K. (Mohandas Karamchand, the Mahatma) Indian lawyer, mystic, weaver, sage who developed Satyagraha and led the freedom movement from the British in South Africa and India; *My Experiments in Truth*; 1869-1948

gandomaki tofu croquettes (Japanese)

Ganesha (Ganapati) Hindu God of Wisdom, Prosperity, and Remover of Obstacles; elephant-headed son of Shiva and Parvati

Ganga 1. the Ganges River. 2. Goddess of the Ganges. 3. (l.c.) potent form of Indian hemp (Sanskrit)

Gangardia Ganges kingdom where invaders were fed a vegetarian diet in order to reform them, in Voltaire's *La Princesse de Babylone*, 1768

Gangtok capital of Sikkim

Ganienkah 'Land of the Flint', spiritual community of Mohawk Indians in the Adirondacks, 1974-

Ganondagan 'Town of Peace', Seneca village

Ganymede cupboarer of Zeus, identified with Aquarius

ganzfeld experiment listening only to white noise and seeing only uniform white light

Garabandal northern Spanish village, where four children saw an angel and heard voices and later began a series of 2000 ecstatic visions of the Virgin, 1961-65

garbanzo a legume or bean; chickpea (Spanish)

Garden of Forking Paths network of all possible times, which approach, fork, break off, and meet one another (Borges)

Garden of Mirth garden in the *Roman de la Rose* in which the poet passes from the Garden of Idleness and Fountain of Narcissus to the Rose

Garfunkel, Art musician; *Bridge Over Troubled Waters*; 1941-

Garrett, Eileen medium, founder of the Parapsychology Foundation; *Many Voices*; 1893-1970

Garrison, William Lloyd Boston abolitionist, suffragist, Indian rights organizer; *The Liberator*; 1805-79

Garuda giant bird, vehicle of Vishnu

gas-belt great cave under the Earth that collapsed allowing Mu and Atlantis to sink (Churchward)

Gaskin, Ina May co-leader of the Farm; *Spiritual Midwifery*; 1940-

Gaskin, Stephen spiritual leader of the Farm community; *Caravan*; 1936-

Gaspar one of the three Magi

Gasparetto, Luiz Antonio Brazilian who has produced more than 20,000 paintings attributed to the spirits of Leonardo, Renoir, etc.

gassho Buddhist mudra expressing gratitude and humility consisting of placing the palms of the hands together, the dominant hand representing the holy, or higher nature, and the other, the world, or lower nature; the two together express One Mind (Japanese)

gate 'gone', first word of a mantra uttered by Avalokiteshvara when he came to the end of an inner struggle and broke ties with the self (Sanskrit)

Gate of the Sun monolithic sculpture at Tiahuanaco carved out of a single block weighing over 10 tons with 48 square figures flanking a flying god

Gateless Gate (Mumonkan, *Japanese*) late Sung collection of Zen koans

gatha 1. 'song', oldest Zoroastrian scripture (Persian). 2. verse inscribed on a Zen painting (Sanskrit)

Gathering of Nations annual powwow and cultural assembly of Native American dancers and singers in New Mexico, 1984-

Gauguin, Paul French post-Impressionist artist; *Noa-Noa*; 1848-1903

Gauquelin, Michel French biologist and investigator of astrology and natural rhythms; *The Cosmic Clocks*

Gauribai Gujarati poetess, saint; 1759-1809

Gauss, Karl Friedrich German mathematician who suggested cutting huge swaths in Siberia to alert extraterrestrials; *Arithematical Disquisitions*; 1777-1855

Gautama (Gotama) surname of Siddhartha before becoming the Buddha

Gautami (Mahaprajapati) Siddhartha's aunt and foster-mother

Gawan (Gawain) knight and nephew of King Arthur; paragon of Arthurian knighthood in *Parzival*

Gawain, Shakti spiritual teacher and author; *Creative Visualization*; 1947-

gay n. or adj. person attracted to someone of the same sex; homosexual or lesbian. n. **gayness**

Gay Cultural Renaissance rediscovery and exploration of the gay cultural heritage expressed through art, music, and literature

Gay Liberation movement to create a society free from defining people on the basis of gender or sexual preference, 1969-

Gayatri prayer to the Sun (Sanskrit)

GCSC Galactic Command Space Complex, 12th density beings that colonized Earth's root races (One World Family)

Geb (Keb, Qeb, Seb) Egyptian God of the Earth

Gebeloc 'idyllic', Guatemala (Mayan)

Geburah Kabbalistic sephiroth of severity and intelligence (Hebrew)

Ged great wizard of Earthsea

Gedo Zen 'wrong way Zen', training done to gain power, unusual experiences, visions (Japanese)

Gedulah Kabbalistic sephiroth of grace,

clemency (Hebrew)

geisha courtesan (Japanese)

Geller, Uri Israeli psychic, spoon and mind bender; *My Story*; 1946-

gelong ordained monk (Tibetan)

Gelugpa (Yellow Hats) one of the four (and least tantric) sects of Tibetan Buddhism, presided over by the Dalai Lama, 14th c. -

gematria art of interpreting the names and attributes of God by letter and number, e.g., A= 1, B=2, C=3, etc.

Gemini twins; third sign of the zodiac; of the airy element; ruler Mercury; keywords: awareness, communicating energy

gen (balancing point) point located near the wrists and ankles that functions as the midpoint of the meridian in terms of the number of sections on the arm or leg (Japanese)

gender socially or culturally determined attributes and behavior patterns attributed to persons on the basis of sex

gender-specific quality unique to a man or woman

Genero, don warrior companion of don Juan in Castaneda's books

generoactive the life-organizing force in the universe (Walter Russell)

genethliacal astrological study of individual birth charts

genjo koan that rises naturally in daily life (Japanese)

genketsu fundamental point of each meridian (Japanese)

genmai miso (brown rice miso) a fermented soybean paste made from brown rice, soybeans, and sea salt, preferred for lighter cooking (Japanese)

gentler someone with a way with snakes

Geo 1. son of Metis and Zeus who was to supplant his father Zeus and rule with an all-loving heart. 2. the Earth Father in the New Age (Shepherd Bliss)

geodesic adj. dome constructed of triangular segments; most economical relationship between two energy points (Buckminster Fuller)

geologian a theologian of the Earth (Thomas Berry)

geomagnetism science dealing with the vital inner energies of the Earth

geomancy 1. divination by tracing figures on the ground. 2. feng-shui: Oriental science of siting, placement, and home and environmental arrangement

geopathic zone area of Earth energies not conducive to human living; correlating with illnesses; strong electric fields, magnetic anomalies, geological fractures, and subterranean water veins

geophysics study of Earth's physical characteristics

geophysiology a planetary science integrating the independent natural sciences into a unified study (James Lovelock)

geopsychic adj. relating to the interrelationship of human and natural relations in a specific region of the Earth

geosophy (from *Gaia*, Goddess of the Earth, and *sophia*, wisdom) Earth wisdom; science of sacred geometry

geosphere solid portion of the Earth, lithosphere

Geraint Arthurian knight and husband of Enid the Fair

germ embryo of the whole grain; part of a cereal that grows and produces new plants; removed in modern refining

Gernsback, Hugo father of modern science fiction, inventor of the word *television* (1909); *Ralph 124C41*; 1884-1967

Gerson, Max German-born physician who associated cancer with the poisoning of modern foodstuffs; *A Cancer Therapy: Results of Fifty Cases*, 1958

Gertrude the Great, St. German mystic; *The Exercises*; 1256-1311

Geser Khan 1. legendary Mongolian hero who is destined to unify and rule the world. 2. medieval epic about his adventures

geshe title of respect for a lama (Tibetan)

gestalt perception of an art work as a whole as distinct from its separate parts (Christian Ehrenfels, 1890)

Gestalt, Homo symbiotic evolutionary strain in Sturgeon's *More Than Human*

Gestalt Therapy integrative growth movement developed by Frederick Perls utilizing methods to expand individual awareness and lessen emotional blocks, including an inner dialogue to resolve conflicts between different parts of the self

get it v. to experience totally (est)

get it together v. to organize oneself or environment, cope (Afro-American)

ghat range of hills, temple steps, cremation grounds, or bathing places (Sanskrit)

ghazal amorous song (Urdu)

Ghazali, al Persian Sufi philosopher; *The*

Revival of the Religious Sciences; 1058-1111

ghee clarified butter (Sanskrit)

gherao laying seige nonviolently (Gandhi)

Ghost Dance mystical dance of the Arapaho, Cheyenne, Shoshone, Pawnee, Dakota, Iowa

ghost vein a dried up vein of water that can cause a dowsing rod to react

Gibbons, Euell forager; *Stalking the Wild Asparagus*; 1911-76

Gibbs, Lois homemaker who led the fight to clean up Love Canal, N.Y., in the 1970s

Gibran, Kahlil Syrian-born mystic, poet, artist; *The Prophet*; 1883-1931

Gichtel, Johann Georg German mystic and celibate, teacher of the Brother of the Angels; 1638-1710

Gift to Be Simple Shaker hymn adapted in a book of the same name by Edward Deming Andrews

Gihon 1. one of the four streams that flowed from the river in Eden. 2. Jerusalem spring

Gilgamesh Mesopotamian epic hero whose story is told on certain sealstones

Gilligan, Carol psychologist and feminist philosopher; *In a Different Voice*

Gilmen, Charlotte feminist; *Women and Economics*; 1860-1935

Gimbutas, Marija archaeologist and explorer of matriarchal civilization; *The Language of the Goddess*; 1921-

Gimel third Hebrew letter: openings, G, 3

ginger (ginger root) a gnarled golden-colored root that is pungent and spicy and used in cooking and for medicinal purposes

ginger compress a compress made from grated ginger root and water, applied hot to an affected area of the body, serving to stimulate circulation and dissolve stagnation; used in macrobiotic home care

ginkgo 1. Oriental tree with fan-shaped leaves that now grows in the Western hemisphere. 2. nut covered with a thin skin inside a hard white shell enclosed by a pink fleshy covering 3. (cap.) macrobiotic detective in fiction by Alex Jack

Ginsberg, Allen legendary North American culture-bearer who attained satori on the Kyoto-Tokyo Express in 1963; shaman, poet, and gay activist; *Howl*;

1926-

ginseng healing root with a human-like appearance, native to Korea

Ginza 'Silver District', downtown area of Tokyo

Giorgi, Francesco Venice friar and cablist; *De harmonia mundi*; 1466-1540

Giotto di Bondone Florentine artist; *Navicella*; ca. 1266-1337

Giovanni di Paolo Renaissance artist; *Expulsion from Paradise*; 15th c.

Giovanni, Nikki poetess; *Gemini*; 1944-

Giraffe Project philanthropic foundation in Langley, Washington, that recognizes people who stick their necks out, 1980s

gita 1. song, poem. 2. (cap.) the *Bhagavad Gita* (Sanskrit)

Gita Govinda 'Song of the Cowherd', mystical love poems about Krishna and Radha by Jayadeva, 12th c. (Sanskrit)

Giver of All the Goddess as giver of life and health, foreteller of spring, increaser (or decreaser) of wealth, and protectress of life and household (Marija Gimbutus)

Gjallarhorn 'ringing horn', Heimdall's trumpet, which will ring at Ragnarok (Norwegian)

GLA (gla) gamma-linolenic acid, abundant in EPO, currants, etc.

Gladsheim 'world of joy', site of Valhalla (Norwegian)

Gladstone Gander Donald Duck's lucky cousin

glasnost openness (Russian)

Glass Bead Game mode of playing with the total contents and values of history, derived from art, music, and chess in Hesse's *Magister Ludi*

Glastonbury site in southwestern England of an Abbey, Tor, and Cross associated with Arthurian Romance and the legend of the Holy Grail

Glastonbury Zodiac pictorial representation of the zodiac covering several square miles, mapped by John Dee and rediscovered in the 1920s by Katherine Maltwood

Glide Memorial Methodist Church peace, freedom, and New Age church in San Francisco

Global Change Encyclopedia animated computer atlas showing land and sea changes over an extended period of time, 1992

Global Forum of Spirituality and Parliamentary Leaders on Human Sur-

vival international movement that grew out of a conference on the Earth in Oxford, England, 1988-

Global 2000 report commissioned by President Carter assessing the probable changes in the world and environment through the end of the century and model for future planning, 1980

Global Village the Earth, unified by modern media (Marshall McLuhan)

Gloriana Faerie Queene in Spenser's poem of the same name

glossalalia speaking in tongues. adj. **glossalalic**

gluten 'glue', 1. the sticky substance that remains after the bran has been kneaded and rinsed from whole-wheat flour; used to make seitan and fu. 2. wheatmeat or seitan. adj. **glutinous** (Latin)

gnome sprite living in the center of the Earth

gnosis knowledge, awareness (Greek)

Gnostic 'one who knows', adherent of an ancient Hellenistic way of life teaching transmigration of souls and a struggle between the forces of light and darkness, 1st c. - 4th. c. n. **Gnosticism**

go 1. (meeting of energy points) point located near the elbows or knees, along the arm and leg meridians, which helps to regulate the flow of energy through the meridians (Japanese). 2. (wei-chi, *Chinese*) game of strategy played on a 19x19 grid with 361 stones illustrating yin/yang philosophy; invented in ancient China, mastered in Japan (Japanese)

Go-i set of five rungs in Zen meditation, relating to pairs of opposites (Japanese)

go to the beach v. to establish a private place in the mind (est)

Gobind Singh tenth and last Guru of the Sikhs who inaugurated the Khalsa and the five K's; 1666-1708

God 1. creator and sustainer of the universe (Judeo-Christianity). 2. transcendent and immanent being who guides and controls the course of planetary evolution (Theosophy). 3. sum total of all that is. 4. lord of the universe who cannot be represented by any form (Islam). 5. the One who plays the game of life by becoming the Many, losing itself in the creation and finding its way back to unity; supreme being, personal friend, teacher, and lover who knows the heart of all beings (Hinduism). 6. indwelling spirit within all beings; one's highest self realized through contemplation or service; eternal, infinite, all-wise, all-knowing, all-loving, ever-free radiant presence (mysticism). 7. impersonal spirit of selfless love (humanism). 8. an infinite sphere whose center is everywhere and circumferance is nowhere (*The Book of the Twenty-Four Philosophers*). 9. that which envelops inside and outside, works through yin and yang; universal spirit, universal oneness, embracing everything (Michio Kushi). 10. pure energy; highest frequency vibration (psychotronics). 11. one who leads us time and again out of our habitual slavery and laziness or self-indulgence into a free horizon (Sherman Goldman)

General Terms for God

Bog	Russian, Polish
Dieu	French
Dio	Italian, Esperanto
Dios	Spanish
El	Hebrew
God	Dutch
Gott	German
Gud	Swedish, Danish, Norwegian
Ilah	Arabic
Ishvara	Sanskrit
Mungu	Swahili
Tanri	Turkish

Creator or Presiding Gods

Ahura Mazda	Zoroastrian
Allah	Islamic
Amma	Dogon
Anguta	Innuit
Awonawilona	Zuni
Brahma, Vishnu, Shiva	Hindu
Chukwu	Ibo
Coyote	North American Indians
Heamavihio	Cheyenne
Jade Emperor	Taoist
Jupiter	Roman
Khnum	Egyptian
Leza	Central African
Make-Make	Easter Island
Marduk	Babylonian
Masau'u	Hopi
Mithras	Persian
Musaga	Pygmy
Ngewo	Sierre Leone
Ol-orun	Yoruba
Ometeotl	Nahuatl
Pacha Camac	Incan
Shang Ti	Chinese
Tirawa	Pawnee
Wakonda	Sioux
Yahweh	Hebrew

Zeus .... Greek

God-image divine symbols spontaneously produced in dreams, fantasies, visions symbolic of wholeness (Jung)

God-realization enlightenment

god seat medium through which the divinity manifests its power, e.g., a ritual mask

God-self inner voice, higher self

Goddard, Dwight American Buddhist organizer; *The Buddhist Bible*; 1861-1939

Goddard, Robert space pioneer who launched the first liquid fuel rocket at Auburn, Mass., March 6, 1926; 1882-1945

Goddess 1. Supreme Being of matriarchal civilization. 2. ancient conceptualization of the powers governing the universe in female form (Riane Eisler). 3. an internal set of images and attitudes. 4. symbol of the power of physical transformation of the godhead as the whirling wheel of life in its birth-bringing and death-bringing totality; the symbol of spiritual transformation (Erich Neumann)

Goddess of Democracy Statue of Liberty-like symbol of the Chinese students in Beijing, 1989

Godwin, William English author and anarchist, husband of Mary Wollstonecraft; *The Inquiry*; 1756-1836

Goenka, S.N. Burmese-born Vipassana meditation teacher

Goethe, Johann Wolfgang von German author, naturalist; *The Sorrows of Young Werther*; 1749-1832

Goetheanum headquarters of the Anthroposophical Society in Dornach, Switzerland

Goetia a text known as the *Lesser Key of Solomon*

gohan meal, rice (Japanese)

gohei paper charms in Shinto temples (Japanese)

gohonzon a Nichiren Shoshu scroll inscribed with the names of the principal enlightened beings mentioned in the *Lotus Sutra* (Japanese)

Gokuraku Pure Land, Buddhist Paradise (Japanese)

Golden Age 1. highest peak of a culture. 2. period of global peace and harmony that existed until about 13,000 years ago when Earth changes and a partial axis shift occurred (Michio Kushi). 3. comic book era of late 1930s and early 1940s. 3. prehistoric era that coincided with the crossroads of the ecliptic and equator and with the ecliptic and the Galaxy, specifically when Gemini and Sagittarius stood firmly at two of the four corners of the quadrangular Earth (Santillana and von Dechend)

Golden Ass occult novel by Apuleius, 2nd c.

Golden Bough 1. certain branch of a tree in Diana's grove at Nemi, plucked by Aeneas before his visit to Hades. 2. pioneer study of mythology by Sir George Frazer, 1890

Golden Bowl 1. symbol of consciousness in the Bible. 2. novel by Henry James

Golden Chain links or steps to wisdom

Golden Dawn English occult fraternity, offshoot of Rosicrucianism, 1887-

Golden Flower 1. symbol of enlightenment in China. 2. Chinese Taoist text possibly influenced by Nestorian Christianity

Golden Ladder blazing golden staircase descended by Dante and Beatrice in Paradise, symbolizing the contemplative life, which by descending causes the soul to rise higher, manifesting countless heavenly splendors wheeling like birds in flight

Golden Legend *History of the Lives of the Saints* by Jacobus de Voragine, 13th c.

Golden Mean (The Good) 1. happy medium, perfect moderate course or position that avoids extremes; Confucian ideal. 2. principle of moderation inscribed at Delphi: 'Nothing in excess'

Golden Plates tablets revealed to Joseph Smith at Cumorah Hill, N.Y., 1827

Golden Race race of mortals created by the Olympian gods when Cronus was king in heaven, who lived free from sorrow and in ease and peace upon their lands with many good things, rich in flocks and beloved of the gods (Hesiod)

Golden Rule 1. Biblical injunction to love others as you would have them love and do unto you. 2. ketch that sailed toward the nuclear-testing zone at Eniwetok, 1958

Golden Section a unique relation in which the small part stands in the same proportion to the large part as the large part stands to the whole; logarithmic proportion reflecting perfect harmony; ratio found in nature and art of 1:1.62...

Golden Stool Ashanti emblem made by a priest, Anotchi, in the 18th c. whose disappearance in 1900 presaged the fall of the nation

Golden Temple sacred temple of the Sikhs in Amritsar, India

Golden Tree tree built by Galahad at Sarras, upon whose completion the Holy Grail appeared to him

Goldman, Emma Russian-born anarchist; *Living My Life*; 1869-1940

Goldman, Sherman macrobiotic editor, author, and teacher; ed. *East West Journal*; 1937-

Goldstein, Emmanuel underground leader in Orwell's *1984*, the Enemy of the People

Golgonooza utopian city in Blake's *Four Zoas*

Gollum a hobbit who once possessed the One Ring and shadowed Frodo in *Lord of the Rings*

goma wakame powder a condiment made from roasted ground sesame seeds and baked or roasted wakame (Japanese)

gomashio sesame seed salt made from dry-roasting and grinding sea salt and sesame seeds and crushing them in a suribachi; used in macrobiotic cooking (Japanese)

gomchen ascetic (Tibetan)

gomoku casserole style of cooking combining five or more ingredients; popular in macrobiotic cooking (Japanese)

gompa solitary place, monastery. **ani gompa** nunnery (Tibetan)

Gondor most important kingdom in Middle Earth

Gondwana 'Land of the Gonds', 1. forest tribe in South Africa. 2. southern continent that formed when Pangaea separated (Plate Tectonics)

gongyo recitation of the *Lotus Sutra* by Nichiren Shoshu (Japanese)

Gont land of wizards in Earthsea

Good Deeds guide of Everyman

good people sin. adj. friend, trustworthy (Afro-American)

Goodman, Andrew civil rights organizer; 1944-65

Goodman, Paul anarchist educator; *Growing Up Absurd*; 1911-72

Goofy buck-toothed gawky buffoon companion of Mickey Mouse

Gopa (Yasodhara) wife of the Buddha

gopi cowgirl, transcendental companion of Krishna (Sanskrit)

gopura elaborate, high gateway of a South Indian temple (Sanskrit)

Gorbachev, Mikhail Soviet leader and architect of freedom in the Communist world; *Perestroika*; 1931-

Gordian Knot tangle cut by Alexander the Great

Gordon, Cyrus pre-Columbian scholar; *Before Columbus*; 1908-

Gordon, Flash radio and comic strip hero, 1930s-

gospel (godspel) 'good news', 1. teachings of Jesus and his Apostles, 2. one of many books about Jesus circulating in the early Church until the 5th c. 3. one of the first four books of the New Testament (Middle English)

Gospel of the Holy Twelve Essene account preserved in a Tibetan monastery, published by Rev. Gideon J. R. Ouseley, 1900

Gospel of Mary gnostic manuscript describing the love between Jesus and Mary Magdalen

Gospel of Philip Gnostic manuscript discovered at Nag Hammadi depicting the union of man and woman as a symbol of healing and peace

Gospel of Truth Christian sermon on the theme of salvation by gnosis attributed to Valentinus

Goswami 'Lord of Cows', 1. epithet of Krishna. 2. Vaishnava priest (Sanskrit)

Gotha world outside the solar system assisting Earth (Aetherius Society)

Gotham 1. legendary medieval village of sages situated somewhere between England and India. 2. hangout of Batman and Robin

Gotterdammerung twilight of the gods, Ragnarok (German)

Gottfried of Stausbourg medieval bard; *Tristan*; 13th c.

Govinda 1. name of Krishna as giver of pleasure to the senses. 2. boyhood companion in Hesse's *Siddartha*

Govinda, Lama (Anagarika Brahmacari) teacher of the Arya Maitreya Mandala; *The Way of the White Clouds*; 1898-

grace 1. divine bounty that increases in exact proportion to the ardor of love that opens to receive it (Beatrice). 2. direct vision of God earned through zealous love. 3. short blessing before a meal (French)

Grad, Bernard psychiatric researcher of healing energy on plants and animals; *A Telekinetic Effect on Plant Growth*;

1908-

Graham, Sylvester W. Presbyterian preacher, vegetarian, inventor of the Graham cracker, friend of hard mattresses and cold showers and enemy of white bread; 1794-1851

Grail Castle 1. castle where the Holy Grail was kept. 2. the home of the highest symbol of the spiritual life carried down from heaven by the neutral angels and capable of being seen only by the worthy (Joseph Campbell)

grain single seed or seedlike fruit of rice, wheat, and other cereal grasses

grain mill a small handmill used to grind grains, beans, seeds, and nuts into various forms, including flour

Gral Holy Grail in the form of a stone

gramdan 'village gift', voluntary communal village movement of Vinoba Bhave where villagers agree to work their land in common (Sanskrit)

Grand Cross (Grand Square) four planets squaring each other, signifying confusion

Grand Inquisitor chapter title and chief torturer of the Church in Dostoevski's *Brothers Karamazov* who is kissed by the returned Christ

Grand Kodo Soka Gakkai headquarters near Mt. Fuji in Japan

Grand Purification 1. (O Horai) ancient chant about a gathering of spirits who decided to make the Earth a peaceful country by washing away humanity's sins. 2. rite celebrated in Japan on New Year's Eve with 108 peals of the gong at midnight to wipe out delusion

Grand Triune three planets each 120 degrees from each other

Grandfathers universal spirits (Black Elk)

Granfaloon false Kerass, mistaking a chance coincidence for a meaningful one (Vonnegut)

granny adj. small, metal-rimmed eyeglasses

granola rolled oats mixed with raisins, nuts, coconut, etc.

Grant, Joan British medium and occultist; *Winged Pharoah*; 1907-

granthi 'knot', obstacle overcome by meditation (Sanskrit)

graphotherapy science of handwriting analysis applied to psychological problems

Grateful Dead rock band (Jerry Garcia, Bob Weir, Ron McKernan, Phil Lesh,

Mickey Hart, Bill Kreutzmann, Tom Constanten); *Anthem of the Sun*; 1960s-

gratitude deep joy in the Order of the Universe (George Ohsawa)

graviton hypothetical massless particle, vehicle of gravitational force

gravity a manifestation of Infinite Expansion which pushes everything on the surface of the Earth toward its center resulting in attraction between yin and yang forces inversely proportional to the square of the distance (George Ohsawa)

Gravy, Wavy California hippie leader

Gray, Elizabeth Dodson ecofeminist and cultural historian; *Green Paradise Lost*

Grdhrakuta 'Vulture Peak', 1. North Indian mountain where Buddha delivered the *Lotus Sutra.* 2. place where truth is alive (Sanskrit)

Great Airship mysterious dirigible-like airship that was seen over North America in 1896

Great Bear constellation Ursa Major, also known as Big Dipper or Charles's Wain

Great Breath the outpouring of all manifested existence from the 'mouth' of divinity

Great Father the chief deity during patriarchal times; a masculine heavenly or sky god

Great God of Sefar magico-religious fresco at Tassili identified as an extraterrestrial

Great Goddess the chief deity during the prehistoric or megalithic period exhibiting creative, destructive, and regenerative powers

Great Mother mother with exaggerated breasts and hips, who gives birth to and nourishes all beings; often represented in art and design holding a child in her lap

Great Purification Earth changes and upheavals prior to the dawning of a new era which will cleanse the world and reunite Heaven and Earth, ushering in a new age of spirituality and light

Great Pyramid of Kulkulcan Mayan structure in Chichen Itza

Great Return journey back to wisdom and the Godhead

Great Spirit Native American name for God

Great Subculture enlightened underground since paleolithic times (Gary Snyder)

Great Wall 1. big wall on China's northern border that is the only human-made object visible from the Moon. 2. dense clusters of galaxies that stretch across the heavens in a wall-like pattern, discovered by Margaret Geller and John Huchra, 1989

Great Web spiral of life

Great Wheel interpenetrating gyres of time, cosmic whirling spirals (Yeats)

Great White Brotherhood occult fraternity said to guide the destiny of the Earth and communicating through various teachers and prophets such as Madame Blavatsky

Great White Lodge brotherhood of masters guarding the planet (Theosophy)

Great Work alchemy

Great Yang two yang lines in the *I Ching* representing Earth and Heaven and the season of summer

Great Yin two yin lines in the *I Ching* representing winter

Greater Benefic Jupiter

Greater Zodiac period of 250,000 years

Greatheart guide in *Pilgrim's Progress*

Greeley, Dana McLean Unitarian minister and social activist; 1908-86

Green 1. political movement based on transformative vision and environmental awareness; originating in West Germany in 1983 and spreading through Europe, America, and elsewhere. 2. member or voter of such a movement. 3. someone who is ecologically aware.

Green Bank Formula estimate of advanced planetary civilizations in the galaxy by scientists at a West Virginia observatory in 1961; about 50 million

Green Belt movement in Africa to establish zones of trees and shrubs to prevent desertification

Green City ecological design model for an urban area including urban wild habitat, diversified transportation, renewable energy, small business zone, etc.

Green Committees of Correspondence U.S. Green political organization, in alliance with the bioregional movement

Green Energy money

Green Guard protectors and restorers of the Earth (Rainbow Family Tribe)

green rice rice cooked with mugwort leaves and having a greenish hue

Green Tara Tibetan Goddess of Success and Salvation

Green Team informal family or community group that gets together to work on environmental and conservation projects

Greenham women's peace camps set up on Greenham Common near a U.S. Air Force Base housing nuclear weapons in Britain, 1981

Greenhouse Crisis Foundation environmental coalition led by Jeremy Rifkin in Washington, D.C., 1980s-

greenhouse effect global warming trend due to the build up of carbon dioxide and other gases which trap heat in the Earth's atmosphere as panes of glass trap heat in a greenhouse

greenhouse gases gases that increase the planet's heat balance, especially carbon dioxide, methane, nitrous oxide

greening 1. rise of the counterculture, especially ecological and environmental awareness. 2. spread or development of honesty, openness, community, and living more harmoniously with the land

greenness index a scale designed to indicate levels of plant productivity and photosynthesis in satellite images and also areas of famine and environmental pollution

Gregg, Richard lawyer and peace acivist; *The Power of Nonviolence*; 1882-1966

Gregory of Nyssa mystical theologian of the Eastern Church; *Life of Moses*; d. 394

Gregory the Great contemplative pope; *Morals on Job*; 540-604

Gregory, Dick comedian, civil rights and peace activist, vegetarian, faster, cross-country walker; *From the Back of the Bus*; 1932-

Grendel the heavy in *Beowulf*

Greyfell Siegfried's horse

Griffin, Susan philosopher and feminist critic; *Woman and Nature*

griffin (griffon) 1. fabulous eagle-lion, guardian of the road to salvation. 2. (cap.) symbol of Christ in the Earthly Paradise in the *Divine Comedy*

Grigorenko, Piotyr Soviet general, organizer for human rights; 1906-87

grihastha householder, second stage of life in Hinduism (Sanskrit)

Grimke, Angela abolitionist and women's rights activist; *Appeal to the Christian Women of the South*; 1805-79

Grimke, Sarah abolitionist and women's rights activist; *Epistle to the Clergy of the Southern States*; 1792-1873

Grimm, Ben Marvel Comics' the Thing

Grimm, Jakob German folklorist; *Fairy Tales*; 1785-1863

Grimm, Wilhelm German folklorist; *Fairy Tales*; 1786-1859

griot West African oral historian

Griscom, Chris New Age healer; *Ecstasy Is a New Frequency*

groats a hulled, usually crushed grain such as buckwheat or oats

Grof, Stanislov psychologist and consciousness researcher; *The Human Encounter with Death*; 1931-

Grogan, Emmet San Francisco Digger and realist; *Rinyolevio*; 1943-

grok v. intuit from within, to dissolve barriers between subject and object (Heinlein)

Groot, Gerard Dutch mystic, founder of the Brotherhood of the Common Life; 1340-84

groove n. or v. intensely enjoyable experience, harmonious interaction, flow. adj. **groovy**

Gross, Sri Darwin current Mahanta of Eckankar

Grossinger, Richard cultural historian and anthropologist; *Planetary Medicine*; 1944-

ground 1. place on the Earth where we were born; rootedness in our own culture, in physical work, in the body (Robert Bly). 2. our native soil; the particular combination of climate, air, light, and vibration coming from the Earth through a certain kind of humus or sand or rock where intuition functions at its peak and the voice of the demiurgos comes through clearly (Sherman Goldman)

grounding 1. living on the ground where you or your ancestors were born or near it. 2. going down into the psyche and bringing into consciousness what is now in the shadows and letting it mingle with the conscious mind (Robert Bly). 3. the process by which electricity, poetry, and the authentic life become possible (Robert Bly)

groupware the combination of intentionally chosen group processes and procedures plus the computer software to support them, 1978

Grousset, Rene French Orientalist; *In the Footsteps of the Buddha*; 1885-1952

Guadalquivir Moorish river

Guadalupe site in Mexico where a vision of Mary appeared in 1531 to an Aztec man running to attend Mass

Guarani native language of Paraguay

Guenon, Rene French esoterist; *The Crisis of the Modern World*; 1886-1951

Guenther, Herbert Buddhist scholar in Canada; *The Tantric View of Life*

guerrilla theater social or political drama performed in the streets or parks

guided imagery an exercise to develop the imagination in which a guide leads people to visualize through suggestions and symbols

Guillaume de Postel French Kabbalist and astrologer; *The Key of Things Kept Secret from the Foundations of the World*; 1510-81

Guilhem IX first troubador; 12th c.

Guinevere wife of Arthur and lover of Lancelot

Gujarat western Indian state bordering Pakistan and the Arabian Sea

gulab jaman sweetmeat of almonds, yogurt, and syrup (Hindi)

guna 1. quality, attribute. 2. one of three modes of energy in the *Bhagavad Gita* (Sanskrit)

rajas	active, passionate
tamas	passive, inert
sattva	balanced

gunavatara incarnation of a quality (Sanskrit)

Gundrun sweetheart of Sigurd

gurbani sacred word of the Sikh Gurus (Punjabi)

Gurdjieff, G. I. (Georges Ivanovitch) Russian-born occultist, magus, and teacher; *All & Everything*; 1872-1949

gurdwara Sikh temple (Punjabi)

gurmukhi script of the Sikh scriptures, pure sound current (Punjabi)

guru (from *gu*, darkness, *ru*, light) 1. teacher, preceptor. 2. spiritual guide who leads the student from darkness to light, personification of truth for the disciple. 3. one who can confer realization. 4. one's highest self appearing to be manifested in a different body. 5. one who contacts the seeker but is never found by him or her. 6. ultimately oneself (Sanskrit)

Guru Poorina day of homage to spiritual teachers, first full moon in July (Sanskrit)

gurubhagini any woman studying under the same teacher (Sanskrit)

gurubhai any man studying under the same teacher (Sanskrit)

gurudev spiritual teacher, more honorific title than guru (Sanskrit)

Guthrie, Arlo folksinger; *Alice's Restaurant*;1947-

Guthrie, Woody grandfather of the folk-protest movement; *This Land Is Your Land*; 1912-67

Gulliver, Lemuel narrator of Swift's *Gulliver's Travels*

Guynvyd heaven of illumined souls (Welsh)

Guyon, Madame French mystic; *Les Opuscules Spirituelles*; 1648-1717

gyalwa 'victorious one', title of a Bodhisattva, honorific name of the Karmapa and Dalai Lama (Tibetan)

Gyatsho, Tenzin (Gyatso, Tendzin) 14th and current Dalai Lama; *The Opening of the Wisdom Eye*; 1935-

gyeling musical reed pipe (Tibetan)

gylany relationship between men and women based on partnership and equality (Riane Eisler) (from *andros* man, *gyne* woman, and letter *l* between for *linking* and *lyos*, the Greek verb which means both analysis and catalysis)

gyn-Ecology 1. new science of understanding women and their relationships, as opposed to *gynecology*, especially by male-oriented doctors. 2. women weaving a world tapestry of their own soil (Mary Daly)

gynaesthesia the new way of seeing and understandiang conferred by becoming a feminist (Mary Daly)

gynarchism social order created by women

gynergy feminist moral values or force (Emily Culpepper, 1975)

gynocentric adj. 1. Goddess-based. 2. woman-centered

gynocritics study of women's literature and writing

gynomorphic a new woman's language or process of creating knowledge (Mary Daly)

gyoji endless training, exertion, unremitting practice (Japanese)

Gypsies (Zigeuener, Zingari, Gitanus) 'Egyptians', vagabond community originating in India

Gyro Gearloose mad scientist friend of Donald Duck

gyromancy divination by whirling in a circle marked with letters and spelling out a prophecy when falling down

gyu tantra (Tibetan)

gyuma (sgyuma) illusion, maya (Tibetan)

Gyume Tibetan monks noted for singing 'one voice chords'; *Tantric Harmonies*

Hh

Habitat for Humanity a Georgia-based ecumenical ministry that builds and repairs homes, 1976-

habs-i-dam Sufi meditation of holding the breath and repeating *La ilaha illa 'llah* as many times as possible in one breath (Arabic)

Hades 1. Greek Underworld. 2. second Uranian planet ruling decay, want, loneliness, misery, healing, and finding value in the past

Hadhayosh 'ever pure', Iranian ox upon whose back people first traversed the sea

hadith tradition going back to the Prophet based on a chain of transmission (Arabic)

Hadjar el Guble 'Stone of the South', dressed Lebanese stone of 2 million pounds of unknown origin

hadron strongly interacting subatomic particle, such as the proton or the pion, divided into categories of baryons and mesons

Haei-Shin Chinese Buddhist traveler who sailed and returned from a land of Painted People, Fusang, identified as the Maya or Incans, 5th c.

ha'guks 'eagle', healing bird of the Iroquois

Hahnemann, Christian Samuel German founder of homeopathy; *The Chronic Diseases*; 1755-1843

Hai fifth Hebrew letter: breath, H, 5

Haight-Asbury hippie district of San Francisco, especially during the Summer of Love, 1967

haiku a short poem expressing the essence of nature and the universe beyond ordinary sentiment and knowledge; traditionally consisting of three lines of 5, 7, and 5 syllables (Japanese)

hajj 'pilgrimage', journey to Mecca (Arabic)

hakata 64 pieces of carved bone cast for divination in Southern Africa

hako 'voice of all things', mantric ceremony of the Plains Indian children

Hakuin Ekaku Japanese Zen master who devised the koan 'What is the sound of one hand clapping?'; 1686-1769

Hakuyu mountain hermit who taught Hakuin inner contemplation; 17th c.

hal 1. (pl. ahwal) 'state', transitory state of enlightenment (Arabic). 2. (cap.) (Heuristically Programmed Algorithmic Computer) supercomputer in *2001*

Hal-il-Maugraby great magician in the *Arabian Nights*

halak dream interpreter (Senoi)

halakhah 'way', Jewish law (Hebrew)

halasana Plow Posture in yoga (Sanskrit)

Hale, Edward Everett Unitarian clergyman; *The Man Without a Country*; 1822-1909

Haleakala 'House of the Sun,' national park in Maui

half-periodic day (half-critical day) day immediately before or after a critical day when subject is exposed to stress in biorhythm

halfling hobbit

Halifax, Joan anthropologist involved with sacred medicine; *Shamanic Voices*

Hall, Manly Palmer esoteric author, founder of the Philosophical Research Society; *Secret Teachings of All Ages*; 1901-

Hall of Records pyramid of secret wisdom including prophecies for 1958-98 in Gizeh (Cayce)

Hallaj 'the wood-carder', (Husain ibn Mansur) Persian Sufi martyred for teaching the union of the soul and God; 858-922

Hallelujah! The Three Rings New Age peace center on the Mt. of Olives in Jerusalem

Haller, Henry Hesse's Steppenwolf

Halley's Comet periodic visitor to our corner of the solar system due next to return in A.D. 2062

hallucination experiencing or perceiving sensory data which have no physical correlation

hallucinogen psychotropic drug that magnifies, distorts, or clarifies sensory perceptions of commonly accepted reality

halo Sun's aura, furtherest reach of its energy field

Halpern, Steven New Age musician, composer, artist, producer; *Spectrum Suite*

halqa Sufi circle (Arabic)

Hamer, Fannie Lou Mississippi civil rights organizer; 1917-77

Hamlet's Mill (Amlodhi's Mill) 1. fabled mill in Norse myth which ground out

peace and plenty but in decaying times ground out salt and later rock and sand, creating a vast whirlpool leading to the land of the dead. 2. title of a book on the astronomical basis of mythology by Giorgio de Santillana and Hertha von Dechend, 1977

hamsa 1. cosmic gander, 2. sound of inhaling and exhaling (Sanskrit)

Han Hsiang Tzu one of the Chinese Eight Immortals, patron of musicians

Hanamatsuri 'Flower Festival', celebration of Buddha's birthday on May 8 (Japanese)

Hanblecheyapi crying for a vision (Lakota)

hand trembler Navajo healer who diagnoses by joining force with a gila monster, which causes his hand to shake and locate the illness

Handel, George Frederick German composer; *Messiah*; 1685-1759

Handsome Lake (Ganyodaiyo) Seneca Prophet who founded the Longhouse religion or Good Tidings movement in 1799

Handy, William C. father of the Blues; *St. Louis Blues*; 1873-1958

hang-up mental or emotional block

Hanged Man Tarot #12: sacrifice, ordeal

Hank (Sir Boss) hero of Twain's *A Connecticut Yankee in King Arthur's Court*

Hannya Haramita Shingyo (the Heart Sutra; Prajna Paramita Hridaya, *Sanskrit*) The Buddha's Teaching of the Essence of Our Infinite Being (Japanese)

Hanuman monkey god who rescued Sita in the *Ramayana*

Hanuman Foundation organization founded by Baba Hari Dass dedicated to service projects and prisoners, 1973-

haoma heavenly tree of immortality on Mount Haraiti (Persian)

happiness 1. mental and psychological health and well-being; the natural state of human beings in harmony with their environment. 2. the endless realization of an endless dream (George Ohsawa)

Hapi Egyptian God of the Nile, prototype of Aquarius

Haqq, al the Real, Sufi term for God (Arabic)

hara 1. (tanden) body's natural center of gravity located in the intestines about three fingers width below the navel; site of the second chakra or energy center (Japanese). 2. (cap.) mountain cave where Muhammad meditated, three miles from Mecca

Harappa Indus Valley culture predating the Vedic civilization

hard adventure physically demanding trip or trek

hard rain revolution, natural disaster (Bob Dylan)

Harding, M. Esther psychiatrist; *Woman's Mysteries*; 1888-1971

Hardwar 'doorway to God', North Indian city (Sanskrit)

Hari title and invocation of Krishna

Hari Mandir (Darbar Sahib) Golden Temple of the Sikhs in Amritsar (Punjabi)

Harivamsha 'Geneology of Hari', sequel to the *Mahabharata* (Sanskrit)

Harlequin invisible sprite of pantomime

Harmonia group of colonies or phalanges founded in mid-19th century by Charles Fourier

Harmonic Convergence New Age day of international prayer and ceremony, Aug. 16-17, 1987

Harmonie utopian community of George Rapp and later Robert Owen on the Wabash River between Indiana and Illinois, 19th c.

Harmony of the Spheres the cosmos as a vast musical harmony (Pythagoras)

Harner, Michael shamanistic trainer and author; *The Way of the Shaman*

Harness, Charles mythological science-fiction writer; *The Ring of Ritornel*; 1915-

Harsha 'exhilaration, joy', Indian monarch who outlawed killing of animals, welcomed Hsuan Tsang; *Nagananda*; ca. 590-647

hartal protest closure of shops and services (Hindi)

Hartmann, Sadakichi avant-garde writer; *Buddha, White Chrysanthemums*; 1869-1944

Harun al-Rashid Baghdad caliph whose realm is featured in the *Arabian Nights*; 8th c.

Harvest Home autumnal pagan festival

Hasan of Basra Muslim ascetic, early Sufi; d. 728

Hashimoto, Ken Japanese scientist who communicated with a cactus and taught it to count to twenty; *Mystery of the Fourth Dimensional World*; 1931-

Hasidism (Chassidism) 'the Pious', mystical Jewish movement founded by Israel ben Eliezer in the Ukraine; major sects include Chabad, Satmer, Belz, Brestlau (Hebrew)

Hastings, Warren British governor-general of India who promoted Sanskrit; 1732-1818

Hastyeyalti (Talking God) grandfather deity in the Navaho pantheon, in whom male and female powers are united

hatali Navajo shaman

hatcho miso a fermented soybean paste made from soybeans and sea salt and aged at least two years (Japanese)

hatha force (Sanskrit)

Hatha Yoga yoga emphasizing asanas, or physical postures, breathing, and diet (Sanskrit)

Hathor cow-headed Egyptian Sky Goddess

hato mugi (Job's Tears, Pearl Barley) small white whole grain traditionally used to eliminate excessive fat and oil from the body and to beautify the skin (Japanese)

Hatshepsut, Queen Egyptian monarchess whose reign is notable for expanding trade and culture; ca. -1500

Hauk's Book chief literary source for the Norse discovery of America, 14th c.

Hauser, Gayelord nutritionist who stressed brewer's yeast, vitamins, wheat germ, yogurt; *Look Younger, Live Longer*; 1895-1984

Hauteville, Jean de French author and pilgrim; *The Man of Many Sorrows*; 12th c.

Hava-Iki homeland of most Polynesian peoples lost in an ancient cataclysm; source of the name for Hawaii

Havasupais 'Blue-Green Water People', Indian tribe which lives in the bottom of the Grand Canyon

Havnor large island in Earthsea, seat of the King of all the isles and center of the world

havoc (haue oc) pagan war cry that is cited as the key to the original universal tongue in Cohane's *The Key*

Hawke, Bob Australian prime minister and environmentalist; *Our Country, Our Future*; 1929-

Hawken, Paul New Age entrepreneur; *Growing a Business*

Hawkman comic book reincarnation of Egyptian prince Knufu

Hawthorne, Nathaniel Transcendentalist, utopian author; *The House of Seven Gables*; 1804-64

Hay, Louise New Age healer and spiritual teacher; *You Can Heal Your Life*; 1927-

hayah divine aspect of the soul in the Kabbalah (Hebrew)

Hayden, Tom peace activist; 1940-

Hayes, Denis coordinator of the first Earth Day; 1944-

Haywood, Bill socialist, IWW leader, miner; 1869-1928

Hazel leader of the rabbits in *Watership Down*

Hazrat Babalan Muslim female saint who kissed Meher Baba's forehead and became enlightened

H.D.L. high-density lipoprotein, one of the good cholesterols

head 1. user of psychedelic drugs or marijuana. 2. the mind or someone who is very mindful

head trip verbal or intellectual path of action; rational, dualistic headspace

headshop store stocking psychedelic paraphernalia

heal v. to restore connections (Wendell Berry)

healing music music that helps to perfect and align the totality of human being and elevate consciousness

health 1. condition of physical, mental, and spiritual wholeness and well-being. 2. letting the universe flow through you. 3. giving yourself completely as a warrior on the playing field where there's no reward for success and you're willing to die because it doesn't matter (Sherman Goldman)

healing crisis brief illness or symptoms that surface in the initial period after making a dietary change or other holistic health adjustment

Health, Seven Conditions of: absence of fatigue; good appetite; sound sleep; good memory; lack of anger; clarity and promptness of thought and action; complete understanding and application of justice for humanity (George Ohsawa)

Health Research esoteric publishers founded by Robert and Mary Wilborn in Mokelumne Hill, Calif., 1952-

health food food eaten for health, including natural, organic, vegetarian, macrobiotic, special diet, and high-nutrient products

Healthy, Happy, Holy Organization Sikh movement founded by Yogi Bhajan

Heamavihio breath of wisdom, God (Cheyenne)

Heard, Gerald English author, mystic; *A Dialogue in the Desert*; 1889-1971

Hearn, Lafcadio Aegean-born novelist, Orientalist; *Gleanings from Buddha Fields*; 1850-1904

heart mind consciousness (Huichol)

heart governor (cheou tsine yin, *Chinese*) meridian from the chest to the extremities of the fingers governing circulation and relating to the physical and emotional aspects of the heart

Heart Sutra (Prajna Paramita Hridaya, *Sanskrit,* Hannya Haramita Shingyo, *Japanese*) sutra expressing the essence of Buddha's teaching

heart-of-foot chakra on the center of the foot

heart-of-hand chakra on the palm of the hand

heat collector part of a solar energy unit where the fluid is heated

Heaven's Force energy from the Sun, Moon, stars, and trillions of galaxies streaming into the Earth; centripetal or yang force going downward and inward

Heavener Inscription runestone of undetermined origin in southeastern Oklahoma on Poteau Mountain

Heavenly Pageant religious masque in which the Church Triumphant appeared to Dante in allegorical guises, including virtues, elders, and evangelists

Heavenly Spheres nine heavenly orbs, one within the next, in medieval Christian cosmology where the good dwelt after life: Moon, Mercury, Venus (Lovers), Sun (Theologians), Mars (Warriors of God, ascetics), Jupiter (Just Rulers), Saturn (Ascetics), Fixed Stars (Patriarchs), Primum Mobile (Trinity)

Heavenly Visitors beings who came to Earth 1.7 million years ago to develop the human race, bringing seeds, the way of agriculture, the way of making fire, the way of cooking, and arts and letters (Michio Kushi)

Heavenly Heart seat of enlightenment

heavy 1. someone respected for his or her weighty ideas or charismatic leadership. 2. adj. overbearing, extreme, too yang. 3. adj. difficult, challenging, burdensome. 4. adj. weighed down by middle class attachments and culture

Hebrew Semitic language of the Old Testament spoken until -250; religious and literary language of Judaism revived in Israel in 1948

Heelstone point at Stonehenge where the Sun rises on the solstice

Hefluland 'Land of Flat Stone', glacial land north of Labrador (Leif Erikson)

hei-koann pressure point three fingers below the wrist; master point of digestion (Chinese)

Heian Japanese era 794-1185

Heide, Wilma Scott feminist social critic; *Feminism for the Health of It*

Heike monogatari Japanese historical romance of the conflict between the Minamoto and Taira clans, 13th c.

Heimdall 'White God', watchman of the Scandinavian gods

Heindel, Max (Carl Louis Van Grasshoff) founder of the Rosicrucian Fellowship; 1865-1919

Heine, Heinrich German lyric poet; *Die Lorelei*; 1797-1856

Heinlein, Robert A. science-fiction author; *Stranger in a Strange Land*; 1907-88

heiwa peace (Japanese)

Hel Norse Goddess of the Dead

heliacal adj. 1. rising of a heavenly body hidden by the Sun. 2. setting of a heavenly body before it becomes invisible again

Heline, Corinne author, musician, healer; *The New Age Bible Interpretation*; 1882-1975

Heline, Theodore Rosicrucian author and editor; *New Age Interpreter*; 1883-1971

helioarianism dietary practice of subsisting plant-like directly on the energy of the Sun

helix spiral in three dimensions. adj. **helical**

hell 1. kingdom of eternal night (Dante). 2. 52-year cycle of spiritual darkness prophesied by Quetzacoatl; nine periods which began with the arrival of bearded white men, 1519-1987. 3. self-created suffering in this life; nonexistent realm in the next life which is completely bright (Michio Kushi). 4. love for the wrong objects; being locked in a particular station in life (Joseph Campbell)

Hellerwork bodywork system combining deep tissue massage with movement re-education and a guided verbal dialogue

Heloise French maiden beloved of Abelard; 1101-64

Helvetius (Johann-Friedrich Schweitzer) Swiss scholar turned mystic after a renowned alchemy experiment; 17th c.

Hemis Buddhist monastery in Ladahk

Henderson, Hazel English-born economist and futurist; *Creating Alternative Futures*

heng pushing through to success, second cyclical movement of heaven (Chinese)

Hennacy, Ammon Catholic pacifist; *The Book of Ammon*; 1893-1970

Henry, Charles French scientist and philosopher who developed a model of the 'atom of life' consisting of three intersecting fields of resonance: the electro-magnetic, gravitational, and biopsychic; 1859-1926

Hensel, Julius German agricultural chemist and nutritionist; *Bread from Stones*, 1894

Hept-Supht 'He Who Keeps Shut', spiritual teacher on Atlantis who helped the Egyptians (Cayce)

Heraclitus of Ephesus Greek philosopher of flux; ca. -6th c.

herb of immortality plant sought at the bottom of the sea by Gilgamesh

herbal tea beverage made from the dried flowers or leaves of various shrubs, plants, or barks

Herder, Johann Gottfried von German romantic, Indologist; *Critical Woods*; 1744-1803

Hering, Constantine German-born homeopathic pioneer; 1800-80

Herland Mother Goddess utopia in Charlotte Perkins Gilman's novel of the same name, 1915

hermaphrodite 1. being with both male and female sexual organs. 2. an archetypal image of the union of opposites

Hermaphroditus son of Hermes and Aphrodite who became united with the nymph Salmacis while bathing

Hermes Greek God of Messages, Commerce, Roads, Theft, Science, Invention, Herds, and Cunning

Hermes Trismegistus legendary Egyptian sage, reputed author of the Tarot, neoplatonism, the Kabbalah, alchemy, and astrology

hermetic adj. secret, occult; especially the Western mystery tradition

hermetic chain links or steps to wisdom

hermetica body of occult wisdom

hermetics science of magic, the occult

Hermine femme fatale in Hesse's *Steppenwolf*

Hermit Tarot #9: wisdom, prudence

Hero Greek priestess of love and beloved of Leander. 2. (l.c.) one who plunges into the darkest part of the wilderness where there is no path to discover truth (Joseph Campbell)

Heron Alexandrian scholar who invented the aeolipile, a steam engine based on turbine principles; 1st c.

Heron People Aztecs

Herrigel, Eugen pistol champion who abandoned shooting for the Japanese bow; *Zen in the Art of Archery*

Herschel, William German-born astronomer, discoverer of Uranus; 1738-1822

herstory 'her story', women's history

Herzeele, Albrecht von German organic researcher; *The Origin of Inorganic Substances*; 19th c.

Herzeloyde Parzival's mother, sister of Anfortas, Trevrizent, Schoysiane, and Repanse de Schoye

Heschel, Abraham Polish-born mystical rabbi; *God in Search of Man*; 1907-72

Hesperides 1. site of the Garden of the Golden Apples sought by Herakles. 2. the maidens there

Hesse, Hermann German mystical author; *Siddartha*; 1877-1962

hesychast 'quiet', hermit, one of a mystical sect of monks at Mt. Athos, 14th c. (from Greek and Latin). adj. **hesychastic** peace of heart and mind toward which all things flow

Hetch Hetchy valley dammed to bring water to San Francisco, opposed by John Muir

Hetep heavenly fields (Egyptian)

Hewavitarne, D. H. (Dharmapala) Ceylonese founder of the Maha Bodhi Society; 1865-1933

hexagram one of 64 six-lined figures in the *I Ching*

Heyerdahl, Thor Norwegian ethnologist; *Kon Tiki*; 1914

H.H. hero of Hesse's *Journey to the East*

Hi Tsugi No Miko 'Respectable Making Fire and Distributor', earliest rulers on the Earth, ca. 1.7 million years ago (Michio Kushi)

Hiamovi high chief among the Dakota and Cheyenne known for peaceful ways

Hiawatha Onondaga chieftain who formed the Confederation of the Five Nations; 15th c.

hibakusha 'explosion affected people', survivors of Hiroshima and Nagasaki atomic bombings (Japanese)

Hickey, Isabel astrologer; *Astrology: A Cosmic Science*; d. 1980

Hicks, Edward Quaker painter; *The Peaceable Kingdom*; 1780-1849

hide traditional English measure of land that can support a family or area worked by one plow during the year

Hiei, Mount site of the headquarters of the Tendai Buddhist school in Japan

Hierarchal Board spiritual governing body of the solar system with headquarters on Saturn (Mark-Age)

hieronics higher energy unknown since the time of Atlantis (Mark-Age)

Hierophantes 'exponent of sacred things', high priest; Tarot #5 (Greek)

Hierosgamos sacred marriage; union of archetypal figures in rebirth mysteries and alchemy (Greek)

Higgs protagonist in *Erewhon* who is jailed for possessing a mechanical object (a watch) and for being ill

high n. or adj. delightful, joyful, ecstatic, conscious, aware, blissful

High Castle novel by Phillip Dick about Japan winning World War II and ruling America through use of the *I Ching* and marijuana

high dream dream with divine or cosmic overtones (Tart)

high-grading cutting the biggest trees in a forest by loggers and developers

High Lama director of the monastery of Shangri-la, ex-priest from Luxembourg in Hilton's *Lost Horizon*; 1680-1931

High Priestess Tarot #2: the female inquirer, the anima

higher moon one of three bodies between Mars and Jupiter, Jupiter and Saturn, and Saturn and Uranus (Rudhyar)

Highlander Folk School civil rights center in Tennessee, 1932-61

Hightower, Jim populist agricultural reformer; *Eat Your Heart Out*

Highwater, Jamake Native American writer and artist; *The Primal Mind*

hikma wisdom (Arabic)

hikuli mescal button of the Huichol and Tarahumara Indians

Hill, Betty and Barney couple said to have been abducted and given a star map by UFO occupants

Hill, Joe Swedish-born Wobblie organizer, poet, song writer, rebel, artist; *The Preacher and the Slave*; 1879-1915

Hillel Babylonian-born Jewish rabbi; ca. -30-9 C.E.

Hillman, James developer of archetypal psychology; *A Blue Fire*

Hilltop Theory theory that the type of

data collected by an investigator is a function of the image among his or her audience (Vallee)

hilluf (timurah) Kabbalistic system of changing the sequence of the same letters to raise common realities to divine ones (Hebrew)

Hilton, James utopian author; *Lost Horizon*; 1900-54

Hilton, Walter English mystic; *The Scale of Perfection*; 14th c.

Himalayan International Institute of Yoga Science and Philosophy yoga and meditation center founded by Swami Rama in Glenview, Ill., now in Honesdale, Pa., 1971-

Himalayas 'Snow Abode', great mountain range between India and Tibet (Sanskrit)

himsa violence (Sanskrit)

Hinayana 'Lesser Vehicle', nontheistic and largely monastic Buddhism of Southern Asia; pejorative term coined by Mahayanists; preferred term by Southern Buddhists is Theravada (Sanskrit)

Hindhede, Mikkel Danish medical official who persuaded the government to shift growing grain for cattle raising to direct human consumption during World War I, sending cancer and death rates plunging

Hindi most widely-spoken Indian language, descended from Sanskrit

Hinkins, John-Roger leader of the Movement for Inner Spiritual Awareness; *The Spiritual Promise*

hip aware, intuitive, wise (from pre-World War II jazz term *hep* or from the African language Wolof word *hipicat* brought over by slaves referring to one who is very aware). n. **hipdom, hipness**

hip bath bath made with sea salt and dried daikon greens immersed in water; used in macrobiotics to help stimulate circulation and treat various skin disorders and female sex organ problems

hippie (hippy) one practicing peace, love, and self-reliance; longhaired freak and drop out from society

Hippocrates Greek philosopher and physician who taught 'Let thy food be medicine, and thy medicine food'; *Airs, Waters, and Places*; ca. -460-370

Hippocratic Oath healing oath formulated by Hippocrates which states 'I will apply dietetic measures for the benefit

of the sick according to my ability and judgment; I will keep them from harm and injustice' and prohibits the use of harmful drugs, surgery, and abortion

Hippolyta bridegroom in *Midsummer's Night's Dream*

Hippolyte 1. Queen of the Amazons. 2. Amazonian leader in *Wonder Woman*

Hiroshige Japanese artist; *53 Views Along the Tokoido*; 1797-1858

Hiroshima 'Broad Island', A-bombed Japanese city that rose from the ashes to become capital of the world peace movement

Hiroshima Day international world peace day celebrated on August 6

Hiroshima Maidens several dozen A-bomb victims who came to the U.S. for physical and psychological treatment and rehabilitation, 1953

Hirschfeld, Magnus German sexologist and pioneer gay activist; 1868-1935

Hisagita-imishi Supreme Being (Creek)

history 1. dark period when the sages relinquished their kingship and let humans govern themselves as people's innate miraculous powers began to atrophy and they began to live by their animal senses and seek out many inventions (Chinese myth). 2. a nightmare from which we are trying to awaken (James Joyce). 3. the last and relatively brief period of human material development that appears as a straight line of progress and achievement because we have forgotten the larger Spiral of History of which it is a small part (Michio Kushi). 4. pattern of events created by heaven but received by East and West in opposite ways as they alternatively face inward toward the Sun or outward toward the dark (Michio Kushi)

hit correct response in an ESP test

Hiten 'flying in heaven', 1. Buddhist god of music. 2. Japan's first moon-bound spacecraft, 1990

hitlahavat ecstasy, God-intoxication (Hebrew)

hito 'spirit-receptacle', human being (Japanese)

Hitopadesa animal tales from India, playful narratives of forest life

Hiva continent that sank beneath the sea and was the original homeland of the first Easter Islanders

hiziki (hijiki) a dark brown sea vegetable which when dried turns black; staple in macrobiotic cooking (Japanese)

H'men 'those who understand and can do', diviners (Mayan)

Ho Hsien-ku one of the Chinese Eight Immortals, patroness of shops and home life

Ho T'u Yellow River Map; *I Ching* arrangement perceived by Fu Hsi in the markings of a dragon horse in the Yellow River showing the diagram of the eight trigrams and five elements

ho shou wu (fo-ti, *Polygonum multiflorum*) Chinese longevity tonic herb

hoa binh peace (Vietnamese)

Hoa-Hao Buddhist sect founded by Huynh Phu So in the Vietnamese Mekong Delta, 1939-

Hoama sacred plant of Zoroastrianism

hobbit one of the good natured small people in Tolkien's sagas

Hod Kabbalistic sephiroth of glory and peace (Hebrew)

Hoffman, Abbie yippie, social activist, madcap underground organizer; *Woodstock Nation*; 1937-89

Hoffmann, Albert Swiss chemist, developer of LSD in 1943

Hoffmann, E. T. A. German Romantic author, musician, artist, Sanskritist; *Tales from Hoffmann*; 1776-1822

Hog Farm (named after land loaned by a farmer in return for caring for his pig) Los Angeles commune active in organizing rock festivals and which served brown rice and veggies at Woodstock

hogan Navajo dwelling, six-sided wall frame with domed, cribbed log roof

Hohokam 'those who have gone', agricultural people of extremely high culture who occupied the Southwest for 1500 years, declined, and vanished

Hokkaido northeastern Japanese island, capital Sapporo; home of Ainu

Hokkaido pumpkin a round dark green or orange squash that is very sweet and harvested in the fall; native to New England, it was introduced to Japan and named after the island of Hokkaido

hokma wisdom (Hebrew)

Hokusai Japanese artist who painted on enormous scrolls or a grain of rice; *The Wave*; 1760-1849

holarchy 'whole order,' synthesis that reflects the order of the totality

Holarctica single continent encircling the North Pole in antediluvian times (Schuchert)

holding together adjacent lines in an *I Ching* hexagram that are alternately yin and yang

holed stone megalithic stone that can be climbed through and which confers the energy of renewal and health associated with the Goddess

Holi spring festival of Krishna in India where people celebrate by squirting each other with enormous water-filled syringes and pastels (Sanskrit)

holism the belief that wholes determine the design, function, and health of their parts rather than the other way around (Jan Smuts)

holistic (wholistic) adj. 1. knowledge or approach that is simultaneously intuitive and rational, scientific and artistic. 2. whole, integrated, comprehensive

holistic health natural, integrative approach to health and well-being utilizing diet, exercise, meditation, chiropractic, acupuncture, macrobiotics, or other noninvasive therapies

Hollow Earth theory that openings at the North and South Poles house warm air worlds peopled by descendents of Atlantis and flying saucers

Holly, Buddy pioneer rock and roll performer; *That'll Be the Day*; 1938-1959

Holmes, John Clennon Beat author; *Go*; 1926-

Holmes, John Haynes Unitarian clergyman, social activist; *My Gandhi*; 1879-1964

Holmes, Mycroft stout older brother of Sherlock

Holmes, Sherlock London detective, student of the Head Lama in Tibet; *Upon the Tracing of Footsteps*; 1854-

Holocene the current geological era dating back about 12,000 years

hologram a three-dimensional photographic image produced by laser light

holographic model paradigm integrating ordinary and alterned states of consciousness (Karl Pribram)

holon entity displaying both independent properties of a whole and dependent properties of parts (Koestler)

holonomics an all-encompassing discipline referring to the study of the principle governing whole systems (George Leonard, 1978)

holonomy the law or principle governing whole systems

Holotropic Breathwork a non-drug journey into nonordinary states of consciousness developed by Stanislav Grof

Holst, Gustav German composer; *Egdon Heath*; 1874-1934

Holt, John radical educator; *Freedom and Beyond*; 1923-85

Holy Grail (Graal, Gral, Sangreal) 1. cup or dish used by Jesus at the Last Supper, preserved by Joseph of Arimathea who brought it to Spain or Britain, and quested for by numerous knights. 2. stone that fell from Heaven, was kept in the Castle of the Holy Grail, and ultimately obtained by Parzival

Holy Kiss spiritual kiss and embrace of the early Christians

Holy Order of Mans Christian spiritual movement centered in San Francisco, Chicago, and Boston

Holy Spirit 1. spirit that is whole. 2. action or agent of the Supreme Being. 3. light

Holy Word divine name or breath

Logos	Greek
Kalma, Ism-i-Azam	Arabic
Nad, Udgit	Sanskrit
Naam, Gurbani, Bani	Hindi
Rauch	Hebrew

Holyway Navajo healing chant

home world original planet of a spaceship

homeopathy (homeotherapy) science of healing based on the principle of 'like attracting like', utilizing tiny doses of natural elements and extracts. adj. **homeopathic**

homeostasis 'the wisdom of the body', equilibrium, self-regulation (Walter Cannon)

Homer Greek poet; *Iliad* and *Odyssey*; ca. -8th c.

homeward journey voyage back to the divine center, Godhead

hominidae family name for all species of the primate order of which only human beings survive (Latin)

hominisation process of evolutionary similarity (Teilhard)

Homo genus of hominoids; family of humans and humanlike ancestors and descendents

Homo habilis	5,000,000 to 1,600,000
Homo erectus	1,600,000 to 75,000
Neanderthal Man	500,000 to 40,000
Cro-Magnon Man	40,000 to 1950
Supermarket Man	1950-

Homo erectus (Sinanthropus, Peking Man) skull from Choukoutien, near Peking, ca. 360,000 B.P. associated with hand axes and a broad diffusion of learned skills and industries; from 1.6 million to 75,000 B.P.

Homo habilis earliest known hominoid and toolmaker whose skull remains were found by L.S.B. Leakey in Tanzania dating from about 5 million to 1,600,000 B.P.

Homo sapiens neanderthalensis (Neanderthal Man) archaic human beings who lived in Europe, toward the close of the great Ice Ages, and who buried their dead and made shrines to slain animals; ca. 500,000 to 40,000 B.P.

Homo sapiens sapiens (Cro-Magnon Man) modern human beings from ca. 40,000 B.P.

Homshuk hero of the Vera Cruz maize legend

homunculus small artificial being of alchemical imagination (Latin)

Honen Shonin Japanese founder of Jodo Buddhism; 1132-1212

honors Sun, midheaven, and their aspects signifying the fame and honor of the native in astrology

Hooghly 1. most westerly channel of the Ganges river in its delta. 2. Indian town

Hook, Captain plumed adversary of Peter Pan

hoopoe 1. bird that carried the letter from Solomon to the Queen of Sheba. 2. leader of Attar's *The Conference of The Birds*. 3. monogamous bird that cares for its parents, sacred to Islam

Hoova planet outside the galaxy that has observed Earth for 20,000 years (Geller)

Hop Karlsefni's first Viking settlement in Vineland

hope certain expectation of future glory, the blessed fruit of grace divine and the good a person has done (Dante)

Hopei coastal province in northern China

Hopi (Hopituh) 'the peaceful ones', 5,500 people living on three mesas in the Southwest and speaking Shoshone whose ancestors arrived in the West via rafts after their Third World was destroyed by floods

Hopi Prophecy ancient teaching of Massau'u, the Great Spirit, restated by the Hopi in 1948, that the white brother would turn from the spiritual path and imperil the continent by upsetting the natural order by talking through cobwebs (telephones), hearing over mountains (radio, TV), building roads in the sky (space flights), and fashioning a gourd of ashes (nuclear weapons) until the Hopi way was reestablished

Hopi Worlds four ages in which humanity was created and was or will be destroyed

First World...............................Tokpela
Second World............................ Tokpa
Third World......................... Kuskurza
Fourth World.................... Tuwaquchi

Hopkinsville site in Kentucky of a cache of Hebrew coins found in 1967 dating to 2nd c.

Horai-san jade island utopia (Japanese)

horary astrology casting the chart for a specific time, usually the present moment

Horbiger, Hans Austrian-born developer of the eternal ice theory; *The Glacial Cosmology of Horbiger*; 1860-1931

horizon 1. *visible*: point 90 degrees below the zenith, varying with the height we are above the surface of the Earth. 2. *sensible*: extension of the visible to the celestial equator. 3. *rational*: sensible taken from the center of the Earth and not from the surface. 4. *Celestial*: combination of the sensible and rational taken at infinity. 5. *cultural*: spiritual boundary (Joseph Campbell)

Horizontal astrological house system based on division of the horizon from the east point by vertical circles

hormone organic cell product transported from one part of the organism to another, which produces specific effects within the cells in another part of the organism

Horn, Paul jazz musician and New Age composer who has recorded in the Great Pyramid, Taj Mahal, and other sacred sites; *Traveler*; 1930-

Horned God consort of the Goddess, the lord of animals and forests, associated with hunting and the forces of death

horoscope picture of the heavens at the moment of birth, or progressed to any future time

Horra Israeli circle dance (Hebrew)

Hosanna 'Save, we pray,' chant hailing Jesus on his entry into Jerusalem

hossen 'dharma battle', dynamic interchange between master and disciple that takes place throughout training (Japanese)

hostel lodge for travelers, especially those on foot or bicycle

hot medium hard, masculine, nonparticipatory or figure/ground-like medium such as print (McLuhan)

Hotei Japanese God of Luck

Hotema, Hilton (George Clements) natural philosopher; *Man's Higher Consciousness*; 1876-1970

Hotevilla third Hopi mesa

Hotinonsonni (Haudenosaunee) People of the Longhouse, the Iroquois

hotline telephone switchboard that dispenses information on health, environment, peace, community resources

Hottentot Khoisan language of South West Africa

Hotu Matua first king of Easter Island who led a migration from Polynesia; ca. 12th c.

houri 'white one', clear-eyed maiden of Paradise (Arabic)

house one of twelve divisions of a horoscope

house of hospitality urban shelter organized by the Catholic Workers

household toxic n. hazardous substance in the home such as furniture polish, toilet cleaners, paints, thinners, batteries, etc. that can pollute the environment if not properly disposed of

Houston, Jean director of the Foundation for Mind Research; *Mind Games*

Houyhnhnms race of supremely intelligent horses visited by Gulliver

Howard, Albert British organic researcher; *Agricultural Testament*; 1873-1947

Howdy Doody companionable TV puppet, 1950s

Howl poem by Allen Ginsberg read at the Six Gallery in San Francisco in March, 1955, that began the Beat movement

Hoxsey, Harry alternative cancer therapist; d. 1974

hozhoni Navajo chant or word expressing the relation between Heaven and Earth; the spirit of Earth and humanity

H.P.B. Helena Petrovna Blavatsky

hri mantric syllable denoting the supreme virtue of modesty (Sanskrit)

hrim great seed syllable devoted to the Lady of the Earth (Sanskrit)

hrossa poets, musicians, and fishermen in C. S. Lewis's space trilogy

Hsi T'zu Great Treatise, or Appended Judgments in the *I Ching* (Chinese)

Hsi Yu Ki 'Journey to the West' (*Monkey*) Chinese epic by Wu Cheng-en about Hsuan Tsang's pilgrimage to India for Buddhist scriptures, 16th c

Hsia prehistoric culture in China

hsiang image in an *I Ching* interpretation

(Chinese)

hsiao 1. line in an *I Ching* hexagram. 2. Confucian tenet of filial piety. 3. straight flute (Chinese)

hsing-i (i ch'uan) martial art based on solid footholds, styles characteristic of animals, and lightning-like energy, 17th c. (Chinese)

hsiu 28 asterisms, or mansions, of astronomy (Chinese)

Hsuan Tsang Chinese Buddhist pilgrim who traversed Central Asia to India for scriptures, developer of the Wei Shih, or Mere Ideation, School; *Travels*; 596-664

Hsuan-tsung (Ming Huang) Chinese emperor of the T'ang Dynasty who presided over one of the most brilliant courts in Chinese history; 713-56

hsueh 'bubbling spring', acupoint on the sole of the foot (Chinese)

hu 1. Sphinx (Egyptian). 2. last syllable of *allahu*, signifying the inmost consciousness of God; Sufi chant (Arabic). 3. jade tiger (Chinese)

hu hsien shape-shifting foxes who attain satori by tricking humans or studying the classics (Chinese)

Hua-shan 'Sacred Flower', sacred mountain in Shensi Province, China

Hua Yen Garland School of Buddhism based on the *Avatamsaka Sutra*, teaching that all beings possess the Buddha Nature; 6th c. (Chinese)

huaca Incan sacred shrine

Hualapais 'pine tree people', Yuman people in the Southwest

huang chung 'yellow bell' the foundation tone of Chinese music; the purest and most perfect audible manifestation of Cosmic Sound

Huang, Chungliang Al Chinese-born tai chi teacher; *Embrace Tiger, Return to Mountain*

Huang Kung-wang (Big Taoist Fool) Chinese artist and hermit; 1269-1354

Huang Po (Obaku, *Japanese*) Chinese Ch'an master, founder of the Obaku sect; *Doctrine of Universal Mind*; d. 850

Hubbard, Barbara Marx New Age author and teacher; *Hunger of Eve*; 1930-

Hubbard, L. Ron philosopher and writer, founder of the Scientology religion; *Dienetics: The Modern Science of Mental Health*; 1911-86

Hue Vietnamese holy city

Huei-wen-t'u revolving chart of Lady Su

Huei composed of 850 characters woven in five colors on a piece of silk; love poem that can be read from different ends in different directions; ca. 3-5th c. (Chinese)

Huemac Toltec astrologer-priest who guided his people to Tula

Hufeland, Christophe von German philosopher and physician; *Macrobiotics or the Art of Prolonging Life*; 1762-1836

Hughan, Jessie Wallace founder of the War Resisters League; 1876-1955

Huginn and Muninn Odin's ravens

Hui-k'o Chinese student who severed his arm to become Bodhidharma's pupil; second Ch'an Patriarch; 487-593

Hui-neng Chinese Ch'an master who attained satori chopping bamboo and was named the Sixth Patriarch while working in the monastery kitchen as a lowly assistant; *The Platform Sutra*; 638-713

Hui-Shen Buddhist monk reported to have sailed to the New World about A.D. 470

Hui-yuan Chinese Buddhist monk, first Patriarch of the Pure Land School; 334-416

Huichol Indians of the Mexican Sierras known for their shamanist deer dance

hukam 1. order, will of God. 2. random passages from the *Siri Guru Granth Sahib* selected to obtain guidance (Punjabi)

hula spiritual dances (Hawaiian)

Hulk existential Comic book creation of Stan Lee

hull the dry outer covering of a grain, seed, or fruit. adj. **hulled** with the outer hull taken off. **unhulled** with the hull still on

hum mantric seed syllable called warrior (Sanskrit)

huma fabulous bird which alights for a moment upon the head of someone destined to become a king (Persian)

human beings 1. featherless bipeds (Aristotle). 2. offspring of the Sun and Moon (Emerson). 3. rocks dancing (John Seed). 4. muscled water (Emilie Conrad-Da'oud)

Human Right's Day December 10

human-scale adj. medium-small scale, harmonious, natural

Humanitas International nonviolent social activism foundation founded by Joan Baez, 1979-

humiliation 1. straying from right conduct or not taking opportunity of the circumstances in the *I Ching*. 2. recognizing the self as small, ignorant, dishonest, greedy, and miserable (George Ohsawa)

humitas corn tamales of Equador and Chile (Spanish)

humito sacred mushroom (don Juan)

hummus (hoomis, humus) a combination of chickpeas and tahini pureed into a smooth thick mixture and used as a dip or sandwich filling, Middle Eastern style

humors qualities or primal nutritive forces that circulate in the body and whose balance produces health or sickness

Greek Humors
Choler	fire, summer, liver
Melancholy	earth, autumn, lungs
Phlegm	water, winter, head
Sanguine	air, spring, heart

Indian Humors
Kapha	Mucus
Vata	Wind
Pitta	Fire

Humpbacked Flute Player Navajo locust kachina who carries seeds of plants and flowers

Humphreys, Christmas English jurist, Buddhist author; *The Way of Action*; 1901-83

humus decomposed organic matter

huna magic and healing practiced by kahunas (Hawaiian)

Hunab Ku 'he who gives measurements', the Mayan name for God

Hunapu heavenly twin heros of the *Popul Vuh*

Hundredth Monkey 1. story told by Lyall Watson in a 1979 book *Lifetide* and popularized by Ken Keyes about monkeys on a Japanese island who washed potatoes and when they reached a critical mass suddenly all the monkeys knew how to wash potatoes, even on other islands hundreds of miles away. 2. metaphor for telepathic group mind

Hunger Project grass roots organization of several million people committed to the end of hunger, 1977-

hungry ghost 1. wandering soul in the spirit world in Buddhism. 2. someone attached to the image of God (Joseph Campbell)

Hunza 1. high valley in the Pakistani Himalayas. 2. people there renowned for longevity due to a natural diet of

unleavened wheat bread, goat's milk, vegetables, and apricots

Husan Hua Chinese-born meditation master, founder of the Golden Mountain Monastery in San Francisco; 1908-

husk outer sheath of the seed, grain, or fruit

Hutchinson Family Singers (Tribe of Jesse) eleven sons and two daughters of Jesse and Mary Hutchinson of Milford, N.H., who were the principal folk singers of the antislavery, temperance, natural healing era; 19th c.

Huxley, Aldous utopian novelist and mystic; *Brave New World*; 1894-1963

Hwang Ho Yellow River (Chinese)

hwarang-do Korean philosophical and martial code (Korean)

Hyades 1. group of Greek nymphs, sisters of the Pleiades. 2. part of the constellation Taurus

Hyakujo Japanese Zen student who became enlightened when Master Baso tweaked his nose during a discussion about flying geese; developer of the first formal rules of Zen training, and formulator of the maxim 'A day without work is a day without food'; 726-814

hydrology science of water in all its states

hydroponics 'floating garden', growing things without soil

hyebea order, destiny, karma (Yoruba)

Hygeia 1. Greek Goddess of Health. 2. model town of health and longevity in Sir Benjamin Ward Richardson's utopian novel of this name, 1876

Hyksos unknown Asian invaders of Egypt, ca. -17th c.

hyle matter (Greek)

hylopsychic adj. relating to exteriorizations of psychic processes in which there is a significant material component (Dennis Stillings)

Hymettus Greek mountain renowned for its honey

Hymn of the Pearl a section of the *Acts of Thomas* relating the journey of a prince to Egypt to get a precious pearl and return to India to don the robe of gnosis

Hynek, J. Allen astrophysicist and pioneer UFO investigator; 1910-86

hyper-real not like a dream or hallucination and usually having a profound transformative effect

Hyperboreans 1. fabulous people in

Greek literature who lived far to the north. 2. second root race (Theosophy). 3. second age in Max Heindel's teaching in which humans began the process of clothing the Spirit in a body

hyperdimensional adj. outside of three-dimensional time

hyperspace 1. fourth dimension conceived of in science fiction as being one physical dimension beyond the ordinary three-dimensional universe; medium through which teleportation occurs. 2. boundary region of the physical universe. 3. (cyberspace) electronic place where people are brought together in computer conferencing

hypertext knowledge web of quotes, information, perspectives, and resources on a computer network

hypnogogic adj. occurring between full wakefulness and sleep

hypnology science of sleep investigation

hypnopaedia learning or memorizing during sleep

hypnopompic adj. occurring between deep sleep and wakefulness

hypnosis state of physical and mental relaxation, utilizing a subject's receptive mode of consciousness for heightened suggestibility to acceptable information. adj. **hynotic**

hypnotherapy hypnosis applied to psychological problems

Hypodorian adj. *ti*-musical mode associated with enthusiasm, ruled by the Sun (from Greek)

hypogeum an egg-shaped underground tomb associated with the Goddess as a symbol of regeneration

Hypolydian adj. *sol*-musical mode associated with the erotic, ruled by Venus (from Greek)

Hypophrygian adj. *la*-musical mode associated with activity, ruled by Mercury (from Greek)

Ii

I Am 1. occult movement centered around the Compte de St. Germain in Mt. Shasta, Calif., 1930s. 2. that which we strive to be able to say and to be permanently within (Bennett)

I Ching (Yi Jing) 'Book of Change', Chinese oracle and philosophical text based on a deep understanding of yin and yang; consisting of sixty-four hexagrams, symbolizing archetypal energies or situations, produced by mirroring the present moment or coming destiny by the configuration of fifty yarrow stalks, three coins, or computerized software; attributed to Fu Hsi who observed the eight basic trigrams on the back of a dragon-horse, ca. -2900; collected by the Duke of Chou, ca. -1500; principal commentary by Confucius (Chinese)

Eight Trigrams

Ch'ien	The Creative	Heaven
K'un	The Receptive	Earth
Chen	The Arousing	Thunder
K'an	The Abysmal	Water
Ken	Keeping Still	Mountain
Sun	The Gentle	Wind/Wood
Li	The Clinging	Fire
Tui	The Joyous	Lake

Sixty-Four Hexagrams

1. Ch'ien.........................The Creative
2. K'un..........................The Receptive
3. Chun.....Difficulty at the Beginning
4. Meng......................Youthful Folly
5. Hsu.............Waiting (Nourishment)
6. Sung....................................Conflict
7. Shih..............................The Army
8. Pi...........Holding Together (Union)
9. Hsiao Ch'u...The Taming Power of the Small...
10. Lu.....................Treading (Conduct)
11. T'ai...................................Peace
12. P'i................Standstill (Stagnation)
13. T'ung Jen...Fellowship with People
14. Ta Yu.Possession in Great Measure
15. Ch'ien...............................Modesty
16. Yu....................................Enthusiasm
17. Sui.....................................Following
18. Ku...........Work on What Has Been Spoiled (Decay)...............................
19. Lin....................................Approach
20. Kuan............Contemplation (View)
21. Shih Ho....................Biting Through
22. Pi.......................................Grace
23. Po............................Splitting Apart
24. Fu.........Return (The Turning Point)
25. Wu Wang.........Innocence (The Unexpected)...
26. Ta Ch'u............The Taming Power of the Great......................................
27. I.............The Corners of the Mouth
28. Ta Kuo...........Preponderance of the Great..
29. K'an............. The Abysmal (Water)

30. Li........................The Clinging, Fire
31. Hsien................Influence (Wooing)
32. Heng..................................Duration
33. Tun.......................................Retreat
34. Ta Chuang..The Power of the Great
35. Chin.....................................Progress
36. Ming I........Darkening of the Light
37. Chia Jen......The Family (The Clan)
38. K'uei.............................Opposition
39. Chien............................Obstruction
40. Hsieh.............................Deliverance
41. Sun.....................................Decrease
42. I...Increase
43. Kuai..Break-through (Resoluteness)
44. Kou........................Coming to Meet
45. Ts'ui.GatheringTogether (Massing)
46. Sheng....................Pushing Upward
47. K'un.........Oppression (Exhaustion)
48. Ching................................The Well
49. Ko..................Revolution (Molting)
50. Ting............................The Caldron
51. Chen.............The Arousing (Shock,
    Thunder)..
52. Ken............Keeping Still, Mountain
53. Chien.......... Development (Gradual
    Progress)..
54. Fuei Mei.......The Marrying Maiden
55. Feng..............Abundance (Fullness)
56. Lu................................The Wanderer
57. Sun....The Gentle (The Penetrating,
    Wind)...
58. Tui........................The Joyous, Lake
59. Huan.........Dispersion (Dissolution)
60. Chieh..................................Limitation
61. Chung Fu........................Inner Truth
62. Hsiao Kuo......Preponderance of the
    Small..
63. Chi Chi................After Completion
64. Wei Chi.............Before Completion

Ialtabaoth craftsman of the world; First Aeon in Gnosticism

Iamblichos neoplatonist philosopher; *de mysteriis Aegyptiorum*; 250-325

Iasos New Age musician; *Crystal Love*

IAT Immuno-Augmentative Therapy, alternative cancer therapy developed by Lawrence Burton

iatrogenesis sickness fostered by doctors or medical treatment

Ibez South American temple, first outpost of the Shambhala fraternity (Bailey)

ibis Egyptian bird sacred to Thoth

Ibis the Invincible comic book magician from ancient Egypt, 1940s

Ibn Arabi, Muhammad Moorish Sufi whose work influenced Dante's *Divine Comedy*; 1165-1240

Ibn Battuta, Muhammad ibn 'Abdul-lah Berber geographer who traveled to China and India; 1304-77

Ibn Rushd (Averroes) Islamic philosopher and Aristotelian from Cordova; *Destructio destructionis*; 1126-98

Ibn Sina (Avicenna) Islamic philosopher and mystic from Persia; 980-1037

Ibo people and language of east-central Nigeria

Ibrahim b. Adham king of Balkh who renounced his throne for the ascetic life, early Sufi; d. 783

Icaria utopian republic of Etienne Cabet's *Voyage to Icaria*, noted for socialist production, street cars, and committees of experts to run things, 1839

Ichazo, Oscar Bolivian-born spiritual teacher, founder of Arica; 1931-

Ichthus 'fish', Christian symbol; acrostic *Iesous Christos, Theous Usios Soter* (Jesus Christ, Son of God, Saviour) (Greek)

id primitive impulses, unconscious forces of the psyche (Freud)

ida subtle nerve on the left side of the shushumna channel; lunar nadi (Sanskrit)

ideogram picture symbol that brings diverse elements into radical juxtaposition

ideomotor movement slight, unconscious muscle movement, facial expression, change in breathing

ideoplasm ectoplasm that can be moulded into any desirable shape

idli flattened bread made from lentils and rice (Hindi)

Idun Norse Goddess of Eternal Youth

Ifa 1. superhuman being and culture bearer of the Yoruba. 2. oracular system using sixteen palm nuts with 256 combinations of single or double strokes in two columns, or knotted cords with eight concave and convex nuts

Ife (Ile-Ife) 'wide', 1. sacred city of the Yoruba in West Africa. 2. celebrated art-style utilizing the bronze lost-wax process

Ignatz Mouse brick-heaving rodent in *Krazy Kat*

Ignatz von Peczely Hungarian doctor who discovered iridology at age ten while playing with a pet owl which broke its leg; 19th c.

ignoramus someone who humbly admits that he or she does not know anything but who believes it is possible to know (George Ohsawa)

ignorance that which obstructs the effortless manifestation of Buddha Nature and which projects into fear and needless craving (Gary Snyder)

ikebana flower arrangement (Japanese)

Ikhnaton 'it pleases Aton', Egyptian pharoah and monotheist; -14th c.

Illich, Ivan Austrian-born scholar, priest, and cultural reformer; *Medical Nemesis*; 1926-

illness condition arising from lack of understanding of the Order of the Universe (George Ohsawa)

illuminator a display base for crystals consisting of a hardwood base with a light bulb

Ilmarinen divine smith of the *Kalevala*

Iltar colonizer from Atlantis, founder of the Mayas (Cayce)

image 1. pattern revealed by a hexagram in the *I Ching*. 2. awareness from the psyche that comes in various forms, such as words, a knowing, or a vision

imaginal (adj.) relating to the world of the imagination that is perfectly real and more coherent than the empirical world (Henry Corbin, 1972)

imagination a little pocket transistor-TV manufactured millions of years ago (George Ohsawa)

Imhotep Egyptian sage and architect who designed the first pyramid; ca. -2780

Immortal 1. deathless sage. 2. one of eight enlightened men and women who guide humanity in Chinese folk tradition

Immovable Spot 1. place where Buddha sat under the Bo tree. 2. a state of mind of one released from phenomenal attachments

impeccability doing one's best in whatever one's engaged in (don Juan)

Imperator leader of the Ancient and Mystical Order Rosae Crucis

implicate order 1. infolded order that is not perceptible but deducible from quantum physics as opposed to the explicate or unfolded order of what we ordinarily see. 2. theory that each flowing 'part' carries within it an implicit image of the continuously changing and unfolding whole (David Bohm)

Impressionism modern art movement emphasizing light hues and fleeting impressions developed from Japanese prints by Monet, Pisarro, Renoir, Cezanne, Seurat

Imum Coeli undersky, meridian point opposite the Medium Coeli (Latin)

in breath breathing in movement

Inayat Moslem Indian painter; *A Group of Ascetics*; 17th c.

Incala priests of Atlantis (Phylos)

incense substance with a fragrant aroma

inconjunct forming no astrological aspect to another heavenly body

Incredible String Band Scottish vocal and instrumental group (Mike Heron, Robin Williamson, Malcolm LeMaistre); *The 5,000 Spirits or the Layers of the Onion*; 1960s

incubation healing art practiced in the sleep temple of Imhotep in Egypt

indicator species a species which indicates the health of the forest such as the northern spotted owl in the Pacific Northwest

individuation process of becoming a psychologically whole person (Jung)

Indo-European world's largest language family including Latin, Greek, Sanskrit, Germanic (including English), Celtic, Slavic, Baltic, Iranian, and Indic languages; ca. -3000 (Thomas Young, 1813)

Indra chief god of the Vedas

induct heating coil part of the solar energy unit that transfers energy from storage tank to the unit to be heated

inductopyrexia fever experienced by a UFO contactee

INFACT Boston-based grass-roots organization that led the boycott against Nestle and on behalf of corporate responsibility

inferior man weak or base person, lower self in the *I Ching*

inferior planet orb between the Sun and Earth

Inferno vast volcanic-shaped pit into which Dante descended while guided by Virgil in the *Divine Comedy*; represented as a contracting spiral with nine circles representing delusional and disorderly states of consciousness terminating in the Ice Hell, where the frozen, fixed, and rigid dwell

inflation ego identification with the persona, archetype, or a religious or historical figure (Jung)

inflexion consciousness coiling inward on itself (Teilhard)

influenced writing inspired psychic communication

infortune problem-bearing planet

infradian adj. relating to rhythmic patterns that repeat in periods of more than 28 hours (Franz Halberg)

inipi 'spirit place', purification lodge (Lakota)

initiation clear shining forth of the inner fire, transition from one point of polarization to another, growing capacity to see and hear on all planes, expansion of consciousness that admits the personality into wisdom attained by the Ego; brief period of enlightenment wherein the initiate sees that portion of the path that lies ahead and shares consciously in the evolutionary plan (Bailey)

initiator a TM instructor

inka seal of approval from the Zen master (Japanese)

inner band team of spirits which helps an individual during his or her incarnation on earth

inner-directed adj. oriented toward the world of inner experience and consciousness as opposed to outer-directed and focused on the external world

inner-heat yoga (tummo, *Tibetan*) yoga through which psychic energy is developed and controlled creating a source of inner warmth and resistance to extreme cold

inner phasing reaching into the subconscious to bring to consciousness and remove the dysfunctional patterns learned early in life

inner space consciousness, the mind

innercise dialoguing with quiet, dormant and hesitant periods that play roles essential to long term health and creativity, including movements, stretches, swings, rocks, and balancing poses (Julie Parker)

innergy 'inner energy', the energy within the tiniest particle (Patrick Flanagan, 1975)

innovator fluctuation that may multiply and cause a whole system to adopt a new mode of functioning (Prigogine and Stenger)

Innuit 'The People', Eskimo name for themselves

instinct capacity to deal with surrounding stimuli; automatically wanting to make balance, through primarily the small brain and the autonomic nervous system (Michio Kushi)

Institute for the Harmonious Development of Man Gurdjieff's school in Fontainebleau, France, 1920s

Institute for the Study of Nonviolence peace center founded by Joan Baez and Ira Sandperl in Carmel Valley, Calif., 1965-

Institute in Culture and Creation Spirituality religious organization founded by Matthew Fox in Oakland, Calif.

Institute of Mentalphysics spiritual center founded by Edwin J. Dingle with headquarters in Yucca Valley, Calif., 1927-

Institute of Noetic Sciences consciousness research center in Palo Alto, Calif.

intaglio prehistoric drawing by unknown people on the desert floor of the Southwest, ca. -10,000

integral dynamic interrelation of spiritual, cognitive, volitional, emotional, and physical elements

Integral Yoga system of yoga developed by Sri Aurobindo that stresses bringing supramental power of divine consciousness down into the ignorance of mind, life, and body to transform and create a divine life in matter

Integral Yoga Institute yoga movement founded by Swami Satchidananda, 1966-

integration yogic transmutation of the many personalities that constitute an individual (Aurobindo)

intellectual judgment understanding of yin and yang; creative, inventive ability; the fourth level of consciousness (George Ohsawa and Michio Kushi)

Intellectual Trinity Aries, Taurus, Gemini

Intensive Journal structured psychological diary for personal growth (Progoff)

intentional community utopian or planned settlement organized around a shared vision

interaction mutual interplay among subatomic particles; of four strengths: strong, electromagnetic, weak, and gravitational

interconnectedness recognition that all of life is inextricably linked with one another and the environment

International Voluntary Services private peace corps in the Third World, headquartered in Washington

interface 1. overlap between two or more activities, interests, or fields of study. 2. (cap.) holistic educational center, Watertown, Mass.

intergalactic adj. between or among galaxies

intermediate technology appropriate technology between the primitive and modern (Schumacher)

internal dialogue 1. inner chatter. 1. ego's commentary on what's happening. 2. that which when stopped is the key to everything (don Juan)

Internal System category of martial arts emphasizing inner qualities such as will, vital energy, strength

International Buddhist Meditation Center educational organization led by Thich Thien-An in Los Angeles, 1970-

International Community of Christ community founded by Gene Savoy in Peru, 1957-

International House of Justice headquarters of the Baha'i Faith in Haifa, Israel

International Society for Krishna Consciousness Hare Krishna community

interreligious adj. relating to two or more religions

intihuatana 'hitching post of the sun,' sculpted mass of granite at Incan sites with possible astronomical significance

intragalactic adj. within a single galaxy

intrapsychic adj. gnostic, presence of God within and out

intrinsic factor (binding factor) substance found in Vitamin B-12, lack of which causes pernicious anemia

introjection personal thoughts and feelings (Karl Pribram)

invariance patterns that remain the same in different contexts

inversion of time appearance of one who has just died to someone closely related

Invisible College 1. building with wings which existed nowhere and yet united the Rosicrucians. 2. informal group of 100 scientists investigating UFOs

invoke v. to open the door to awareness with the mind (Bodhidharma)

involution inward movement of consciousness or energy into more dense or physical form as opposed to evolution, the outward movement toward higher consciousness

Inyanga African site of Azanian culture, stone dams, conduits, and hilltop forts

Iona (Argyllshire) Scottish island, site of ancient Celtic Christianity

IPM integrated pest management; transitional farming practice of introducing selected natural predators into fields to cut down on pesticide use

Ippen itinerant Japanese Buddhist sage; 1239-89

intuition 1. undoubting conception of a pure and attentive mind which comes from the light of reason alone (Descartes). 2. harmonizing the self with totality, the infinite universe; perceiving far away or future things; seeing if someone can be healed or seeing his or her destiny; the judgment of the infinite working through us, received primarily by the mid-brain and the body as a whole (Michio Kushi)

invisible adj. to live like the new moon, hardly noticed; to resemble clear water running over a stream bed (Robert Bly)

Iqbal, Muhammad Indian Moslem poet and visionary; *Javia-Nama*; 1873-1938

irada desire to seek the path and discipline of the way (Arabic)

Irene (Eirene) personification of peace (Greek)

irenics feminist style of writing or non-confrontational rhetoric (Moira Ferguson, 1986)

irfan gnosis, especially in Shi'ite Islam and among Persian dervishes (Arabic)

iridiagnostician a practitioner of iridology

iridology science of detecting and diagnosing disease through examination of the irises of the eyes developed by Ignatz Peczely in 1880

iriko small dried fish (Japanese)

Irish moss a seaweed found in the Atlantic and valued for its natural gelatinous properties

iron man immovable, imperturbable, and indestructible Buddha Nature within one; aspect of the dharmakaya

Isa Jesus (Arabic)

Isaac the Blind Jewish Kabbalist from Provence; 12th c.

Isaak, Rabbi Zashkenazi teacher of the Kabbalah; 1534-72

Ise shrine in southeast Japan sacred to Amaterasu

Isherwood, Christopher Vedantist author, gay activist; *A Meeting by the River*; 1904-

Ishi last of the Yana Indians of northern California; ca. 1861-1916

Ishizuka, Sagen (Dr. Daikon) Japanese medical doctor and grandfather of macrobiotics; *A Chemical Nutritional Theory of Long Life*; 1850-1910

Ishmael 1. son of Abraham and Hagar, progenitor of the Arabs. 2. narrator of

Moby Dick

ishraq illumination (Arabic)

ishtam spiritual ideal of the aspirant (Sanskrit)

ishvarakoti person spiritually illumined from birth, companion of an avatar (Sanskrit)

Isipatana site near Benares where Buddha preached the Fire Sermon; present-day Sarnath

Isis 1. Egyptian Goddess of the Nile, sister-wife of Osiris, mother of Horus. 2. transneptunian planet ruling aspiration, situated at the galactic center in 26.5 degrees Sagittarius

ISKON International Society for Krishna Consciousness

Islam 'submission to the will of God', way of life of the followers of Muhammad (Arabic)

Island Lake body of water near Silvertown, Colo., where the first man and woman and the Navajo people emerged from a world below

Islandia utopian novel by A. T. Wright about people of Karain, a subcontinent in the southern hemisphere, 1942

Isle of the Blest 1. St. Brenden's Island. 2. celestial paradise of Taoism

Isohara Scrolls Japanese documents relating to pre-Columbian contacts between East and West, the ancient one world language, and Jesus's possible visit to Japan

Isolt (Isolde, Yseut, Essylt) heroine of the Pictish romance *Tristan and Isolt*

isolation tank sensory deprivation device

Isra' Muhammad's night journey to Jerusalem during which he met Abraham, Moses, and Jesus (Arabic)

Israel 'God wrestler', 1. spiritual seeker. 2. Jewish people. 3. ancient northern kingdom, including the ten tribes. 4. modern Middle Eastern state, 1948- (Hebrew)

Israfil Islamic angel who will sound the trumpet on Resurrection Day

Issa Japanese haiku master; 1752-1817

Isvara (Ishvara) Lord, personal god (Sanskrit)

ito soba a very thin type of soba noodle (Japanese)

Ittoen 'Garden of a Single Light,' commune and way of life emphasizing community service founded by Tenko Nishida near Kyoto, 1903- (Japanese)

Itzamna Mayan culture hero who introduced maize, cocoa, writing

Itzpapalotl obsidian butterfly, symbol of the soul (Nahuatl)

IUMMA star around which the planet UMMO revolves

Ivanhoe, Wilfred of knightly hero in the novel *Ivanhoe* by Sir Walter Scott

IWW International Workers of the World, anarchist labor union, early 20th c.

Ix day of obsidian, jaguar; day on which Heaven and Earth embraced (Mayan)

Ixbalanque 'little jaguar', one of the heavenly twin heroes (Mayan)

Ixchel rainbow, consort to Votari (Mayan)

Ixtaccihuatl 'sleeping lady', sacred volcano in Amecameca, Mexico

Iyengar, B. K. S. Indian yoga teacher; 1918-

Izanagi 'Male-Who-Invites', central figure in the Japanese creation myth; with Izanami, the eighth pair of brother and sister gods after Heaven and Earth separated from chaos

Izanami 'Female-Who-Invites', female twin to Izanagi in the Japanese creation myth

Jj

J 1. Judean source in the Hebrew Bible, associated with the Davidic line; who is possibly a woman and who writes about women and the divine aspect of mercy. 2. (psi) subatomic particle

Jabberwock fabulous creature in Carroll's *Through the Looking Glass*

Jabir (Geber) Abbasid Islamic alchemist; *The Book of Venus*; 8th c.

Jachin black pillar in Solomon's temple

Jack hero of the Jack tale cycle of south Appalachia, from 18th c. British, Scot, and Irish immigrants

Jack, Billy Indian folk protest hero in films by Tom Laughlin and Dolores Taylor

Jack, Gale (Barbara Gale Fields) macrobiotic teacher and counselor; *Promenade Home*; 1939-

Jack, Homer A. Unitarian minister and social activist; *The Gandhi Reader*; 1916-

jackfruit pineapple-like Indian fruit

Jackson, Jimmy Lee Alabama civil rights worker; 1938-65

Jackson, Wes environmentalist and pioneer agricultural researcher and director of the Land Institute near Salina, Kansas; *Altars of Unhewn Stone*

Jacob 1. Hebrew patriarch, second son of Isaac, progenitor of the Israelites. 2. (Jacob the Just) second son of Joseph and Mary, brother of Jesus, leader of the Nazoreans

Jacob of Marvege rabbi who settled disputes by submitting the question to heaven before going to sleep; *Responsa from Heaven*; 12th c.

Jacobson, Michael biochemist and founder of the Center for Science in the Public Interest

Jacopone da Todi Italian lawyer, Franciscan mystic; *Spiritual Songs*; 1228-1306

Jade Emperor (Yu Huang) supreme deity of Taoism

Jade Pass (Yu-men, Yu-kuan, Yu-men-kuan, *Chinese*) gateway or divide between China and Turkestan, now in the western part of Tun-huang district, Kansu Province

Jagannatha 'world-lord', 1. epithet of Krishna. 2. temple at Puri in Orissa

Jagerstatter, Franz Austrian Catholic nonviolent resister; *Farewell Letter*; 1907-43

Jaidev (Jayadeva) Bengali poet; *Gita Govinda*; 12th c.

Jain 'conquerer', one on the path to conquering one's inner enemies; follower of Mahavira and Jainism (Sanskrit)

Jainism Indian way of life stressing ahimsa founded by Mahavira, -6th c.

Jaipur pink-rose Indian city renowned for art, jewelry, fabrics, palaces, and observatory in Rajasthan

jakugo word or phrase expressing the inner meaning of a koan (Japanese)

Jalandhar north Indian site of a great Buddhist council at which Buddhism divided into Northern and Southern schools

jam i jam 'Jamshid's mirror', divine mirror of the human heart (Arabic)

Jambhala Indian God of Wealth, depicted holding a mongoose

jambo greeting (Swahili)

James (Jacob the Just) brother of Jesus, leader of the Nazoreans; d. 62

James, William psychologist, philosopher, psychic researcher; *The Varieties of Religious Experience;* 1842-1910

Jammastami Krishna's birthday celebration in August

Jampolsky, Gerald G. holistic doctor; *Goodbye to Guilt and Teach Only Love*

Janaka Indian monarch and father of Sita in the *Ramayana*

Janan divine beloved (Arabic)

jan tao way of human beings, reason (Chinese)

japa repetition of the divine name (Sanskrit)

Japanese language of Japan, unrelated to any other extant language, which adopted Chinese pictographs in the 3rd c. and is written vertically from the right

Jaredite member of the first Lost Tribe of Israel to emigrate to America, ca. -600 (Joseph Smith)

Jarrett, Keith musician and song writer; *Changes*

Jarvis, DeForest Clinton Vermont country doctor; *Folk Medicine*; b. 1881

Jason 1. leader of the Argonauts. 2. planet postulated between Saturn and Uranus ruling inner freedom

Jataka Tales accounts of the Buddha's previous lives in and around Benares as various animals to show that all beings have Buddha Nature

jati birth, origin, rebirth, existence (Sanskrit, Pali)

jayanthi birthday (Sanskrit)

Jaynes, Julian consciousness researcher; *The Origin of Consciousness in the Bicameral Mind*

Jebel Uri ruined stone city in Daffur, Central Africa

Jedi Knights Peacekeepers of the Old Republic in *Star Wars*, strongest and most revered beings in the galaxy

Jeffers, Robinson California poet and voice of rivers, mountains, and hawks; *Tamar and Other Poems*; 1887-1962

Jefferson Airplane rock group (Marty Balin, Jorma Kauokonen, Jack Casady, Spencer Dryden, Paul Kantner, Grace Slick, Joey Covington); *Surrealistic Pillow;* 1960s

Jefferson, Thomas farmer, architect, statesman, inventor, and author who smuggled brown rice out of Italy and introduced it to Virginia and the Carolinas;*Notes on the State of Virginia*; 1743-1826

Jehosaphat a valley outside Jerusalem

popularly believed to serve as the scene of the Last Judgment

jen benevolence, goodness, love; greatest Confucian virtue (Chinese)

jenn mo vessel of conception; meridian along the ventral line of the body (Chinese)

Jeremiah pre-exilic Hebrew prophet; ca. -650

Jerusalem 'peace and wholeness,' 1. heavenly city whose earthly type is located in Israel. 2. site where the waters of the Flood arose from beneath its central rock and afterwards subsided. 3. scene of Abraham's sacrifice, the crucifixion of Jesus, and Mohammed's ascent to heaven. 4. utopian Christian community in New York based on Jeremiah Wilkinson's teachings, 1788-1821

Jesus (Jeshua, Yeshua, Joshua) 'salvation of Yahweh', Prince of Peace, Son of Man, Jewish ethical teacher; ca. -4-30

Jesus Christ Superstar rock opera by Andrew Webber and Tim Rice

Jesus Movement contemporary wave of Evangelists, Conservatives, Liberals, Neo-Pentacostalists, and Fundamentalists who live communally, preach the Gospel on street corners, and practice asceticism, 1969-

Jharna-Kala 'Fountain Art', Sri Chinmoy's paintings (Bengali)

ji 1. word ending referring to a temple (Japanese). 2. word ending denoting familiarity, affection; diminutive of a name, e.g., Gandhiji (Sanskrit). 3. (u.c.) Amidaist school of Japanese Buddhism, led by Ippen, 1275-

Jibril (Jabrail, Gabriel) angel who revealed the *Qur'an* to Muhammad

jihad inner warfare, mystical striving (Arabic)

jikkenchi 'testing station', commune, new community (Japanese)

Jikonsaseh (Mother of Nations or the Peace Queen) Seneca spiritual leader

Jim wise companion and adviser to Huck Finn

jimsonweed (datura) hallucinogenic plant of the Southwest

jin mei order of human beings; hereditary destiny; human constitutional factors (Japanese)

Jin Shin Jyutsu 'Art of Circulation Awakening', acupressure treatment founded by Jiro Murai, 20th c. (Japanese)

jina 'conqueror', title given to the five

chief manifestations of Buddha-wisdom and prophets of Jainism (Sanskrit)

jinenjo a light brown wild mountain potato or yam that grows to be several feet long and two to three inches wide (Japanese)

jinenjo soba noodles made from jinenjo and buckwheat (Japanese)

jinn spirits (Arabic)

jiriki 'self-power', salvation by self-discipline (Japanese)

Jittoku legendary Zen poet, subject of many Japanese paintings, respected as an incarnation of Manjusri

jiva 1. empirical self in Buddhism. 2. individual soul behind personality or ego in Hinduism (Sanskrit)

jivanmukta one liberated in this life. adj. **jivanmukti** (Sanskrit)

Jizo (Kshitigarbha, *Sanskrit*) Bodhisattva who will save all beings from the time of Sakyamuni's death until the coming of Maitreya (Japanese)

JMH (Justin Moreward Haig) spiritual teacher of the Brotherhood of Adepts of East and West working with artists and musicians as described in the *Initiate* books of Cyril Scott

jnana knowledge, wisdom of reality (Sanskrit)

Jnana Yoga path of wisdom arrived at through discrimination and discipline of the mind (Sanskrit)

Jnaneshvar Indian mystical poet; *Inoneshvari*; 1271-96

jnani follower of the path of wisdom (Sanskrit)

j.n.d. just noticeable difference; smallest observable difference between two stimuli (Fechner)

Joachim of Fiore Christian mystic who divided history into ages of the Father, Son, and Holy Spirit; 1132-1202

Joan of Arc Maid of Orleans, visionary prophetess, clairvoyant, soldier; 1411-31

Joaquim, Jose (Al Capone) Portuguese safecracker who became macrobiotic in prison and influenced many prisoners in a healthy direction; 1944-

Job 1. calamity-struck householder who learned the lesson of faith; -6th c. 2. book of the Hebrew Bible

Jodo 1. school of Japanese Buddhism founded by Honen emphasizing nembutsu mantra and faith, 1175- . 2. martial art utilizing a cylindrical stick of wood against a sword. 1955- (Japanese)

Jodo Shin 'True Pure Land', Japanese Buddhist sect of Amidaism founded by Shinran, 1224-

John Zuni man with natural instincts in Huxley's *Brave New World*

John, Prester son of Feirefiz and Repanse de Schoye, Christian priest-king in India

John of the Cross, St. poet and contemplative, disciple of St. Teresa in Spain; *Dark Night of the Soul*; 1542-91

John, St. (John, son of Zebedee, St. John the Divine) mystical Christian gospelist; traditional author of the *Book of Revelation*; 1st c.

John XXII, Pope (Angelo Guiseppe Roncalli) peace advocate and founder of Vatican II; *Pacem in Terris*; 1881-1963

Johnny's Selected Seeds organic, natural gardening seed company in Albion, Maine

Johnson, Raynor C. mystic and author; *Imprisoned Splendor*; 1901-

Johnson, Robert A. psychologist and author of one-syllable books: *He, She, We*

Johnson, William H. mystical artist noted for black madonnas; *Jesus and the Three Marys*; 1901-70

Johor emissary from Canopus in Doris Lessing's *Shikasta*

Johrei 'Purification of Spirit,' a method or teaching to heal the spirit through the channeling of light (Japanese)

Jois, Pattabhi Indian yogi and Sanskrit scholar; 1915-

jolt healing instant cure from addiction (Sylvia Cary)

Jomon Japanese culture noted for its superb pottery, ca. -3000

Jonah Biblical hero who was swallowed by a whale

Jonas, Eugen Czech psychiatrist, director of Astra; *Predetermining the Sex of a Child*; 1928-

Jones, Casey (John Luther Grant) bodhisattva locomotive engineer who rode the Cannonball Express to his death to save others; d. 1900

Jones, Rufus Quaker mystic; *The Luminous Trail*; 1863-1948

Jones, Tristan Welsh sailor who has crisscrossed the world alone many times; *The Incredible Voyage*; 1924-

Jones, William (Oriental) English jurist, pioneer Indologist, and founder of the Asiatic Society of Bengal; tr. *Saconta-*

la; 1746-94

Jonsson, Olof psychic who carried out ESP tests from Earth with Edgar Mitchell on the Moon; 1923-

Joplin, Janis hard living blues singer; *Kozmic Blues*; 1943-70

Jord Norse Earth Goddess

Josaphat 'bodhisattva', medieval Christian saint of Asia

Joseph 1. Hebrew patriarch, son of Jacob, noted for dream interpretation. 2. father of Jesus

Joseph, Chief (Hinmaton-Yalaktit) Nez Perce who led his people on a 1000-mile march toward Canada; ca. 1840-1904

Joseph of Arimathea Jerusalem merchant who claimed Jesus's body and figures in the Holy Grail legends

Josetsu Japanese Zen artist; *The Three Doctrines*; 15th c.

Joshu Jushin (Chao-chou Ts'ung-shen, *Chinese*) Chinese Ch'an master who formulated the Mu koan; 778-897 (Japanese)

Joshua Tree National Park in California's Mojave Desert

jouissance total joy that includes the physical, mental, sexual, and spiritual (French)

Journey to the East novel of spiritual pilgrimage by Hesse, 1932

Journey to the West (Hsi Yu Ki, *Chinese;* Monkey) novel of Hsuan Tsang's pilgrimage to India for Buddhist scriptures by Wu Cheng-en; 16th c.

joy 1. a harmony of all the emotions as opposed to a single emotion; quality felt in the heart (Yellow Emperor's Classic) 2. the fruit of great difficulties (George Ohsawa)

jubjub fantastic bird in Carroll's *Through the Looking Glass*

judgment 1. interpretation of events, direction in which the situation is headed in the *I Ching*. 2. level of understanding (George Ohsawa). 3. Tarot #20, transmutation, change

judo no-holds-barred martial art developed by J. Kano in Japan, 1882-

judoka student of judo (Japanese)

Judy Essene leader who tutored Jesus (Cayce)

juju ritual associated with charms and amulets in Africa

juku traditional Oriental way of education in which students and teachers live together in a small, intimate household

(Japanese)

Julia heroine of Orwell's *1984*

Julian of Norwich English mystic; *The Shewings*; 1343-1413

Julian the Apostate Roman Emperor who turned from Christianity and became a pagan mystic; 332-63

Jumbo beloved English zoo and American circus elephant; 1860s-85

Jundishapur southwestern Persian city, principal seat of learning in western Asia of exiled Greeks and Christians at the time of the Arab conquest

Jungk, Robert German-born pacifist; *Brighter Than a Thousand Suns*; 1913-

Jupiter 1. Roman ruler of the gods. 2. planet ruling fortune, philosophy, expansive energy

justice 1. Tarot #11 force. 2. natural law; the absolute joy of life revealed in every phenomenon at every moment (George Ohsawa)

Jyoti, Swami Amar Indian yogi who founded many centers and ashrams in India and the U.S.; 1928-

jyotih illumination, effulgence (Sanskrit)

jyotisa Hindu astrology (Sanskrit)

Kk

K 1. (pl.) five kakkas or symbols worn by initiated Sikhs: kara (steel bracelet), kanga (wooden comb), katcha (underwear), kirpan (steel sword), kesh (uncut hair) (Punjabi). 2. antihero of Kafka's *The Trial*

ka double, astral body (Egyptian)

Kaaw 11th Hebrew letter: hollow, Q, 20

Ka'ba 'cube', sacred shrine in Mecca (Arabic)

Kaba Aye World Peace Pagoda in Rangoon, 1954

Kabbalah (Qabbalah, Cabala) 'Tradition', Jewish mysticism; chain of inner transmission of the secrets of esotericism (Hebrew). n. **Kabbalist**. adj. **Kabbalistic**

Soul Aspect

yehida	archetype
hayah	divine emanation
neshamah	thought, principles
ru'ah	spirit
nefesh	species, animal soul

Ten Emanations (Sephiroth)

Kether	Crown	Top of Head
Hockmah	Wisdom	Right of Brain
Binah	Understanding	Left of Brain
Hesed	Mercy	Right Arm
Pechad	Strength	Left Arm
Teferet	Beauty	Heart
Nezah	Victory	Right of Pelvis
Hod	Glory	Left of Pelvis
Yesod	Foundation	Genitals
Malkhut	Kingdom	Genitals

Worlds

azilut	world of emanations
b'riyah	creative world
y'zirah	world of forms
assiah	world of object

Levels of Interpretation

Psht	literal
Rmz	symbolic
Drsh	intuitive
Sud	spiritual

Kabir Indian weaver and poet; *Kabir-Granthavali*; 1440-1518

kabocha Hokkaido pumpkin (Japanese)

kabod materialization of the divinity in the form of a cloud (Hebrew)

Kachina 1. Zuni and Hopi dolls with moveable arms representing the spirits of plants, birds, animals. 2. dance performed by masked impersonators

kadesh prayer for the soul of the dead (Hebrew)

kado sacred sun dance of the Kiowa

Kaempfer, Engelbert German physician who introduced knowledge of moxibustion to the West; *The History of Japan*; 1651-1716

Kaf (Qaf) 1. Caucasus Mountains. 2. range of mountains that ring the Earth (Arabic, Persian)

kagami Shinto sacred mirror (Japanese)

Kagawa, Toyohiko Japanese reformer and Christian social worker; 1888-1960

kagura Shinto dance (Japanese)

kahuna Hawaiian shaman

Kaianerekowa 'Great Peace', Great Law of the Iroquois Five Nations

Kaibara, Ekken Japanese Confucian educator and health reformer; *Yojokun*; 1630-1716

Kaid planet in Iranian astrology revolving retrograde in a period of 144 years

Kailas Shugendo 'Way of Spiritual Power', esoteric Buddhist sect in San Francisco (Japanese)

Kairos major and minor periods of illumination (Kelman, from Greek)

Kairouan (al-Qayrawan) city and

mosque in Tunisia, fourth major Islamic pilgrimage site

kaivalyam state in Jainism of unconditional isolated perfection in timeless omniscience (Sanskrit)

Kakuzo, Okakura Japanese scholar and translator; *The Book of Tea*; 1861-1913

Kal-El Superman's given name on Krypton

kala 1. time (Sanskrit). 2. (cap.) ape who raised Tarzan

kalachakra 'cycle of time', 1. tantric deity, mystical aspect of the teacher, depicted with 24 arms, embracing a consort. 2. name of this tantra (Sanskrit)

Kalahari African desert home of the Bushman

Kalapa capital of Shambhala

kalavinka legendary Himalayan bird with a wondrous voice that appears before the coming of a Buddha

Kalevala 'Land of Heroes', Finnish epic

Kali 'black', Great Goddess, wife of Shiva in wrathful aspect, signifying destruction of the ego, illusion (Sanskrit)

Kali Yuga (Dark Age, Iron Age) fourth and current age in Hinduism signifying loss of faith, calamity, and disease, which began on Krishna's death at 12:00 a.m., Feb. 17, -3102 and will last 432,000 years

Kalidasa Indian poet and dramatist; *Shakuntala*; 4th or 5th c.

kalimba African finger piano

Kalki (Kalkin) avatar of Vishnu who will come at the end of the Kali Yuga on a white horse with drawn sword

Kaho'olawe sacred Hawaiian island where the gods were brought from Tahihi and which was used by the U.S. Navy for bombing practice

kalpa inconceivably vast period between the creation of a universe and the destruction preceding its recreation; 4,320,000,000 years (Sanskrit)

Kalpalata wishing tree of paradise (Sanskrit)

Kalu Rinpoche Tibetan abbot of a monastery in Sonada, India

Kama 1. the Lord of Desire who flung weapons at the Buddha which were transformed into flower offerings. 2. the Hindu God of Love

kama-loka desire-world, after-life, or a state of mind or consciousness marked by desire or attachment (Sanskrit)

kama-rupa desire body (Sanskrit)

Kama Sutra 'Love Text', sex manual attributed to Vatsyayana, ca. 1st c. (Sanskrit)

Kamakura Japanese era 1185-1333

Kamakura Buddha 15-meter bronze statue of Amida at Kamakura, Japan, 1252

Kamala courtesan in Hesse's *Siddartha*

Kami nature gods of Shintoism (Japanese)

Kammerer, Paul Austrian biologist; *The Law of Series*; 1880-1926

Kamo Chomei Japanese essayist; *Record of a Ten-foot Square Hut*; 1153-1216

Kampfer, Englebert German-born scientist who first described Zen in English; *History of Japan Together with a Description of the Kingdom of Siam*, 1727

Kampo Chinese medicine (Japanese)

k'an water, the abysmal; one of eight trigrams in the *I Ching* (Chinese)

Kana 1. Japanese alphabet devised by Kobodaishi. 2. 'name of God', sound through the human mouth in Kototama (Japanese)

Kanagi-Guruma Ancient Spiritual Eternal Calendar which was the origin of yin and yang and the nine stages of energy transformation (Michio Kushi)

Kancheepuram (Conjeeveram) South Indian holy city, capital of the Pallava Dynasty

Kanchenjunga, Mt. 'Great Snow of the Five Treasures', Sikkim's highest peak and divine protector, 28,146 feet high

kanda root of the nadis; egg-shaped nerve center below the navel (Sanskrit)

Kandel, Lenore Beat poet; *Word Alchemy*; 1932-

Kandinsky, Wassilly Russian-born expressionist; *On the Spiritual in Art*; 1866-1944

Kandy Sri Lankan city, site of the Temple of the Buddha's Tooth

Kang Rinpoche Mount Kailash in western Tibet (Tibetan)

Kanisch, Peter founder of the Pikarti sect holding that God was indwelling in any person who served spirit; 15th c.

Kanishka Indo-Scythian king and patron of Mahayana Buddhism; 1st c.

kanji Chinese characters used by the Japanese (Japanese)

Kanjur (Kah-gyur) scriptures of Lamaism (Tibetan)

Kannon (Kwannon, Kanzeon) Bodhisattva Kuan Yin (Japanese)

kanpyo dried gourd strips; used in sushi

or to tie cabbage rolls and other special vegetable dishes (Japanese)

kanten a jelled fruit dessert made from agar-agar (Japanese)

Kanthaka 'garland', Prince Siddartha's horse who set him on the path to enlightenment and, after dying of grief upon the Future Buddha's departure, became a celestial bodhisattva (Sanskrit)

Kanyakubja (Kannauj) ancient North Indian city, Harsha's capital, 7th c.

Kanzan legendary Zen poet who wrote on trees and rocks, respected as an incarnation of Samantabhadra

Kanzeon (Kannon, Kwannon) Kuan Yin, the bodhisattva who hears the calls of the world and personifies the Great Compassion and Mercy which arise as a result of true training (Japanese)

Kapilavastu Buddha's birthplace near present-day Piprawa, Nepal

Kapleau, Philip spiritual teacher, founder of the Zen Center in Rochester, N.Y.; *Three Pillars of Zen*; 1912-

kappa fabulous creatures that live in pools (Japanese)

kara age deep-fry style of cooking (Japanese)

karamat miracle (Arabic)
mu'jiza (miracle)....... sign of a prophet
karamat (favor)........... wonder working
ma'unat (help) .... ordinary person's wonderful works or by accident.............
istidraj (stealth) .... magic

Karamazovs three brothers in Dostoevski's novel *The Brothers Karamazov*: Alyosha, the mystic; Ivan, the intellectual and atheist; and Dmitri, the soldier

karana reason, cause, potential cosmic energy (Sanskrit)

karana-sharira causal body (Sanskrit)

karate 'Chinese hand art', open hand martial art from Okinawa, 17th c.-

Kardec, Allan (Hyppolyte Leon Denizard Rivail) clairvoyant after whom a large spiritualist church in Brazil is named; 19th c.

kare sansu dry landscape garden with 15 rocks in Ryoanji Zen Temple in Kyoto

kareteka skilled practitioner of karate

Kargyudpa Buddhist sect in Tibet founded by Marpa stressing Oral Transmission, 11th c.- (Tibetan)

Karlsefni, Thorfinn leader of the first settlement in Vinland, 11th c.

karma (karman) 'action', 1. measure of attachment, one's worldly circumstanc-

es, psychological development, and level of consciousness, often distinguished as good or bad karma, though in Indian tradition, all karma is to be transcended; imperfections that are washed or burned by yoga, meditation, service, cultivating the dharma, or other spiritual practice. 2. that which is created so long as one doesn't realize one's original nature (Bodhidharma) 3. consequences of a thought, word, or deed; reaping what is sown. 4. sum of the consequences of one's thoughts, words, or deeds in this and previous lifetimes. 5. chain of moral cause and effect. 6. force generated by consciousness or actions that conditions this and future lives. 7. fate, the natural and necessary happenings of one's lifetime, preconditioned by one's past lifetimes. 8. moral debt, worked out and repaid, usually gradually, for past actions. 9. that which the individual has instituted, carried forward, endorsed, omitted to do, or has done right, through the ages until the present moment of ripe harvest (Bailey). 10. balance, compensation; what you yourself produce to keep a smooth journey of eternal life (Michio Kushi). 11. vibrations, aura (Sanskrit). adj. **karmic**. n. **sanchita karma** accumulated actions of all past lifetimes. **prarabha karma** portion of karma allotted for being worked out in this life. **agami karma** current karma created by the individual. **kusala karma** good karma. **akusala karma** bad karma (Sanskrit)

Karma Dzong 'fortress of karma', Tibetan Buddhist practice center in Boulder, founded by Chogyam Trungpa; 1971-

Karma Yoga path of selfless service, teaching of Krishna in the *Bhagavad Gita* (Sanskrit)

karma yogi one on the path of service (Sanskrit)

Karmapa 'Man of Action', 1. founder and lineage-holder of the Karma-branch of the Kargyudpa sect; leader of the Black Hat Buddhists of Tibet. 2. most recent Karmapa was Rangjung Ringpe Dorje; 1924-81 (Sanskrit and Tibetan)

Karmathians Islamic sect that regarded the *Qur'an* as allegorical, rejected revelation, fasting, and prayer, and lived communally, 9th c.

karmic debt moral or spiritual lesson that

is learned through experiencing difficulty or sorrow or other unpleasant experience

Karmu (Edgar Warner) Cambridge car mechanic, healer, psychic; d. 1989

Karnak temple in Luxor, Egypt

karshipta mystical bird of Zoroastrianism (Persian)

karuna compassion (Sanskrit)

Kasdan, Laurence film director; *The Big Chill*

kasha coarse, cracked buckwheat groats, millet, or barley

kashf revelation, spiritual discrimination (Arabic)

Kashi 'City of Light', traditional name for Benares (Sanskrit)

Kashmir beautiful valley north of India

Kaster, Hans journeyer in Mann's *The Magic Mountain*

Kasyapa 1. Buddha immediately preceding Sakyamuni. 2. (Mahakasyapa) close disciple of Buddha, first Zen Patriarch

kata 1. method of formal exercise in the martial arts; choreographed movements by training partners (Japanese). 2. white scarf given to high Tibetan lamas (Sanskrit)

Katakamuna cosmology of the ancient spiritual One World preserved in a poem written on deerskin in an ancient spiral script describing the genesis of the universe and the beginning of human life on Earth; dating back to more than 13,000 years ago and revealed by a sennin in the mountains of Japan after World War II

Kataragama city sacred to Hindus, Jains, Muslims, and Sufis in Sri Lanka

Katchongva, Dan Hopi Sun Clan teacher; ca. 1865-1972

Katha 1. Hindu sage. 2. Upanishad in which Nachiketas wins three boons from Death. 3. tale, story, history, narrative (Sanskrit)

Kathak Indian classical dance

katsu (ho, *Chinese*) Zen exclamation to counter egoistic thoughts (Japanese)

katun period of twenty years (Mayan)

Katzen, Mollie vegetarian cook; *Moosewood Cookbook*

Kaur 'princess', female Sikh initiate (Punjabi)

Kautantouwits Great God of the Algonquians who introduced corn and beans to humans

kavvahah (pl. kavvanot) 'devotion', permutations of the divine name in the Kabbalah (Hebrew)

Kawamoto, Ichiro Japanese day laborer and saintly pied piper of Hiroshima after the bombing

Kawthar 'abundance', river in Paradise visited by Muhammed (Arabic)

Kayser, Hans German mathematician and researcher of plants and music; *Akroasis: The Theory of World Harmonics*; 1891-1964

kayu cereal grain porridge that is soft and creamy (Japanese)

Kazantzakis, Nikos Greek novelist; *The Last Temptation of Christ*; 1883-1957

kazoo small mouth-blown musical instrument

Ke-T'eng 'vines and wisteria', entanglements, nature of a koan (Chinese)

Keats, John English Romantic poet; *Hyperion*; 1795-1821

Kebnzeh spiritual science of the Caucasuses

Kedarnath 1. name of Shiva. 2. pilgrimage place, temple, or mountain in the Himalayas. 3. temple in Benares

Keen, Sam storyteller and encounter group leader; *The Passionate Life*

keepers of the threshold spirits, dragons, or other divine manifestations that stand between the realms of existence

kefir cultured, whole pasteurized milk with fruit flavorings

Kegon (Hua-yen, *Chinese*, Avatamsaka, *Sanskrit*) Chinese school of Buddhism founded by Tojun, 7th c., which flourished under Hoso, and was introduced to Japan by Dosen in 736 (Japanese)

Kehaar far-seeing black-headed gull who helps the rabbits in *Watership Down*

Keillor, Garrison radio broadcaster and humorist; *Prairie Home Companion*; 1942-

Keitoku Dento-Roku 'Transmission of the Lamp', records of 1700 Indian and Chinese Zen masters (Japanese)

Keizan Jokin one of Soto Zen's two great Patriarchs, founder of Sojiji Temple; *Denkoroku*; 1267-1325

Kellogg, John H. Seventh Day Adventist, naturopath; *How to Have Good Health*; 1852-1943

kelp a large family of sea vegetables that grows in northern ocean latitudes

kemal perfection beyond polarity (Arabic)

Kempo (Shorinji Kempo) Japanese-style Chinese martial art utilizing blinding fast hand techniques and explosive focus of energy (Japanese)

ken mountain, keeping still; one of eight trigrams in the *I Ching* (Chinese)

kendo 'way of the sword', martial art, 18th c. (Japanese)

Kennett, Roshi Jiyu British-born Zen abbess, founder of Shasta Abbey; *Zen Is Eternal Life*; 1924-

Kenobi, Obi-Wan (Ben) Jedi Knight in *Star Wars*, wise and grizzled sage who tutors Luke Skywalker in the ways of the Force and use of the lightsabre

kensho 'to see into one's own nature', enlightenment, satori (Japanese)

Kensington Stone runestone found in Douglas County, Minn., in 1898 by farmer Olof Ohman commemorating an expedition from Vinland in 1362

Kent, Clark mild mannered reporter for the *Daily Planet*, alter-ego of Superman

Kent State site of the slaying of four students (Jeff Miller, Allison Krause, William Schroeder, and Sandy Scheuer) during a Cambodian peace rally by National Guardsmen on May 4, 1970

Kepler, Johann German astronomer and mystic; *Harmonice Mundi*; 1571-1630

kerass group of people who are unknowingly working together toward some common goal fostered by a larger cosmic influence (Vonnegut)

Kere Nyaga 'Mount of Brightness', Mt. Kenya

Kerista 'love', flower tribe, utopian lifestyle on the West Coast, 1960s (Greek)

Kern, Frank macrobiotic corrections official who took sugar out of the diet of juvenile defenders at the Tidewater Detention Center in Chesapeake, Vir., and reduced infractions and aggressive behavior by 45 percent

kernel a grain or seed enclosed in a hard husk or the inner, usually edible, part of a nut or fruit

Kerouac, Jack Beat writer; *On the Road*; 1922-69

Kervran, Louis French scientist and associate of George Ohsawa; *Biological Transmutations*, 1972

kerygma 'preaching', proclaiming the Christian gospel (Greek)

Kesdjan second body, higher than the physical (Gurdjieff)

Kesey, Ken poet, novelist, Merry Prankster; *One Flew Over the Cuckoo's Nest*; 1935-

Kether Crown sephiroth in the Kabbalah (Hebrew)

ketjak monkey chant from the *Ramayana* (Indonesian)

ketsu acupressure point (Japanese)

ketu descending lunar orbit, dragon's tail (Sanskrit)

kevala 'single', absolute (Sanskrit)

Key, The book by John Philip Cohane that posits an original Earth language based on the study of geographical and mythological names, especially the syllables *Og* and *Howa*, 1969

Keyline whole earth agricultural system designed by P. A. Yeomans in Australia described in *The City Forest*, 1954

keyword descriptive term in astrology for a planet or sign; mneumonic device

Kffwa island city and medieval Swahili center of East Africa

khafi hidden or mysterious one; one of the five lata'if (Arabic)

Khajuraho Central Indian site of Jain and Hindu erotic sculptures, 10th c.

Khalkha Mongolian tongue written vertically from the left in Uigur script until 1941 when Cyrillic was adopted

Khalsa 'Pure Ones', Sikh Brotherhood (Punjabi)

Khan, Hazrat Inayat founder of the Sufi Order; *The Sufi Message*; 1882-1927

Khan, Vilayat Inayat Sufi teacher; *Toward the One*; 1916-

Khanda the symbol of Sikhism, comprising three parts: the double-edged sword, symbol of truth, justice, and one God; the two cutting swords representing spiritual authority and temporal power; and the circle, the continuity of life and unity of people

Khaneghah and Maktab Islamic group founded by Pir Maleknia Naseralishah in Teheran, 1970-

Khayyam, Omar Persian mathematician, astronomer, Sufi poet; *Ruba'iyat*; d. 1123

khenpo abbot (Tibetan)

Khepher the sacred beetle in ancient Egypt

kherp oarblade, paddle (Egyptian)

Khidr (Abu'l-'Abbas Malkan) 'seagreen', legendary immortal Sufi saint (Arabic)

khilvat Sufi hermitage or retreat (Arabic)

Khmer 1. language of Cambodia. 2. people who dominated Southeast Asia from 9-12th c. 3. present-day Cambodians

Khnum (Khnemu) Egyptian Creator God who fashioned people out of clay on a potter's wheel

Khoisan non-Bantu languages of South Africa including Bushman and Hottentot

Khotan ancient Central Asian kingdom, former center of Mahayana Buddhism

Khyenpa, Dusum first Tibetan Karmapa, disciple of Gampopa who received a crown made from the hair of 100,000 Dakinis; 1110-93

ki (ch'i, *Chinese*) 1. universal life energy (Japanese). 2. the natural electromagnetic energy of Heaven and Earth that carries consciousness as well as energy to the meridians, chakras, and cells (Michio Kushi). 3. vitality, strength; e.g., 'he or she has strong ki'. 4. 'luck', mythical cock symbolizing peace and courage (Vietnamese)

ki kai ocean of ki, where sperm and egg meet and the baby grows from; the region of the hara (Japanese)

Kiai-jitsu Japanese martial art based on the ability to resonate ki with loud shouts (Japanese)

kibbutz (pl. kibbutzim) Israeli collective farm community (Hebrew)

Kidd, James Arizona hermit and miner who willed his property to anyone who could prove the existence of a soul at death (awarded to the American Society for Psychical Research); d. 1956

Kierkegaard, Soren Danish philosopher; *Stages on Life's Way*; 1813-55

kigo season word in a haiku (Japanese)

Kiichizan, Nancho Zen priest-painter; *Five Hundred Arhats*; 1352-1431

kikmongwi Hopi village leader

Kikuyu 1. largest tribal group of Kenya. 2. their Bantu language

Kim Chi Ha Korean poet; *Cry of the People*; 1941-

Kim Qui golden tortoise who granted a king use of her claws to form a crossbow to drive back invaders in Vietnamese mythology

Kim van Kieu national epic of Vietnam by Nguyen Du; allegorical Buddhist poem about the trials and tribulations of young Kieu, 18th c.

Kimbangu, Simon Congolese healer, pacifist, founder of the Church of Christ on Earth; d. 1951

kimchi highly spiced Chinese cabbage pickle (Korean)

Kimnara fabulous beings, half-human, half-animal; musicians of Indra (Sanskrit)

kimochi sensing of another's intuitive field (Japanese)

kinako roasted soybean flour (Japanese)

kinesics body language. adj. **kinesthetic** relating to touch, sensory, or tactile awareness

kinesiology muscle testing in which the person holds the substance in question while being tested for muscular resistance responses

king ideal ruler who is gentle and beneficent, perfect and taciturn, but capable of turning the entire world upside down (George Ohsawa)

King, Katie spirit daughter of buccaneer Henry Morgan who appeared to William Crookes in ESP experiments

King, Martin Luther Jr. Baptist minister, civil rights leader, disciple of Gandhi; *Why We Can't Wait*; 1919-68

Kingdom of Heaven (Kingdom of the Father) 1. infinite universe as a whole which 'is spread upon the Earth and humans do not see it' (Jesus, *Gospel of Thomas*). 2. paradise entered by freely applying yin and yang to the daily use of consciousness; intellectual awareness, the fourth level of judgment, (Michio Kushi)

Kingston, Maxine Hong Chinese-born author; *Warrior Woman*; 1940-

kinhin walking meditation (Japanese)

Kinkakuji Golden Pavilion in Kyoto, replica of a 14th c. original

Kinnell, Galway poet; *Body Rags*; 1927-

kinpira style of sauteing in which root vegetables are cut in very thin slices or shaved and seasoned with tamari soy sauce (Japanese)

Kiowa D. H. Lawrence's community in New Mexico

Kirgiz 1. Soviet Republic bordering China, capital Frunze. 2. Turkic tongue spoken there

Kirillov philosophical engineer in Dostoevski's *The Possessed*

Kirk, James commander of the *Starship Enterprise* in *Star Trek*

Kirlian photography aura or energy field photography developed by Semyon and Valentina Kirlian in Russia, 1939

kirtan repetition in song of the names of God (Sanskrit)

Kisa Gautami nun and friend of Buddha

kismet destiny, fate (Turkish)

kiss of peace Christian embrace

kiswa 'robe', black brocade curtain covering the Ka'ba (Arabic)

Kitab-I-Iquan 'Book of Certitude', Baha'i scripture by Baha'u'llah

Kitaro (Masanori Takahashi) multi-instrumentalist, composer, and one of the foremost exponents of New Age music; *Tunhuang*; 1953-

Kitatani, Kitsuhide Japanese-born administrator who founded the U.N. Macrobiotic Society; 1931-

kitchen the headquarters for world peace; the place of food preparation where life and consciousness, including a calm, peaceful mind, are produced (Michio and Aveline Kushi)

kitsch camp, endearingly in bad taste

kiva Pueblo house or community center

Klee, Paul Swiss intuitive artist; *Man on a Tightrope*; 1879-1940

Kleito daughter of Leukippe and Euenor, wife of Poseidon

klesha 1. karmic defilement, hindrance to enlightenment (Sanskrit). 2. obstacles, poisons, mixed-up feelings, mean notions, angriness, sneaky exploitations (Gary Snyder)

klieg conjunctivitis soreness or inflammation of the eyes resulting from an encounter with a UFO

Klingons grim, violent brawny humanoids in *Star Trek*, opposed to humans in perpetual war with the Federation

Knecht, Joseph master of the Glass Bead Game in Hesse's *Magister Ludi*

Kneipp, Sebastian German priest, hydrotherapist, natural healer; *My Water Cure*; 1821-97. **kneipping** natural healing

Knight, J. Z. channeler of Ramtha

Knight of the Rueful Countenance Don Quixote

knish a piece of dough stuffed with vegetables or other ingredients and baked or fried in the traditional Jewish style

Knot of Eternity Tibetan meditation symbol of the never-ending discriminating awareness of wisdom

knowledge understanding that can raise a human being's temperature and change his or her life (Robert Bly)

Ko Hung Chinese alchemist; *Pao P'u Tzu*; 4th c.

koan (kung-an, *Chinese*) 'public case', 1. statement, story, or riddle used by a Zen master as a teaching device to help a disciple realize his or her True Nature; paradoxical formulation of truth solved by deep meditation in Rinzai Zen. 2. any spiritual barrier or fundamental problem in one's training which one needs to face, penetrate, clarify and transcend, especially one naturally arising in daily life in Soto Zen (Japanese)

Kobo Daishi (Kukai) Japanese artist and teacher who introduced Shingon Buddhism to Japan; 774-835

Kodaijungu inner shrine at Ise, Japan, housing the mirror of the Sun Goddess

Koestler, Arthur Hungarian-born British novelist and psychic investigator; *The Roots of Coincidence*; 1905-83

Kohler, Jean professor of music who healed terminal pancreatic cancer with macrobiotics; *Healing Miracles from Macrobiotics*; 1917-80

koi koku a rich thick soup made from carp, burdock, bancha tea, and miso (Japanese)

Koinonia Farm partnership farming and civil rights community in Georgia founded by Clarence Jordan, 1942-

Koinonia Foundation ecumenical training center in Baltimore, 1951-

Koko a female gorilla trained by Francine Patterson to use sign language

Kokopelli the flute player, ancient Hopi symbol of abundance

koji a grain inoculated with bacteria and used in making fermented foods such as miso, tamari soy sauce, amasake, natto, and sake (Japanese)

Kojiki 'Records of Ancient Matters', Japanese chronicle spanning the creation to the Imperial court, 712

kokkoh ground cereal and seed gruel for infants (Japanese)

kokoro heart, mind, spirit (Japanese)

kombu a wide, thick, dark green sea vegetable that grows in deep ocean water and is used in macrobiotic cooking to make soup stocks, condiments, stews and cooked as a separate dish or with vegetables, beans, or grains (Japanese)

kombu powder a condiment made by roasting kombu in a skillet and crushing it in a suribachi

komori 1000-day meditation on a mountain top (Japanese)

Kon-Tiki raft piloted by Thor Heyerdahl which sailed from Peru to Polynesia proving the possibility of pre-Columbian contact, 1947

Konark site of the Sun Temple in India, 13th c.

Kondanna Brahman who predicted at Siddartha's birth that he would become a Buddha

Konjaku-monogatori 'Tales of Long Ago', collection of Indian, Chinese, Japanese tales, ca. 1050 (Japanese)

Konkokyo Japanese way of life combining elements of Shinto, Buddhism, Christianity, 1859-

Konya Sufi holy city in central Turkey

kopavi vibratory center on the top of the heaven (Hopi)

Kore divine maiden of the Greeks

Korean language of Korea unrelated to any other, with an alphabet of 25 letters invented in the 15th c.

Koretz, Rabbi Pinhas Shapira Kabbalist, disciple of the Maggid, shamanistic teacher; ca. 1726-1801

Kornfield, Jack Vipassana meditation teacher; *A Clean Forest Pool*; 1944-

Koros, Csoma de Hungarian traveler who visited Tibet and compiled a dictionary; d. 1842

Korzybski, Alfred Polish-born engineer and founder of General Semantics; *Science and Sanity*; 1879-1950

kosha sheath, subtle body enclosing the soul (Sanskrit)

Koshala Indian kingdom during Buddha's time

Koshiway, Jonathan Oto teacher and founder of the peyote cult, the Church of the First Born; 18th c.

Kosmon amalgamation of all present races (Oahspe)

Kosmos government sponsored spiritual center in Amsterdam with a natural foods restaurant, sauna, library, and gallery

Koster site near St. Louis of a prehistoric Native American culture that lived peacefully for 9,500 years

kotatsu heater placed on the floor with a low table over it (Japanese)

koto unfretted long zither (Japanese)

Koto-Dama (kotodama, kototama) 'spirit of words', 1. spirals of sound representing the powerful forces of heaven and Earth able to carry a true vision of nature and the universe. 2. science of the fifty sounds developed by Kuji Ogasawara (Japanese)

Kotzsch, Ronald macrobiotic teacher and author; *Macrobiotics Yesterday and Today*; 1944-

Kovic, Ron Vietnam vets spokesman; *Born on the Fourth of July*

Koya, Mount (Koya-san) mountain in Japan with ten thousand Buddhist temples; headquarters of Shingon Buddhism founded by Kukai

Kozel, Jonathan radical educator; *Death at an Early Age*; 1936-

KPFA first alternative radio station, Berkeley, Calif., 1946-

kra (okra, kla) life-soul, spirit that reincarnates; seven types corresponding with the days of the week (Yoruba)

kraal native village of Africa, usually built in the form of a circle, surrounded by a protective fence

krabi-krabong sword and staff martial art (Thai)

Krakatoa volcanic island in Indonesia vaporized in 1883

Krazy Kat disingenuous feline, surrealist comic strip by George Herriman, 1913-44

Kripalu Yoga Ashram meditation center founded by Yogi Amrit Desai in Sumneytown, Pa., and Lenox, Mass., 1970-

Kris Balinese mystical Dagger Dance (Indonesian)

Krishna (Krsna) 'all-attractive, black or dark blue (to the human senses)', singer of the *Bhagavad Gita*, adviser to the Pandus in the *Mahabharata*, incarnation of Vishnu, Supreme Personality of Godhead, the wisdom of the wise (Sanskrit)

Krishna, Gopi Kashmiri yogi, scientist; *The Biological Basis of Religion and Genius*; 1903-

Krishnamurti, Jiddu Indian philosopher and educator who emphasized direct experience and observation and relying on one's own intuition; *The First and Last Freedom*; 1895-1986

Krita Yuga first world age of truth in Hinduism (Sanskrit)

Kritias Plato's great uncle or distant cousin in whose house the story of the war between Atlantis and Athens is told in the *Timaios*

kriya 'completed action', exercise or set of exercises that awaken and channelize energy to the higher centers; automatic cleansing movement (Sanskrit)

Kriya Yoga discipline of opening the spiritual centers through activation of the shakti (Sanskrit)

kriyaban follower of Kriya Yoga or Swami Kriyananda

Kriyananda, Swami (J. Donald Walker) spiritual teacher, disciple of Yogananda, founder of Ananda Cooperative Village; 1927-

Kronos fourth Uranian planet ruling authority, government, and the highest point of development

Kropotkin, Prince Peter Russian anarchist; *Mutual Aid*; 1842-1921

Krotona Theosophical school and center near Hollywood, 1912-26, and in Ojai, Calif., 1926-

krypton 1. element linking the astral and physical body according to UMMO. 2. (cap.) Superman's home planet

ksana instant; shortest period of time in Buddhism (Sanskrit)

kshama supporting all pleasant and unpleasant things with patience (Sanskrit)

kshatriya member of the warrior or governing class of Hinduism (Sanskrit)

Kshitigarbha Bodhisattva of benevolence and mercy who watches over Earth between the time of Sakyamuni and Maitreya

Ku K'ai-chih wildly unconventional Chinese Taoist artist; *The Fairy of the Lo River*; 344-406

kua trigram or hexagram in the *I Ching* (Chinese)

Kuan-hsiu Chinese Ch'an artist renowned for exaggerated arhats with bony skulls, huge eyebrows, and Indian features; *West Peak Collection*; 832-912

Kuan Yin (Avalokiteshvara, *Sanskrit*; Kannon, *Japanese*) Bodhisattva of compassion and mercy who answers all prayers (Chinese)

Kubler-Ross, Elizabeth Swiss-born psychologist; *On Death and Dying*; 1926-

Kubrick, Stanley film director; *2001: A Space Odyssey*; 1928-

Kucha ancient Gobi city with a high Sanskrit culture, ca. 7th c.

k'uei 1. dragon motif on Shang bronzes. 2. sacred tortoise. 3. discarnate spirit. 4. lingam (Chinese)

Kuen-luen fabulous mountain at the center of Earth, site of the peaches of life, source of the Yellow River and the Phoenix, ruled over by the Fairy Queen of the West (Chinese)

Kufic angular script used for decorative purposes (Arabic)

kufu naturalness in bodily action, Zen effortlessness (Japanese)

Kuhlman, Kathryn faith healer; *Noth-*

ing Is Impossible with God; d. 1976

kukicha bancha tea; the older twigs, stems, and leaves of the tea bush (Japanese)

Kukkutapada mountain in Magadha where Makakashyo died or is still waiting for Maitreya (Sanskrit)

Kuksu northern California/southern Oregon bioregion, subdivision of Turtle Island continent

Kukulcan Quetzalcoatl (Mayan)

Kulvinskas, Viktoras raw foods author; *Survival into the 21st Century*; 1941-

Kumano shrine to the God of Food and Way of life near Matsue, Japan

Kumara one of the seven highest beings in the solar system (Theosophy)

Kumarajiva Indian-born scholar and founder of the Madhyamika school of Buddhism in China; 344-413

Kumari Ghar Temple of the Living Goddess in Katmandu (Nepaii)

Kumbha Mela 'Pitcher Fair', Indian pilgrimage festival held every twelve years just outside of Allahabad, India, where the Ganges, Yamuna, and the mythical Saraswati Rivers meet; the gathering on Feb. 6, 1989, with 15 million people in attendance was the largest spiritual gathering in history (Hindi)

Kumbi Saleh capital of ancient Ghana

kumiss fermented mare's milk (Mongolian)

Kumuhonua first man in Hawaiian myth from whose right side was fashioned a wife, Ke-ola-Ku-honua or Lalo-nana

kundalini 'burn', 1. primordial cosmic energy coiled up like a serpent with three and a half coils with head downwards at the spinal base in the muladhara chakra. 2. a yoga designed to release and creatively use this energy (Sanskrit)

Kundrie witch who counseled Parzival not to abandon the quest

kung the foundation tone or musical note expressing celestial order (Chinese)

kung-fu task, work performed, special skills, strength; generic term for exercise (Chinese)

Kunz, Dora Dutch East Indian-born cofounder of Therapeutic Touch

kupuri life energy (Huichol Indians)

Kurdish Iranian language spoken by the Kurds

Kurdistan Kurdish region in Turkey, Iran, Iraq, Syria, and U.S.S.R.

Kurgan hypothetical mother-culture of

the Indo-Europeans; ca. -5000-3000 (Marija Gimbutas)

Kurma tortoise incarnation of Vishnu

Kurosawa, Akiro Japanese film director; *The Seven Samurai*; 1910-

Kurozumikyo Japanese way of life devoted to the Sun Goddess founded by Kurozumi Munetada, 1814-

Kurukshetra 'field of the Kurus', 1. battlefield in North India, site of the *Bhagavad Gita*. 2. field of life (Sanskrit)

Kush ancient African land south of Egypt

kusha Indian grass used for meditation mats and cushions and feed

Kushi, Aveline (Tomoko Yokoyama) Japanese-born macrobiotic teacher; *How to Cook with Miso*; 1923-

Kushi-inada-hima Princess of the Ricefields who was saved from the eightheaded dragon by the Wind God who set out eight barrels of sake and slew the dragon when he got drunk (Japanese)

Kushi Institute macrobiotic educational organization with headquarters in Brookline and Becket, Mass. and affiliates around the world founded by Michio and Aveline Kushi, 1978-

Kushi, Michio Japanese-born educator and macrobiotic teacher; *One Peaceful World*; 1926-

Kushinara (Kusinagara) North Indian site of Buddha's death where he passed into parinirvana

Kuthumi 1. Mahatma referred to by Blavatsky. 2. Brother who speaks through Ray Stanford. 3. (Kut Humi) Chohan of the Second Ray in Mark-Age

Kuvalayananda, Swami Indian guru and pioneer in physical education; 1883-1966

Kuyundlik (Nineveh) Sumerian excavation site of a calculation of 15 digits

kuzu (kudzu) a white starch made from a prolific wild vine used in macrobiotic cooking to thicken soups, gravies, sauces, desserts, and for medicinal beverages (Japanese)

Kwan Saihung Taoist master described in *The Wandering Taoist* by Deng Ming-Dao

kwatz 1. loud cry uttered by Zen masters to cut through attachments and fetters of their disciples. 2. musical progression of the drum, cymbals, and small bell (Japanese)

Kyogen comic interlude between episodes in No drama (Japanese)

Kyongju Korean city noted for Bulguksa and Sukkulam temples and the God Bell

Kyos Greek island of 400 monasteries

kyosaku awakening stick used to prod meditators and massage stiffness (Japanese)

Kyot (Laschantiure, 'The Provencal') the Spanish source who learned the Grail story from a Muslim magician in Wolfram's *Parzival*

Kyrie Eleison 'Lord have mercy', prayer in the Catholic mass, remnant of Greek liturgy (Greek)

Kyrios Lord (Greek)

kyu martial arts class (Japanese)

kyudo Zen archery (Japanese)

Kyushu southernmost island of Japan

Kyushu Kyokyaku eccentric Zen artist; *Plum Blossoms*; 14th c.

Ll

L-Field electro-dynamic field of radionics (Harold Saxon Burr)

L-rod dowsing rod in the shape of an L

L'Anse aux Meadows site of the first Viking settlement in America, discovered in Newfoundland in 1960 (French)

La Catalina warrioress in the don Juan books; worthy opponent of Castaneda

LaChapelle Dolores feminist educator and author; *Earth Wisdom*

La Crescenta site in California of the Ananda Ashrama established by Swami Paramananda, 1923-

La Leche League network of mothers promoting breast-feeding and natural childbirth

La Vita Nuova 'the New Life,' Dante's book about his early life and meeting with Beatrice on a bridge in Florence

labor-credit communal work arrangement whereby credits are given for labor contributed

labor-intensive adj. system of agriculture utilizing large quantities of labor as opposed to capital or technology; traditional farming

labyrinth maze, archetype of the circuitous quest for wisdom; the five great ones in antiquity were at Cnossus and

Gortyna, Crete; Lemos, Greece; Clusium, Etrusca; and Lake Moeris, Egypt. Labyrinths have also been depicted on pillar scratches at Pompeii, in floor tiles of Toussaints Abbey in France, 18th c. Rajasthani manuscripts, in traditional Zuni sand drawings, the notebooks of Paul Klee, and among Chiriqui rock drawings in Panama. adj. **labyrinthine** (from Latin via Greek)

Lacandon Indian tribe descended from the Mayans in Mexico and Guatemala

Lady of the Lake hand which offered Arthur the sword Ecalibur

laetrile (nitrilosides, amygdalin, Vitamin B-17) anti-cancer drug from apricot pits developed by Drs. Ernest Krebs, Sr. and Jr.

laghu intricate footbeats in dance (Sanskrit)

Lahiri Mahasaya Indian spiritual teacher, disciple of Babaji, guru of Sri Yukteswar; 1828-95

Laing, R. D. (Ronald David) Scottish psychiatrist; *The Politics of Experience*; 1927-89

Lake Wobegone mythical Minnesota setting of *Prairie Home Companion* where all the men are shy and the women good-looking

Lakhovsky, Georges Russian-born engineer and pioneer in cellular oscillation; *The Origin of Life*; 1870-1943

Lakshmi (Sri) Hindu Goddess of Beauty, Wealth, Youth; wife of Vishnu; mother of Kama

Laliat al-Mir'aj festival of Muhammad's Night journey, in July (Arabic)

Lalleswari (Lalla) Kashmiri yogini, mystical poetess; 14th c.

lama learned priest or layperson (Tibetan). adj. **lamaistic**

Lama Foundation spiritual community in San Cristobal, N.M.

Lamanites disorderly tribe that controlled America by 420 (Joseph Smith)

Lamarck, Jean French naturalist; *Zoological Philosophy*; 1744-1829. adj. **Lamarckian** evolutionary theory of the inheritance of acquired characteristics

Lamaze, Fernand French obstetrician who developed psychoprophylaxis; *Painless Childbirth*; 1890-1957

Lamaze method natural childbirth approach pioneered by Fernand Lamaze

Lambarene site of Schweitzer's hospital in Gabon, West Africa

lamed-vovniks thirty-six hidden saints upon whose merit the existence of the world depends (Yiddish)

Lames 12th Hebrew letter: extention, L, 30

Lan Ts'ai-ho troubadour among the Chinese Eight Immortals, patron of florists

Lan-chi I-hsuan Chinese Ch'an master whose teachings inspired Rinzai Zen; d. 867

Lancelot Arthurian knight turned monk

land earth or soil serving as both mother and father; receiver of seed, bearer and nurturer of the young, raiser of seedstalk, bearer and shredder of seed (Wendell Berry)

land-ark seed bank

land trust land held cooperatively, usually under legal auspices

Lane, Charles English-born reformer, mystic, transcendentalist, co-founder of Fruitlands; 1800-70

Lane, Lois Superman's sweetheart

Lang, Andrew Scottish poet and folklorist; *The Blue Fairy Book*; 1844-1912

Languedoc Cathar area in France; region southward from the Loire to the Pyrenees down into Arragon and eastward to the Rhone; the most highly civilized area of Western Europe during the Middle Ages

Lanka (Sri Lanka) Ceylon (Sanskrit)

Lankavatara Sutra 'Entrance to Ceylon Text', Mahayanist scripture expounding subjective idealism (Sanskrit)

Lao-tzu (Lao-tse, Lao Zi, Li Er) 'Old Guy', Chinese civil servant, philosopher, and sage whom Confucius described as appearing like a dragon rising to the clouds; *Tao Te Ching*; -6th c.

Lapchi-Kang Mt. Everest (Tibetan)

lapis (*Lapis philosophorum*) the stone, or philosopher's stone of alchemy; the agent of transmutation of base metals into gold

Lappe, Francis Moore food and world hunger activist; *Diet for a Small Planet*; 1944-

Las Casas, Bartoleme de Spanish priest and defender of the Indians; *Destruction of the Indies*; 1474-1566

Lascaux paleolithic cave in Spain with paintings of a bird-headed person and bison

Last and First Men science-fiction novel by Olaf Stapledon describing future history culminating in an awakened planet of telepathically aware individuals united in a group planetary mind,

1930

Laszlo, Ervin general systems analyst; *The System View of the World*

lata'if organs of spiritual apprehension; Sufi system of spiritual energy centers (Arabic)

nafs (ego) ....navel
qalb (heart) ....left side of chest
ruh (spirit) ....right side of chest
sirr (secret) ....middle of chest
khafi (hidden) ....forehead
akhfa (deeply hidden) .... brain

Laurasia northern continent formed when Pangaea separated (Plate Tectonics)

Lavater, Johann Swiss physiognomist; *Essays on Physiognomy*; 18th c.

laver Scottish seaweed, similar to nori

law of similars principle that like shall be cured by like

Law, William English mystic; *Serious Call to a Devout and Holy Life*; 1686-1761

Lawrence, D. H. (David Herbert) English-born novelist; *The Plumed Serpent*; 1885-1930

Lawrence, L. George Silesian-born engineer and radiesthesiologist; *Intersteller Communications Signals*; 1925-

Lawrence, T. E. (Thomas Edward) (Lawrence of Arabia) Welsh poet and Near Eastern adventurer; *The Seven Pillars of Wisdom*; 1888-1935

laya yoga technique of altering consciousness by sound and rhythm

laying of hands healing with the hands or palms

Lazaris entity channeled through Jach Pursel; *The Sacred Journey: You and Your Higher Self*

Lazarus brother of Mary and Martha whom Jesus raised from the dead

L.D.L. low-density lipoprotein, one of the bad cholesterols; associated with saturated fat consumption

Le Plongeon, Augustus French excavator of Mayan ruins and Atlantist; *Queen Moo and the Egyptian Sphinx*; 1826-1908

Lead, Jane English mystic; *The Enochian Walks with God*; 1623-1704

Leadbeater, C. W. British Theosophist; *The Chakras*; 1847-1934

leading houses first, fourth, seventh, and tenth houses in astrology, signifying action and pioneering

Leah wife of Jacob, symbol of the active life of the soul

Leary, Timothy psychologist and pioneer LSD experimenter; *Politics of Ecstasy*; 1920-

LeBoyer, Frederick natural childbirth educator; *Birth Without Violence*

lecithin group of fatty substances occurring in animal and plant tissues such as soybeans, corns, egg yolk; emulsifying agent for cholesterol

Led Zepplin English rock group (John Paul Jones, John Bonham, Robert Plant); *Houses of the Holy*; 1960s

Lee, Ann (Mother Wisdom) English-born mystic, founder of the Shakers in America; 1736-84

Leek, Sybil witch, numerologist; *Diary of a Witch*; 1917-82

left-brain more receiving, accepting consciousness; analytical, rational hemisphere of the brain that governs language, speech, mathematical and scientific reasoning and that controls the right side of the body. adj. **left-brained**

left-handed path tantric path, way of magic, occultism

left-handed spiral clockwise spiral that follows the path of the sun or hands of a clock

left-hemisphere brain region associated with analytical consciousness

legominism work of conscious art from past ages (Bennett)

legume plant bearing nitrogen-fixing bacteria on its roots, such as beans, alfalfa, lentils

Leibnitz, Gottfried Wilhelm von German philosopher and mathematician who discovered binary numbers and studied the *I Ching*; *Discourse on the Natural Theology of the Chinese*; 1646-1716

Lemstrom, Selim Finnish scientist and plant researcher; *Electro Cultur*; 1838-1904

Lemurean 1. inhabitant of Lemuria. 2. third root race (Theosophy). 3. third age in Max Heindel's teaching in which the Archangels helped the Lords of Form create the desire body around the vital body

Lemuria 1. hypothesized Afro-Indian peninsula explaining the distribution of lemurs (Philip L. Sclater, 19th c.). 2. (Mu) large continent submerged in the Pacific according to occult tradition

Lenape 'The People', Delawares' name for themselves

Lennon, John English-born Beatle, peace activist; *Imagine*; 1940-80

lenticular adj. lens shaped, especially flying saucers

lentils small green or red beans, originally a staple of the Middle East

LeGwin, Ursula K. science-fiction writer; *The Lathe of Heaven*; 1929-

Leo the Lion, fifth zodiacal sign; of the fire element; ruler the Sun; keywords: creativity, courage, energy

Leo, Alan (Frederick William Allan) English astrologer; 1860-1918

Leonard, George educational reformer; *Education and Ecstasy*; 1923-

Leonard, Gladys Osborne English trance medium; *My Life in Two Worlds*; 1882-68

Leonardo da Vinci Florentine artist, sculptor, engineer, scientist, vegetarian; *Mona Lisa*; 1452-1519

Leopold, Aldo father of the modern deep ecology movement; *Sand County Almanac*, 1886-1948

Lepchas indigenous forest people of Sikkim

lesbian a woman who identifies with women, especially sexually

Lesbos Aegean Greek island, home of Sappho

LeShan, Lawrence holistic psychologist and healer; *The Medium, the Mystic, and the Physicist*; 1920-

Leslie, Joseph spiritualist who reconstructed the entire Atlantean civilization; *Submerged Atlantis Restored*

lesser benefic Venus

Lessing, Doris English novelist; *Shikasta*; 1919-

Lethe river of oblivion in Greek myth

Levant Near East

Levelers English Diggers

Levertov, Denise English-born poetess and peace activist; *With Eyes at the Back of Our Heads*; 1923-

Levi (Levi H. Dowling) preacher, doctor, visionary; *The Aquarian Gospel of Jesus the Christ*; 1844-1911

Levi, Eliphas (Alphone Louis Constant) French Catholic occultist; *The History of Magic*; 1810-75

Levin, Cecile macrobiotic teacher and counselor; *Cooking for Regeneration*

Levis (from Levi Strauss, manufacturer) blue jeans; denim pants

levity upward, outward force the opposite of which is gravity

Lewis, C. S. (Clive Stapes) British theo-logian, science-fiction writer; *Out of the Silent Planet*; 1898-1963

Lewis, Samuel L. (Murshid, Sufi Ahmed Murad, Chisti) Sufi teacher; *Saladin*; 1896-1971

ley (ley line) 'grassland,' straight road or path constructed in prehistoric times connecting ancient landmarks (Alfred Watkins)

Leza 'cherished', supreme being among Africans from northern Kalahari to Congo, Zambia, and Tanzania

Lha supernatural being who planned to incarnate on Earth as a human during the third root race (Theosophy)

Lhasa 'Lord's place', capital of Tibet, founded by King Songtsen-gampo; seat of the Dalai Lamas until the Chinese invasion in 1959, 7th c.- (Tibetan)

li 1. fire, the clinging; one of the eight trigrams in the *I Ching*. 2. usefulness that furthers, third cyclical movement of Heaven. 3. ritual vessel, tripod. 4. morality, rites (Chinese)

Li Ch'ing-chao Chinese poetess; 1084-1151

Li Ehr 'Plum Ear', given name of Laotze (Chinese)

Li Ju-chen Chinese novelist; *Mirror of Sounds*; 1763-1830

Li Po Chinese Taoist alchemist, poet, wanderer; *Banished Immortal*; 701-62

Li T'ieh-kuai one of the Chinese Eight Immortals; a begger with an iron crutch and orange gourd, patron of healing

Liang K'ai (Crazy Fellow) Chinese Ch'an artist; *The Sixth Patriarch Tearing a Sutra*; 13th c.

Liang, T. T. Chinese-born T'ai Chi master; *T'ai Chi Chuan for Health and Self-Reflection*

Liber Mundi 'book of the world', nature (Latin)

Liberating the Living (ho-jo, *Japanese*) Buddhist ceremony of purchasing live animals from meat or fowl markets and freeing them

liberation 1. enlightenment. 2. cultural movement for greater freedom, opportunity, and justice, e.g. gay, women's, animal, theological. n. **lib**, **liberationist**. adj. **liberated**

Liberation News Service alternative communications network established in New York City, 1967

liberatory education radical education method of Paulo Freire

Libra the balance or scales; seventh zodical sign; of the airy element; ruler Venus: keywords; justice, beauty, harmonizing energy

libranomancy divination with incense

Library of Alexandria Egyptian gnostic center of learning burnt by Julius Caesar in -48 and destroyed by Christian Emperor Theodosius in 389

Liebknecht, Karl German antimilitarist, anarchist, companion of Rosa Luxemburg; 1871-1919

Lieh Tzu Chinese Taoist sage; *Lieh Tzu*; -4th c.

life 1. energetic property of all living beings including mountains, rivers, and valleys. 2. the passage of energy through changing forms. 3. consciousness, awareness, the eternal play of freely creating and erasing images (Michio Kushi). 4. infinitely amusing and wonderful adventure with awareness of absolute justice (George Ohsawa). 5. the capacity for self-motion. 6. living system characterized by a comprehensive unity, incessant activity, the capacity to grow and develop its own parts, increasing differentiation through time, the power of regeneration and repair, the ability to transform other materials into itself, the initiation of natural action from within, and the ability to reproduce itself. 7. a self-organizing system characterized by an actively sustained low entropy and things bounded by walls, membranes, skin, or waxy coverings; using energy directly from the Sun and indirectly from food, incessantly acting to maintain their identity and integrity; even as they grow, change, and reproduce and which do not lose their visible, recognizable entities (Lovelock). 8. sorrow (Buddha). 9. the ability to move upstream against the flow of time (Schrodinger). 10. carbon flesh activated and maintained by a genetic code (modern view)

life column megalithic symbol of life energy rising from the womb, cave, or water

life energy cosmic life force that animates and circulates throughout creation; natural electromagnetic energy of the infinite universe composed of waves, ray, and vibrations that remain undetected by modern science

animal magnetism ....Mesmer
arunquiltha ....Australians
astral light ....Blavatsky
baraka ....Arabs
biomagnetism ....de la Warr
bioplasma ....Vicktor Inyushin
chi.. Chinese
eck ....Ekankar
ectoplasm ....Charles Richet
elan vital.................................. Bergson
eloptic energy ....Hieronymous
ether...alchemy
etheric formative force ....Steiner
facultas formatrix ....Kepler
ferho ....Gnostics
fohat ....Tibetans
Holy Spirit ....Christians
huaca ....Incas
ki..Japanese
libido ....Freud
magnale magnum................van Helmot
mana ....Polynesians
manitou ....Algonquians
megbe ....Pygmies
motor force................................Keely
mulungu ....Ghanians
mumia ....Paracelsus
N-rays..Blondlot
negative entropy..............Schroedinger
noetic energy ....Charles Muses
ntoro ....Ashanti
ntu... Bantu
odic force ....Reichenbach
oreda ....Iroquois
orgone ....Reich
pneuma ....Greeks
prana ....Indians
psi faculty ....Rhine
psychotronic energy .... Pavlita
ruach ....Israelites
sila..Innuit
soul............................ Afro-Americans
synchronicity ....Jung
tane ....Hawaiians
telesma .... Hermes Trismegistus
telluric force .... Bovis
ton .... Dakota
universion ....Lakhovsky
X force...Eeman
waka ....Sioux
yesod .... Kabbalists

life-line series of lives

life reading clairvoyant description of past lives, as by Edgar Cayce

lifeform being or organism that has life

light n. or adj. 1. spiritual illumination. 2. spirit. 3. God as light. 4. (cap.) the guide in *The Blue Bird* who leads the children to understanding and happiness. 4. loose, open, young in spirit, staying close to the Earth, humble

light being entity with a highly developed consciousness in one of the spiritual worlds

light show stroboscopic display of lights, colors, slides, films, music

light worker spiritual guide

lightsaber a yard-long beam of blue-white light that can cut through anything in *Star Wars*

lila God's play, pastime, or sport; inscrutable cosmic playfulness (Sanskrit)

Lilith 1. Adam's first wife exiled from Eden for insisting on equality. 2. planet postulated between Mercury and Venus. 3. women's liberation symbol

Liljequist, Nils Swedish iridologist; *Diagnosis from the Eye*; 19th c.

Lilliput land of small people visited by Gulliver

Lilly, John scientist, physician, consciousness researcher; *The Mind of the Dolphin*; 1915-

Lily Dale spiritualist town in western New York

Lima (after Lima Ohsawa) macrobiotic food distributor and community in Belgium, 1950s-

liminal experience betwixt and between different dimensions or levels of awareness (Victor Turner, 1969)

limit what gives form to the limitless (Pythagoras)

Lincoln, Abraham statesman, nature mystic, clairvoyant; 1809-65

Lincos 'lingua cosmics', universal, extraterrestrial language under construction by Dutch logician Hans Freudenthal

Lindisfarne 1. island off the coast of Northumberland, England; site where St. Aiden built a monastery in 635, burial site of St. Cuthbert. 2. New Age community in Southampton, N.Y., founded by William Thompson

line one of six constituents of an *I Ching* hexagram which shows the nature of the situation and its future shape

ling sacred unicorn (Chinese)

Ling Lun a minister of Huang Ti sent to search for a unique set of bamboo pipes to bring earthly music into conformity with universal harmony

lingam 'mark, characteristic', stylized phallic symbol, emblem of Shiva's creative power (Sanskrit)

lingasharira subtle body, psychic body constituting sheaths of intelligence, mind, and vital energy, activated during dreaming (Sanskrit)

Linnaeus, Carl von Swedish botanist; *Plants of the Bible*; 1707-78

Linton, Charles blacksmith who at age twenty-two transcribed psychically *The Healing of Nations*, a 340-page book in KJV style in 1854

Lippi, Filippino Florentine artist, son of Fra Lippi; *Tobias and the Angel*; 1457-1504

Lippi, Fra Filippo Florentine artist, Carmelite monk; *Madonna and Child*; ca. 1406-69

Lisaura tragic lover of Tanhauser

literature writing that heartens us by showing us new and true possibilities and how much may be achieved in life and art by conscious endeavor (Gary Snyder)

Little Prince story of little prince who leaves his tiny planet and comes to Earth where he learns from a fox the secret of what is important in life in Antoine de Saint-Exupery's book of the same name

Little, Stuart adventurous mouse in T. B. White's book of the same name

Liuzzo, Viola Gregg housewife and civil rights marcher; 1925-65

live food uncooked, freshly grown food, especially sprouts

Living Father moving, changing eternal universe (Jesus, *Gospel of Thomas*)

living in the moment Zen-like awareness of letting the universal or emptiness shine through every instant

Living Love Center consciousness center established by Ken Keyes in Berkeley, Calif.

living theater free-form play stressing improvisation, audience participation, open-air performance

Livingston-Wheeler, Elizabeth holistic cancer immunologist

Lixus 'golden city' built by unknown Sun-worshipers south of Gibralter where the ocean current sweeps toward the Gulf of Mexico; burial site of Herakles (Greek)

llama wooly being of the high Andes

Llan Illtud Fawr old Celtic sanctuary near Llantwit Major in Glamorgan, Wales, and site of one of the Perpetual Choirs of Britain

Llano cooperative community established in California, later Louisiana; 1914-36

Lo Shu 'Writing from the Lo River', *I*

Ching arrangement based on numbers (Chinese)

Lo-yang district in Honan, China; principal city of the T'ang Dynasty and former capital of China

Lobsang Rampa, Tuesday (Cyril Hoskins) English plumber and Tibetan lama; *The Third Eye*; 1911-81

local adj. ecological

local mean time true time at the place of birth

locale I the region of the astral world similar to the Earth world (Robert Monroe)

locale II that region of the astral world that is governed by different laws and inhabited by different beings (Robert Monroe)

Locana 'Earth Diamond', female counterpart to Vairocana (Sanskrit)

Lochner, Stephen Cologne artist; *Adoration of the Magi*; d. 1451

lodge esoteric organization in the physical or astral world working on behalf of human evolution

Lodge, Sir Oliver English physicist, educator, psychical researcher; 1851-1940

Logia (Q) 'sayings', collection of sayings of Jesus; source from which Matthew and Luke were compiled

logarhythmic spiral spiral with successive stages growing in harmonic proportion based on the ratio of the Golden Section from the center outward or inward, manifested in everything from galaxies to seashells, from the human constitution to the unfolding of history

logion (pl. logia) one of 114 sayings of Jesus in the *Gospel of Thomas*

logos 1. Word, reason, universal principle of life. 2. Jesus Christ (St. John). 3. (pl. logoi) angels (Greek)

logotherapy existential analysis developed by Viktor Frankl from his experience at Auschwitz

Logres King Arthur's Kingdom

lohan arhat, spiritual adept (Chinese)

Lohengrin (Helyas) a scion of the Grail family in medieval myth; son of Parzival and Condwiramurs; the Swan Knight

loihtija wise women (Finnish)

loka 'world', one of six states of mind produced by the three fires of greed, hate, and delusion: heaven, human, animal, asura, hungry ghost, hell (Sanskrit)

Loki mischievous figure in Scandinavian mythology

Lollards John Wycliffe's followers in England, 14th c.

London, Jack dharma bum and author; *The Call of the Wild*; 1876-1916

Looking Backwards utopian novel of Edward Bellamy set in Boston in 2000 noted for credit cards and stereos, 1889

looking glass dream dream involving messages or subjective reactions to people and events in the external world (Ann Faraday)

looking inward dream dream that shows us a picture of how we feel about our private, inner world (Ann Faraday)

looking outward dream dream that provides valid information about people or situations in the external world (Ann Faraday)

Looking-Glass Land chess-like realm traversed by Alice where time flows backward as well as forward

Lorentz transformations formulae to determine the difference in time aged between space travelers and people on Earth

Lorenzo Monoco Florentine artist and Carmaldolite monk, teacher of Fra Angelica; *Adoration of the Magi*; ca. 1370-1425

Los peronification of the soul in Blake's poetry

lotus (padma, pundarika, *Sanskrit,* renge, *Japanese*) Hindu and Buddhist symbol for training, enlightenment, compassion and purity; roots in the mud represent the suffering of daily life, the stem spiritual training, and the blossom enlightenment

lotus root root of the water lily, brown-skinned with a hollow, chambered off-white inside, used in macrobiotic dishes and for medicinal preparations

lotus seeds edible seeds of the lotus root plant, often cooked along with brown rice or other grains

Lotus Sutra (Sutra of the Lotus of the Wonderful Law, Saddharma Pundurika, *Sanskrit*, Myoho Renge-kyo, *Japanese*) Mahayanist text relating the final discourse of the Buddha at Vulture Peak before entering nirvana, 1st c.

Lourdes French pilgrimage site and resort celebrated for miraculous cures since a vision of the Virgin Mary before Bernadette Soubiros, an invalid child, in 1858

lovage garden herb associated with transmuting desires into reality

love 1. the force that moves the Sun and the other stars (Dante). 2. the heaven that encircles all (Dante). 3. a spiritual motion that can never rest short of the thing that fills it with devotion (Dante). 4. the essence of God, the universe, nature. 5. divine expression of compassion, mercy, affection, and tenderness. 6. selfless or egoless state of consciousness in which you don't mind to die for the beloved, humanity, or the world (Michio Kushi). 7. the cliff you jump off to learn to fly (Sherman Goldman). 8. hitching your wagon to a star. 9. accepting or choosing another individual exactly as he or she is and giving him or her the space to be that way (est). 10. deep affection and warmth toward a friend, child, parent, stranger. 11. sexual passion or desire. 12. attraction between man and woman, the strong and weak, the learned and ignorant, rich and poor, the creative and destructive, the healthy and sick. 13. universal polarity and attraction; yin and yang in balance; what makes the world go around. 14. the binding force (Joseph Campbell). 15. state of unconditional acceptance where only endless happiness and infinite freedom are experienced (George Ohsawa)

agape	Greek
ahavah	Hebrew
ai	Japanese
amo	Esperanto
amor	Spanish, Portuguese
amore	Italian
amour	French
ask	Turkish
elskor	Danish
houb	Arabic
iuloire	Rumanian
karlek	Swedish
laska	Czech
libe	Yiddish
liebe	German
liefde	Dutch
lyubov	Russian
milose	Polish
prema	Sanskrit
rakkaus	Finnish
szeretet	Hungarian
tjinta	Indonesian
upendo	Swahili

Love Canal sitein upper New York state of a major toxic waste confrontation in the 1970s

love feast Moravian communal meal

Lovejoy, Elijah abolitionist printer; *The St. Louis Observer*; 1802-37

Lovejoy, Sam ecology activist who toppled a 500-foot tower in Montague, Mass., in 1974 in protest of nuclear power

Lovelock, James British scientist; *The Ages of Gaia*; 1919-

Lovers Tarot #6: passion, choice

Lovewisdom, Johnny American-born natural healer living in the Andes; *Eternal Youth Life Newsletter*; ca. 1915-

Lovins, Amory B. appropriate technologist; *Soft-Energy Paths: Toward a Durable Peace*

low-flow adj. toilets or showers that are energy-efficient

Lowell, Percival astronomer who predicted Pluto; *Soul of the Far East*; 1855-1916

Lowen, Alexander developer of Bioenergetics; *Love and Orgasm*; 1910-

lower self that part of the mind that is attached and living in the world of delusion

lowerworld realm of shamanic journey

Lozanov, Georgi Bulgarian parapsychologist; *Suggestology and Suggestopedia*

LSD (lysergic acid diethylamide) 1. powerful hallucinogen synthesized by Albert Hofmann in Switzerland in 1943. 2. sacrament, avatar of God for the Atomic Age, spiritual alternative to the A-Bomb (Leary)

LST local sidereal time in astrology

Lu Shih legendary student who dreamt his whole life at the hut of Taoist hermit Nam Kha (Vietnamese)

Lu Tung-pin one of the Chinese Eight Immortals, patron of the sick

Luang Prabang ancient capital and holy city of Laos

Lucas, George film director; *Star Wars*; 1944-

Luce, Don Vermont agriculturist who exposed the Tiger Cages in Vietnam; *The Unheard Voices*; 1934-

Lucifer 'Light Bearer', 1. Venus as the morning star. 2. prince of the fallen angels. 3. hero of Milton's *Paradise Lost*. 4. (Rex) planet postulated between Mars and Jupiter ruling birth, intuition, delays

Lucis Trust service organization founded by Alice and Foster Bailey in New York City, 1922-

Lucky Dragon Japanese fishing boat caught in a radiation storm near Bikini Atoll in 1954

Luddites English craftspeople who resisted textile plants, 19th c.

Lueken, Veronica the Bayside Seeress who experienced visions and messages from Mary from 1970-

Lug Celtic Messenger God

Luke, St. physician, gospelist; *Acts of the Apostles*; 1st c.

Lully, Raymond Majorcan mystic; *The Art of Contemplation*; ca. 1235-1315

Lulu Moppet, Little liberated comic strip heroine

Lumbini park near Buddha's birthsite

lumen gratiae divine light of grace (Latin)

Luna Roman Goddess of the Moon

lunar mansion one of the twenty-eight divisions of the Moon's path

lunar month (synodic month) interval between two new moons, 29.531 days; time of one revolution of the Moon around the Earth

lunar year 12 lunar months, 354.3 days

lunation new moon

Lund, Diderich H. Norwegian pacifist; *Resistance in Norway*; 1888-

Lundbergs (Harlan, Homer, Eldon, and Wendell) pioneer family of brown rice farmers and natural food producers in Richvale, California

lung one of twin bodily organs that internalizes air and electromagnetic energy and removes wastes

lung-gompa (lum-gompa) runners who can span long distances effortlessly through meditative and breathing techniques (Tibetan)

lung-mei 'dragon-paths', ley lines or paths that run between astronomical mounds and high mountains (Chinese)

Lung Wang Chinese Dragon King

Lungmen Buddhist cave complex in western China

Lunisad Celtic summerfest, August 1

Luria, A. R. Soviet physiologist; *The Mind of a Mnemonist*

Luthuli, Albert Zulu chief, freedom activist; *Let My People Go*; 1898-1967

Luxor modern name for ancient Thebes in Egypt

Lynd, Staughton radical historian, Quaker activist: *Nonviolence in America*; 1929-

Lytton, Lord Edward English utopian novelist; *Zanoni*; 1803-73

Mm

ma spacial experience surrounding a pole (Japanese)

ma-la peppery method of Szechuan cooking (Chinese)

Ma-Wang-Tui Texts 51 ancient Chinese texts including the earliest *Tao Te Ching,* ancient medical texts, and the *I Ching* found in 1973 in a Chinese tomb dated to -168

Maat Egyptian Goddess of Truth and Justice portrayed with a feather

Mab Queen of the Fairies in English mythology

Mabinogion Welsh epic tales

Macarius, St. Egyptian anchorite; ca. 295-386

MacCumal, Fionn hero of Fenian Irish cycle

Machen, Arthur Welsh occultist; *The Great God Pan*; 1863-1947

Machu Picchu Incan holy city in present-day Peru

Maclaine, Shirley actress and student of reincarnation; *Out on a Limb*; 1934-

Macrina 'blessed', Christian saint, sister of Gregory of Nyssa; 4th c.

macro adj. large, cosmic, macrobiotic

macrobiotics (from *macrobios,* 'long life' or 'great life,' Hippocrates, -6th c., *Greek)* 1. the way of health, happiness, and peace through biological and spiritual evolution and the universal means to practice and harmonize with the Order of the Universe in daily life, including the selection, preparation, and manner of cooking and eating, as well as the orientation of consciousness toward infinite spiritual realization (Michio Kushi). 2. the everyday guide to absolute health and infinite happiness (George Ohsawa). 3. looking at life from the largest view, that of the infinite universe. 4. the ecological way of life practiced by humanity for thousands and thousands of generations. 5. the adventure that seeks out challenges and the greatest difficulties in order to realize the greatest happiness

macrocosm the order of the universe

macrocosmic orbit energy flow including the entire meridian system in Taoism

Macumba Brazilian spiritualism

Mad Hatter frenzied being in *Alice in Wonderland*

Madhavadasaji, Paramahansa Indian yogi; 1798-1921

Madhyamika Middle Path school of Buddhism, forerunner of the Mahayana founded by Nagarjuna, 2nd or 3rd c. (Sanskrit)

Madoc, Prince (Madag) Welsh seafarer said to have landed in Alabama and inspired a Welsh-speaking tribe of now extinct Mandan Indians, 12th c.

Madri wife of Vessantara who followed her husband to forest exile

madrigal 'womb', 1. poetic form with a pastoral theme, 14th c. 2. sectional, secular polyphonic vocal, 16th c. (from Greek)

Maeterlinck, Maurice Belgian poet and playwright; *The Blue Bird*; 1862-1949

Maezumi-roshi, Taizan Japanese-born director of the Zen Center in Los Angeles

Mag Mel Celtic paradise

Magadha ancient Indian kingdom in Bihar

Magdalene, Mary sweetheart of Jesus

Magdalenian most advanced paleolithic culture in Europe (French)

Maghrib 'the West', northwestern Africa (Arabic)

Magi (sin. magus) Zoroastrian astronomer-priests (Persian)

magic 1. accomplishment of ends through the application of psychic technology. 2. the art of changing consciousness at will (Starhawk)

Magic Maiden archetypal nymph of the Aquarian Age

Magic Mirror mirror that reflects all of history; attributed to Iskander Zu al-Karnayn, Kai Kosru, Tariq ibn-Ziyad, Lucian of Samosata, Jupiter, Merlin

Magic Mountain novel by Thomas Mann

Magic Theater place for madmen only in Hesse's *Steppenwolf*

Magic Table grid of numbers that add up the same horizontally, vertically, and diagonally, especially the basic numbers of Nine Star Ki which are used in astrology, numerology, calendar, and destiny studies

Magician Tarot #1: the inquirer

magick the science and art of causing change to occur in conformity with will (Aleister Crowley)

Magister Ludi 'master of the game', novel by Hesse also known as the *Glass Bead Game*

magma someone to whom the terrestial future is more important than the present (Teilhard)

Magna Mater Great Mother (Latin)

Magnesia model city-state ruled by sacred number described in Plato's *Laws*

magnetic field gradient postulated field that dowsers pick up

Magnetic Star the star HD 37776 in Orion that is the only object in the heavens ever observed to have a predominantly quadrupole magnetic field, discovered 1990

Magnetic Zero the state of rest, source of life, God, mind (Walter Russell)

magnetism 1. complementary antagonistic force to electricity, arising more in colder temperatures; property on the Earth only of iron, cobalt, and nickel but if temperatures drop, other elements start to become magnetized. 2. natural attraction between the human body and One Infinity; as we become more yang, our intuition, our deep thinking, begins to work, especially as a result of ingesting more minerals and salt and experiencing cold weather (Michio Kushi)

magnetobiology science dealing with the effects of magnetic fields on living things

magnetotherapy the use of magnetic fields to heal

Magnus, Albertus German alchemist and Dominican monk; *Book on Minerals*; ca. 1193-1280

Mahabalipuran (Mamallapuram) South Indian site of the Seven Pagodas, 7th c.

Mahabharata 'Great India', great Indian epic of 18 volumes of which the *Bhagavad Gita* is a small episode, ca. -1800 (Sanskrit)

Mahakala 'Great Time', Tibetan tantric protector, depicted as wrathful, black, holding a skull-cup and chopper (Sanskrit)

Mahakasyapa (Kasyapa) Buddhist disciple who smiled when Sakyamuni held up a flower thereby receiving transmission of the dharma and becoming the first Zen Patriarch

mahamantra 'great recitation', chief mantra of a group (Sanskrit)

mahamudra 'great gesture', the Middle Way, union of opposites (Sanskrit)

Mahanta 'Light Giver', title of Eckankar leaders (Sanskrit)

mahapralaya 'great deluge', destruction of the universe at the end of a cosmic cycle (Sanskrit)

Maharaj ji 1. (Nimkroli Baba) Indian saint. 2. (Guru Maharaj ji) Indian head of the Divine Light Mission; 1958-

Maharishi Mahesh Yogi Indian physicist, founder of Transcendental Meditation; *The Science of Being and the Art of Living*; 1918-

Maharishi University yogic teaching center in Fairfield, Iowa

mahasamadhi an enlightened death (Sanskrit)

Mahasaya, Lahiri Indian yogi; 1827-95

mahatma 'great soul', 1. title of respect. 2. (cap.) Gandhi (Sanskrit)

Mahatma Letters epistles to Madame Blavatsky reportedly from various hidden masters expounding the Secret Doctrine

Mahavamsa 'Great Chronicle of Ceylon', Pali epic, 5th c.

Mahavira 'Great Hero', last in the line of twenty-four Jain prophets, teacher of ahimsa; -599-27

Mahavishnu (John McLaughlin) English musician; *My Goal's Beyond*; 1942-

Mahayana 'Great Vehicle', Northern Buddhism of Tibet, China, Korea, and Japan which stresses the Bodhisattva ideal (Sanskrit)

Mahayana scriptures chief texts of Mahayana Buddhism include:
Buddhacharita kavya....... Buddha's life
Prajnaparamita....... emptiness, wisdom
Vajrachchhedika ....diamond wisdom
Saddhamapundarika (Lotus of the True Law) .... supreme last teaching
Mahaparinirvana...................... nirvana
Avatamsaka (Garland)........ 10 stages of enlightenment ....
Lankavatara (Ceylon) .... teachings
Lalita-vistara................... Buddha's life
Vimalakirti .... Buddha within
Srimaladevi ....one vehicle
Surangamasamadhi .... samadhi
Sukhavati-Vyuha (Pure Land) .... after death ....
Bodhi-charavatara................ discipline

Mahayuga Great Cycle of 4,320,000 years which began on Feb. 18, 3102 B.C. (Sanskrit)

Mahdi twelfth inman of Islam believed to have hidden himself until the appropriate time (Arabic)

Mahikari 'True Light', spiritual movement focusing on palm healing and giving light

Mahinda son of Ashoka; Indian monk who introduced Buddhism to Ceylon

Maillard, Keith Canadian novelist; *Two Strand River*; 1942-

Maimed King Pellinor, custodian of the Grail Castle

Maimonides (Moses ben Maimon) Spanish-born Jewish philosopher of Cairo; *Guide for the Perplexed*; 1134-1204

Maison Ignoramus 'House of Ignorance,' George Ohsawa's school in Japan, 1947-53

maithuna meditative sexual union (Sanskrit)

Maitreya (Metteya, *Pali,* Mi-lo-fo, *Chinese,* Miroku, *Japanese*) 'loving one', Buddha who is to come in the future, currently waiting in the Tushita heaven as a bodhisattva (Sanakrit)

Maitreyi female sage in the *Brihadaranyuka Upanishad*

majlis (pl. majalis) 1. Sufi gathering. 2. collection of a saint's sayings (Arabic)

Majnun legendary Persian lover who pined for Laila in Sufi literature

Major Arcana archetypal 22-card section of the Tarot

major planets outer planets from Earth

makara 1. syllable *m*, mystical letter concluding Aum. 2. five forbidden things in Hinduism or practiced things in the tantra (Sanskrit)

Make-Make chief god of Easter Island

maki sushi a style of sushi in which rice is rolled up in nori with vegetables, pickles, fish, tofu, or other ingredients and sliced into small spiral rounds (Japanese)

making the two one understanding and using movement and rest, and other complementary opposites; entering paradise, living in the Kingdom of Heaven (Jesus, *Gospel of Thomas*)

makko-ho five-minute physical fitness program (Japanese)

makoto 'sincerity', chief virtue in Shinto (Japanese)

makyo hallucinations that may arise during meditation, usually due to incorrect breathing, posture, or stress (Japanese)

mala rosary (Sanskrit)

Malacandra (Mars) perfect world in C. S. Lewis's space trilogy

malakut dominion, the world of form (Arabic)

male-practice medical malpractice and domination of women's health concerns by men (Robert Mendelsohn)

Maledil Martial god in C.S. Lewis's space trilogy

malefic difficult and problematical planet in a chart

Mali great African empire espousing Islam, 14th c.

Malindi great iron-working and commercial city of medieval Zanj

Malinke West African language of the Niger-Congo family

Malkuth sephiroth of the world, kingdom, realization in the Kabbalah (Hebrew)

Mallinatha Indian princess who became the 19th Jain Tirthankara

maloka Indian longhouse of the South American tropical rainforests

mama child's first words, expressing its journey from the infinitely small (*m* sound) to the infinitely large (*a* sound) (Michio Kushi)

Mambrino Spanish king whose magical helmet rendering invisibility was perceived in a barber's basin by Don Quixote

mana life force (Polynesian)

Manabusch 'Big Rabbit', culture-bearer of the Algonquins

manas mind (Sanskrit). adj. **manasic**

Mancha Don Quixote's homeland

Manco Capac Incan culture-bearer, founder of Cuzco

mandala intricate pattern of concentric circles, squares, polygons, and other geometric or artistic symbols representing the Order of the Universe used for instruction or meditation (Sanskrit). adj. **mandalic**

Mandate of Heaven sanction to govern in China or Vietnam which can be lost by misrule and restored by anyone on behalf of universal order

Mandean (Nazorean) member of a Christian gnostic sect in Persia and Iraq, possibly descended from the original Jewish Christians

Mandeville, Sir John English traveler to the Holy Land and Far East; *Travels*; 1322-72

mandorla almond-shaped figure formed by two intersecting circles symbolizing celestial union

Mandrake the Magician comic book wizard initiated in Tibet designed by Lee Falk and Phil Davis; 1934-

Manetho Egyptian high priest; *History of Egypt*; -3rd c.

mango heavenly-tasting tropical fruit

Mani 1. Scandinavian Moon God. 2. Persian prophet and muralist; ca. 215-73. 3. stone piled up near a monastery to fulfill a prayer (Tibetan). n. **Manichee** follower of Mani

manifestation 1. materialization. 2. expression of the Godhead

manifesting the ability to bring into reality that which is desired

Manikarnika burning ghat in Benares

manipura navel chakra (Sanskrit)

Manipuri Indian school of dance illustrating pastoral loves of Krishna

Manitou spirit of the Fox people

Manjusri Bodhisattva personifying meditation and great wisdom, usually depicted sitting in meditation on a lion (the wild self), holding the sword of wisdom which cuts through all delusion

Mann, Thomas German author; *The Magic Mountain*; 1875-1955

Manoa lost Brazilian City of Gold reported by explorers, 18th c.

Mantegna, Andrea Italian artist; *St. Jerome in the Wilderness*; 1431-1506

Mantiq uttair 'Parliament of Birds', poem by Attar on the Sufi path

mantra (mantram) formula composed of syllables (meaningful or meaningless) whose sounds produce psychic or spiritual effects; sacred sound (Sanskrit). adj. **mantric**

Manu the first human being in Hindu myth who saved humankind from a deluge by building a ship and taking aboard all manner of seeds; archetypal law giver

Manushi-Buddhas three Buddhas of the preceding kalpa and the first four of a thousand of this kalpa: Vipasyin, Sikhin, Visvabhu, Krakuccanda, Kanakamun, Kasyapa, Sakyamuni

manvantara period of Manu's rule, 71 celestial yugas (Sanskrit)

Maori 1. inhabitants of New Zealand who originated from Tahiti in waves until the 14th c. 2. their language

map guide to consciousness and life; e.g. primal arrangement in the *I Ching*, reconciliation of opposites in mysticism, myth of the Eternal Return in primitive culture, *solve et coagula* in alchemy

map dowsing locating water, oil, missing objects, etc. with a pendulum and map rather than actually being on the site

Mappo third and last period of the destruction of the Buddhist dharma from A.D. 1000 to the present (Japanese)

Mapungubwe ancient site of a mysterious culture of gold and terraces excavated in the Transvaal, 1932

maqam (pl. maqat) stage or degree on the Sufi path; place of manifestation where a saint has revealed his or her presence and at which he or she can be reached (Arabic)

Mara 'Death' master of delusion who appeared with his daughter and army to unseat the Buddha and make him abandon his resolve and who was told to put away his malice and go in peace; the ego, the small self (Sanskrit)

Marceau, Marcel French pantomimist; 1923-

March Hare frenetic being in *Alice in Wonderland*

March on the Pentagon mammoth anti-Vietnam war protest in Washington, D.C., Oct. 21, 1967

March on Washington large civil rights march led by Martin Luther King, Jr. in Washington, D.C., Aug. 28, 1963

Marchahuasi central Peruvian plateau with a complex of sculptures attributed to a Masma culture predating the Incas

Marcuse, Herbert German-born neo-Freudian and Marxist philosopher; *Eros and Civilization*; 1898-1979

Mardana Islamic drummer, companion of Guru Nanak

Marduk chief Babylonian deity

marg (marga) way, path (Sanskrit)

Margulis, Lynn biologist and co-founder of the Gaia hypothesis

ma'rifa (ma'rifat) mystical intuitive knowledge of God, perfect knowledge of divine things, wisdom revealed from on high (Arabic)

Marion, Maid sweetheart of Robin Hood

Mark the lover of Isault in the Arthurian Romances

Mark Age 1. period between the Old and New Age. 2. Earth plane aspect of the hierarchical plan. 3. spiritual name of El Morya in his present incarnation. 4. spiritual unit operating on Earth with headquarters in Miami

Mark, John Christian Jewish gospelist; *Gospel of Mark*; 1st c. adj. **Marcan**

Marlowe, Christopher English poet, freethinker, and possible author of the Shakespearean Canon; *Dr. Faustus*; 1564-?93

Marmion Way Jesus's home street in Nazareth (*Aquarian Gospel*)

Marpa (The Translator) Tibetan Buddhist, disciple of Naropa, teacher of Milarepa, who utilized dreams and omens; 1012-97

marriage 1. an ordeal, a spiritual battleground in which antagonistic energies are transmuted into a unified force (Joseph Campbell). 2. union of man and woman and the community in a vow of sexual responsibility toward each other (Wendell Berry)

Mars 1. Roman God of Health and Combat. 2. planet ruling force, energy, health, outgoing energy

Marshack, Alexander ethnologist who decoded Ice Age reindeer bone marks which revealed a high astronomy in Paleolithic times; *The Roots of Civilization*; 1918-

martial arts a form of meditation-in-action developed from Ch'an Buddhism in China, especially by Bodhidharma at the Shaolin temple as an exercise to keep monks from falling asleep during sitting meditation and to remain centered in the midst of daily activity and strife

China

kung fu	generic term for martial arts
t'ai-chi chuan	subtle yielding
hsing-i	footholds, direct energy
pa-kua	circular movement
mo ming kung	nameless, formless
kenpo	Chinese-style karate

Okinawa

karate	open hand
tae kwon do	empty hand
cireum	wrestling

Japan

judo	no holds barred
aikido	rhythmic
jodo	stick vs. sword
kendo	sword
ia-do	sword
sumo	wrestling

Burma

bando	boxing, wrestling

Thailand

krabi-krabong	sword and staff

Indonesian

pentjak-silat	tiger-motions

Martin, St. French ex-soldier turned saint, Bishop of Tours, founder of the first Western monastery; 316-97

Martineau, Harriet English radical author and Unitarian; *Autobiography*; 1802-76

Martini, Simone Sienese artist; *Christ Returning from the Temple*; 1284-1344

Marx, Bernard dissident in Huxley's *Brave New World*

Marx, Karl German-born philosopher, father of Communism; *On Religion*; 1818-83

Mary 1. mother of Jesus. 2. symbol of a woman who has no Kali energy and no Artemis energy; Demeter without the snakes (Robert Bly). 3. (the other Mary) mother of Jacob and Joseph at the scene of the Crucifixion

masa fresh dough made from whole corn kernals soaked with limestone or wood ash and used in making arepas, tortillas, and other traditional South American dishes (Spanish)

masala spices, herbs, and seasonings ground or pounded as a base for curry sauce (Hindi)

Masau'u Great Spirit (Hopi)

masculine n. or adj. characteristics that are primarily yang but may appear in either sex including aggressiveness, competitiveness, logical thinking, fairness, and going out on a physical or spiritual quest

masculine signs Aries, Gemini, Leo, Libra, Sagittarius, Aquarius

masjid mosque (Arabic)

Maslow, Abraham humanist psychologist; *Toward a Psychology of Being*; 1908-70

Masolino di Panicale Florentine artist; *Healing of the Cripple*; 1384-1447

Massey, Gerald British author; *A Book of the Beginnings*; 1828-1907

master 1. one who has mastered a spiritual discipline and teaches or guides others. 2. (pl.) hidden teachers who rule the spiritual evolution of Earth (Theosophy)

master ship #10 Sananda's spacecraft in etheric orbit around Earth since 1885 (Mark-Age)

Masters, Edgar Lee peace poet; *Spoon River Anthology*; 1869-1950

Mat Fool in the Tarot (French)

Matagiri Aurobindo community in Mt. Tremper, N.Y., 1968-

Matakiteranai 'Eyes Looking at the Stars', native name for Easter Island

Matatu-Araracuanga underground city reported in the Amazon; abode of flying saucers and hidden rulers

matcha (hikicha) powdered green tea (Japanese)

material civilization the dark half of the spiral of the northern sky during which the Earth receives less electromagnetic energy from the Milky Way and human society is more chaotic and warlike; approximately -12,000 to A.D. 2100 (Michio Kushi)

material world visible part of the spiritual world (Michio Kushi)

materialization 1. translation from one frequency vibration to another. 2. translation of chemical, electronic, and auric fields of a person or object

Maternal Trinity Cancer, Leo, Virgo

Mathnawi epic poem by Sufi mystic Jalalu'l-din Rumi

Matilda friend in Purgatory who explains to Dante natural order

Matohoshila Sioux who introduced corn to his people

matriarchal (matrifocal) cultures that are led or guided by women and are more nurturing, agrarian, egalitarian, democratic, and peaceful

matricentic the era characterized by spontaneities and nurturing qualities (Thomas Berry)

matrilinear adj. culture or family traced through the mother

matrilocal practice of a husband going to live with his wife's family or clan

matrism mother-identification (G. Rattray Taylor)

matristic adj. Mother Goddess-oriented culture

matrix framework of interdependent interrelationships

matrix inversion instead of arising from the action of an external object on the sensorium, the 'perception' event may be primary, with the external object arising as a secondary phenomenon (Otto Schmitt)

matrix time everyday experience of living in two worlds and regarding the second world as occurring in 'matrix time', i.e., at the same time but in another dimension as ordinary clock time (John Heron)

Matsuwa, don Jose Huichol shaman 1880-

Matsya fish incarnation of Vishnu

matter 1. gravitationally trapped light. 2. substance-like phenomena, physical manifestation. 3. energy form with a heavier, slower vibration than mind or spirit. 4. dense or crystallized spirit, the end result of the spiral of materialization (Michio Kushi)

matutine rising of a planet before the Sun

matzah (pl. matzot) unleavened bread (Hebrew)

Maui trickster and culture-bearer of Polynesia

Maurin, Peter French social activist; cofounder of the Catholic Worker Movement

Mawlawiyya Sufi order derived from Rumi, located chiefly in Turkey, popularly known as Whirling Dervishes (Arabic)

Mawlidan-Nabi celebration in April of Muhammad's birth (Arabic)

Max, Peter pop artist; *The New Age Organic Vegetarian Cookbook*; 1937-

May, Rollo psychologist; *Love and Will*; 1909-

Maya 1. ancient people of southeast Mexico and Central America with a high culture, especially in astronomy, whose descendents still live in the Yucatan, Guatemala, and Honduras. 2. (l.c.) phenomenal world, illusion (Sanskrit). 3. thinking that the phenomenal world is not God (Swami Rama, Sanskrit). 3. external energy of the Lord, which seems incomprehensible (Sanskrit). 4. (cap.) Buddha's mother

Maya owichapaha the old woman who judges souls along the Spirit Path after death (Sioux)

Mayan linguistic family and language of the Maya, still spoken by several million Indians; originally written in hieroglyphs which are partially deciphered; three surviving texts are the *Dresden Codex* (astronomy), *Codex Perezianus* (ritual), *Tro-Cortesianus Codex* (astrology)

Mayan Great Cycle, era which began in -3113 and ends in A.D. 2011

Mayapan Mayan city built by Kukulcan

Mayda crescent-shaped island paradise of Moorish imagination in the north Atlantic

Mayo Irish county, site of neolithic and medieval monastic ruins, associated with St. Patrick's ministry

Mazdanism Persian way of life antecedent to Zarathustra

Mazdaznan Zoroastrian movement founded by Otoman Zar-Adusht Ha'nish with headquarters in Los Angeles

McAbre, Sarcophagus vulture in *Pogo*

McAlister, Sister Elizabeth peace activist; 1939-

McCarrison, Robert British surgeon who discovered the disease-free Hunza culture in 1904-11; *Nutritional and Nutural Health*; b. 1878

McCarthy, Eugene (Clean Gene) politician who inspired youthful dissidents to work within the system to end the Vietnam War; 1916-

McClure, Michael Beat poet; *The Ghost Tantras*; 1932-

McCoy, Leonard (Bones) doctor on the *U.S.S. Enterprise* in *Star Trek*

McDougall, John A. holistic medical doctor; *The McDougall Plan*

McGovern Report (*Dietary Goals for the United States*) historic Senate report linking the modern diet with six of the ten leading causes of death; chaired by Senator George McGovern, 1976

McLuhan, Marshall Canadian educator and philosopher of the Global Village; *Understanding Media*; 1911-80. adj. **McLuhanesque** participatory, cool, oral, nonlinear

McTaggart, David Canadian-born sailor and inspirator of Greenpeace

Mead, Margaret anthropologist; *Coming of Age in Samoa*; 1901-78

Measling, Wolf Polish-born psychic, subject of ESP tests by Stalin, Freud, Gandhi; Russian telepathist; 1899-

Mecca holy city of Islam in present-day Saudi Arabia

mechanicals androids, cyborgs, and robots in any form in *Star Wars*

Mechthild of Hackborn, St. German mystic; *Revelations*; 14th c.

Medamothy 'nowhere', utopian island visited by Pantagruel

Medea sorceress who aided Jason in Greek mythology

mediatrix mother, muse, distributer of energy and creator of forms

medicine (from *medi*, 'middle' or 'center', *Latin*) 1. that which brings you back to the center. 2. healing agent of the North American Indians. 3. allopathic medicine; modern medicine; conventional approach to health and sickness

Medicine Buddha (Yakshi Nyorai, *Japanese*) Buddha with the power to heal everyone

medicine bundle (medicine bag) collection of stones, feathers, leaves, or other personal objects of high electromagnetic vibration that can be used for healing or protection

Medicine Eagle, Brook Native American medicine woman; *Moon Lodge*

medicine, energetic medicine that deals with the blood and electromagnetic energy exchange through a change of diet, mental adjustment, physical exercises; preventive in orientation

medicine for humanity medicine that deals with life as a whole, especially guiding people through a more philosophical and educational orientation (Michio Kushi)

medicine, symptomatic medicine that eliminates symptoms or changes the condition using various invasive methods and techniques including surgery, radiation, acupuncture, and moxa

Medicine Wheel (Medicine Circle) 1. Plains Indians' way of life symbolizing a dynamic, spirallic understanding of the universe. 2. (l.c.) an ancient stone circle that has been used for thousands of years by Native people as a place for prayer, ceremony, and self-understanding (Sun Bear)

Medina 'the city', 1. site of Muhammad's migration in 622, in present-day Saudi Arabia. 2. old town of Fez

meditation n. or adj. 1. art and science of contemplation and concentration spanning Paleolithic hunting rituals, Neolithic vegetative mysteries, and historic religious traditions East and West, especially Zen, Yoga, Sufism, and Coptic, Carmelite, Trappist, and Quaker Christianity. 2. contemplation, reflection, intuition, doing nothing; in duration from a moment to a kalpa, though most frequently for periods of ten minutes to several hours or days; performed anytime, anywhere, or in any position or activity, though often sitting on the Earth, floor, a chair, rock, or pinnacle, standing straight or holding a posture, walking, dancing, jogging, making love; sometimes accompanied by chanting silently or aloud, alone or with a group; focusing on the breath, the chakras, the mind, parts of the body, light, sound, God, a tutelary deity, symbols, archetypes, a candle, or another internal, external, or transcendental object. 3. practice leading to cosmic consciousness, enlightenment, truth-consciousness-bliss, absorption

with the divine, union of skillful means and perfect wisdom. 4. practice of centering the whole being, developing body consciousness, rooting in the here-and-now, perfecting harmony and balance with the Earth. 5. discipline of mind, awareness and control of thoughts, emotions, and states of consciousness. 6. return to the source or emptiness to erase delusions, refresh ourselves day to day and begin anew (Michio Kushi). 7. exercise or practice of just being; experiencing ourselves as whatever we are, without any extra thing added (Gary Snyder). 8. going into the mind to see wisdom for yourself—over and over again, until it becomes the mind you live in (Gary Snyder). 9. space to work on fears, hopes, neurotic games, self-deception (Trungpa). 10. self-analysis, self-cultivation, self-enlightenment (Swami Rama). 11. thought-form building, bringing down to the concrete levels of the mental plane abstract ideas and intuitions and shattering of forms; establishing of a direct channel between the monad and the purified personality, and between the seven centers in the human etheric vehicle; freedom to work on any path (Bailey). 12. the Tao of cats. n. **meditator, meditativeness.** adj. **meditative.** v. **meditate** (from *meditari*, Latin)

medium intermediary, especially a trance psychic who serves as a channel for communication between the living and the dead

Medium Coeli middle of the sky, midheaven in astrology (Latin)

Medjugorje site in Yugoslavia where six children saw the Virgin holding the infant Jesus on a hill near the village in 1981

Medusa Greek Goddess with snakes rising from her head whose look turned to stone, signifying energy that is so great it stops the developing masculine consciousness in its tracks (Robert Bly)

mega-vitamin therapy (orthomolecular therapy) nutritional approach based on making up for deficiencies with vitamin and mineral supplements

megalithic yard prehistoric unit of measure at Stonehenge; 2.72 feet (Thom)

Meher Baba (Merwan S. Irani) Indian-born prophet of Persian lineage who taught Sufi wisdom and kept silent for

44 years; 1894-1969

mehitabel cat in *Archy & Mehitabel* who believed she was the reincarnation of Cleopatra

mei mon acupoint on the lower back, behind the hara, which is traditionally given moxa to bring a dying person back to life (Japanese)

mei-toku bright shining grace (Japanese)

Meier, Eduard 'Billy' Swiss caretaker who experienced a series of close encounters with UFO visitors from the Pleides beginning in 1975

Meiji Japanese era from 1868-1911

mejaz illusion, that which makes nothing appear as everything (Arabic)

mekabu root of the wakame sea vegetable (Japanese)

mela spiritual festival (Hindi)

Melchior one of the three Magi

Melinda (Meander, *Greek*) Greek ruler of the Punjab, inquirer in a Buddhist discourse *The Questions of Melinda*; ca. -150

Melkor rebellious Holy One in Tolkien's sagas

Melville, Herman author and Tahitian adventurer; *Moby Dick*; 1819-91

Mem 13th Hebrew letter: woman, M, 40

memory 1. (episodic memory) recall of specific events. 2. (semantic memory) recall of knowledge and facts. 3. (implicit memory) recall of skills one exercises automatically such as speaking with proper grammar or hitting a baseball. 4. (spiritual memory) recall of past lives or ancient civilizations. 5. (universal memory) recall of one's eternal journey and purpose on the Earth. 6. (yin) vision of the future. 7. (yang) vision of the past

men's liberation movement among males to free themselves from stereotypical sex roles and exploitation of women, 1970s

Mendeleyev, Dmitri I. Russian chemist who discovered the periodic table of elements in a dream; 1834-1907

Mendelsohn, Robert holistic physician; *Confessions of a Medical Heretic*; 1926-88

Mendelssohn, Felix German composer; *Elijah*; 1809-47

Menehune native Hawaiians

Meng, Lady old woman who makes the Broth of Oblivion for reincarnating souls in Chinese mythology

Meng-ste sage who guided Jesus in Tibet

(*Aquarian Gospel*)

menhir natural or roughly shaped standing stone, alone or in a group

Menninger, Karl J. psychiatrist and explorer of the role of the emotions in healing; 1893-

Mentastics 'mental gymnastics'; Trager therapeutic approach

mentation placing one's consciousness and a specific idea in a specific part of the body

Mephistopheles Prince of Darkness, tutor in Marlowe's *Dr. Faustus*

Mercury 1. Roman God of Communication. 2. planet ruling commerce, language, writing, and versatile, mental energy

Meriadoc (Merry Brandybuck) companion of Frodo in *Lord of the Rings*

meridian 1. one of fourteen channels of electromagnetic energy in the human body, according to traditional Far Eastern medicine, that supplies energy to the organs and functions, tissues and cells. 2. the great circle passing through the poles of the Earth, 24,883.2 miles. 3. East West division of longitude, measured from Greenwich, England. 4. (cap.) house system based on the equal division of the equator by hour circles in astrology

Traditional Pairs of Meridians

Lungs............................Large Intestine
Spleen and Pancreas................Stomach
Heart............................Small Instestine
Kidney......................................Bladder
Heart Governor.................Triple Heater
Liver...................................Gall Bladder
Conception Vessel....Governing Vessel

Merkabah 'chariot', ascension to higher realms (Hebrew)

Merlin (Myrddin) bard and magician of Celtic romance

Meroe ancient Kushite kingdom in Africa whose mystery schools preserved the wisdom of ancient Egypt. adj. **Meroitic**

Merry Pranksters psychedelic gypsies led by Ken Kesey, 1960s

Merswin, Rulman Strasbourg visionary; *The Book of the Nine Rocks*; 1307-82

Merton, Thomas (Father M. Louis) Trappist monk and Zen commentator; *The Seven-Storey Mountain*; 1915-68

Meru 1. mountain in the center of the universe. 2. (l.c.) guru bead of a rosary (Sanskrit)

Mesa one of three fingers of land above the Arizona desert, home of the Hopi

Mesa Verde site in Colorado abandoned by Anasazi in 1300s, rediscovered in 1874

mescalin drug derived from Peyote, regarded as divine by native Mexicans

Mescalito personification of the peyote plant

Mesmer, Franz Antoine Austrian doctor who developed animal magnetism; 1733-1815

Mesoamerica pre-Columbian period of civilization in Mexico and Central America

mesocosm order of the attuned society

mesocosmic adj. taking a part for the whole

mesolithic the culture at the end of the last glaciation, ca. -8000

message transmission from God to humanity affecting the spiritual orientation from age to age (Sufi term)

MEST matter, energy, space, and time; force created by the Thetan (Scientology)

meta act experience toward which millions of individual actions are tending which will collectively 'deliver us' as a co-creative species (Barbara Marx Hubbard)

metabelief belief about belief (Lilly)

metachory abstract synthesis of dance-motion, poetry, music, geometrical form, color, perfume (Rudhyar)

metagnomy knowledge gained without use of normal senses

metalinguistics science of language and consciousness

metanoia 'repentance', new state of consciousness (Greek)

metaphoron the characteristic hylopsychic and cyberbiological expression of the symbolic nature of a discrete substance as it acts within or upon living entities, as in homeopathy and alchemy (Dennis Stillings)

metaprogram consciousness-raising pattern (Lilly)

metapsychiatry study of the relationship between psychiatry and mysticism (Stanley Dean)

Metcalf Stone stone discovered near Fort Benning, Ga. in 1966 by Manfred Metcalf with signs of an Aegean syllabary of the late Bronze Age

Metcalfe, William English-born author of the first book on vegetarianism in the U.S.; *Abstinence from Animal Flesh*; 1788-1862

Metonic Cycle (after Meton, -5th c. Greek) 19-year lunar cycle after which the new moon occurs on the same day of the year

Metropolis Earth home of Superman

Metsys, Quentin Flemish artist; *Triptych of the Lamentation of Christ*; 1466-1530

metta love; one of the Buddhist heavenly states of mind (Pali)

Mevlevi Order Sufi dervish society founded by Rumi, 13th c. -

MHD magnetohydrodynamics; study of the motions of electrified gases in stars and interstellar space

Mi Cao Bu holy woman of Burma; 1393-1468

Miao-Hsin female Chinese Ch'an master; *Commentary on the Wind and Flag Koan*

Miao Shan Chinese princess identified with Kuan Yin; -7th c.

miasm nonphysical agency that produces disease by blocking the life energy (Hahnemann)

Michael 'who is like God', archangel on the right hand of God, guardian of Israel (Hebrew)

Michelangelo Buonarroti Florentine sculptor, painter, poet; *Pieta*; 1475-1564

Michelson-Morley experiment physics experiment showing that the speed of light traveling in the direction of the Earth's rotation is the same as that of light traveling at right angles to the Earth's orbit

microcosm order of the individual

microcosmic orbit energy path consisting of the loop formed by the governing and conception vessels in Taoist philosphy and medicine

microenterprise development lending money to people in Third World countries to start businesses, feed their families, and develop independence and self-esteem

microorganism one of the less underrepresented forms of life (Lovelock)

Middle Earth main continent and setting of *Lord of the Rings*

Middle Way (madhyama-pratipad, *Sanskrit*) path between indulgence and asceticism taught by the Buddha

Midgard Earth in Scandinavian myth

midheaven point overhead in the sky, the medium coeli

midpoint 1. point in space exactly midway between two planetary bodies. 2. technique of Cosmobiology

Midsummer Ritual of Caerron Stonehenge festival, June 21

midwife a wise woman or priestess, especially one who assists in the birthing process

Mies van der Rohe, Ludwig architect and originator of the concept 'Less is more'; 1886-1969

Mifune, Toshiro samurai extraordinaire in Japanese films; *The Seven Samurai*; 1920-

Migadaya deer park at Sarnath near where Buddha preached his first sermon and set in motion the Wheel of the Dharma

mihrab niche in a mosque which marks the direction of Mecca (Arabic)

Mikkyo esoteric Buddhism (Japanese)

Mil (Gael) Celts of eastern origin

Milarepa (Milaraspa) Tibetan Buddhist sage, disciple of Marpa, teacher of Gampopa; *The 100,000 Songs*; 1052-1135

Milford Track gorgeous 33-mile hike on South Island, New Zealand

Milky Way 1. the Pollen Path in Lakota mythology. 2. Grains of Isis in Egyptian mythology. 3. the heavenly river separating the herdsman and weaving maiden in Far Eastern mythology. 4. the scar left by run away horses of the Sun Chariot in Greek mythology. 5. thin silver stream of stars in the night sky. 6. home galaxy of the solar system and planet Earth. 7. galactic center which when directly overhead during the precession of the equinox showers natural electromagnetic energy on Earth, energizing plants and human beings, giving a bountiful natural harvest, more highly charged consciousness, and stimulating a Golden Age; the last time this happened was about 20,000 years ago and the next time 10,000 years hence (Michio Kushi)

Millay, Edna St. Vincent New England poet; *Renascence and Other Poems*; 1892-1950

millennium 1. a spiritual condition of one thousand years of peace to be brought about by divine providence. 2. an age of happiness to be brought about by human effort

Millenium Falcon spaceship in *Star Wars*

Miller, Norman Thomas mystical composer; *The Call of Camelot*

millet a small yellow, red, or black grain native to China and Africa and now other parts of the world that can be prepared whole, added to soups, salads, and vegetables dishes or baked

Milne, A. A. British author; *Winnie the-Pooh*; 1882-1956

Milton, John English poet; *Paradise Lost*; 1608-74

miming a spontaneous expression of the capacity of becoming physically and psychically one with the animal (Gary Snyder)

Mimir Norse custodian of the foundation of wisdom

Minamata Japanese fishing and farming town, site of mercury poisoning and strong ecology movement

Minas Tirith capital of Gondor famed for its House of Healing in *Lord of the Rings*

mind 1. discriminating faculty that constantly evaluates, judges, and reasons. 2. awareness whose basic nature is empty, neither pure nor impure. 3. root from which all things grow (Bodhidharma). 4. the watcher. 5. seat of the senses, which must be controlled and mastered to attain enlightenment. 6. types of mind include: angry, calm, clerical, disorderly, doubting, empty, fearful, floating, grasping, greedy, happy, lustful, mistrustful, orderly, original, peaceful, revengeful, spiritual, unruly, and many others

mind blowing adj. psychedelic, shocking, exciting, tumultuous

mind machine machine to stimulate brain wave activity, biofeedback, or a meditative state

Mind Seal nonverbal transmission of authority from a Zen master to student

Mindanao Philippine island noted for a Stone Age tribe, the Tassaday

mindfulness 1. awareness of each moment; paying attention without preconceptions, judgment, or evaluation. 2. Buddhist meditation technique to develop such awareness

Minerva Roman Goddess of Wisdom who filled the sails of the heavenly ship as Dante and Beatrice ascended to the sphere of the Moon

ming 1. fate, will of Heaven. 2. (cap.) 'brilliant', Chinese dynasty 1368-1644 (Chinese)

mini-blackhole bubble that constantly

appears, disappears in the geometry of space. **mini-whitehole** antiparticle to the mini-blackhole

minimum-impact adj. camping or visiting sites, treating the land respectfully, and not leaving any trace of your visit

Ministry of Truth department that rewrote all books and refashioned all ideas in *1984*

Minor Arcana 56-card section of the Tarot from Aces through Kings

Mira Bai Rajasthani princess, mystic, poetess; *Padavali*; 1498-?1546

miracle a divine intervention in the mind which heals thought patterns (A Course in Miracles)

mi'raj ascension, Muhammad's night journey to Heaven (Arabic)

Miranda heroine of *The Tempest*

mirin a sweet cooking wine made from sweet rice (Japanese)

Mirkwood ancient forest in the north of Middle Earth

Miroku Maitreya (Japanese)

Mirtala New Age musician; *Mandalas: Visions of Heaven and Earth*

Mishna first part of the *Talmud*

Mishong Crow Clan leader who brought his followers to Hopi from the San Francisco peaks; ca. 1200

Mishongnovi Hopi village, founded in the 12th century, where the Snake Dance is held in odd-numbered years

Mislimov, Shirali (Baba) Transcaucasian farmer, world's oldest documented living person, whose wife of 102 years survived him; 1805-1973

miso a fermented paste with a sweet taste and salty flavor made from soybeans, sea salt, and usually rice or barley, used in macrobiotic cooking for soups, stews, spreads, baking, and as a seasoning (Japanese)

missing time amnesic fog liftable only by hypnosis following a purported UFO abduction

Misty Mountains mountain range in Middle Earth

Mitchell, Edgar D. astronaut, moonwalker, founder of the Institute of Noetic Sciences; 1930-

Mitchell, Joni Canadian musician; *Both Sides Now*; 1943-

Mithras 1. ancient Persian God of Light and Truth. 2. deity worshiped by Utopians in More's novel

mithril true-silver; the prized metal of dwarves in Middle Earth

mitzvah blessing (Hebrew)

Mixolydian *fa*-musical mode: Moon, meloncholy (Greek)

Miyako ancient Kyoto, capital of Japan, 794-1868

MLD Manual Lymph Drainage; a massage therapy to boost immune response and rejuvenate body tissues

Mm 14th Hebrew letter: son, N, 50

mmoatia little people of the forest (Yoruba)

Mnajdra mysterious megalithic ruins in Malta

Mo Shan female Chinese Ch'an master; late T'ang

moai small wooden statue of Easter Island

Moby Dick great white whale in Melville's novel of the same name

mochi a cake or dumpling made from cooked, pounded sweet rice and a favorite snack in macrobiotic cooking (Japanese)

Modern Utopia title of H. G. Wells's ideal commonwealth, notable for use of money to guarantee freedom, 1905

Modred treacherous nephew of King Arthur

Mogen David Star of David, two overlaid equilateral triangles (Hebrew)

Moggallana (Maudgalyayana) close disciple of Buddha

Mogollon prehistoric Southwestern people known for stone masonry and adobe architecture

Mohaves (Aha-makave) 'beside the water', people in Arizona and California speaking a Shoshonean language

moha 'delusion', one of Buddhism's three cardinal roots of imbalance (Sanskrit)

Mohawk 1. people originally from the Mohawk Valley, now in St. Regis, N.Y., and parts of Ontario and Quebec. 2. their Iroquoian language

Mohenjodara 'City of the Dead', pre-Aryan North Indian site, 400 miles from Karachi; site of a high culture that flourished at the time of Harappa, ca. -2500

mokugyo musical wooden percussion instrument shaped like a sphere and carved in the likeness of a fish, representing every-minute awareness (Japanese)

Molay, Jacobus last Grand Master of the Templars; 14th c.

moldavite a rare green tektite that fell to

Earth 14.8 million years ago

moly magic herb given to Odysseus by Hermes to resist Circe

Momaday, N. Scott Native American writer and poet; *The Way of Rainy Mountain*

Momoyama Japanese era 1573-1614

monad unit of force comprised of an active and passive components that does not manifest in the phenomenal world but exists inside actualized manifestation as potential; likened to a series of clocks that manage to keep time without being connected (Leibniz). adj. **monadic**

Mond, Mustapha World Controller in Huxley's *Brave New World*

Monday Night Class communion class taught in San Francisco by Stephen Gaskin

mondo 'question and answer', Zen spiritual exchange likened to two arrows in mid-air that meet (Japanese)

Mongol Persian period 1256-1353

Monkey restless genius of the Chinese epic *Journey to the West*

Monks Mound largest earthwork in the Western hemisphere in Cahokia; 800-1500

Monlam prayer festival afer the Tibetan New Year in February

Monophysite 'one nature', Copt who believes solely in Jesus's divine nature

monopole hypothesized subatomic particle that is the basic unit of magnetism

monosaccharide simple sugar such as glucose, fructose, or galactose that enters the bloodstream rapidly and may lead to imbalance

Monroe, Robert A. consciousness researcher; *Journeys Out of the Body*

Montague, Ashley anthropologist; *The Natural Superiority of Women*; 1905-

Montanism (New Prophecy) Christian movement stressing ecstasy and asceticism founded by Montanus, 2-9th c.

Monte Abiegno mystic mountain in Rosicrucianism, source of its texts

Monte Alban Zapotec city

Monte, Thomas macrobiotic author and teacher; *Recalled by Life*; 1950-

monthly number number in numerology secured by adding the destiny number to the digit of any month and year

Montsalvat mountain of salvation in the Grail legends

Montsegur Cathar mountain citadel associated with the Grail quest

Montserrat Spanish town whose 9th c. monastery is said to house the Holy Grail

Monument Valley Navajo region in Arizona and New Mexico; site of mesas, buttes, natural bridges, earthworks, canyons, gorges

Moody Blues English rock group; On the *Threshold of a Dream*; 1960s

Moody, Raymond, M.D. investigator of near-death experiences; *Life After Life*

Moon 1. heavenly body orbiting a planet, especially the Earth's, signifying soul, fruitfulness, mother, magnetic energy. 2. mandala figure of the Peyote cult. 3. Tarot #18: danger, enemies. 4. symbol of consciousness in time (Campbell)

Moon country a land whose symbol or flag is traditionally the Moon, especially in the Middle East and South Asia, where flour and grains are eaten, where a mystical and metaphysical way of thinking developed, and which will 'conquer' the world spiritually through the spread of religious teachings (Michio Kushi)

moontime menstrual period

Moor Moslem of mixed Arab and Berber descent living in northwest Africa or Spain in the Middle Ages. adj. **Moresque**

Moore, William mailman, civil rights pilgrim; 1927-63

mooring hole hole chiefly in Great Lakes regions on boulders near waterways, possibly left by Vikings to moor their ships

Moosewood Restaurant vegetarian natural foods restaurant in Ithaca, N.Y., 1972-

morality bringing wisdom back out in the way you live, through personal example and responsible action, ultimately toward the true community of all beings (Gary Snyder)

Mordor dark land in Middle Earth where the shadows lie

More, Sir Thomas English author, cleric, visionary; *Utopia*; 1477-1535

Moreno, J. L. founder of group therapy and psycho-drama; *Who Shall Survive?*; 1892-

Morgan, Juliette librarian who compared the Montgomery Bus Boycott with the Gandhian movement in India and influenced Martin Luther King, Jr. and the civil rights movement to adopt a nonviolent philosophy; 1914-57

Morgan le Fay 1. Irish goddess. 2. sister of King Arthur. 3. heroine in Dion Fortune's *The Sea Princess*

Morgan, Lewis Henry New York lawyer, defender of the Iroquois; *Ancient Society*; 19th c.

Morgan, Robin women's activist and pioneer radical feminist; *Sisterhood Is Powerful*

Moria greatest dwarf dwellings in Middle Earth

Moriarty, Dean hero of Kerouac's *On the Road*

Moriarty, Professor James mathematician whose face oscillated from side to side in a curiously reptilian manner; the Napoleon of Crime, Sherlock Holmes' archrival; *Treatise on the Binomiall Theorem*; 1852-?94

Morinus astrological house system based on equal division of the equator by hour circles

Mormon 'More Good', last chief of the Nephites who engraved the Golden Plates, which his son Moroni finished for Joseph Smith

Morning Star Ranch hippie commune in Sonoma County, Calif., founded by Lou Gotlieb, 1966; branch in Taos, N.M., 1967-

Moroni Nephite historian who buried the records of the Ten Lost Tribes near present Manchester, N.Y., in 421

Morpheus Greek God of Dreams, son of the God of Sleep

morphogenetic field a subtle patterning field generated by a natural system that organizes subsequent similar systems

Morris English version of Moorish dance

Morris, William English author; *News from Nowhere*; 1834-96

Morton, Julius Sterling founder of Arbor Day; 1832-1902

Morton, Thomas New England poet who set up the Maypole at Mare Mount; *New English Canaan*; d. 1647

Morya transneptunian planet postulated by Sutcliffe and Hodson

Moses (Hosarsiph) Biblical prophet who led the Israelites out of slavery in Egypt to the Promised Land and received the Ten Commandments; ca. -1300

Moses, Bob (Bob Parris) taciturn civil rights organizer; 1944-

Moses de Leon compiler of the *Zohar*; 1250-1305

Moses, W. Stainton medium; *Spirit Teachings*; 1839-92

moshav Israeli commune with private dwellings

Moslem (Muslim) follower of Islam

moth intimate friend and helper of Mexican sorcerers since time immemorial; symbol of knowledge (don Juan)

mother 1. Tao. 2. (cap.) (Mira Alfassa) spiritual teacher, associate of Aurobindo; *White Roses*; 1878-1973

Mother Goddess 1. natural mother of all things, mistress and governess of all the elements, the initial progeny of worlds, chief of the powers divine, queen of all that are in hell, the principal of them that dwell in heaven, manifested alone and under one form of all the gods and goddesses, at whose will the planets of the sky, the wholesome winds of the seas, and the lamentable silences of hell are dispersed (Isis). 2. archetypal feminine aspect of the Godhead. 3. mediatrix, creator of forms, the celestial energy that gives birth to the world and all beings. 4. Mother Earth, Mother Nature. 5. space, the void, field of consciousness. 6. time, who devours all her children. 7. Tao, way of gentle turning back (Lao-tzu)

Ala	Ibo
Amaterasu-omi-kami	Shinto
Anoba	Gaelic
Aphrodite	Cypriot
Asasa Ya	Yoruba
Astarte	Phoenician
Athena	Greek
Bellona	Roman
Benten	Japanese
Brigid	Celtic
Ceres	Eleusinian
Ceridwan	Celtic
Chicomecoatl	Nahuatl
Chomo Lhari	Bhutanese
Coatlicue	Nahuatl
Cybele	Phrygian
Danu	Druidic
Demeter	Greek
Devi Sri	Balinese
Diana	Cretan
Estanatlehi	Navajo
Fortuna	Roman
Freya	Scandinavian
Frigg	Scandinavian
Gaia	Greek
Hathor	Egyptian
Hecate	Greek
Hel	Norse
Ilamatecuhtli	Aztec
Isis	Egyptian

Ishtar.....................................Babylonian
Ixchel ....Mayan
Jord .... Norse
Juno .... Roman
Kali ....Indian
Kuan Yin ....Chinese
Lakshmi ....Indian
Lilith.. Hebrew
Luna ....Roman
Magna Mater...............................Latin
Mary ....Christian
Mawu ....Dahomean
Mayahuel .... Nahuatl
Minerva ....Greek
Morgan Le Fay ....Irish
Nut...Egyptian
Ostara....................................Germanic
Pachamama .... Incan
Persephone ....Greek
Pi-hsia Yuan-chun.....................Taoist
Rangda .... Balinese
Sagarmathe .... Himalayan
Saraswati .... Indian
Sophia .... Gnostic
Tara .... Tibetan
Taurt .... Paleolithic
Tlazolteotl .... Aztec
Venus .... Roman
Venus of Willendorf ....Neolithic
Venus of Menton .... Neolithic
Venus of Lespugue .... Neolithic
Venus of Lanssel ....Neolithic
White Goddess ....Druidic

Mother Jones (Mary Harris) Irish-born union organizer; 1830-1930

Mother of the Book (Umm al-Kitab, *Arabic*) *Qur'anic* term for the heavenly archetype from which divine scriptures are derived (Arabic)

Mother-Right n. or adj. matrilineal, Mother-Goddess oriented

mother ship large UFO from which smaller craft emerge and return

Mott, Lucretia Quaker minister, co-founder of the women's rights movement; *Discourse on Women*; 1793-1880

Mou-Shin diagnosis by listening to the sound and tonal quality of a person's voice (Chinese)

mound 1. megalithic site in Europe associated with the pregnant belly of the Mother Goddess. 2. Native earthwork of the Mississippi Valley and Southeast

Mouni Sadhu German-born disciple of Sri Ramana Maharshi; *The Tarot*

mount one of seven slightly raised portions of the palm: Jupiter (base of index finger), Apollo (ring), Mercury (little),

Saturn (middle), Venus (thumb), Moon (side opposite thumb), Mars (between Mercury and Moon)

Mount Analogue spiritual island continent in the South Pacific with a mountain of the same name in Rene Daumal's novel *Le Mont Analogue*, 1952

Mount Baldy Zen Center Buddhist community located in the San Gabriel Mountains under the guidance of Joshu Sasaki-Roshi, 1971-

Mount Cuchama (Mt. Tecati) mountain on the California-Mexican border associated with Aztec myth and legend

Mount Doom site where Frodo took the One Ring

Mount Madonna Center a mountaintop community founded by Baba Hari Dass, overlooking Santa Cruz, 1974-

Mount Shasta sacred California mountain known by Native Americans as Wyeka, 'Great White'; 14,162 feet high

Mountain Ark macrobiotic trading company in Fayetteville, Ark., 1982-

mountaineering mystical mind-body practice of moving on a vertical plane in a realm that is totally inhospitable to human beings (Gary Snyder)

Mountains and Rivers Sutra essay by Dogen on the depths of consciousness to be learned from nature

Mounte Sainte-Odile Alsacian town, home of visionary healer St. Odile and retreat of Treverezent, teacher of Grail wisdom

mouth place of freedom where spirit and body meet through breathing, chanting, eating, drinking, silence, and expression; the key point in life, uniting spiritual and physical structures (Michio Kushi)

Movement the wave of individual and social activity devoted to achieving a more peaceful and just society, 1960s-

Movement of Spiritual Inner Awareness consciousness group led by John-Roger Hinkins in Rosemead, Ca., 1960s-

moving line line that changes into its opposite in the *I Ching*

Mowat, Farley Canadian wilderness writer; *Never Cry Wolf*; 1921-

moxa 1. dried mugwort preparation placed on the skin and burned to stimulate energy in the meridians. 2. liberation (Japanese)

moxibustion traditional Far Eastern healing technique of burning an herb on the skin

Mozart, Wolfgang Salzburg composer; *The Magic Flute*; 1756-91

Ms. feminine title: Miss, Mrs.

mu 1. 'nothing', immaculacy, Buddha Mind; usually referring to Joshu's reply to a koan 'Has a dog the Buddha Nature?' (Japanese). 2. herbal tea made of ginseng and various herbs (Japanese). 3. water (ancient Egyptian). 4. (cap.) lost continent in the Pacific, believed wiped out by a cataclysm ca. -9,500 (from Bishop Diego de Landa's alphabet, of two symbols for *M* and *U* as deciphered by Brasseur from a Mayan text in 1864). adj. **Muvian**

mu tea a tea made from a variety of herbs that warms the body, strengthens the female organs, and has other medicinal properties (George Ohsawa)

Mu-Kyoku 'non-polarization,' One Infinity (Japanese)

Mucalinda serpent-king who shielded Buddha with his hood during a storm following enlightenment

mudhif Near Eastern reed architecture, often of cathedral appearance

mudita delight in the happiness of others (Pali)

mudra 1. gesture that expresses or encourages different attitudes of mind, e.g. compassion (Buddhism). 2. gesture producing psychic responses in Hinduism. 3. third M in the tantra, aphrodisiac. 4. sinuous hand movement in dance (Sanskrit)

Mueller, Gottfried German spy who became a vegetarian in a World War II prisoner of war camp and vowed to devote his life to others if spared; founder of Salem Childrens' villages

Muesli natural breakfast cereal invented by Bircher in Switzerland

Muessa Muhammad's cat who slept in his sleeve and awakened him at prayer time

MUFON Mutual UFO Network group investigating UFOs and extraterrestrial contact

Mughal (Moghal) 1. Indian era from 1530-1658 dominated by Moslem influence. 2. school of Indian miniature painting 1526-1717

mugi cha roasted barley tea (Japanese)

mugi miso (barley miso) fermented soybean paste made from barley, soybeans, sea salt, and water favored for daily miso soup in macrobiotic cooking (Jap-

anese)

mugwort a wild plant that can be dried and made into a tea, used in cooking, or prepared into moxa

Muhammad (Mohammed, Mahomet) Arab peacemaker, mystic, founder of Islam; 570-632

Muhammad Ali (Cassius Clay) boxer, poet, conscientious war objector; 1942-

Muhammad the Horse horse who could extract cube roots and tap answers with its feet in Elberfield, Germany, 19th c.

Muia the Hopi's original home, an island in the Pacific which their ancestors left following a natural disaster

Mu'inu-d-Din Chisti Sanjari Ajmeri Sufi who introduced the Chisti Order into India; ca. 1142-1236

Muir, John Scottish-born naturalist who arrived at his glacial theory by lying down on glacial polished granite in order to think like a glacier; founder of the Sierra Club; *Our National Parks*; 1838-1914

Muktananda, Swami Indian spiritual teacher; *Guru*; 1908-82

muladhara first chakra at the base of the spine (Sanskrit)

Muller, Friedrich Max German Indologist; *Sacred Books of the East*; 1823-1900

Muller, Robert United Nations administrator and social theorist; *Global Spirituality*; 1923-

Mulligatawny 'pepper-water', Indian soup (from Tamil)

multiverse universe with many dimensions beyond the familiar framework of space time

Mum, Mr. health-bar freak in the comics

Mumford, Lewis cultural historian and architect; *The City in History*; 1895-1990

Mumonkan 'The Gateless Barrier', book of 48 koans by Chinese Ch'an master Mumon Ekia (Japanese)

munbano rainbow, hem of the Sun God's coat (Samoyed)

Munchkin 1. country in Oz where a tornado set down Dorothy Gale's house. 2. an inhabitant of Oz who looks like a child, dresses in blue, and wears a round hat with bells around the brim (Baum)

mundane astrology study of current and future events

Mungo, Raymond founder of Liberation News Service; *Cosmic Profit*; 1946-

muni (mouni) 1. one following silence as a discipline. 2. Jain monk (Sanskrit)

municipal foreign policy movement where cities and towns send lobbyists to the national capital, set their own international trade policy, and monitor human rights abuses

Munster German communal movement led by Anabaptist John Leider, 1534

Muntzer, Thomas German radical Protestant reformer, leader of the Peasants' Revolt; d. 1525

Muramoto, Noboru Japanese-born macrobiotic teacher and food producer; *Healing Ourselves*

muraqaba (murakkaba) meditation, self-observation (Arabic)

Murasaki, Lady Shikibu Japanese author; *The Tale of Genji*; 975-1025

Muridiyya black Sufi order founded by Ahmad Bamba with central mosque at Touba, Senegal

Muromachi Japanese era 1333-1573

Murphy, Bridey past reincarnation of Ruth Simmons brought out in Colorado housewife Virginia Tighe under hynosis by Morey Bernstein; in 1952; 1798-1864; 1923-

Murphy, Gardner psychologist and psi researcher; *The Challenge of Psychical Research*; 1895-1979

Murray, Judith Sargent English feminist; 1751-1820

murshid (morshed) 'guide', Sufi master. (f.) **murshida** (Arabic)

Musa, Mansa Kankan Mali monarch, pilgrim to Mecca from Timbuktu; d. 1332

Musashi, Miyamoto Japanese samurai, poet; *A Book of Five Rings*; d. 1645

Musawarat es Safra palace and temple ruin near Meroe

muscular armor sum total of the muscular attitude that an individual develops as a block against the breakthrough of emotional and organ sensations (Reich)

Muses, Charles Swiss consciousness researcher; *Illuminations on Jacob Boehme*; 1919-

Museum of the Machines place in Erewhon where technology and mechanical inventions are kept as they are considered counterproductive to society

mushin state of no-mind in Zen (Japanese)

music 1. perfection of sound arising when the world is at peace, when all things are at rest, and when all obey their su-periors through all life's changes (*Spring and Autumn Annals*). 2. temporal sound flow or rhythm, alternating between high and low notes, mounting and descending, soft and hard, smooth and rough shadings, working together as one pattern

music of the spheres celestial vibrations; Pythagorean theory of correspondences between planets and the musical scale

music therapist one who makes contact with the patient through music and guides towards a freeing of the emotions

music therapy use of music to heal and elevate consciousness like David, Apollo, Aesculapius

Musical Banks vaults where the people of Erewhon trade in currency

musician one who is able to produce within audible sound a music in harmony with celestial order

mustafa chosen one; Muhammad (Arabic)

mustard seed grain associated with faith in Christian and Buddhist parables

Muste, A. J. Dutch-born clergyman, peace organizer; *Of Holy Disobedience*; 1875-1967

mutable signs Gemini, Virgo, Sagittarius, Pisces, expressive of conciliating and restless energy

Mutanabbi, al Ahmad Ibn al-Husain Arabic poet and wanderer; 915-65

mutma'inna tranquil; state of the soul that has found peace (Arabic)

mutual reception planets in each other's signs

MWI Many Worlds Interpretation of quantum mechanics in which the universe can be viewed as constantly branching through alternate realities (Hugh Everett and John Wheeler, 1957)

Mxyzptlk, Mr. adversary from the fifth dimension who Superman tricks into saying his name backwards

My Lai (Song My) Vietnamese village, site of a massacre of men, women, and children by U.S. troops, 1968

Mycenaean dagger mysterious carved dagger on a stone at Stonehenge

Myers, Frederick English classicist, founder of the Society for Psychical Research; *Phantasms of the Living*; 1843-1901

Mygatt, Tracy founder of the War Resisters League; *Stranger on the Earth*; 1886-1974

Myshkin, Prince Christlike hero of Dostoevski's *The Idiot*

Mysteries ancient Greek cults practicing rebirth ceremonies and teachings of purity and righteousness; associated with Demeter, Dionysus, Kore, Orpheus (from a Greek translation of the Egyptian *hrysst* 'he who is over the secrets', i.e. Anubis)

Mystery Hill (Pattee's Caves, America's Stonehenge) cluster of 22 small dry-walled structures, including some set in sky alignments, in North Salem, N.H., of megalithic origin, ca. -2500

mystic n. or adj. 1. one who has experienced God directly. 2. believer in intuitive knowledge of God, especially through contemplation. adj. **mystical**

Mystic Cross Kabbalistic pentacle with four arms with three circular convexities on each end

Mystic Rose supreme state where Dante and Beatrice behold the heavenly souls appearing like a white rose in the eternal springtime of the radiance of God

Mystical Traveler spirit that exists simultaneously on all levels of consciousness in total awareness and can teach individuals who request its assistance and free themselves from reincarnation (John-Roger Hinkins)

mysticism 1. communication that God makes of his or her spiritual light to the depths of the human heart (Dhu'n-Nun Misri). 2. the art and science of establishing conscious relation with the absolute (Evelyn Underhill). 3. states characterized by ineffability, that is, they defy expression, and a noetic quality, that is apparent states of knowledge (William James). 4. feeling of union with all life. 5. awareness of a dazzling light that fills the mind and heart. 6. experience of being bathed in emotions of joy, awe, wonder. 7. intuitive flashes of awareness and understanding of the universe. 8. merging with the creation, creator, nature. 9. feeling of transcendental love and compassion for all living things. 10. renewed sense of energy and vitality and health. 11. sudden vanishing of suffering and fear of death. 12. enhanced appreciation of art and beauty and less attachment to material things. 13. appearance of ESP and enhanced intellect, gifts, and powers. 14. renewed sense of purpose and mission in life. 15. change in personality and inner and outer radiance

myth 1. traditional story of gods, goddesses, or epic heros and heroines illustrating spiritual and psychological truths, or historical, social, or natural developments. 2. symbols that communicate between the psyche and the unconscious. 3. story whose function is a) to awaken and maintain in the individual a sense of wonder and participation in the mystery of the universe. b) to fill every particle and quarter of the current cosmological image with its measure of this mystical import. c) to validate and maintain whatever moral system and manner of life-customs may be peculiar to the local culture. d) to conduct individuals in harmony through the passages of human life, from childhood to maturity to old age and death (Joseph Campbell). 3. allegories for inner processes of spiritual transformation; stories that are symbolically but never factually true tales of the world which resemble each other as dialects of a single language (Joseph Campbell). 4. a public dream in contrast to dream which is a private myth (Joseph Campbell). 5. the common language of humanity concentrated on numbers, motions, measures, overall frames, schemas, structures, geometry, and ciphers for celestial activity, a language for the perpetuation of complex astronomical data; a preliterate form of science through which culture, especially astronomy, was transmitted (Santillana and Duchend). 6. sacred system of musicology ground on a protoscience of number and tone (Ernest McClain) (from *Latin*)

mythographer myth maker

mythology organization of insights made known by way of works of visual art and verbal narration (scriptural or oral) and applied to communal life by a calendar of symbolic rites, festivals and manners, social classification, pedagogic initiation, and ceremonies of investiture, by virtue of which the community is itself mythologized (Campbell)

mythogenic adj. relating to archetypal vision, growth, or development

mythologize v. to become metaphorical of transcendence, participating with the universe in eternity (Campbell)

Mytyl woodcutter's daughter and seeker of happiness in *The Blue Bird*

Nn

naan flat white bread (Hindi)

nabe a traditional one-dish meal prepared and served in colorful casserole dishes and accompanied with a dipping sauce or broth made of tamari soy sauce or miso and various garnishes (Japanese)

nabi (pl. anbiya) prophet (Arabic)

Nachiketa seeker and questioner of Death in the *Katha Upanishad*

nada mystic sound; primordial sound behind all creation; inner music (Sanskrit)

Nader, Ralph consumer advocate; *Unsafe at Any Speed*; 1934- . **Naderite** consumer activist

nadi nerve channel (Sanskrit)

Naes, Arne Norwegian ecologist; 1912-

nafl-athbat Sufi meditation of bringing up *La ilaha* from the navel, expelling it with a jerk toward the right shoulder, uttering *illa 'llah* and jerking the head toward the heart to imprint the words on it (Arabic)

nafs experiencing, lower self (Arabic)

Nafzawi, Shaykh Islamic author; *The Perfumed Garden*; 16th c.

Nag Hammadi Egyptian site where thirteen Coptic manuscripts, including the *Gospel of Thomas*, were found in 1945

naga 1. snake of Hindu mythology; semi-divine being who has the power to turn a drop of water into a torrent (Sanskrit). 2. (cap.) member of a predominantly Christian hill tribe in northeast India

Nagarjuna Indian sage, founder of the Madhyamika school of Buddhism; 14th Zen Patriarch; 2nd or 3rd c.

Nagarkot beautiful hiking spot thirteen miles southeast of Katmandu

Nagasaki Japanese city noted for A-Bomb Memorial, Chinese Temple, and Spectacles Bridge

Nagasaki Day August 9, peace observance

nagual part of the self for which there is no description (don Juan)

Nahash astral serpent of the Kabbalah (Hebrew)

Nahua 'one who speaks with authority', linguistic group of pre-Aztec Mexico

Nahuatl language of pre-Conquest Mexico adopted by the Aztecs and still the most spoken Indian language today; originally pictographic, now utilizing a Roman script

naisan visiting a Zen master secretly any time of day or night (Japanese)

Nakayama, Miki Japanese founder of Tenrikyo; 1798-1887

nakshatras twenty-eight stars or lunar mansions of Hindu astrology (Sanskrit)

Nalanda ancient Indian city near Bodh Gaya, site of a Buddhist university, 2-9th c.

nam 'name', word of God, spiritual sound current (Hindi, Punjabi)

Nam Kha old Vietnamese Taoist whose cooked millet sent Lu Suih into a long dream about the vanity of life

Nam Myoho Renge Kyo Infinite Miraculous Law of the Lotus Flower Sutra; Buddhist chant and prayer, especially among the Nichiren sects (Japanese)

namaste (namaskarum) greeting with palms joined together and a slight bow of the head, symbolizing recognition of the divine within (Sanskrit)

name number number in numerology secured by transferring the letters in a person's name to numbers

Nana St. Bernard nurse in *Peter Pan*

Nanabozho trickster and culture-bearer of the Algonquians

Nanak, Guru Indian teacher, founder of the Sikh Dharma; first of ten gurus; 1469-1539

Nandi 'happy', one of Shiva's devotees and his mount in the form of a bull chosen to contain his ecstatic devotion

nanotechnology split-second technology, especially computer technology

Naqshbandi Sufi order noted for kindness to animals founded by Muhammad Naqshband, 14th c.

nara 1. man (Sanskrit). 2. (cap.) Japanese city noted for a Deer Park and Great Buddha. 3. (cap.) Japanese era 710-94

Nara Sinha 'man-lion', early avatar of Vishnu (Sanskrit)

Naranjo, Claudio psychologist, consciousness researcher; *The Healing Journey*

Narayan, Jayaprakash Indian statesman, Sarvodaya leader; 1902-79

narayana one who pervades all things; sleeper on the waters; Vishnu (Sanskrit)

Naropa Bengali Buddhist, disciple of Tilopa, teacher of Marpa; 1016-1100

Naropa Institute Tibetan Buddhist educational center in Boulder, Co., founded by Trungpa, 1974-

nasip 'portion' the share of spiritual wealth one stands to inherit from one's spiritual line (Turkish)

Nashoba community of freed slaves founded by Frances Wright in Tennessee, 1826-28

Nasrudin, Mulla humorous character in Sufi teaching stories

natal astrology study of individual birth charts

Nataraja Lord of the Dance, Shiva

Nathan, Abie Middle East peace activist who operates the Peace Ship off Israel and Egypt; 1926-

nation imaginary political or geographical state that does not exist in nature

National Center for Appropriate Technology renewable energy sources and appropriate technologies clearinghouse, Butte, Montana

National Gay Pride Day June 27

National Public Radio listener-supported radio

Native American Church peyote cult formalized in 1941

nativity 1. birth of Jesus. 2. birth chart

Natsume, Soseki Japanese zenic novelist; *I Am a Cat*; 1867-1926

natto a sticky dish with long strands and a strong odor made from soybeans that have been cooked and mixed with beneficial enzymes and fermented for 24 hours (Japanese)

natto miso a spicy condiment made from shortly fermented soybeans, grain, ginger, and kombu (Japanese)

Natura Naturans 'nature which creates nature', absolute (Spinoza, *Latin*)

natural n. or adj. 1. ecological, environmentally based, sustainable, organic. 2. open, honest, humble, simple, lacking in self-consciousness or sophistication. 3. unpredictable, unprogrammable, nonstandardized. 4. liberated. 5. counter to synthetic, artificial, mechanical

natural agriculture 1. the return to a more natural and wild state of food production based on principles of non-weeding, non-tilling, non-fertilizing, non-spraying, non-seeding, and non-pruning. 2. original agriculture practiced in the ancient world before domestication of plants. 3. farming philosophy taught by Masanobu Fukuoka

natural astrology study of earthquakes, tidal waves, and other climatic and environmental influences

natural foods whole foods; foods grown or processed with a minimum of refining, additives, preservatives, hormones, chemical fertilizers, or pesticides; often but not necessarily organic

natural farming traditional way of agriculture which avoids planting, weeding, and plowing in favor of peaceful, gentle methods such as softening the soil, scattering many seeds together and allowing many species to grow, playing music and singing songs to the growing plants, picking up the harvest after it grows by itself, and leaving about 20% of the seeds to come up naturally the next year (Michio Kushi)

Natural Gourmet Cookery School whole foods and wellness center in New York City founded by Annemarie Colbin

natural living living harmoniously with other beings by not exploiting or harming them for civilized comforts

natural medicine any therapy that stimulate's one's own healing powers; that places responsibility upon oneself rather than the doctor, healer, or any exterior source; that utilizes nontechnological means and medicine

nature ('self-thus', *Chinese*) a living system that is not programmed, generating its own rules from within (Gary Snyder)

Nature Conservancy environmental organization based in Chicago that buys parcels of undeveloped land for preservation

nature religion a symbolic center and the cluster of beliefs, behaviors, and values that encircles it based on wilderness identification as well as a passionate concern for place and mastery in society (Catharine Albanese)

naturopathy science of treating sickness through natural remedies, e.g., air, sunshine, saunas, as opposed to drugs or medication

natya dance (Sanskrit)

Naui-Atl 'Four Water', fourth world in Nahuatl myth destroyed by a deluge, survived by a single couple

Naui-Eecatl 'Four Wind', second world of Nahuatl myth destroyed by a tempest

Naui-Ocelotl 'Four Jaguar', first world of Nahuatl myth destroyed by wild beasts

Naui-Ollin 'Four Movement', current and fifth world age in Nahuatl myth symbolized in the center of the Aztec Calendar

Naui-Quiauitl 'Four Rain', third world of Nahuatl myth destroyed by rain

Navajo 100,000 people in Navajo, Canoncito, Puertocito, and Ramah in the Southwest who call themselves Dine, 'The People', and speak an Athapaskan language (from the Tewa word for cultivated fields)

Nazarite 'separated, consecrated', Israeli ascetic at the time of Jesus noted for long hair, abstention from alcohol and other foods (Hebrew)

Nazca Peruvian site of huge animals drawn on the sand whose contours and intersecting lines are visible only from the air

Nazorean 1. original Jewish follower of Jesus. 2. (pl.) name the Mandaeans call themselves today

NDE near death experience; powerful experience, often following an accident or sickness, in which the journeyer approaches a bright light through a long tunnel in which spirits float and enters a world of light, love, and bliss; the person is often suffused with a sense of peace, love, and innocence that lasts long after the immediate experience

Neak Pean 'coiled serpent', small chapel of Avalokiteshvara in a pool at Ankor Wat (Khmer)

Nearing, Helen natural philosopher; *Living the Good Life*; 1904-

Nearing, Scott socialist, radical reformer, and organic farmer; *Living the Good Life*; 1883-1983

nectar meditation curling the tongue around and back in the esophagus to taste the divine dew within

Needleman, Jacob author and theologian; *A Sense of the Cosmos*

Neferiti Egyptian queen, wife of Ikhnaton; -14th c.

nefesh animal soul in humans in the Kabbalah (Hebrew)

Nefilim 1. mysterious people who interbred with the daughters of men in the Bible. 2. a superior race from the planet Marduk who seeded the human race (Zecharia Sitchin)

negentropy (negative entrophy) 1.

showing no similarity or identity in psychical research experiments. 2. measure of how organized a natural community is, how much it is structured, how much energy is trapped for use

negredo alchemist term for darkness (Latin)

Nei Ching (*Book of the Yellow Ancestor* or *Yellow Emperor's Classic of Internal Medicine*) world's oldest medical text; foundation of Far Eastern medicine, describing yin and yang and the five transformations; dating back 5000 years, with oldest extant copy to the -2nd c.

Neil, A. S. British educator, founder of Summerhill; *Neill! Neilli Orange Peel!*; 1885-1974

Nelissen, Adelbert Dutch macrobiotic teacher and counselor

Nelson, Gaylord senator, environmentalist, founder of Earth Day

nembutsu 'to think on Buddha', repetition of the Buddha's name; used instead of sitting meditation as a form of concentrated prayer and expression of eternal gratitude (Japanese)

Nemo, Captain captain of the Nautilus in Verne's *20,000 Leagues Under the Sea*

neoagrarian one who believes in agriculture or farming values as the foundation for modern society

neocatastrophism school of science that believes in evidence of global cataclysms, especially in respect to extinction of the dinosaurs, the onset of the Ice Ages, and events in the Bible or Plato's account of a lost continent

neolithic last period of the Stone Age when animals were domesticated and simple agriculture developed

neopaganism movement devoted to nature worship, polytheism, Goddess worship, ancient tribal religions

neoplatonism syncretistic mystical philosophy teaching emanations radiating through the universe from the ultimate One, 2nd c.

neo-Reichian self-actualization movement based on the methods of Wilhelm Reich

Nepal small independent Himalayan kingdom whose seven million people are about half Buddhist and half Hindu

Nephesh ghost, phantom in the Kabbalah (Hebrew)

Nephite member of a lost Hebrew tribe defeated by the Lamanites (Joseph Smith)

Nephthys wife of Set, sister of Osiris and Isis in Egyptian mythology

Neptune 1. Roman God of the Sea. 2. planet ruling dreams, the psychic, mellow energy

neshamah angelic aspect of the soul in the Kabbalah (Hebrew)

nest 1. paradisical community in Heinlein's *Stranger in a Strange Land* and the Church of All Worlds. 2. a coven

Nestorian Christian believing in two separate Christs (historical and divine), rejecting the Virgin Mary; as a group the Nestorians were driven out of Asia Minor and brought to China by Syrian monk A-lo-pen in 635 and greatly influenced the Mongols of the Yuan Dynasty (from Nestorius, Bishop of Constantinople)

neter (pl. neteru) holy, sacred, god, principle (Egyptian)

neti not this; repeated twice or more symbolizing reasoning negatively to arrive at eternal truth (Sanskrit)

networking v. to communicate actively with others, sharing information, contacts, experiences, insights, etc. that contribute to the benefit of the whole. n. **network**

Netzah sephiroth of victory and justice in the Kabbalah (Hebrew)

Neumann, Erich psychologist; *The Great Mother*; 1905-60

Neurolinguistic Programming (NLP) a psychology of communications which recognizes the link between linguistics and physiology understanding such factors as tone of voice, pitch, body posture, eye movements (neurolinguistic coined by Korzybski)

neurologic n. wisdom built into the functioning of the nervous system (Leary)

neuromuscular therapy a form of deep massage combining shiatsu, acupressure, and Western methods (Paul St. John)

neurotoxicity study of the effects of chemicals on the nervous system

neutrino massless subatomic particle belonging to the lepton category

neutron subatomic particle belonging to the baryon category and constituting one of the building blocks of atomic nuclei

Neve Shalom New Age community between Jerusalem and Tel Aviv

Neverland island of pirates, fairies, Indians, lost boys in Barrie's *Peter Pan*

New Age 1. movement of emerging planetary consciousness devoted to making Earth a healthier, happier, and more peaceful place to live based on respect for humanity's diverse traditional ways of life in harmony with the environment. 2. holistic community in general, including practitioners of yoga, meditation, natural foods, spiritual development, humanistic psychology, environmental and peace activism, psychic arts and sciences, and many other approaches and disciplines. 3. Aquarian Age, coming era of peace and spiritual understanding. 4. age of group interplay, group idealism, and group consciousness (Bailey). 5. an added dimension to our daily, ordinary living; a sense of empowerment and enthusiasm arising from the presence of the unexpected in our lives (David Spangler). 6. waking up from our somnambulistic existence, turning the lights on 'inside', and letting go of beliefs that no longer serve us or the planet, dropping fear and letting love fill its place (Swami Virato). 7. a major and unprecedented cultural transformation (Riane Eisler). 8. journal of the utopians of Ham Common, England, 1843. 9. journal of the Guild Socialists, England, 1920s. 10. adj. utopian. n. **new ager** believer in the New Age. n. **New Ageism** phenomenon of the spread of New Age awareness

New Age Fusion type of music combining New Age and Jazz Fusion

New Age Interpreter quarterly founded by Theodore Heline, published in La Canada, Calif., 1939-

New Age Journal holistic magazine published in Boston, 1974-

New Age Music 1. genre or individual composition based on harmony and consonance, rather than dissonance and percussive rhythms, encouraging the integration of the inner and the outer being, offering an audio portrait of world peace (Stephen Halpern). 2. music that actually vibrates the body's psychic energy centers and transforms our awareness (David and Steve Gordon). 3. music characterized by sounds of other dimensions, aural fragrances, radiant liquid pools of sound, shimmering and pulsing, crystal essences that seem like seeds of vast galactic swirls of hidden music taking us beyond ourselves and through ourselves, in which we seem to melt (Stephen Hill)

New Age politics movement for a more conscious, environmentally aware society

New Age Press publishers in La Canada, Calif., devoted to the works of Theodore and Corinne Heline, 1948-

New Alchemy Institute experimental fishpond, solar dome, and windmill station in Falmouth, Mass., started by John Todd and Bill McLarney, 1969-

New Atlantis 1. utopia of Francis Bacon ruled by scientists, 1624. 2. America (Cayce)

New Canaan Massachusetts site of the Maypole where Puritans danced with the Indians

New City city to be destroyed in an earthquake in Nostradamus's verse

New Dimensions pioneer New Age radio program syndicated from San Francisco, 1972-

New England Salem Children's Village vegetarian children's home in Rumney, N.H., 1979-

New Father a man who expresses his male, yang energy and is also developing the more yin, female side of himself (Robert Bly)

New Harmony utopian community in Indiana led by George Rapp and later Robert Owen, 1825-27

New Jerusalem 1. holy city that will appear on Earth as described in *Revelation*. 2. New England as conceived by the Pilgrims. 3. mystical utopia of William Blake

New Lanark industrial utopia founded by Robert Owen near the Fall of Clyde, Scotland

New Lebanon Shaker community in New York, 1787-1947

New Left radical movement devoted to participatory democracy, economic freedom, decentralization of authority, 1960s

New Story the ongoing story of the creation of the universe; a meaningful new cosmology and mythology needed by humanity as it enters the new era (Thomas Berry)

New Thought mind development movement founded by Phineas P.

Quimby, 19th c.

New Vrindavan community of the International Society of Krishna Consciousness in West Virginia

new wave 1. adj. avant-garde, on the cutting edge. 2. (cap.) French cinematic movement of Truffaut, Godard, et. al.

ney Sufi reed flute (Arabic)

Newbrough, John Ballou channel for the *Oahaspe Bible*; b. 1828

Newport Tower controversial small stone structure in Rhode Island said to date to Viking times

News from Nowhere utopian novel by William Morris, 1890

Nezahualcoyotl 'Hungry Coyote', ancient Toltec poet-philosopher

Ngewo Supreme Being of the Mede of Sierra Leone

ngondro foundation practices (Tibetan)

Nguyen Du Vietnamese poet; *Tale of Kieu*; 1765-1820

Nhat Hanh, Thich Vietnamese Zen master, poet, peace activist; *Being Peace*; 1926-

niacin water-soluble vitamin that contributes to the health of the tongue, skin, and other organs and tissues; aids in fat synthesis, carbohydrate utilization, and tissue respiration; protects against pellagra; found in whole grains, beans, vegetables especially shiitake mushrooms and green peas; sea vegetables especially nori and wakame, seeds and nuts

Nibelungenlied 'song of the Nibelungs', 1. Middle High German epic poem, 13th c. 2. Wagner's operatic cycle *The Ring of the Nibelung*

Nicaea, Council of Christian assembly called by Emperor Constantine which edited out all textual references to karma, rebirth, and abstinence from alcohol, flesh foods, and sexual indulgence in the Gospels and substituted a supernatural faith, 325

Nichiren fiery founder of a Japanese Buddhist sect; 1222-82

Nichiren Soshu Japanese Buddhist movement devoted to Nichiren's teachings

Nichols, Mary Gove leader of the Boston Ladies' Physiological Society; 1810-84

Nichols, Thomas Low New York physician and proponent of natural foods; *Eating to Live: The Diet Cure*; 1815-1901

Nicoll, Maurice Scottish author and student of Gurdjieff; *Dream Psychology*; 1884-1953

nidana 'fetter', one of twelve links in the Buddhist chain of dependent origination (Sanskrit)

nidra valuable idea obtained in sleep (Sanskrit)

Niekerk site of Azanian culture in Zimbabwe noted for 50 square miles of intensive terracing

nigari hard crystallized salt made from liquid droppings of dampened sea salt and used in making tofu (Japanese)

nigari sushi small pieces of vegetables or seafood served on top of clumps of rice and wrapped with thin strips of nori (Japanese)

Night Chant 8 1/2-day Navajo healing ceremony

Night of Nights Islamic event when the secret doors of heaven open wide and water in jars becomes sweeter

nigredo disintegration stage in alchemy (Latin)

Nihongi 'chronicles of Japan', Shinto texts (Japanese)

Nikko Japanese city noted for Toshogu Shrine, Sacred Bridge, Rinnoji temple

Nikkyo Japanese disciple of Nichiren who started Nichiren Soshu; 13th c.

Nila-kantha 'blue-throated', epithet of Shiva for drinking poison and saving the world when the gods churned the ocean for nectar (Sanskrit)

Nim a male chimpanzee trained by Herbert Terrace who acquired a 125-word vocabulary after four years

Nin, Anais French-born writer; *Dairies*; 1903-77

1984 1. Orwell's dystopian novel, 1948. 2. time of a Soviet utopian novel by Alexandra Cajanov (Ivan Kremaev) about a peasant waking up in 1984 in a world controlled by five powers, 1920

Nine Star Ki (Kyu Sei Ki-Gaku, *Japanese*) system of Oriental astrology, numerology, directionology, and study of destiny based on a Magic Table of nine basic stages of energy flow; derived from the Later Heaven Diagram of the *I Ching*

1. White Water.Gentle Flowing Energy
2. Black Soil.............Nourishing Energy
3. Emerald Tree...........Budding Energy
4. Green Tree.....Branching Out Energy
5. Yellow Soil............Centering Energy
6. White Metal...........Gathering Energy
7. Red Metal.............Reflecting Energy
8. White Porcelain Soil.Shining Energy
9. Purple Fire.................Active Energy

ninety-minute cycle a normal REM pattern of dreaming that repeats every hour and a half

Ninomiya, Sontoku Japanese farmer and sage; early 19th c.

ninth house segment of the horoscope dealing with travel, the law, philosophy, dreams

nirguna without qualities; attribute of Brahman (Sanskrit)

nirmanakaya 'transformation body', physical Buddha; one's own true body (Sanskrit)

nirodha control of the thought process (Sanskrit)

nirvakalpa highest form of samadhi in which there is no distinction between the knower, the known, and knowledge (Sanskrit)

Nirvana 'to blow out, to extinguish', 1. cessation of attachment to desire and delusion; enlightenment; Buddha mind; state beyond life, death, or rebirth attained through awareness or at death. 2. emptiness; the ultimate aim or state of a Buddha or bodhisattva. 3. a dying out in the heart of passion, hatred, and delusion. 4. samsara: nondualistic perception of the phenomenal world (Sanskrit)

Nirvana Sutra (Mahapari-nirvana sutra, *Sanskrit*) Mahayana text containing Buddha's last words

nishime long, slow style of boiling popular in macrobiotic cooking in which vegetables or other ingredients give strong, peaceful energy; often referred to as 'waterless cooking' since the vegetables cook mostly in their own juices (Japanese)

Niskayuna 'grows good maize', site of the Shakers' original settlement north of Albany, N.Y.

Nisroch Babylonian winged god with long beard and arrows in hand

nitensoji work at a Zen monastery (Japanese)

nitsuke an intermediate style between quick and slow boiling (Japanese)

nitty-gritty heart, guts, essence (Afro-American). **real nitty-gritty** essence of the essence

nituke sauteed vegetables (Japanese)

nitya eternal, permanent (Sanskrit)

Nityananda, Bhagawan Indian Shaivite teacher and guru; 1896-1961

niyama positive rules for living; second step of Raja Yoga (Sanskrit)

Nizami, Ilyas ibn Yusuf Persian romancer; *The Treasury of Secrets*; ca. 1140-1209

nkomoa beneficient spirit that comes upon the future shaman (Yoruba)

nkrabea 'manner of taking leave', impulses on dying that set the karma for the next round (Yoruba)

NLP neurolinguistic programming

N o (Noh) classical Japanese drama with music and dance, combining a play about the gods, a warrior, a woman, a mad person, and devils or festivity (Japanese)

no blame (no error) situation in the *I Ching* where one can correct one's mistakes

No-Eyes a blind Chippewa medicine woman, living alone in the Rocky Mountains, subject of the book *Spirit Song* by Mary Summer Rain, 1985

No Nukes no nuclear weapons; the slogan of the Nuclear Freeze Movement

no-tech adj. nontechnological

Noble Eightfold Path way to end suffering taught by the Buddha (Sanskrit):
samyagdrishti........................ right view
samyagrak ....right speech
samyaksamkalpa ....right resolve
samyakkarmanta ....right conduct
samyagajiva ....right livelihood
samyagvyayama.................. right effort
samyaksmriti ....right recollection
samyaksamadhi......right contemplation

noctural arc lower half of a horoscope, night path of the sun symbolizing the unconscious, what is to be worked upon

nodes lines of force of a heavenly body on the intersecting ecliptic, usually applied to the Moon's upward or downward journey

noetic adj. paranormal episodes

noetics science of consciousness and its alterations (Muses)

nomadics art and science of wandering

non-credo ('do not believe', *Latin*) macrobiotic motto (George Ohsawa)

non-irradiated adj. food that has not been irradiated

non-Zen scriptural, formal

noncompetitive adj. cooperative

nonhierarchical adj. without gradation or leaders

noninterference environmental princi-

ple of respecting the environment and letting nature take its course

nonlinear adj. intuitive

nonlocal adj. hidden, invisible (David Bohm)

nonordinary reality dimension or experience beyond ordinary consciousness

nonpatriarchal adj. nonsexist

nonrenewable adj. used up when consumed, e.g. fossil fuels

nonsexist adj. nonchauvinistic in respect to sexual distinctions or roles

nonsoul immortal nonessence of living beings in Buddhism

noodynamic dynamic spiritual energy; necessary tension of the quest (Teilhard)

noogenesis spiritual evolution; opposite of entropy (Teilhard)

Noor-e-Ilahi divine light in the *Qu'ran* (Arabic)

noosphere thinking envelope around the Earth (Eduard Le Roy and Teilhard)

norbu wish-granting gem (Tibetan)

nori thin sheets of a dried sea vegetable that are black or dark purple but which turn green when roasted over a flame; used as a garnish, to wrap rice balls, in making sushi, or as a condiment (Japanese)

Norse, Harold poet and gay cultural activist; *Hotel Nirvana*; 1916-

north place where one reports to the master on accomplishments in the *I Ching*

North Beach area of San Francisco frequented by the Beats of the 1950s and the hippies of the 1960s

northern signs Aries through Virgo

Northrop, F. S. C. philosopher; *The Meeting of East and West*; 1893-

Northrup, Christiane macrobiotic physician and educator

Nostradamus, Michel de French physician and prophet; *Centuries*; 1503-66

Not Man Apart newsmagazine of Friends of the Earth

Notarikon Kabbalistic practice of taking the letters of a word individually as initials of other words (Hebrew)

Notre Dame 'Our Lady', Parisian cathedral build on an ancient Celtic and Roman worship site of mystical design attributed to alchemists and astrologers, 1163 (French)

nous higher mind, spiritual soul (Greek)

nova 1. unnamed new star. 2. old star

that suddenly brightens

Novalis (Friedrich von Hardenberg) pen name of a German romantic poet and visionary philosopher; *Hymns to the Night*; 1772-1801

Novanoah I Paulo Soleri's design for a floating city of 40,000 persons

Novus Ordo Seclorum 'A New Order of the World', motto inscribed below the scroll on the Great Seal of the U.S.

NOW National Organization for Women founded by Betty Friedan, 1966-

NPR National Public Radio

NPU net protein utilization; measure of available amino acids in a food

NREM nonrapid eye movement sleep, nondream period of sleep

ntoro life-force, collective unconscious of the clan (Yoruba)

Nu Wa female creator and protector of humanity who created human beings with clay (Chinese)

Nubia southern Egypt

Nuclear Free Zone (NFZ) zone created by law, referendum, and resolution in cities, towns, and countries banning the manufacture and storage of nuclear weapons and the location of nuclear armament industries in the area; approximately 3,775 by 1990

nuclear trigrams two trigrams in the center of an *I Ching* hexagram

nucleation threshold point at which fluctuations spread to the whole system (Prigogine and Stenger)

nucleus positively charged center of an atom consisting of protons and neutrons and comprising nearly all the atom's mass

nuka rice bran, used to make a pickle (Japanese)

Nulantis continent which will appear in the south Atlantic at the next root race (Banning)

Null Korzybski's non-Aristotelian system of logic

Null, Gary natural foods advocate and health broadcaster; *The New Vegetarian*; 1945-

number the archetype of creation; that which is behind all things and is the bond which holds everything in nature together (Plato)

numen divine will or power; used in the sense of libido or psychic energy bound up in a complex, especially in the unconscious (Jung)

Numenor the historical repository of humanity's past greatness (Tolkein)

Numerica fifth and next root race (Banning)

numerology science of numbers, associated with Pythagoras, the Kabbalah, and witchcraft

Numinor Celtic Atlantis of the north

numinosity a light in the aura attracting psychic energy and inspiring the individual to develop his or her spirituality and psychic understanding (Jung)

numinosum inexpressible, mysterious, terrifying divine experience (Otto)

numinous adj. sacred, magical, awe-inspiring (from Latin)

Nummo spirit progenitors (Dogon)

Nunavit proposed Innuit province in northern Canada, 1976

nur al anwar light of lights (Arabic)

Nur Muhammadi primal precreation, the Light of Muhammad from which all creation springs (Arabic)

nurse log dead and decaying log from which hemlock seedlings and other shade-tolerant plants take root

Nussbaum, Elaine wife and mother who healed herself from terminal uterine cancer with macrobiotics; *Recovery*; 1939-

Nut Egyptian Sky Goddess

Nux Elegia 'Nut Tree's Lament', short elegy of a tree's complaints of stones thrown at it by passers-by, attributed to Ovid (Latin)

NVS nonviolent struggle

Nyame (Nyankonpon, nyambe) Supreme Being (Yoruba)

nyasa process of charging a part of the body with a specified power through touch (Sanskrit)

nyim thun all day meditation (Tibetan)

Nyingmapa Tibetan Buddhist tradition emphasizing tantric practice

Nyingma Institute Tibetan Buddhist teaching community guided by Tarthang Tulku in the Berkeley Hills of California, 1973-

nyoi 1. jewel capable of granting any wish and removing all suffering; symbol for the dharma. 2. wooden or jade staff, occasionally with a twisted dragon around its length, symbolizing the nyoi jewel (Japanese)

Nyorai (tathagata, *Sanskrit*) 'thus come', Buddha's appellation for himself (Japanese)

Nyro, Laura rock singer; *Eli and the 13th Confession*; 1947-

Oo

O 'Metaphysic', spiritual and temporal head in Campanella's *The City of the Sun*

O Harai Grand Purification chant describing how spirit beings gathered to purify the Earth and make it a peaceful planet and introduce cereal grains to humanity (Michio Kushi, ancient spiritual One World language)

Oahspe (Oahspe) 'the Spiritual Record of the Earth and Sky', book received psychically by John Newbrough concerning the past 24,000 years; *Kosmon Bible*, compiled in 1880-81 (from the exclamation *Oh, awe, ah,* and spirit *espe*)

Oannes mythical aquamarine culture-bearer of Sumeria

oats whole cereal grain native to northern Europe and North America; usually available as whole oats (most complete form), oatmeal (rolled), and Scotch oats (cut)

Obaku one of the three Zen schools in Japan, brought by Ingen Ryuki, a Chinese Ch'an master combining Zen and Pure Land practices, with head temple, Mampukiii, at Uji in Kyoto, 1654-

OBE (OOBE) out of body experience

OBEer person who has an out-of-body experience

Obelix fat supplier of menhirs in Asterix comics

Oberon 1. King of the Fairies in *A Midsummer Night's Dream*. 2. satellite of Uranus

objective consciousness stilling the mind and becoming one with the world as a whole (Gurdjieff)

O'Brien chief agent of Big Brother in Orwell's *1984*

occulation eclipse of a heavenly body by another

occult n. or adj. hidden, secret

occultism science of secret knowledge

Oceana utopian novel of James Harrington, 17th c.

Ochs, Phil singer and peace activist; *I A'int A-Marchin 'Anymore*; 1940-76

octave range of waves of vibrational frequency

octet truss structure of alternating octahedra and tetrahedra, capable of filling space in all directions

oden stew made with tofu or deep-fried tofu simmered with a variety of other ingredients (Japanese)

Odic force (od) life energy (Reichenbach)

Odom King of the Trees (Yoruba)

Odoru Shukyo Dancing Religion; Japanese sect noted for ecstatic worship, founded by Kitamura Sayo, 1945-

odu sign of the Ifa oracle

Odysseus wily Greek warrior and wanderer in Homer's *Odyssey*

offbeat adj. hip, fantastic

off day critical day in biorhythm

Offissa Pup canine constable in *Krazy Kat*

ofuro 'honorable bath', traditional bath in a wooden tub with very hot water (Japanese)

Og 1. King of Bashan at the time of Exodus. 2. survivor of the Flood who rode on top of Noah's ark. 3. (As, On) pre-Incan Peru (Cayce). 4. tributary of the Thames running past Stonehenge

ogam early Celtic writing based on Latin with perpendicular and oblique dashes above and below a straight line

Ogotemmeli wise Dogon elder who transmitted teachings on cosmology and star contacts to Marcel Griaul in *Conversations with Ogotemmeli*

Ogygia Calypso's island. adj. **ogyian** prehistoric

ohagi a rice cake popular in macrobiotic cooking made from cooked pounded sweet rice and coated with azuki beans, chestnuts, sesame seeds, roasted soybean flour, or other ingredients (Japanese)

Ohashi, Wataru Japanese-born founder of workshops on shiatsu and natural childbirth; 1944-

ohitashi light boiling in which vegetables are cooked in a small volume of bubbling hot water for up to a few minutes or just dipped in and out to take out their raw or bitter taste and preserve their bright fresh color (Japanese)

Ohlone original people living on the shores of San Francisco and Monterey Bay; discovered by the Spanish in the 1770s and virtually extinct in 50 years

Ohrmazd Zoroastrian Creator

Ohsawa, George (Georges Ohsawa) (Yukikazu Sakurazawa, Nyoichi Sakurazawa) modern founder of macrobiotics who healed himself of terminal tuberculosis as a teenager; lived and taught in Paris in the 1930s; predicted Japan's defeat during World War II and spent the end of the war in jail under sentence of death; authored 300 books and booklets; and undertook 'the journey of a penniless samurai' in the 1950s and 1960s around the world, visiting Dr. Schweitzer in Africa, Vietnam, India, Europe, and North America; *The Book of Judgment*; 1893-1966

Ohsawa, Lima (Sanae Tanaka) macrobiotic teacher and wife of George Ohsawa; *The Art of Just Cooking*; 1899-

Ohta river in Hiroshima

Oimcalc Celtic winter festival, Feb. 2

ojas vigor, spiritual energy (Sanskrit)

Ojibwa (Chippewa) Algonquian tongue

okara coarse soybean pulp left over when making tofu and used in soups or cooked with vegetables (Japanese)

Oki, Masahiro Korean-born martial artist, Japanese yoga teacher, founder of Okido; *Meditation Yoga*; 1921-85

Okido (Oki Yoga, Dynamic Zen) 'way of Oki', yoga school and system of corrective exercises developed by Masahiro Oki (Japanese)

Okigbo, Christopher Ibo poet; *Heavensgate*; 1932-67

Okina oldest No play, performed on New Year's by an actor playing the God of Longevity (Japanese)

okriki divine songs (Yoruba)

Ol-orun 'Owner of the Sky', Yoruba Supreme Being

Olcott, Henry Steel journalist, colonel, co-founder of the Theosophical Society, Buddhist educator; 1830-1907

old true, right, normal: in the flow of the universe (Gary Snyder)

Old Chronicle Egyptian era covering a period of twenty-five Sothic cycles (36,525 years), beginning with the first line of princes, the Auritae, followed by the Mestraens, and the Egyptians

Old Europe Europe's first civilization, focused in southeastern Europe, -7000-3500

old growth forest characterized by large trees hundreds of feet high and from 250 to 1000 years old or more, a multilayered canopy, large standing dead trees, and large dead trees on the ground and in streams

Old Oraibi longest inhabited town in North America, by the Hopis from A.D. 1100

Old Religion witchcraft or paganism that continued into the Middle Ages

old soul one who has reincarnated many times and is more spiritually mature than most people

oldie old tune or song, usually golden and memorable

Olduvai site in Tanzania where *Zinjanthropus australopithecus* (world's oldest anthropoid) was discovered by Dr. Leakey in 1959

Ollie Dragon long-toothed, eye-rolling companion of Kukla and Fran

Olmec ancient Mexican civilization around Vera Cruz noted for huge stone heads

Olmstead, Frederick Law planner and landscape architect; father of Central Park in New York and first director of Yosemite; 1822-1903

Om (Aum) 1. the imperishable Brahman, the universe; whatsoever has existed, whatsoever exists, whatsoever shall exist hereafter; whatsoever transcends past, present, and future (*Mandukya Upanishad*). 2. sacred syllable symbolizing the sum total of all energy; first cause; omnipresent sound; lasting peace (Sanskrit). v. **oming** chanting for peace

Om Mani Padme Hum 'Om jewel in the Lotus Hum', Tibetan -national mantra (Sanskrit)

Om Namah Shivaya mantra of Shiva's name (Sanskrit)

Om Vaira Pani Hum 'Hail to the Holder of the Dorje', Tibetan mantra (Sanskrit)

omedeto 'congratulations', a porridge made from azuki beans and roasted brown rice (Japanese)

Omega 1. last letter in the Greek alphabet. 2. symbol of the Apocalypse. 3. symbol of the Vietnam antiwar draft resistance movement

Omega Point universal center of divine convergence; the apex of the evolutionary process (Teilhard)

omega-3 marine fatty acids, fish oil; common in linseed, walnut, rape, soybean

omega-6 polyunsaturated fatty acids with the first double bond on the sixth carbon, e.g., GLA, common in corn oil, EPO, currant, hops, oats

Ometeotl 'God of the Near and Close', Nahuatl Creator

omnicentric universal view; looking at things from totality (Thomas Berry)

Omoto 'Teaching of the Great Origin', Japanese way of life noted for anti-atom activities, art, and Esperanto founded by Deguchi Nao, 1892-

omphalos 1. navel. 2. megalithic stones so shaped (Greek)

on joyfulness in distributing infinite freedom and eternal happiness (Ohsawa, *Japanese*)

on-line adj. active, up and running, functioning; referring originally to computers and nuclear power plants but now to people as well

One Grain, Ten Thousand Grains the spirit of endless giving; principle of universal distribution; macrobiotic motto (George Ohsawa and Michio Kushi)

One Infinity source of all life encompassing the beginningless beginning and the endless end; process of universal life, appearing and disappearing in the endless universe; the absolute world beyond space and time, yin and yang; God, the eternal, your real self (Michio Kushi)

One Peaceful World 1. era of planetary peace and harmony synthesizing the material and spiritual. 2. an ancient era of world unification characterized by stone circles and pyramids for energy collection and generation, natural agriculture, a predominantly grain and vegetable diet, a single world calendar and language, flying saucer-like aircraft, and the division of people by races of black, red, yellow, blue, and white rather than by nations; first one occurring ca. 50,000 B.P.; the second one, ca. 20,000 B.P.; the coming one, ca. A.D. 2100-12,000. 2. book by Michio Kushi and Alex Jack on realizing personal, family, and planetary peace, 1987. 3. international friendship society, educational and cultural organization, and information and communications network founded by Michio and Aveline Kushi, 1986-. 4. periodical of the One Peaceful World society, 1989-

One Peaceful World Village educational and spiritual community in Becket, Mass., 1990-

One-Pillar Pagoda (Chua Mot Cot, *Vietnamese*) lotus-shaped shrine in Hanoi

One Ring object of great and terrible power forged to bring all under Sauron's rule in *Lord of the Rings*

one-sidedness overemphasis on conscious pursuits to the exclusion of unconscious creative promptings (Jung)

one vehicle Buddha path referred to in the *Lotus Sutra* in which Buddha reveals the unity behind the three ways of achieving liberation

One Word word that will inaugurate the spiritual world on Earth, promised by Meher Baba but never spoken

onearth planetary culture (Findhorn)

Oneida utopian community in New York State, practicing Perfectionism and free love, led by John H. Noyes, 1848-81

onikare sweat lodge made of young willows (Sioux)

Onisaburo (Kisaburo Ueda), leader of Omoto in Japan, 1871-

Ono, Yoko Japanese-born artist and partner of John Lennon; *Grapefruit*; 1933-

ontogeny 'being origin', natural history of changes in the life cycle of an individual beginning with the fertilized egg (from Greek)

Oothoon America personified as a young girl (Blake)

open-form adj. Ginsberg-style poetry

open-land movement to free or turn over land to anyone who wants to live or cultivate it, 1960s-

open-pollinated traditional Indian corn that is pollinated by the wind as opposed to hybrid corn; also known as standard corn

Ophir 1. Noah's great-grandson. 2. legendary land of gold in Arabia

Opitsaht a village on Meares Island off the west coast of Vancouver Island which has been continously inhabited for more than 5000 years

opposition planets 180 degrees or six houses apart in a chart; a major unfavorable aspect

optophone invention in Alexander Moszkowski's romances that transmutes any object into its musical equivalent, 1922

oracle 1. prophet, place, book, etc. relating the past, present, or future. 2. (cap.) San Francisco underground paper, late 1960s

Orage, A. R. editor and student of Gurdjieff; *The New Age*; 1871-1932

Oraibi a Hopi village, one of the oldest settlements in North America, 1150-

orb point of an aspect in astrology; arc of influence

Orbeliani, Sulkhan-Saba Georgian fablist; *Bouquet of Words*; 1658-1725

Orbiston Scottish utopian, vegetarian community founded by Abraham Combe, 1825-27

orbit 1. elliptical path of a planet around the Sun. 2. high experience

Orc 1. personified spirit of revolution (Blake). 2. goblin in *Lord of the Rings*

order principle or law governing nature, the universe, and all of life

dharma....................Hindu and Buddhist
li...Chinese
logos..Greek
neter...Egyptian
rita..Hindu
tao...Chinese

Order of the Golden Dawn London magic circle, including Waite, Yeats, Crowley, early 20th c.

Order of the Universe 1. the order whose heavenly nature holds from the center and spins all else around it (Dante). 2. that which sustains, animates, destroys, and transmutes everything, the visible and invisible, and is Absolute Justice (George Ohsawa). 3. the eternal principles of change and harmony; the moving infinite creation; the Living God; the laws of yin and yang (Michio Kushi)

Oredson, Olivia macrobiotic teacher and cook; *Macrobiotic Palm Healing*

Oregon New Age Jazz fusion band; *In Performance*

orenda life energy, spirit power (Iroquois)

Organa, Princess Leia heroine in *Star Wars* held prisoner by Darth Vader on the Death Star

organic adj. 1. way of life based on experiencing basic processes of growth, change, and renewal; embracing whole, natural foods, natural childbirth, breastfeeding, breadbaking, gardening, and other traditional crafts and customs that are in harmony with the environment. 2. foods processed, packaged, transported, and stored to retain maximum nutritional value, without the use of artificial preservatives, coloring, or other additives; irradiation; or synthetic pesticides and which are grown in accordance with ecological farm management practices, which rely on building soil humus through crop rotations, recycling organic wastes, and applying balanced mineral amendments and as necessary, mechanical, botanical, and/or biological controls with minimum impact on health and environment are implemented (Organic Food Production Association of North America). 3. produce grown in soil containing at least 3 percent humus content (Robert Rodale). 4. produce grown without chemicals for at least three years (Bread & Circus). 5. life-forms or chemical compounds containing carbon

Organic Brotherhood prehistoric vegetarian, monogamist, nonresistant people from whom the prophets appeared (Oahspe)

organics living beings as opposed to mechanicals in *Star Wars*

orgasm unitary involuntary convulsion of the total organism at the acme of the genital embrace (Reich)

orgone primordial cosmic energy obtained from the orgasm reflex or repeated expansions and contractions as the basic formula of all living functioning (Reich)

Organon principal work by Samuel Hahnemann introducing homeopathy, 1810

Orgone Box (accumulator) device for focusing orgone energy (Reich)

Orgueil site in France where a meteorite fell on May 14, 1864, containing organic molecules suggesting life on Earth could come from outer space

orichalcum 'mountain copper', the sparkling metal found in Atlantis (Plato)

Oriental Zodiac astrology system prevalent in the Far East, based on the order in which the animals arrived to pay tribute to the Buddha, the rat jumping off the ox's back to win

rat .... April
ox .... May
tiger ....June
rabbit ....July
dragon .... August
serpent .... September
horse .... October
sheep .... November
monkey .... December
cock .... January
dog .... February
boar .... March

origami the art of folding colored paper into decorative objects (Japanese)

Origen Christian theologian, believer in rebirth and karma; *Commentaries*; ca. 185-254

Original Mind fresh, childlike awe at the wonder and beauty of creation; Buddha mind

Oriphiel Hebrew Angel of Solicitude

Orisha humanized gods and goddesses with whom worshippers often merge through dance in neo-African religion

Orishanla 'Great God' who fashioned humanity from clay at Ife (Yoruba)

orizuru folded paper crane (Japanese)

Orphalese city in which Kahlil Gibran's *Prophet* will return

Orpheus Greek musician whose lyre enchanted people, rocks, animals, trees and Hades itself in a quest to free his wife Eurydice

Orphic mystical doctrines attributed to Orpheus or Dionysus

Orphic bards first human rulers who kept order by music alone, enchanting whole countries with a cycle of songs in harmony with the changing seasons

Orphism modern art movement stressing pure color and dynamic contrasts developed by Apollinaire

orthonoia commonly accepted mind state; normality (Greek)

Orun-mila 'Heaven knows salvation', Yoruba god of the Ifa oracle

oryoki Zen eating utensils: set of three bowls, spoon and chopsticks, scraper and cloth-ended stick (Japanese)

Osadhi Yoga yogic healing through herbs (Sanskrit)

Osage 1. Missouri people forced to move to Oklahoma. 2. their Siouan language

Osaka Japan's second largest city; commercial and folk arts center

OSC ordinary states of consciousness

Oshogbo Yoruba spiritual center

Osiris 1. Egyptian culture-bearer, Lord of the Underworld, brother-husband of Isis, father of Horus. 2. Guide of the Aquarian Age (*Book of Truth*). 3. transneptunian planet ruling inner peace

osmotic energy theoretically derived by fresh water rising through a pipe sunk deep into the ocean

Ostara German Goddess from whose name Easter comes

Osun Yoruba River Goddess

OT Operating Thetan; next stage after *clear* in which one is free of time and space (Scientology)

other n. double, astral body

Other Shore Buddhist term for Nirvana

Other Side after-death realm

otherworld life after death

Otomi 1. people of the high Mexican plain, descendents of the Aztec survi-

vors. 2. their language, said to have links to Chinese

Ott, John Nash discoverer of the harmful radiation effects of TV and fluorescent lights; *Health and Life;* 1909-

Ouija ('yes yes', *French* and *German*) board on which psychic messages are spelled out

Our Common Future landmark statement on human survival by the U.N. World Commission on Environment and Development, 1987

Our Lady of Vladimir Russia's sacred icon in Moscow's Tretyakov Gallery

Ouroboros alchemical dragon biting its own tail (Greek)

Ouspensky, Peter D. Russian mathematician and associate of Gurdjieff; *In Search of the Miraculous*; 1878-1947

out breath breathing out cycle

out-of-earth experience experiencing from beyond our planet ourselves as cells in a living body

out-of-sight fantastic, marvelous; invisible like the Divine (Afro-American)

out-of-the-body experience awareness of the astral body detaching from the physical body, either voluntarily or involuntarily, awake or dreaming

outer band spirits in the astral world who assist humans in creative tasks and achievements

ovalar adj. 'egglike', beginning essence of a train of thought that has the potential to grow in importance

Ovana deva of a 200-year-old Oak, New Age guide (*Beauty Unknown*)

overmind 1. plane of consciousness beyond mind; creator of truth (Aurobindo). 2. force sent to Earth to save humanity from self-destruction in Clarke's *Childhood's End*

Oversoul Absolute, Brahman (Emerson)

overt n. contrasurvival act against one or more Dynamics (Scientology)

Ovid Roman poet; *Metamorphoses*; ca. -43-17

ovo-lacto-vegetarian vegetarian who eats eggs and dairy products

ovula 1. tiny proturberance hanging down in the back of the mouth. 2. the point of disconnection in the Spiritual Channel between Heaven and Earth's force governing human freedom and destiny (Michio Kushi)

ovulatory cycle 13-day fertile period in women counted from the 16th day after menstruation, plus six days before and after

Owen, Robert English industrialist and utopian socialist, founder of New Harmony in Indiana; 1771-1858

owsla ruling council of strong rabbits in *Watership Down*

Oxfam International emergency food and development agency founded in Oxford, England, 1942-

Oxherding Pictures ten pictures and verses illustrating the steps to enlightenment, attributed to Chinese Ch'an master Kuo-an Shih-yuan, 12th c., Japanese version by Shubun

1 ....looking for the ox
2............................. seeing its footprints
3.. seeing the ox
4.................................... catching the ox
5.................................... herding the ox
6 ....returning home on its back
7.. the ox forgotten, the human remains
8 ....both human and ox forgotten
9...............................returning to the source
10............................... entering the city

Oxomoco first man in Nahuatl myth

Oxyrhynchus site in Egypt where three papyri manuscripts of the original Greek text of the *Gospel of Thomas* were found in the late 19th c.

Oz fabled land and site of the adventures of Dorothy Gale, the Tin Woodman, Scarecrow, and Lion in L. Frank Baum's stories

ozan horizontal canopy around the lining in the rear half of a tipi that prevents rainwater from splattering the floor (Sioux)

OZMA first experiment to pick up radio signals from outer space intelligences at Green Bank, W.Va., 1960

ozone form of molecular oxygen containing three atoms produced in the high atmosphere by ultraviolet radiation from the Sun

ozone layer atmospheric strata that absorbs ultraviolet radiation from the Sun some 25-35 kilometers above the Earth, endangered by environmental pollution

Pp

P 1. priestly source in the Hebrew Bible who depicts Yahweh as more cosmic,

less personal, with an emphasis on justice and punishment. 2. probability; ESP test measure of the expected frequency of a given result from chance alone

Pa Hsien Eight Immortals (Chinese)

pa kua 1. eight trigrams. 2. martial art emphasizing circular evasion and attack, 18th c. (Chinese)

paan betel nut, spice, and lime paste mixture chewed after meals (Hindi)

Paccari tambo three mythical caves from which the Incas' ancestors emerged

Pacha Camac Incan Creator God

Pachamama Incan Earth Goddess

Pacific Rim countries bordering the Pacific Ocean such as Japan, U.S., Korea

Pacioli, Luca Renaissance mathematician and student of the Golden Secton; *Divina Proportione*; 16th c.

pada short song conveying instruction on the spiritual life (Sanskrit)

padayatra foot pilgrimage, especially Vinoba Bhave's walks (Sanskrit)

padma lotus (Sanskrit)

padmasana lotus posture (Sanskrit)

Pagan ancient Buddhist temple complex on the Irrawaddy in Burma;

Pagels, Elaine religious scholar and feminist; *The Gnostic Gospels*

pagoda structure containing Buddhist relics (from Portuguese, Persian)

Paige, Leroy R. (Satchel) ageless pitcher and baseball wonder; 1906-82

Paine, Thomas English-born rebel and pamphleteer; *Commonsense*; 1737-1809

pakora deep-fried savory of eggplant or cauliflower (Hindi)

Pakshi, Karma the second Karmapa and teacher to Kublai Khan, 1204-83

Pala Buddhist pacifist utopia in Aldous Huxley's *Island*, 1962

Palace of Love dwelling place of the heavenly king and holy souls in the Kabbalah

Palenque site of ancient Mayan ruins in Chiapas, Mexico

paleolithic prehistoric Stone Age characterized by nomadic, patriarchal, hunting tribes

paleothaumic era whose technology was magical (Roszak)

Pali scriptural language of Theravada Buddhism

Pali Canon collection of Buddhist texts recorded from oral traditions, -1st c.

Pallava South Indian dynasty, 7th c.

palm healing natural healing method utilizing the palms of the hands to focus energy on various parts of the body

Palmer, Daniel David developer of chiropractic; *The Art, Science and Philosophy of Chiropractic*; 1845-1913

Palmer, Raymond A. editor of *Amazing Stories* and promoter of the flying saucer legend; 1911-77

palming exercises to correct eye problems by covering the eyes with the palms of the hands (Bates)

palmistry science of interpreting the palms of the hands

Pan 1. Arcadian God of Flocks. 2. large antediluvian continent in the northern Pacific (Oahspe). 3. transplutonian planet ruling disputes discovered by Charles Muses

pan-fry to saute with a little oil over a low to medium heat for a moderate to long time, turning or stirring minimally

panch shabd '5 sounds', divine sound current resounding through the five inner planes (Sanskrit)

Panchatantra '5 books', collection of Indian animal fables popularly known in medieval Europe as the *Fables of Bidpoi* [Pilpay] (Sanskrit)

Panchen Lama (Tashi or Teshu Lama) former head of the Tashilunpo Monastery, Tibet; the most recent was Ngoerhtehni; 1939-89 (Tibetan)

panchkosi 50-mile pilgrimage circuit around Benares (Sanskrit)

Pandavas five sons of King Pandu: Yudhisthira, Arjuna, Bhima, Nakula, Sahadeva; heros of the *Mahabharata*

pandit learned person (Sanskrit)

panethnicity cross-cultural, accepting from all cultures and traditions

Pangaea single, giant continent that existed 200 million years ago (Plate Tectonics)

Panini Indian grammarian; *Grammar*; ca. -4th c.

panj piare five beloved ones; first Khalsa Sikhs who baptised and were baptised by Guru Gobind Singh

panpsychic adj. seeing consciousness everywhere

panspermia theory that the templates of life arrived in the form of microscopic spores which escaped the donor planet by means of air currents or volcanic eruptions (Svante August Arrhenius)

Pantaloon hero of the commedia dell' arte

Panza, Sancho Don Quixote's squire

paotze steamed vegetable dumplings (Chinese)

Papago 'bean people', Indian tribe of the Southwest who call themselves Toho'-no-o-otam, 'Desert People'

pappadam light, puffed crisp bread made from lentil flour (Hindi)

Papus (Gerard Encausse) French Kabbalist; *Tarot of the Bohemians*; 1865-1917

para supreme, other, enemy (Sanskrit)

parabrahman 'beyond Brahman', absolute (Sanskrit)

Paracelsus Swiss magus; 1493-1541

Paraclete Christian spirit of Truth manifested in the world

paradigm 1. a set of deep concepts about the nature of reality that shapes language, thought, perceptions, and system structures. 2. unconscious dogmas and assumptions which make ordinary scientific practice possible (Thomas Kuhn)

paradigm shift spiritual or mental axis-shift; change in perception or world view such as the Copernican, Darwinian, Freudian, or quantum revolutions

paradise (from *pairi-daeza,* 'a walled or enclosed garden', *Avestan* [Old Iranian]) 1. heaven or perfected state of being in the next life. 2. earthly garden of delights. 3. a psychological or spiritual state; the essence of nirvana, ecstasy, divine union, cosmic consciousness. 4. an age or era of happiness and prosperity that periodically recurs in human history. 5. place from which the hero returns to the ordinary world with a healing balm and whose knowledge and existence must be shared. 6. that place ever found in thinking of my lady and looking into her eyes (Dante). 7. that realm or place where friend meets friend (Joseph Campbell). 8. the transcendent beatitude expressed in intimate forms of bodily and spiritual delight (Thomas Berry). 9. the union of yin and yang in harmony; intellectual judgment (Michio Kushi)

Garden of Eden	Hebraic
Dilmun	Sumerian
Garden of Yima	Iranian
Tep Zepi	Egyptian
Golden Age	Greek
Krita Yuga	Sanskrit

Paradise Island Pacific home of Wonder Woman

Paradise, Sal hero of Kerouac's *On the*

Road

Paradisio heavenly realm visited by Dante and his guide, Beatrice, where he experienced the Divine Light of Love and observed Christian saints and blessed figures from the past

paradoxical intention logotherapeutic technique in which the patient is asked to do exactly what is feared (Frankl)

Paraiba Inscription copy of a Canaanite text found on a Brazilian rock in 1872 describing a transatlantic voyage in -531 from the Red Sea with a secret acrostic made by the Jewish scribe

parallel distance of planets from the celestial equator

parallel lives simultaneous multiple incarnation by the same oversoul (Dick Sutphen)

parallel worlds science-fiction theme of what might have been historically

parama-anu subatomic particles known only through meditation by the Buddhist Sarvastivadins; 84,000 or countless such atoms in a human body

Paramahamsa 'supreme swan', title of a perfected yoga master (Sanskrit)

paramartha absolute truth (Sanskrit)

paramita 'reaching the other shore', a perfection; quality arising out of the mind of meditation and representing the life of the Bodhisattva; sign of enlightenment (Sanskrit)

giving... dana
keeping the precepts........................ sila
patience..................................... kshanti
vigor ....virya
meditation.................................. dhyana
wisdom.. prajna
skillful means............................. upaya
commitment....................... pranidhana
strength.. bala
knowledge .... jnana

paramnesia deja vu

paranormal n. or adj. faculties and phenomena beyond normally understood causal factors

paraphysics the study of laws that govern psychic phenomena

parapsychic someone who scores high on psi tests (J. B. Rhine)

parapsychology science of measuring and investigating extrasensory perception and behavior. adj. **parapsychical** extrasensory

parasamgate completely gone beyond (Sanskrit)

paratha Indian-style whole wheat bread fried on a griddle (Hindi)

parents 1. all living beings (Shinran). 2. the original bodhisattvas (Dalai Lama)

parinirvana 'complete annihilation', 1. complete cessation of rebirth. 2. final passing away of a Buddha (Sanskrit)

Parker, Theodore Unitarian clergyman, antislavery firebrand; 1810-60

Parks, Rosa church worker whose sitting down in the front of a bus in Montgomery, Ala., on Dec. 1, 1955, sparked the civil rights movement; 1913-

paroptic sense faculty of seeing with the astral body, without physical eyes

Parousia 1. archetypal presence in Platonism. 2. Advent in Christianity

parsah ego barrier in the Kabbalah (Hebrew)

parsec astronomical unit equal to 3.26 light years

Parshva 22nd Jain Jina, founder of the Nirgranthas order; 9th c.

Parsi (Parsee) 'Persian', modern Zoroastrian in India

participatory democracy movement for more individual involvement and grassroots participation in decision-making at all levels, 1960s-

partnership spirituality cooperative male/female spirituality that preceded and surpassed historic religion and philosophy (Riane Eisler)

Parvati 'mountaineer', daughter of the Himalayan God and wife of Shiva

Parzival legendary hero of Wolfram's Grail epic of the same name

pas-i-anfas Sufi meditation of inhaling and imagining the sound *Allah*, seeing the word engraved in luminous Arabic letters on one's left breast, and exhaling making the sound *hu* (Arabic)

Pascal, Blaise French mathematician, mysti- cal poet; *Les Pensees*; 1623-62

Pashubhava state of the animal-human; first stage of the tantras (Sanskrit)

Pashupatinah Nepalese holy town, site of Shiva Lord of Animals Temple

past-life therapy method of searching for the roots of a person's current situations in previous lifetimes

Pasternak, Boris Russian poet; *Dr. Zhivago*; 1890-1960

Pataliputra 'City of Sweet Scented Flowers', Ashoka's capital near modern Patna, India

Patan (Lalitpur) Buddhist city near Katmandu, Nepal, 3rd c.-

Patanjali Indian philosopher; *Yoga Su-*

tras; ca. 2nd or 5th c.

Patchen, Kenneth poet; *The Journal of Albion Moonlight*; 1911-72

path 1. eternal movement of the absolute downward to the sphere of manifestation, upward to the unmanifest. 2. way from ignorance to knowledge, or from suffering to enlightenment traversed, beaten, and trod by previous journeyers, especially a slender, narrow, hazardous, and easily lost one. 3. one of innumerable avenues back to Godhead, the center, the spiritual home. 4. spiritual discipline, movement, or school. 5. eternal odyssey (as opposed to a trip). 6. that which exists but not the traveler on it (Visuddhi Magga). 7. train you cannot get off (Suzuki Roshi). 8. Buddha Mind, True Self, enlightenment. 9. Tao, the way. 10. energy connection, direct channel to the source

Pathan member of a fierce tribe in northwest Pakistan converted to nonviolence by Gandhi

pathbreaking adj. crusading, novel, cutting edge

pathfinder spiritual guide, help, or tool

pathworking spiritual practice

paticca-samuppada Chain of Dependent Origination in Buddhism; twelve links in the cycle of life, death, rebirth (Pali)

Patmos Greek island where *Revelation* was written

patriarchal adj. 1. the rule of a senior male over an extended family or tribe. 2. male-dominated political state characterized by a high degree of occupational specialization, commerce, social stratification, and warfare. n. **patriarchy**

Patriarchs Zen meditation masters in a line of transmission; twenty-eight in India, six in China

patrilinear culture or family traced through the father

patrilocal practice of the wife going to live with the family or clan of her husband

patrism father-identification (G. Rattray Taylor)

Paul, Alice suffragette, organizer of the Women's Peace Society, and introducer of the Equal Rights Amendment; 1885-1977

Paul of Thebes first Egyptian desert saint, ca. 250

Paul, St. (Saul of Tarsus) tentmaker and

Nazorean persecuter who converted after a mystical vision on the road to Damascus; *Acts*; ca. d. 68

Paula Amazonian scientist in *Wonder Woman*

Pauling, Linus chemist, peace activist; *Science and World Peace*; 1901-

pax peace (Latin)

Pax Gaia 'the Peace of Earth', understanding the Earth as a single community that must survive in its integrity (Thomas Berry)

Paxton, Tom folk and protest singer; *Whose Garden Was This*; 1937-

pea-pod ship flying saucer sent down by a mother ship

Peabody, Elizabeth Transcendentalist; *The Dial*;1804-94

peace 1. 'grain and mouth', the original Chinese ideogram for peace (*wa*) represents the calm state of mind produced by eating whole grains as principal food. 2. inner calm; serenity; enlightenment; that which passes all understanding. 3. harmony with the environment; state of concord and mutual friendliness among persons, animals, and plants. 4. repose, quiet, tranquillity. 5. greeting, salutation, mantra to begin or close a meeting, speech, or letter. 6. nonviolence, ahimsa, satyagraha. 7. nuclear disarmament, absence of war, conflict, hostility or tension. 8. truce, armistice. 9. hexagram #11, Tai, in the *I Ching*, uniting Heaven and Earth in harmony with strength on the inside and devotion on the outside. 10. (cap.) a comedy by Aristophanes, -421. (from Middle English *pees, pois*). adj. **peaceable**, **peaceful**. adv. **peaceably**. n. **peacemaker**, **peace marcher**, **peace offering**

amani	Swahili
beke	Hungarian
fred	Norwegian, Swedish, Danish
frieden	German
heiwa	Japanese
hoa binh	Vietnamese
irini	Greek
mir	Russian, Czech
pace	Italian, Rumanian
paco	Esperanto
paix	French
pax	Latin
paz	Portuguese, Spanish
perdamaian	Indonesian
pokoi	Polish
ruaha	Finnish

salaam... Arabic
scholim.......................................Yiddish
shalom...................................... Hebrew
shanti ....Sanskrit, Hindi
sulb.. Turkish
t'ai .... Chinese

Peace Brigades International (PBI) Philadelphia-based group that trains people for nonviolent conflict resolution in Central America and elsewhere

Peace Links grass roots anti-nuclear organization, Washington, D.C.

peace movement international effort to end war and the nuclear arms race and devote the Earth's resources to peaceful, harmonious ends

Peace Pilgrim penniless female pilgrim who walked 25,000 miles for peace; d. 1981

peace shield creative meditation to produce coherent brain waves to allow for the waging of peace in the world by the Pentagon Meditation Club and SDI (Spiritual Defense Initiative) visualizing a peace shield around the Pentagon, the country, and the world; founded by Edward Winchester, retired U.S. Air Force officer, 1990

peace sign first two fingers held up in the shape of a V

Peace Sunday international peace concert-rally in Pasadena, California on June 6, 1982, where 85,000 came to hear speeches and music in support of the U.N. Special Session on Disarmament and a freeze on nuclear weapons

Peace Week June 6-12, 1982, culminating in a demonstration at New York's Central Park by 800,000 to 1 million people in support of disarmament and the Nuclear Freeze

Peacemakers antidraft group organized to promote tax refusal and mutual support, 1948-

PeaceNet global computer network working for peace, based in San Francisco

PeaceTrees ecology project for publishers to plant new trees for each tree used in their publications

peacework activity contributing to peace

peaches of immortality heavenly fruit of Chinese mythology

peak experience ecstatic event, supreme moment in one's life (Abraham Maslow)

Pearce, Joseph Chilton consciousness researcher; *The Crack in the Cosmic Egg*

pearl barley (Job's tears, hato mugi, *Japanese*) a small white barley valued for its medicinal and cosmetic properties in traditional Oriental medicine

pearled barley a polished form of barley

peasant cuisine ethnic soups, stews, grains, and bean dishes

Pechad Kabbalistic sephiroth of severity, intelligence (Hebrew)

Peck, M. Scott author and educator; *A Different Drum*; 1936-

Pecos Bill legendary cowboy culture-bearer of the American West, Ausralia, and Argentina

peer group bonding method using loud wholesome screaming to stir long-forgotten memories; work proceeds in couples, one of each sex, who hold each other closely (Daniel Casriel)

Pegleg Pete wooden-legged adversary of Mickey Mouse

Pei 17th Hebrew letter: open mouth, P, 80

Pele 1. Hawaiian Fire Goddess. 2. a volcano

pelican 1. wise bird with an advanced throat chakra. 2. form of circulatory still in alchemy. 3. medieval symbol of Christ

Pelletier, Kenneth psychologist; *Healthy People in Unhealthy Places*; 1946-

Pendle Hill Quaker retreat in Wallingford, Pennsylvania

Pendu, Le Hanged Man in the Tarot (French)

pendulum dowsing and radionics instrument consisting of a bob suspended by a short cord held in the fingers

Penelope patient and resourceful wife of Odysseus

P'eng Tsu Chinese Methuselah

Penn, William English-born Quaker, founder of Pennsylvania; *Essay Towards the Present and Future Peace of Europe*; 1492-1559

Pentacles Tarot suit symbolic of fortune and enterprise

pentagram five-pointed star

pentjak-silat Indonesian martial art originated by a peasant woman who subdued her berating husband after watching the movements of a tiger and large bird

people power 1. community action and self-government. 2. the movement led by Corazon Aquino in the Philippines that came to power nonviolently

people's art anonymous art done in a public place

People's Park empty lot in Berkeley owned by the University of California where several hundred people planted vegetable seeds on April 20, 1969, and which became a symbol of the ecology movement

Pepperland country beyond the Sea of Green with bright psychedelic colors in the Beatles' *Yellow Submarine*

peradam magical crystal on Mount Analogue

Perceval (Percival) hero of Chretien de Troyes's Grail epic

percipient 1. subject of an ESP test. 2. UFO observer

perennial plant that continues a cycle of new growth and flowering for many seasons between germination and death

Perennial Philosophy belief in a divine reality permeating all things and periodically blossoming in the human mind and the myths and religions of all peoples (Leibnitz)

Perennis unfinished pyramid engraved on the $50 U.S. note, 1778

perestroika restructuring (Russian)

Perfect Masters those who sustain the spiritual development of Earth; five in Meher Baba's teaching

perfect number number which is equal to the sum of its factors such as 6 or 28

perfume piano instrument that exudes odors to correspond to its music in Kurt Lasswitz's *Bilder aus der Zukunft*, 1878

peripheral isolate event on the fringe that results in sudden and unpredictable changes in whole systems (Eldredge and Gould)

periplus ancient ship captain's log (Greek)

Perls, Fritz psychologist, developer of Gestalt Therapy; *In and Out of the Garbage Pail*; 1893-1970

permaculture 'permanent agriculture', conscious design of agriculturally productive ecosystems (Bill Mollison, 1975)

pero cereal beverage of malted barley, chickory, rye, molasses

Perpetual Choir sacred bards and musicians who governed in Britian before the Druid era

Perrault, Father founder of Shangri-La, 1681-1931

Persephone Greek princess carried off to the Underworld

Perseus Gorgon- and dragon-slayer; rescuer of Andromeda in Greek myth

persona 'mask', 1. the face an individual presents to the world (Jung). 2. role that society allows us to play (Joseph Campbell)

personalization process of cosmic consciousness (Teilhard)

Pert em Hru *Egyptian Book of the Dead*, or *The Coming Forth by Day*

PETA People for the Ethical Treatment of Animals; animal rights organization, 1980s

Petaku Effect discovery that the longer the time of exposure to x-rays or other artificial electromagnetic radiation, the smaller the total dose needed to damage living tissue (Abram Petkau, 1972)

Peter Pan eternal child in a story by James Barrie

Peter, Paul, and Mary folk rock group of Peter Yarrow, Paul Stookey, Mary Ellen Travers; *Puff the Magic Dragon*; 1960s-

Peter, St. (Simon Peter) Galilee fisherman, first Pope, and heavenly denizen who danced three times around Dante and Beatrice in Paradise; *Epistles*; ca. d. 67

petroglyph image engraved on stone

Peyote small cactus found along the Rio Grande in Mexico containing the hallucinogen mescaline

Pfeiffer, Ehrenfried biodynamic chemist; *The Compost Manufacturer's Manual*; 1899-

Phaeton 1. son of Apollo who drove the chariot of the sun, lost control, and was slain by Zeus's thunderbolt. 2. planet between Mars and Jupiter theorized to have disintegrated and crashed as planetoids into Earth (Niolai Rudenko)

Phanerozoic ancient geological time of the plants and animals

Phanes 'Manifestor or Revealer', golden winged primordial being in Greek myth, particularly Orphic thought, who was hatched from the Cosmic Egg

Phantasos 'dream', son of Sleep who bestows visions in Greek mythology

phantom leaf effect removal of a portion of a plant leaf prior to photographing the whole of the corona by Kirlian photography

pharmacognosy science encompassing those phases of knowledge relating to natural products which are generally of medicinal value and primarily of plant origin

phase aspect of the Moon, Mercury, or Venus

phassa sense-impression; a link in the Buddhist chain (Pali)

phi 1. Golden Section; the principle underlying beauty of form used by architects, painters, and sculptors through the ages, represented by a rectangle with sides in the proportion 1:1.61803 (Greek). 2. nature spirit (Thai)

Philae Egyptian island, site of the Temple of Isis

Philemon Phrygian who, with his wife, offered hospitality to the disguised Zeus and Hermes and received an inexhaustible pitcher

Philo, Judaeus Greek Jewish author; *On the Contemplative Life*; ca. -30-45 C.E.

Philokalia writings of the fathers of the Eastern Catholic Church, compiled 18th c.

Philosopher's Stone 1. universal medium of alchemy which transmutes base metals into gold. 2. key to life

Phobos 'fear', moon of Mars, said by some scientists to be a hollow, artificial satellite (Greek)

Phoebus planet postulated between Mercury and the Sun

Phoenix 1. fabulous Egyptian bird that rose out of its own ashes to be reborn. 2. Egyptian period of 1460 years. 3. a Phoenician. 4. purple or deep crimson color. 5. city in Arizona. 6. yacht sailed by the Reynolds family into the Pacific A-bomb test area, 1958. 7. Quaker peace ship that carried medical supplies to Hanoi, 1967

photochromotherapy color healing

photon massless subatomic particle representing the unit of electromagnetic radiation and acting as the vehicle of the electromagnetic force

photovoltaic adj. direct conversion of solar energy into electricity

Phrygian ecstatic *re*-musical mode ruled by Jupiter (Greek)

phylogenetic adj. evolutionary

Phylos the Tibetan Atlantean adept who channelled through Frederick Spencer Oliver; *A Dweller on Two Planets*, 1884

physic healing substance or preparation

Physicians for Social Responsibility medical society that educates the public and legislature about the effects of nuclear testing and the danger of the nuclear arms race, 1970s-

physiognomy the art of judging character and disposition from the features of the face or the form and lineaments of the body generally

physiology the science concerned with living systems seen holistically

phytotherapy use of plants for therapeutic purposes

pi the ratio of the circumfrence of a circle to its diameter (Greek)

Pi-hsia Yuan-chun Taoist Goddess, the Princess of the Motley Clouds, Patroness of Women, Children, Foxes

Pi Sheng Chinese printer, inventor of moveable type from clay, ca. 1041

Piaget, Jean Swiss psychologist; *The Origin of Intelligence in Children*; 1896-1980

Piankoff, Alexandre French Egyptologist; *The Litany of Re*; d. 1966

pickle press a small enclosed glass or plastic container with a screw-plate for making pressed salad or light, quick pickles

Pico della Mirandola, Giovanni Florentine philosopher who posted 900 theses on comparative religion, astrology, the Kabbalah, and Islam and challenged the Church Fathers to a debate; *Heptaplus*; 1463-94

picture mind image based on a belief system; a barrier (est)

Pierrot artist in love with Columbine in the commedia della' arte

Piers Plowman English allegorical poem of William Langland, 14th c.

Pig-Pen 1. dirty little rascal in *Peanuts*. 2. term of endearment for a messy person

Piggy intelligent child in Golding's *Lord of the Flies*

Pigsy brutish companion of Tripitaka in *The Journey to the West*

pikadon 'thunder, lightning', atomic-bombing of Hiroshima (Japanese)

Pike, James A. Episcopal bishop, psychic explorer; *The Other Side*; 1913-69

pilaf fluffy rice (Persian)

pilgrim spiritual seeker; one on the road who knows he or she travels not alone (Bailey)

Pilgrim's Progress allegorical work by John Bunyan received in a dream, 1678

Pima Indian tribe of the Southwest who call themselves Ah-Kee-Muh-O-O-Tam, 'River People'

Pine Ridge Lakota reservation in South Dakota

pineal endocrine gland in the forebrain;

physical counterpart of the Third Eye (from pine cone)

pingala subtle nerve channel on the right side; solar nadi (Sanskrit)

Pippin (Peregrin Took) companion of Frodo in *Lord of the Rings*

pir elder; Iranian or Indian Sufi director (Persian)

pir-i-gha'ib invisible saints (Arabic)

PIRGS U.S. Public Interest Research Groups; citizens' organizations educating on toxics and solid-waste issues

Piri Reis Map map made in 1513 by Turkish Admiral Piri Reis with features of North and South America predating much later discoveries, especially the flora and fauna and a perfect outline of Antarctica before the last Ice Age; rediscovered in 1929, traced to an Alexandrian original of the 1st c. by Charles Hapgood in *Maps of the Ancient Sea-Kings*

Pirsig, Robert author and traveler; *Zen and the Art of Motorcycle Maintenance*

Pisces Fishes; twelfth sign of the zodiac; of the watery element; ruler Neptune; keywords: sympathy, compassion, gentle energy

Pishon one of four heavenly streams that flows from the Garden of Eden (Hebrew)

pistachio olive-shaped nut native to the Orient and Mediterranean

pit lower room in the Great Pyramid

Pitcairn Island site in Polynesia of a communal society founded by mutineers of the Bounty and local women, 1825-

pitha center of worship of a female tantric deity (Sanskrit)

Pitman, Sir Isaac English vegetarian and promoter of a phonetic English language; 1813-97

pitri father; progenitor of the human race (Sanskrit)

pituitary gland a small gland in the head with two lobes that governs the hormonal system

pity the feeling which arrests the mind in the presence of whatsoever is grave and constant in human sufferings and unites it with the human sufferer (Joyce)

PK psychokinesis; influence of mind upon matter

place a particular environment that is deeply experienced or lived in. v. **living in place**

placemaking art of geomancy

placement test PK test in which the subject tries mentally to influence falling objects to come to rest

Placidian equal division of the equator using house circles, but with a correction for the cuspal declination (Placidus de Tito, 15th c. monk)

Plan n. divine purpose for which the One has deemed it wise to submit to incarnation (Bailey)

planchette Ouija board pointer (French)

Planck's Law equation expressing the variation of the intensity of black-body radiation with wave length at a given temperature (Max Planck)

plane level or realm of manifestation

planet a heavenly body that forms from a comet that gradually increases in density in the center of a solar system (Michio Kushi)

Planet Drum ecology foundation in San Francisco

planetary n. or adj. 1. international, global, universal. 2. decentralist, seeking biological and spiritual rather than technological solutions

planetary awakening spreading awareness that we share a single planetary home and must be responsible for our environment

planetary consciousness awareness and experiencing the Earth as a living entity

planetary family the Earth as a whole; awareness of global citizenship and universal brother- and sisterhood

planetary hours heavenly rulers of the hours calculated on Sun time

planetary precognition inner experience expressing our creativity as vital members of a planetary system; shared experience of planetary oneness (Barbara Marx Hubbard)

planetesimal swirl of gas and solid particles at the edge of hydrogen clouds that form stars

planetization totalization of human consciousness (Teilhard)

plants products of the vegetable kingdom, something like our mother who cannot be controlled or changed (Michio Kushi)

plastic n. or adj. fabricated, artificial, synthetic, impressionable, malleable, false, saccharine, stagnant, lifeless

Plastic Man (Plas) rubbery comic strip hero of Jack Cole, 1930s-60s

Plate Tectonics geological theory of one gigantic continent 200 million years ago preceding continental drifts

Platform Sutra Buddhist text by Hui-neng, 7th c.

Plato Greek philosopher who studied with Socrates and the priests in Egypt; *The Republic*; -427?-347

Platonic year a Great Cycle of 25,920 years

play natural purpose of human beings on this Earth, to marvel at life and enjoy every moment from morning to night without tiredness to realize our endless dream (Michio Kushi)

Pleiades 'weepers', constellation in Taurus; seven daughters of Atlas and Pleione

Pleiadian messages series of UFO teachings conveyed to Eduard Meier, 1975-

Pleroma 'fullness', transcendental field of Gnosticism (Greek)

Plotinus Greek neoplatonist; *Enneads*; ca. 204-70

Plum Blossom intuitive method of casting the *I Ching* developed by Shao Yung

Plurabelle, Anna Livia (Maggi) wife of the dreamer in Joyce's *Finnegans Wake*

pluriverse universe of multiple dimensions

Pluto 1. Roman God of the Underworld. 2. planet ruling power, crusading energy. 3. dogged companion of Mickey Mouse

PMIR psi-mediated instrumental response; synchronistic phenomenon (Stanford)

PMS premenstrual syndrome

pneuma vital spirit, life energy (Greek)

p'o animal, or lower human, spirit (Chinese)

po a stage in creative thinking, neither yes nor no (Edward de Bono)

Po Chang Chinese Ch'an master who developed the basic Zen monastic code; 720-814

p'o mo ink-splash painting technique (Chinese)

pochtecas guild of itinerant vendors devoted to Quetzalcoatl and the quest for the Land of the Sun

pod 1. group of whales. 2. (cap.) Tibet proper (Tibetan)

poesis use of self-created symbols (David V. Forest)

poetry the stuttering voice of revelation that guides lovers toward ecstasy, gives witness to the dignity of old people, intensifies human bonds, elevates the community, and improves the public spirit (Gary Snyder)

Pogo satirical comic strip of Walt Kelly set in the Okefenokhe swamps

Polarea polar sacred land; home of the First Root Race (Theosophy)

Polarian first stage of human evolution in Max Heindel's teaching in which the human spirit was lightly veiled in an aetheric aura

Polaris the present North Star which will pass directly overhead in about A.D. 2100, coinciding with the end of the Spiral of History and the beginning of a new Golden Age that will last about 10,000 years (Michio Kushi)

polarity balancing (polarity therapy) wholistic system that balances the life energy through releasing blocks in the physical body

polenta a traditional Latin or Mediterranean dish made with corn and beans or vegetables

politics the flow of power within society (Gary Snyder)

Pollen Path mystic way of spiritual ascent (Navaho)

pollution the wonderful ground from which we set out to seek paradise and create a new world (Michio Kushi)

polo rice (Persian)

polygenesis independent origin of similar folk tales

Polyphemus one-eyed Cyclops of Greek mythology

polyphony simultaneous use of two or more meters (from Greek)

polysaccharides complex sugars that gradually become absorbed during digestion, including starch and cellulose found in whole grains and vegetables

polyunsaturated adj. class of fats of primarily vegetable origin whose molecules consist of carbon chains with many double bonds unsaturated by hydrogen atoms; associated with low cholesterol in the blood

polyunsaturated fats essential fatty acids found in high concentration in whole grains, beans, seeds, and in smaller quantities in fish

pom copal resin incense of Central America

Pon-nyu, U Burmese poet; *Vessantara*; ca. 1807-66

Pondicherry former French colony in South India; site of Aurobindo's ashram

Pongal South Indian rice harvest festival

Popocatepetl 'warrior prince', sacred volcano in Amecameca, Mexico

Popol Vuh 'Book of the Community', sacred book of the Kiche Maya of Central America in romanized Kiche telling of the creation

poppy seed tiny white seed with a sweet, nutlike taste

Porphyry neoplatonic philosopher; *On Abstention from Animal Food*; 232-305

Port Huron Statement SDS manifesto calling for participatory democracy drafted by Tom Hayden, published in Pt. Huron, Michigan, 1962

Portola Institute educational organization, publishers of the *Whole Earth Catalog*, in Menlo Park, Calif.

Poseidia first portion of Atlantis prophesied to rise near the Bahamas (Cayce)

Poseidon 1. Greek Sea God. 2. sire with Kleito of the original Atlanteans (Plato). 3. eighth Uranian planet, ruling novelty, creative illumination

Posidon Temple temple at the center of the inner island of Atlantis

Posidonius Greek stoic who first believed India could be reached via the Atlantic; *Historia*; ca. -135-50

position planet's place in a horoscope

possibility-binding science-fiction practice of making all of what might be, part of what is

Post, Charles W. ulcer patient at the Battle Creek Sanitarium who invented Postum and Elijah's Manna (Grape Nuts); 1854-1914

postcapitalist adj. post-Exxon, IBM, AT&T

postcognition memory or flashes of a past life

postindustrialism movement away from mass production, waste, consumption

postpatriarchal adj. nonsexist, participatory governance emerging from present modern society

postum malt and barley beverage

Potala 1. heavenly residence of Avalokiteshvara. 2. palace in Lhasa where the Dalai Lamas lived, 1694-1959

poultice soft mass of fresh vegetable matter, usually heated, spread on cloth, and used in natural healing

Poussin, Nicolas French artist; *Landscape with St. Matthew and Angel*; 1594-1665

power realm of higher consciousness; active, impersonal force interacting with human existence (don Juan)

power object object with the ability to call in spirit forces

power place site or place with strongly charged natural electromagnetic energy

power plant plant or flower with psychotropic qualities or energies

power point (psychic vortex) spot or place along an Earth meridian with a capacity to amplify and transform energy, especially where two such paths interconnect

Poya weekly holiday in Sri Lanka, day of Moon's quarter phase and preceding half day

prabha halo (Sanskrit)

prabhakari illumination; third stage of the Bodhisattva path (Sanskrit)

Prabhavananda, Swami Indian Vedantist; *Vedic Religion and Philosophy*; 1893-1976

Prabhupada one at whose feet all other spiritual masters surrender (Sanskrit)

practice the intensification of what is natural and around us all of the time; being fully conscious of the dignity and pride of one's life and work (Gary Snyder)

prajna 'wisdom', seeing clearly; wisdom beyond discriminatory thought arising naturally from meditation, love, and compassion (Sanskrit)

Prajnaparamita 'perfection of wisdom', large collection of Mahayana texts on realizing wisdom and assisting others (Sanskrit)

prakriti matter (Sanskrit)

pralaya state of latency between cycles of the universe (Sanskrit)

pramudita delight; first stage of the Bodhisattva path (Sanskrit)

prana life energy (Sanskrit)

pranam respectful salutation with folded palms, prostration, or touching the dust of the feet (Sanskrit)

pranava Aum; the sacred syllable (Sanskrit)

pranayama control of life energy through breathing (Sanskrit)

prarabdha portion of karma initiated in past lives that must run its course; unalterable conditions (Sanskrit)

prasad consecrated food (Sanskrit)

Pratap, Vijayendra Indian yogi who founded the SKY Foundation in Philadelphia in 1972

Pratt, J. Garther psi researcher; *Para-*

psychology: An Insider's View of ESP; 1910-

Pratyeka Buddha nonteaching Buddha who stays in the nirvanic realms

prayer arrow ceremonial arrow in Native American communities, Shinto, and other traditions that conveys messages or energy between Heaven and Earth

prayer position meditation with the thumbs on the sternum, finger tips touching lightly

pre-cast perception of probabilistic factors that predispose it toward a given state (Adrian Dobbs)

pre-Raphaelites symbolist art movement associated with William Hunt, John Millais, Dante Gabriel Rossetti, mid-19th c.

preatomic particles energy that appears in the form of numerous particles of spirally moving energy (Michio Kushi)

precept (sila, *Sanskrit*) way of living in accordance with the dharma

precession of the equinoxes path of the vernal equinox along the ecliptic over a 25,800 year cycle; the Great Year or Cycle whose months make up the Age of Pisces, Age of Aquarius, etc.

preclear beginner, aspirant (Scientology)

precognition psychic knowledge of future events

precycling buying only items that will not pollute the environment (Edmund Benson)

preestablished harmony theory that the universe consists of individual monads containing an image or pattern of the universe as a whole (Leibnitz)

prelucid dream dream in which the subject debates whether he or she is dreaming; false awakening (Ann Faraday)

prema 1. ecstatic divine love in Hinduism. 2. spiritual sublimation of love in Tibetan Buddhism (Sanskrit)

premie 1. lover of the divine. 2. initiate in Guru Maharaj Ji's Divine Light Mission (Sanskrit)

prepatriarcy matricentric period of Old Europe lasting until the Aryan invasions, -6500-3500

present the whole spiral of life, without beginning and end

pressed salad salad prepared by pressing sliced vegetables and sea salt in a small pickle press or with an improvised weight

pressure cooker an airtight metal pot that cooks food quickly by steaming under pressure at a high temperature

preta 1. hungry ghosts with giant appetites and throats no bigger than needles. (Sanskrit) 2. modern societies (Gary Snyder)

Pribam, Karl neuropsychologist and developer of the holonomic theory of brain functioning; *Languages of the Brain;* 1919-

Price, Weston dental surgeon who investigated traditional human cultures free of degenerative disease; *Nutrition and Physical Degeneration*, 1945

Prieure Gurdjieff's school near Paris

Prieure de Sion secret society devoted to restoration of the Merovingian Dynasty and bloodline from Jesus, 12th c. -

Prigogine, Ilya Russian-born chemist and theorizer of the self-organizing processes of the natural world; *Order Out of Chaos: Man's New Dialogue with Nature*; 1917-

Primal Scream therapeutic method of reliving deep-rooted experiences developed by Arthur Janov

Primal Therapy a highly structured and controlled individual process which increases the pressure upon repressed early emotions until they explode outwards, followed by a reintegration program (Arthur Janov)

primary productivity rate at which radiant energy from the Sun is stored by green plants in the form of organic substances that can be used as food

primary trigram dominant trigram in an *I Ching* hexagram

prime vertical great circle that crosses the meridian of the birth place at right angles

primitive (from *primus*, 'first') original human society or way of being

primordial image archetype

primum mobile crystal firmament; ninth heavenly sphere visited by Dante and Beatrice in the *Divine Comedy* (Latin)

Prince, Diana Wonder Woman

principal food main food; whole grains; the staff of life

principalities planetary powers governing wisdom

Pringle, Cyrus Vermont Quaker, pacifist; *The Civil War Diary*; 1838-1911

prisoner of conscience someone imprisoned because of his or her beliefs, religion, or human rights

Prisoners for Peace Day December 1

priti delight, pleasure in the Lord (Sanskrit)

Pritikin, Nathan dietary and health pioneer; *The Pritikin Program*; 1915-85

Probert, Mark deep-trance medium, co-founder of Mark Age; 1907-

process 1. v. to refine, can, freeze, or dehydrate food. 2. (cap.) Church of the Final Judgment founded by Robert de Grimston teaching Christ and Satan's unity, 1963- . 3. (l.c.) non-judgmental self-observation (est)

process meditation meditation using a mantra out of one's own experience (Progoff)

Proclus neoplatonic philosopher; *Two Treatises*; ca. 412-90

Procol Harum surreal British rock group (Keith Reid, Gary Brooker); *A Whiter Shade of Pale*; 1960s

Proconsul humanoid whose skull is regarded as the probable ancestor of both humans and the apes

Progoff, Ira depth psychologist, founder of Dialogue House; *At a Journal Workshop*; 1921-

program unconscious pattern of behavior (Lilly)

progress 1. the art of preserving order amid change and change amid order (Alfred North Whitehead). 2. what was left over after you met an impossible problem (Norman Cousins)

progressed horoscope chart derived from the radix and transits indicating the planetary positions subsequent to the time of birth

project v. to have a clear image and send it

Project Cyclops proposed network of 10,000 radio dish telescopes in New Mexico for extraterrestrial contact

projectionist someone who makes an astral projection

Prometheus Greek mythological hero who stole fire from heaven on behalf of humanity

Promised Land heaven, utopia, perfect society, ideal commonwealth

promittor (promissor) planet signifying something important in a chart in the future

proofing stage in bread-making in which the dough sets and rises to proper lightness

proper name dream dream symbol that puns on a proper name

prophet (f. prophetess) inspired person, especially one who foretells future events (from Greek)

Prophet, Elizabeth Clare founder of the Church Universal and Triumphant; 1940-

proprioceptive 'from within', a meditational writing practice with roots in stream-of-consciousness, free writing

proprium desire to become something (Allport)

prosperity consciousness visualization or meditative approach to realizing material wealth

Prosperos 1. magician in *The Tempest*. 2. Fourth Way School founded by Thane Walker and Phez Kahlil, 1956-

Proterozoic the middle age of the Earth, spanning the first appearance of oxygen until communities of cells gathered to form new collectives

proton positively charged subatomic particle belonging to the baryon category; hydrogen atom nucleus

Proudhon, Pierre-Joseph French libertarian anarchist; *What Is Property*; 1809-65

proving taking small doses of poisonous substances in preparation for healing in homeopathy

Provos Dutch anarchists influenced by the Beats, early 1960s

Prydain mythical Welsh realm of Druids and large oaks (Celtic)

Pseudo-Dionysius the Areopagite neoplatonic Byzantine mystic; *The Heavenly Hierarchy*; ca. 500

psht (pshat) plain or literal reading of a Kabbalistic text (Hebrew)

psi 1. 23rd Greek letter associated with 7, 70, 700. 2. general term for ESP. 3. (J) subatomic particle. adj. **psi-activating** generating psychic energy. adj. **psi-conducive** facilitating psychic abilities

psi bank a planetary information storage and retrieval system whose primary function of holonomic recollection operates or manifests through the binary code (Jose Arguelles)

psi-field postulated ESP zone analogous to a gravitational field

psi-hitter person who scores high on ESP tests

psi-mediated adj. psychically influenced

psi-misser person who scores low on ESP tests

psi-trailing long-distance trekking of animals after their masters (J. B. Rhine and Sara Feather)

psion 1. smallest, most essential unit into which consciousness may be divided (Henry Frazier and Yogi Yukteswar Sri Babajhan, 1950s). 2. psi information structures that continuously circulate between humans and the planet (Jose Arguelles)

psionics 1. the study or investigation of psi or the paranormal (John Campbell, 1956). 2. Soviet term for radionics

psitron particle of imaginary mass that can travel faster than the speed of light (Adrian Dobbs)

psy-tech adj. relating to the psychic and technological

psyche 'breath', 1. soul, spirit, mind. 2. mental or psychological structure of the personality. 3. (cap.) young woman beloved by Eros in Greek myth. 4. second emanation of the One, world spirit in neoplatonism (Greek)

psychedelic n. or adj. 1. mind-expanding. 2. hallucinogenic. 3. bright, fluorescent, paisley colors or sounds in undulating wave patterns with psychic resonances

psychenaut spiritual journeyer (Jean Houston)

psychic n. or adj. 1. trance medium. 2. realm of the paranormal, occult, or astral (Flammarion)

psychic being soul or spark of the Divine Fire supporting the individual evolution (Aurobindo)

psychic dentistry spontaneous instant healing of teeth or gums in a group setting with a psychic or holistic dentist

psychic surgery healing or removal of diseased tissue without instruments

psychist psi researcher or student

psychoactive adj. mind-expanding, especially hallucinogens

psychoatmospheric density (PAD) increasing incidence of artificial conditioning factors in the planetary environment (Jose Arguelles)

psychobiology study of the relation between mind and body

psychobiomimesis the metaphorical expression of individual and collective unconscious processes within the form and content of scientific theories and technologies; e.g., on a very rudimentary level, the modeling of human mental processes in computer technology (Dennis Stillings)

psychocalisthenics fluid series of exercises practiced with an emphasis on breathing developed by Oscar Ichazo in Chile in 1958

psychodrama a form of group therapy where patients act out roles depicting their situations (J. L. Moreno)

psychoenergetics interaction of consciousness, matter, energy

psychogenesis 1. process of psychological development. 2. evolution (Teilhard)

psychogeny process of mind development

psychograph paranormal appearance on photographic material

psychographics studies based on psychological characteristics and profiles as distinct from demographics

psychography direct writing

psychoid the materialization of an archetype in the physical world (Jung)

psychoneuroimmunology interactions between the brain, the endocrine system, and the immune system (Robert Ader, 1980s)

psychokinesis (PK) mind over matter. n. **psychokinetics** its study

psychometry 'measure of the soul', faculty of obtaining paranormal information from touching or holding an object. adj. **psychometric** (J. R. Buchanan, 1842, from Latin)

psychonization the trend toward increasing artificialization of human consciousness (Michio Kushi)

psychopharmacology science or study of psychoactive substances

psychophon direct voice receiver developed by Franz Seidl

psychophysical complex concept that social, economic, technological, and attitudinal forces are so interrelated that systematic alternatives are needed for meaningful change

psychophysics 1. science relating physics and consciousness (Fechner). 2. study of the physics of the mind-body relationship

psychopompos 'conductor of souls', spiritual guide, especially through the Underworld (Greek)

psychoprophylaxis natural childbirth method developed in Russia

psychopter the winged self, evolving spirit (Arthur Young)

psychosexual adj. psychological and sexual interrelationships

psychosomatic adj. unity of mind and body, especially mentally-caused diseases

psychosynergy 1. wholistic integration. 2. synthesizing traditional polarized concepts to create a new result

Psychosynthesis psychological and educational approach to integration utilizing Eastern and Western methods to enable the Self to emerge and manifest in daily life developed by Johannes Schultz and Roberto Assagioli, 1910-

psychotechnology a method or system to induce a change in consciousness, especially a shift from left-brain to right-brain thinking (Marilyn Ferguson)

psychotherapist attendant of the soul (James Hillman)

psychotherapy psychological counseling that treats the mind and body as a whole

psychotronics application of consciousness to technology

psychotropic adj. hallucinogenic

Pu-tai potbellied, bald wandering beggar of Zen legend, identified with Maitreya

Pu-t'o-shan Chinese island off the coast of Ningpo identified with the Taoist Isle of the Blessed; pilgrimage spot of devotees of Kuan Yin

public-access television community TV, primarily local programming

Public Citizen activist organization of consumer protection and corporate accountability founded by Ralph Nader, Washington, D.C.

Puck 1. mischievous sprite in *A Midsummer Night's Dream.* 2. plucky black and white cat who was healed of congestive heart failure through a macrobiotic diet and palm healing; 1978-89

Pueblo Bonito best known feature of Chaco Canyon, occupied from A.D. 900 with 800 rooms and 37 kivas

puella aeternus eternal daughter; archetypal woman who never grows up (Latin)

puer aeternus eternal boy; archetypal boy who never grows up (Latin)

pufa polyunsaturated fatty acid

Puharich, Andriya psychiatrist, psychic investigator; *Uri*; 1918-

puja worship (Sanskrit)

pulau rice cooked with spices, vegetables, lentils, or beans (Hindi)

pulque agave beer, fermented juice of the maguey cactus in Mexico

pulse 1. legume. 2. heart beat or the beat of one of the inner organs. 3. ancient civilizational center (Jose Arguelles)

pulse diagnosis Oriental healing method

of measuring pulses for indications of the state of internal organs

pulse points areas of enhanced electromagnetic energy where ancient civilizations developed (Jose Arguelles)

puncturated equilibria nonlinear model in which evolution proceeds neither quickly or slowly but in spurts (Eldredge and Gould)

pundit learned person (Sanskrit)

Punjab region divided between India and Pakistan, home of the Sikhs

Punjabi 1. (pl.) people of the upper Indus Valley. 2. their language

punya merit, virtue (Sanskrit)

purana 'ancient', one of eighteen Hindu mythological texts (Sanskrit)

Pure Land Buddhism Mahayana school originating in China teaching faith in Amitabha Buddha, invoking his name to win rebirth in his Pure Land; major scriptures are the *Sukhavati-vyuhas* and the *Amitayur-dhyana;* 4th c.-

puree v. to mash food in a suribachi, bowl, mill, or food processor until smooth and even in consistency

Purgatory mountain between light and darkness where the soul is healed depicted in the *Divine Comedy* rising from an island with seven cornices representing various forms of egotism to be purged; ascended by Dante along a spiral path ending at the Earthly Paradise

Puri 1. seashore town in Orissa, India; Hindu holy city. 2. (l.c.) fried bread puffs (Hindi)

Purim feast of lots commemorating Queen Esther (Hebrew)

Purna Yoga integral yoga of Sri Aurobindo

Purple Hall of the City of Jade Confucian term for the Third Eye

Purple Hills Chinese term for paradise

purusha human being, soul (Sanskrit)

Purvis, Ann spiritual teacher and peace promoter; 1944-

Purvis, Harry Hale manufacturer and peace activist; 1915-68

Pushkar 'blue lotus', lake and temple in Rajasthan with a four-faced image of Brahma (Sanskrit)

Pushkin, Alexander Russian poet; *Evgeny Onegin*; 1799-1837

pushing hands T'ai Chi exercises performed by two partners

Puss in Boots marvelous cat of Scandinavian folklore

PWA people with AIDS

Pythia an ecstatic female trance medium through whom Apollo or Zeus spoke at the Delphic Oracle

pyramid 'fire in the middle' 1. large tetrahedral stone structure, such as in Egypt or Central America. 2. any such structure with four or three sides, whether of stone, paper, wood, etc. 3. tetrahedral shape commonly found in chemical elements. 4. high energy storage place or human-made mountain built throughout the ancient spiritual One World (Michio Kushi) adj. **pyramidal, pyramidic, pyramidical**

pyramid energy life energy accumulated or conducted within any pyramidal-shaped construction aligned square along a North-South axis; natural preservative energy radiated at the point or base of the pyramid

pyramidology science or study of pyramids, especially their preservative qualities or historic use as receptacles of ancient wisdom

pytalin enzyme in saliva that breaks down starchy foods into simple sugars upon thorough chewing

Pythagoras Greek philosopher from Samos noted for his doctrine of the Harmony of the Spheres and teaching that all is number; -6th c.

Qq

Q 1. heavenly body with a period of 25,900 years discovered by Dr. Pickering at Harvard in 1909, identified as a twin companion of the Sun, 875 AU distant. 2. (quelle) 'source', hypothetical collection of Jesus's sayings embodied in the Gospels of Matthew and Mark (German)

Q-Oph 19th Hebrew latter: submerged stratum, K, 100

Qabalah Jewish mysticism; this spelling refers to the magical/occult use of the Kabbalah beginning in the mid-1800s, including Tarot and systems of correspondences

qabd period of spiritual contraction (Arabic)

Qadiriya Sufi order stressing the repetition of God's name, founded by 'Abd al-Qadir, 12th c.-

Qalandar order of wandering Sufis

qalb heart; one of the five lata'if, meeting place of physical and spiritual forces, center of the holy war (Arabic)

qawm 'folk', mystic people, Sufis (Arabic)

qi (ch'i) life energy (Chinese)

Qi Gong (Chi Kung) martial art with slow, circular movements (Chinese)

Qizil Central Asian site near Kucha with Cave of Maya frescoes

quadrant quarter of a circle; arc of three houses in astrology

quadruplicity group of four

Quang-Duc, Thich Vietnamese monk who immolated himself on June 11, 1963, to focus attention on Vietnam's sufferings

quantity 1. measure or volume. 2. that which changes quality (George Ohsawa)

quantum unit of electromagnetic radiation; photon

quantum electrodynamics theory of electromagnetic interactions between subatomic particles, combining elements of quantum mechanics and relativity theory

quantum field theory theory combining quantum mechanics and relativity theory to describe the force fields and mutual interactions of subatomic particles

quantum mechanics (quantum theory) theory of atomic phenomena worked out by Planck, Einstein, Bohr, Heisenberg, Schrodinger, Pauli, De Broglie, Dirac, 1920s-

quantum number integral number specifying the location or shape of an atomic orbit or an integral or half-integral number specifying a certain property, such as charge or spin

quark (from 'three quarks for Muster Mark' in Joyce's *Finnegans Wake*) theoretical subatomic particle underlying all particles (Murray Gell-Man)

quartz mineral or rock crystal, hexagonal in form, used in healing, weather control, dematerialization, and protection from harmful electromagnetic energy

quasar quasi-stellar radio source; distant heavenly body of large mass emitting radio waves, first photographed in 1885

quaternity an archetype associated with the symbolic arrangement of things or ideas in fours or multiples of four; associated with the Self by virtue of the attributes of balance and perfection (Jung)

quatrain rhymed four-line verse containing Nostradamus's *Centuries*

Quechua 1. language of the Incas. 2. tribal name of four million Andean people

Queen of Hearts regent of cards and croquet players in *Alice in Wonderland*

quena Incan flute

querent inquirer in a Tarot reading

quest 1. search for the Holy Grail. 2. traditional spiritual practice of Native Americans seeking a personal vision

Question compassionate inquiry required of Sir Galahad or Parzival at the Castle of the Grail

Quetzalcoatl 'most precious twin', compassionate culture-bearer of ancient Mexico who could not kill animals or pick flowers; the feathered serpent; the planet Venus

Quiche Mayan descendents in Guatemala

Quigley, Joan astrologer who cast Gorbachev's horoscope before President Reagan's first summit meeting in 1985 and told Mrs. Reagan that 'Ronnie's *evil empire* attitude has to go'

Quimby, Phineas Parkhurst metaphysical healer; 19th c.

quinary group of five elements

quincunx 1. Mayan cross. 2. (inconjunct) planets 150 degreess apart; a minor unfavorable aspect

quindecile planets 24 degrees apart: a minor favorable aspect

quinoa (pronounced keenwa) ancient grain of the Incas traditionally grown in the high mountains of Peru and Bolivia and now elsewhere

quintile planets 72 degrees apart; a minor favorable aspect

quipu Incan knot record

Quivira legendary Golden City of southwest Mexico

Qumar Ali Dervish Sufi saint whose mosque near Poona, India, contains a boulder that can be levitated when exactly eleven people touch index fingers and chant his name

Qumran Essene site northwest of the Dead Sea where 500 scrolls were found between 1947-56

Qur'an (Koran) 'reading', Islamic sacred scripture revealed to the Prophet Mu-

hammad; as written, a compilation of Muhammad's teachings ordered by Abu Bekr a year after his death based on memory; present one is a second edition compiled eleven or twelve years later by Caliph Othman after the originals were destroyed

qurb realization of the nearness of God (Arabic)

qutb 'pole', saint (Arabic)

Rr

R heavenly body discovered by Dr. Pickering at Harvard with a period of 500,000 years, possibly a sister Sun or large planet

R2-D2 small, bullet-shaped robot in *Star Wars* that communicates in electronic bleeps

Ra Sun (Egyptian and Polynesian)

Ra Expeditions two reed vessel voyages organized by Thor Heyerdahl from Safi, North Africa, to the Bahamas showing the possibility of pre-Columbian contact, 1969

Ra Ta High Priest of Egypt from a group of invading Caucasians, ca. -11,000 (Cayce)

Raai Egyptian monarch under whom peace first came; -11,000 (Cayce)

Rabbit trickster of the southeastern American Indians

Rabelais, Francois French poet and savant; *Gargantua and Pantagruel;* 1494-1553

Rabi'a al-'Adawiyya Sufi saint, mystic, and poet from Basra; 717-801

Rachel wife of Jacob, symbol of the contemplative life of the soul

Radha gopi sweetheart of Krishna

Radha Soami 'Lord of the Soul', spiritual movement founded by Shri Dayal; offshoot of Sikhism, 19th c. (Sanskrit)

Radha, Swami Sivananda (Sylvia Hellman) yoga teacher and leader of the Yasodhara Ashram near Vancouver; 1911-

radical software people's video systems

radiesthesia sensitivity and ability to detect biological radiations and resonances; clairvoyant healing

radionics instrumental form of radiesthesia; interaction of mind and matter

radiosonic sensory fusion technology (Jose Arguelles)

radix natal birth chart

raga 'love', musical note or harmony (Sanskrit)

Ragnorok 'twilight of the gods', Scandinavian apocalypse (Norse)

Rahab the harlot of Jerico who helped Joshua gain the Promised Land and the first soul to ascend to heaven with Jesus after the Crucifixion

Rahman 'merciful', title of Allah (Arabic)

rahu northern lunar node: dragon's head (Sanskrit)

Rahula 'impediment', son of Prince Siddartha; ordained a Buddhist monk at age eight by his father

Raiatia one of the Society Islands; Polynesian holy land with a flowering plant on a sacred mountain that will grow nowhere else on Earth

Raikov, Vladimir Soviet parapsychologist; *Reincarnation by Hypnosis*

rainbow 1. arc of prismatic colors arising from the reflection of rain drops or a waterfall. 2. reminder of a bridge that once existed between Heaven and Earth and was accessible to all people. 3. seven colors of the rainbow symbolizing the seven heavens of many religions and myths. 4. symbol of the covenant between Yahweh and the Israelites

Rainbow Bridge Earth's largest natural bridge, 290 feet high and 270 feet across a canyon in Utah

Rainbow Family Tribe human race

Rainbow Gathering annual gathering of tribes/people from around the continent and world to live and celebrate life for a week without money, electricity, bureaucratic laws and artificiality; 1972-

Rainbow Warrior Greenpeace ship that sailed into the nuclear testing zone in the Pacific and was attacked by the French

rainforest tropical wilderness that is the source of much of the world's oxygen and home to a majority of the Earth's plants, animals, and birds; a vast region, including the Amazon, rapidly vanishing from human development, logging, mining, and clearing for the grazing of cattle and other lifestock for animal food production

Rainforest Action Network global organization to protect the rainforests, based in San Francisco, Calif.

Rainforest Information Centre environmental group founded by John Seed

Raj Ghat memorial to Gandhi in Delhi

Raja Yoga 'King of Yogas', spiritual science developed by Patanjali emphasizing regulation and control of the mind (Sanskrit)

Rajneesh, Bhagwan Shree (Rajneesh Chandra Mohan; Osho) Indian-born teacher of tantric and Sufi heritage with a weakness for Rolls Royces; 1931-90 n. **Rajneeshees** disciples

Rajneeshpuram town near Antelope, Oregon, set up by Rajneesh disciples, 1981-85

Rajagriha site in India near Vulture Peak; seat of the first Buddhist council

rajas passion, motion, action; one of the three gunas (Sanskrit)

Ralahine English utopian community founded by John Scott Vandeleur, 1831-33

Ram Dass fourth Sikh Guru, founder of the city of Amritsar and the Golden Temple; 1534-81

Ram Dass, Baba (Richard Alpert) seeker and teacher; *The Only Dance There Is*; 1932-

Rama (Ram) avatar of Vishnu preceding Krishna, hero of the *Ramayana*

Rama, Swami 1. Indian spiritual teacher; 1903-72. 2. Indian teacher, founder of the Himalayan International Institute of Yoga Science and Philosophy; *Living with the Himalayan Masters*; 1925-

Ramacharaka Indian sage who sent a disciple, Baba Bharata, to the Chicago Fair in 1893; 1790-1893

Ramadan ninth month of the Islamic calendar; period of fasting, commemorating sending down of the *Qur'an*

Ramakrishna (Gadadhar Chatterji) Bengali saint, ecstatic worshipper of the Divine Mother; 1836-86

Ramakrishna Math and Mission movement spreading Ramakrishna's teachings, with center at Belur, India, 1886-

Ramana Maharishi, Sri Hindu saint who taught at Arunachala Ashram near Madras; 1879-1950

Ramanuja Tamil qualified nondualistic philosopher; *Commentary on the Gita*; 1017-1137

ramapithecus fossil ape; ancient hominoid found in India

Ramayana Sanskrit epic poem by Valmiki narrating the story of Rama

RAMC right ascension of the MC; used in determining a horoscope's axis

ramen a Chinese-style noodle that has been deep-fried and dried

Ramtha 35,000-year-old entity from ancient Lemuria channeled by J. Z. Knight, a Washington state housewife

Rangjung Rigpe Dorge sixteenth and most recent Tibetan Karmapa; 1924-81

Rankin, Jeannette pacifist, suffragist, first Congresswoman; 1880-1973

Ransom hero in C. S. Lewis's space trilogy

ransyo raw egg in the shell mixed with tamari (Japanese)

rap 1. informal conversation. 2. black style of music, 1980s

rap group consciousness raising group, especially an activist cell serving as a medium for social change

Rapanui native name for Easter Island

Raphael 'healing of God', 1. Hebrew archangel standing behind God's throne. 2. (Raffaello Santi) Renaissance master; *Sistine Madonna*; 1483-1520. 3. (Robert Cross Smith) English astrologer; 1795-1832. 4. being who channels through Ken Carey in *The Starseed Transmissions*

Rapp, George German-born utopian; founder of Harmony and Economy; 1757-1840

raqs Sufi dancing (Arabic)

Ras Shamra Ugarit Phoenician excavation site in Syria, 1930

rasa essence, fluid, flavor; Krishna's love (Sanskrit)

Rashid-eddin Mongol minister, author of world's first universal history; ca. 1300

Rastafarian Jamaican culture synthesizing African and Biblical themes

rasul (rassoul, rasool) 'messenger', prophet, saviour (Arabic)

rat Chinese constellation of Aquarius, bringer of water

Rati Hindu Goddess of Love

Ratnasambhava Matrix of the jewel Bodhisattva (Sanskrit)

Raudive voices voices appearing psychically on tape (Konstantine Raudive)

Ravenna wrathful adversary in the *Ramayana* who kidnaps Sita

Ravidas (Raidas) Indian cobbler, mystic, teacher of Mirabai; 17th c.

raw foods diet of uncooked vegetables and sprouts

Ray one of seven channels through which all being in the solar system flows (Theosophy)

I ....will, power
II...love, wisdom
III...intelligence
IV ....art, harmony, beauty
V.....................scientific understanding
VI...devotion
VII............................... ceremonial order

Ray, Satyajit Bengali film director; *The Apu Trilogy*; 1922-

Raza 'the race', Chicanos (United Farmworkers, *Spanish*)

Razi Islamic alchemist; *The Book of the Secret of Secrets*; ca. 825-925

Raziel angel from whom Adam received a Kabbalistic book

rddhi sensual delight, wealth; yogic obstacle (Sanskrit)

Re (Ra) Egyptian Sun God

real work the work of really looking at ourselves, of becoming more real; cultivating ecological consciousness and re-inhabiting the continent (Gary Snyder)

Realistic Advaita yogic philosophy upholding the reality of the world as a manifestation of the Real (Aurobindo)

reality check empirical feedback

reality principle theory that human survival is the basic motivating factor (Freud)

reality-tunnel model, especially a limited one

reason n. 1. ordered thought. 2. critical understanding, intellect, as distinct from intuition. 3. basis or cause for belief, action, or an event. 4. purpose, object, aim. 5. justification or explanation of a belief or action. 6. the handmaiden of faith (Dante). 7. center of assemblage, mirror reflecting that which is outside of it (don Juan). 8. (cap.) ideal commonwealth based on education and equality in William Hodgson's utopian romance, 1795. 9. v. to think logically, step-by-step, inductively, deductively, or dialectically; to infer, conclude, judge, argue, convince, persuade

Rebecca 1. wife of Isaac. 2. Jewish maiden, secret love of Ivanhoe in Scott's novel

rebirthing process of releasing repressed attitudes and emotions gained by deep breathing techniques and a re-enactment of the birth process (Elizabeth Lehr)

recall remembering past events while remaining in the present state of mind

receive v. to be empty and attract vibrations or energy from Heaven and Earth

received   language language that the psyche has not absorbed and interpenetrated; dead language (Robert Bly)

receiver 1. person receiving energy in palm healing. 2. channel in ceremonial magic

reconnect v. to go back to the source

rectification astrological technique for detemining the exact birth time when it is not known precisely

recycle v. to reuse things and materials in order to create a sustainable environment

recyclables things that can be reused

Red   Books catalogue of threatened and endangered species published by the International Union for Conservation of Nature and Natural Resources, including some 800 species of higher animals: Asian elephant, snow leopard, polar bear, grizzly, jaguar, cheetah, pronghorn antelope, giant ibis, condor, black-necked   swan,   golden   eagle, whooping crane, paradise parrot, ivory-billed woodpecker, whales, and others

red   giant star of intermediate evolution, with large volume, low surface temperature, and reddish hue

red   miso a short-time fermented miso made from koji, soybeans, and sea salt

red   rice rice cooked with azuki beans and having a nice red color

red   road the path running north and south, the good or straight way, as opposed to the blue or black road, running east and west, the path of error and destruction (Sioux)

red   squirrel tiny endangered being that feeds on pine cones and lives on top of Mt. Graham in the Coronado National Forest, Arizona

Red   Tree book title and prehistoric record of humanity's past 20 million years by psychic Christine Hayes

Red   Zinger zesty herbal tea produced by Celestial Seasonings

redemption of the sparks descent into the underworld in Judaism

Redon,   Odilon French symbolist artist noted for rich colors, magical themes, soft forms; 1840-1916

Redwood   Creek a watershed in California inhabited by old-growth redwoods,

black bear, elk, egrets, otter, salmon and the Chilula Indians

Redwood   National   Park nature preserve in northern California, 1968-

Reeb,   James   J. Unitarian minister, civil rights activist; 1927-65

Reed,   John radical journalist; *Ten Days That Shook the World*; 1887-1920

re-entry return to ordinary consciousness after a psychedelic experience

reenchantment rediscovery, especially of the Earth as a living reality

reflexion process of collective human consciousness (Teilhard)

refined   oil cooking oil that has been chemically processed to alter or remove its natural color, taste, and aroma

reflex   balls (tai-chi balls) metal balls that when rotated in the palm contribute to balanced energy flow

reflexology a healing system based on the manipulation of reflex points on the feet or toes

reformhaus health food store (German)

Regeneration   Institute organization dedicated to environmental, agricultural, and cultural regeneration founded by Robert Rodale, Emmaus, Penn.

Regeneratrix the Great Goddess in her aspect of renewing life

reggae Jamaican music

Regiomontanus (Johann Muller) German archbishop and astrologer, developer of a house system based on equal division of the equator; 1436-76

regression 1. a backward chronological movement of behavior patterns from mature to less mature (e.g., infantile behavior) (Freud). 2. a condition brought about by energetic forces of archetypes attempting unsuccessfully to find expression in conscious symbols (Jung). 3. reexperiencing past events including emotions, behavior, and general state of mind

regression   therapy past-life research and therapy

Regulus Lion's Heart, fixed star in 5 degrees of Leo

rei spiritual body (Japanese)

rei-do spiritual   movement;   unusual movement produced without the participation of consciousness (Japanese)

rei-kai the spiritual world, encompassing the Milky Way (Japanese)

Reich,   Wilhelm Austrian-born psychoanalyst, discoverer of orgone energy; *The Function of the Orgasm*; 1897-

1957

Reichian   Therapies variety of regression methods based on Reichian Character Analysis involving breathing, voice, massage, and movement techniques as well as talking, thinking, and social encounter to access material suppressed in the past by releasing muscular and mental tensions

Reik,   Theodore analyst; *Listening with the Third Ear*; 1888-1969

Reiki 'Spirit Energy,' a spiritual movement developed by Mikao Usui emphasizing laying on of hands to heal and experience peace and harmony, 19th c.-

Reiki monogatari 81-volume 'Tales of the Spiritual World,' by Onisabura

reincarnation rebirth in various bodies from one lifetime to the next

Reisch 20th Hebrew letter: self, progress, R, 200

reishi (ganoderma) mushroom of immortality (Chinese)

Rejdak,   Zdenek Czech parapsychologist; *Telepathy, Telegnosis, Dowsing, PK*

relativity theory (special theory of relativity) Einstein's formulation of space-time providing a common framework for mechanics and electrodynamics (1905), extended in 1915 to the general theory of relativity to include gravity

religion (from *religare*, to bind back, *Latin*) 1. way or ways that people orient themselves in the world with reference to both ordinary and extraordinary powers, meanings, and values (Catharine Albanese). 2. institution whose function is to protect us from an experience of God (Jung)

REM rapid eye movement; correlated with dreaming sleep, occurring at 90-minute intervals every 2-60 minutes

Rembrandt   Harmensz   van   Rijn Dutch artist; *The Jewish Bride*; 1606-69

remember v. 1. to recover your dream, seeing clearly what you came here to accompish in this life (Michio Kushi). 2. to awaken (Gurdjieff)

remythologize v. to affirm that divinity and spirit are immanent in nature, the body, our life and work, and daily life (Joseph Campbell)

remote viewing clairvoyant perception of a distant location

renewer Islamic renovator whom Muhammad predicted would come every

century

Rennes-le-Chateau site of parchments found in the south of France pertaining to the Grail mystery

Repanse   de   Schoye Grail-bearer; wife to Feirefiz and mother of Prester John

repertorization matching symptoms with remedies that produce and relieve affliction in homeopathy

reproductive   trinity Libra, Scorpio, Sagittarius

Reps,   Saladin   Paul Zen author, painter; *The Gateless Gate*; 1895-

Republic 1. Plato's utopia ruled by philosopher kings. 2. Chinese period 1912-49

Resistance draft resistance movement, 1967-68

resonance extremely short-lived type of unstable particle belonging to the hadron category

resonant   field   model image of reality developed by Charles Henry consisting of three intersecting fields: the electromagnetic, gravitational, and biopsychic

resonate v. to strike a similar chord

rest 1. the receptive principle; yin energy; complement to motion (Jesus, *Gospel of Thomas*). 2. infinite speed

restoration 1. healing the land and returning it to its near original condition. 2. a silent retreat (Fransisters)

restoration   ecology 1. movement to resore the environment to its original, natural condition by tree-planting, preserving wetlands and watersheds, bringing back native prairies and grasslands, restocking salmon streams, returning humus to eroded farmlands, and other hands-on activities. 2. shaping the land, transforming the human spirit; restoration as a technique for basic research, a way of raising questions and testing ideas about the systems being restored (University of Wisconsin Arboretum)

restorationist ecologist who restores the land

Restoring the Earth organization that helped launch the restoration ecology movement; based in Berkeley, Calif.; 1988-

RESULTS grass-roots organization devoted to getting political leaders to end world hunger, Washington, D.C., 1981-

Retallack,   Dorothy operatic soprano, discoverer that plants thrive on classical, Indian music, and jazz and wilt on acid rock; *The Sound of Music and Plants*

retas seed, semen (Sanskrit)

retreatant one on a spiritual retreat

retrocognition paranormal knowledge of past events

retrofit v. to renovate and make more energy-efficient. **retrofitting**

retrograde apparent backward motion of a heavenly body

Reverence for Life ethical doctrine of Albert Schweitzer first experienced in the African jungle when he realized that 'I am life that wills to live in the midst of life that wills to live'

reversal pun dream symbol that spells out an emotion or quality

re-vision 1. recreating or reflecting on one's own past or experience. 2. reviewing woman's past and creating a new history and future

revolution annual path of a planet

Rexroth, Kenneth poet, father of the Beats; *The Heart's Garden and the Garden's Heart*; 1905-82

Reynard crafty fox in the medieval French beast epic

Reynolds, Barbara Quaker world peace activist and founder of the Hiroshima/Nagasaki Memorial Collection; 1915-90

rgna pole drum (Tibetan)

Rhadamanthys son of Zeus, ruler of the Elysian Fields

rhapsodomancy divination by opening a book of poetry at random

Rhijne, Willem Ten Dutch physician who visited Japan and composed the first comprehensive description of acupuncture in the West, 1647-1700

Rhombus 4-D computer that programed Sprectra hundreds of light years ago (Geller)

Rhys-Davids, T. W. British civil servant who founded the Pali Text Society; 1843-1922

ri'aya method for the pursuit of the mystical life (Arabic)

ri-bi 'separateness-mysterious', Zen term for working of the One in creation (Japanese)

ribat Sufi center (Arabic)

Ricci, Matteo Italian Jesuit priest who arrived in Peking disguised as a Buddhist monk and who introduced modern science to China; *True Meaning of the Lord of Heaven*; 1552-1610

rice cake a light round cake made of

puffed brown rice, popular as snacks and eaten plain or with a spread

rice fast eating just brown rice for several days to recover health, clarify the mind, or develop spiritually

rice kayu bread a whole grain bread developed by George Ohsawa made from baking softly cooked rice with whole wheat flour

rice paddle flat spatula used for toasting grains, seeds, and flour, and for serving foods

rice syrup (yinnie syrup) a natural sweetener made from malted brown rice

Richard of St. Victor medieval mystic; *Benjamin Major and Minor*; 12th c.

Richards, Reed limb-stretching scientific genius of *The Fantastic Four*

Richards, Sue Storm invisible heroine of *The Fantastic Four*

rida contentment (Arabic)

Rider-Waite Tarot deck designed by Pamela Colman Smith under Arthur Waite's direction

Rifkin, Jeremy political activist, economist, and organizer against genetic experimentation; *Algeny*; 1945-

Rig-din Emperor of Shambhala who waged war against, and subdued, the three Lords of Materialism: Form, Speech, and Mind (Tibetan)

Rig Veda (Rg Veda) chief Vedic hymn

Right Action 1. activity or behavior that is balanced and consciously directed toward the good of all. 2. sweeping the garden (Gary Snyder)

right ascension measurement along the equator in astrology

right-brained adj. creative, intuitive, mystical

right-hand path journey to wisdom based on faith, light, and avoidance of sensual pleasures; the perfections

right-handed spiral counterclockwise spiral

right-hemisphere brain region associated with creative, artistic consciousness, as opposed to the left-hemisphere associated with rational, analytical consciousness

Right Livelihood work that is consciously chosen, individually satisfying, performed with full awareness and care, and for the common good

Right Practice paying attention to the details of whatever you're doing (Gary Snyder)

Right View first step on the Eightfold Buddhist Path; understanding that the real values are within nature, family, mind, and into liberation, not in saving time or making money (Gary Snyder)

Rikon Tibetan refugee center in Switzerland

Rilke, Rainer Maria German lyric poet; 1875-1926

ring circular pattern visible on the surface of the ground left by UFOs

ring-pass-not confining barrier that acts as a separator or a division between a system and what is external to it (Bailey)

Rinnoji temple in Nikko, Japan, of the three monkeys who see, hear, and speak no evil

Rinpoche (Rimpoche) 'Precious Teacher', title of honor, especially referring to Padma Sambhava who introduced Buddhism into Tibet, 747 (Tibetan)

Rinzai (Lin-chi, *Chinese*) Zen school founded by Chinese Ch'an master Rinzai Kigen utilizing koan technique, 9th c.; brought to Japan by Eisai, 1191 (Japanese)

Ris city on the astral plane with a temple of wisdom (Eckankar)

rishi sage, singer of hymns (Sanskrit)

Rishikesh Indian holy city on the upper Ganges with many ashrams

rising sign ascendent; sign on the eastern horizon at the time of birth signifying the personality as viewed by others

Rissho Kosei Kai 'Society for the Establishment of Righteousness and Friendly Intercourse', Japanese Nichiren Buddhist sect founded by Niwano Shikazo and Naganuma Masa emphasizing group therapy, peace, tolerance, 1938-

rita law, order, custom (Sanskrit)

rites the measurement of Heaven and Earth (Chinese)

Ritornel predestinarian, cyclical religion in Harness's *The Ring of Ritnornel*

ritual 1. ceremony to restore balance with nature and the world and bring back lost harmony and sacredness. 2. periodic, repetitive behavior to create, recreate, enforce, reinforce certain tendencies and potentialities in the biopsyche (Gary Snyder)

Rmoahalls first Atlantean sub-race (Steiner)

Rmz (Ramaz) 'hint', intellectual or symbolic level of Kabbalistic text interpretation (Hebrew)

Roanoke 'shell beads', island off North Carolina where Raleigh established a colony, subsequently lost, 1585-86

Robbins, John social and environmental activist; *Diet for a New America*

Roberts, Estelle English psychic; *Forty Years a Medium*; 1890-1970

Roberts, Jane psychic and channel for Seth; 1929-84

Robertson, Laurel cooking teacher and author; *Laurel's Kitchen*

Robins, John and Mary English parents of a new messiah who planned to lead 144,000 vegetarian pilgrims to the Holy Land, 17th c.

roc fabulous bird which carried Sinbad out of the Valley of Diamonds (Arabic)

Rock Around the Clock pioneer rock and roll song by Bill Haley and the Comets, 1955

rock dust organic fertilizer first popularized by German chemist Julius Hensel

rock people Native Indian name for stones and crystals; mineral beings with consciousness

rocker rock 'n roll dancer or performer

Rocky Mountain Institute appropriate energy institute in Colorado founded by Amory and Hunter Lovins, 1984-

Rodale, Jerome Irving organic farmer, publisher; *The Healthy Hunzas*; 1898-1971

Rodale, Robert publisher, organic gardener; *Our Next Frontier*

Rodgers, Buck radio hero of the 1940s transported into A.D. 2400

Rodin, Auguste French sculptor; *The Thinker*; 1840-1917

Roerich, Nicholas Russian mystical artist and spiritual philosopher who inspired the Roerich Peace Pact Treaty, signed in 1935, to preserve cultural monuments in times of war; *Mother of the World*;1874-1947

Rohan realm in Middle Earth famed for wild horses

Rohanda an Edenic planet in Doris Lessing's *Shikasta* that succumbs to disobedience and degenerative disease

Rohirrim men of Rohan, famed for horsemanship who helped in the War of the Ring

Rolfing a stringent muscular realignment therapy used mainly for back and neck problems developed by Ida Rolf; structural integration v. **rolf** to give a Rolfing session. **be rolfed**to get one

roll back 'to open the door and welcome the robber', basic T'ai Chi posture yielding to the opponent and letting him or her come forward and going with that person's incoming energy

roll in way of reentering the body after an astral projection (Robert Monroe)

roll out turning over and over to leave the body in an astral projection (Robert Monroe)

Rolland, Romain French pacifist, author; *The Life of Sri Ramakrishna*; 1866-1944

Rolle Richard English hermit, mystic; *The Fire of Love*; 1300-49

rolled oats oats that have been rolled and flattened; common oatmeal

Rolling Stones British rock group (Mick Jagger, Charlie Watts, Keith Richard, Brian Jones, Bill Wyman, Mick Taylor); *Let's Spend the Night Together*; 1962-

Roman de la Rose French allegorical love poem by Guillaume de Lorris and Jean de Meung, 13th c.

Romance of Alexander medieval epic attributed to Callisthenes, companion of Alexander the Great

Romany language of the Gypsies derived from Sanskrit and Indic tongues

Romulans warlike aliens in *Star Trek* who sometimes live in peace with humans

Ronach middle level of existence, astral world in the Kabbalah (Hebrew)

Rongo Maori God of Agriculture and Peace

rongo-rongo undeciphered writing of Easter Island

ronin masterless samurai (Japanese)

Ronstadt, Linda singer and song writer; *Hand Sown, Stone Grown*; 1946-

root chakra lowest energy center; sexual center

root race one of successive races of human evolution: Polarian, Hyperborean, Lemurian, Atlantean, Aryan, and two to come (Theosophy)

rose flower symbolic of youth, love, and spiritual attainment

rose hips seed pods of roses

Rosenkreuz, Christian German originator of Rosicrucianism; 15th c.

Rosetta Stone basalt slab found in 1799 near the Nile's mouth which provided the key to hieroglyphics

roshgulla cottage cheese balls cooked in syrup flavored with rose water (Hindi)

roshi 'reverend master', title of a Zen master conferred upon the worthiest of disciples (Japanese)

Rosicrucian member of a medieval European secret society professing esoteric knowledge, founded by Christian Rosenkreuz, 15th c.

Rosicrucian Fellowship esoteric Christian organization founded by Max Heindel, 1909-

Rosinante Don Quixote's horse

Rossetti, Christina English poet; *Goblin Market*; 1830-94

Rossetti, Dante Gabriel English poet and artist; *The House of Life*; 1826-62

roti bread (Hindi)

Rotiianerson 'Nice People', chiefs of the People of the Longhouse

Round Table seat of twelve Arthurian knights (originally made by Merlin for Uther Pendragon who gave it to Arthur on his wedding) at which the Holy Grail appeared

Rousseau, Henri French artist; *La Charmeuse de Serpents*; 1844-1910

Rousseau, Jean-Jacques French romantic philosopher; *The Social Contract*; 1712-78. adj. **Rousseuian** relating to Rousseau's ideal concept of the noble savage; back-to-nature

Routa northern island of Atlantis that resulted from a cataclysm 200,000 B.P. (Rudolf Steiner)

Rowena Saxon maiden and wife of Ivanhoe

Roxane sweetheart of Cyrano de Bergerac

Roy, Ram Mohan Bengali reformer, founder of the Brahmo Samaj; 1772-1833

Royal Science astronomy

RSI repetitive strain injury such as caused by working on a computer

ruach spirit of God (Hebrew)

ruah human soul in the Kabbalah (Hebrew)

Rub' al-Khali 'Empty Quarter', Arabian Desert (Arabic)

rubedo the property of redness in alchemy (Latin)

Rubin, Jerry yippie activist turned yuppie stockbroker; *Growing Up at 37*; 1938-

Ruckelshaus, William (Mr. Clean) first director of EPA and one who banned DDT; 1932-

rucksack all-purpose pack

Rudhyar, Dane musician, painter, astrologer; *The Planetarization of Consciousness*; 1895-1985

Rudi (Albert Rudolph, Swami Rudrananda) American-born Shaivite teacher; 1928-73

rudraksha 'eye of Shiva', berries whose seeds are worn as a rosary (Sanskrit)

ruh breath, spirit (Arabic)

Ruhani Satsang 'spiritual gathering', movement founded by Sant Kirpal Singh (Sanskrit)

ruku Muslim prayer posture with head bowed and the palms of the hand placed on the knees (Arabic)

rulership planetary influence

Rumi, Jalal al-Din Persian Sufi mystic, founder of the dancing dervishes; *Mathnawi*; 1207-73

Rumtek site of a monastery in Sikkim; Tibetan center headed by the Karmapa, 1962-

run group of trials in ESP, usually 25 cards or 24 single die throws

rune 1. letter in the old Scandinavian script. 2. divinatory system utilizing rune stones inscribed with a letter from the Viking alphabet. adj. **runic**

runestone stone on which runes have been carved

rupa matter, form, body (Sanskrit)

Ruskin, John British socialist, critic, mystic; *Unto This Last*; 1819-1900

Russell, Bertrand British philosopher, pacifist, eccentric; *Principia Mathematica*; 1872-1970

Russell, Eric Frank English science-fiction writer, theorizer that Earth is owned by other galactic beings; *Sinister Barrier*; 1905-

Russell, Lao wife and creative partner of Walter Russell; head of the School for Science and Understanding

Russell, Walter artist, sculptor, philosopher who attained satori and went on to develop a metaphysical teaching based on the cosmic spiral; *The Universal One;* 1871-1963

Rustin, Bayard labor leader, civil rights leader; *Down the Line*; 1910-87

Rutas sunken continent in the Indian Ocean (Louis Jacolliot)

Ruth sister of Jesus (Cayce)

Ruysbroeck, John the Blessed German mystic; *The Book of the Twelve Beguines*; 1293-1381

Ryoanji Zen temple garden in Kyoto

Ryogon (Surangama, *Sanskrit*) Mahayanist sutra dealing with the steps to en-

lightenment, 1st c. (Japanese)

ryokan Japanese-style inn (Japanese)

Ryokan, Daigu (Big Fool) Japanese Zen monk-calligrapher; *Heaven and Earth*; 1757-1831

Ryonin Japanese founder of Amida Buddhism; 1072-1132

Ryozen Japanese Zen monk-painter; *White-Robed Kuan Yin*; 14th c.

ryu 'family group', martial arts school or tradition (Japanese)

Ss

Sabarmati place in India where Gandhi set out on his Salt March to the sea

Sabbath seventh heaven; highest level of awareness (Jesus, *Gospel of Thomas*)

sabi 1. effortlessness in execution; Zen art term. 2. loneliness, the color of a poem. 3. the quality of being aged or worn by nature (Japanese)

Sabian 1. Jew or Christian named in the *Qur'an* as a believer in God. 2. symbol or degree of a zodiac sign

Sabina, Maria Mexican shaman; 1894-1988

Sabra sweetheart of St. George and the Dragon

Sacajawea Shoshone woman who guided Lewis and Clarke; d. 1884

sach khand 'True Region', fifth spiritual plane where the work of the Sikh Guru ends (Punjabi)

sacralize v. to make sacred, holy

Sacred Barley Queen divine incarnation of the Druid Moon and Earth Goddess

Sacred Books and Epics

Alf laila wa-laila.... Arabian Nights
Angas............................. Jain scriptures
Avesta .... Zoroastrian scriptures
Bardo Thodol.............Tibetan Book of the Dead...
Bhagavad Gita.................. Hindu poem
Bharata Yuddha............. Javanese Epic
Ch'a' Ching......... Chinese Tea Classic
Conte del Graal, Le............ French epic
Chilam Balam........... Mayan scriptures
Dhammapada.................... Buddhist text
Dilasani............. stories of the Pit River
Divine Comedy ....Christian epic

Eddas..........................Scandinavian epic
Gesar Khan.................. Mongolian epic
Hebrew Bible ....Jewish scripture
Heike-monogatari........... Japanese epic
Hsi Yu Ki .... Chinese epic
I Ching........ Chinese Book of Changes
Ifa .... Yoruba oracle
Iliad .... Greek epic
Kalevala .... Finnish Epic
Keitoku Dento-Roku Zen wisdom tales
Kim van Kieu........... Vietnamese poem
Kitab-l-lquan ....Baha'i scripture
Kitab-el-Hikmet ....Druze scripture
Kojiki ....Shinto scripture
Lotus of the Wonderful Law Sutra ...
Mahayana Buddhist text.......................
Mabinogian .... Welsh epic
Mahabharata ....Indian epic
Mahavamsa ....Ceylonese epic
Mathnawi ....Sufi poem
New Testament ....Christian gospel
Nibelungenlied .... German epic
Nihongi ....Shinto scripture
Odyssey ....Greek epic
Paradise Lost ....Christian epic
Pert em Hru.............. Egyptian Book of
the Dead...
Philokalia ....Orthodox Catholic texts
Pilgrim's Progress.... Christian allegory
Popol Vuh ....Mayan scripture
Prajnaparamita................Buddhist texts
Qur'an..........................Islamic scripture
Ramayana........................... Hindu epic
Romance of Alexander....medieval epic
Secret Doctrine ... Theosophy scripture
Sefer Yetzirah ....Kabbalist text
Shahnamah ....Persian epic
Shariyat-ki-sugmad ....Eckankar text
Siri Guru Granth Sahib ....Sikh text
T'abula Smaragdina ....alchemy text
Tantras ....Hindu & Buddhist texts
Tao Te Ching ....Taoist text
Tomenika MS........... Easter Island text
Upanishads................. Indian scriptures
Vedas ....Indian scriptures
Volsung............................Teutonic saga
Volsung........................Icelandic saga
Walam Olum..........Delaware chronicle
Waniyetu Wowapi......Dakota chronicle
Way of a Pilgrim ....Russian text
sacred circle life; what we're all in to-
gether
sacred geometry art and science of de-
scribing the universe by number and
universal patterns
Sacred gymnastics Gurdjieff exercises
sacred hoop vision of Black Elk seeing
the life and community of the Sioux as
one of many hoops that make one circle
wide as daylight and starlight
Sacred Islands the world's holy islands
include:
Delos ....Greece
Iona...Scotland
Kyos ....Greece
Lamu ....Kenya
Philae ....Egypt
Pu-t'o-shan ....China
Raiatia................................. Polynesia
Turtle Island.............................. U.S.A.
sacred number 1. number derived from
eternal standards in nature. 2. the art
and science of numbers and proportions
which constitute the order of the universe
Sacred Oak King incarnation of the
Druid Sky God
sacred pipe (peace pipe, *chanunpa*, Lakota) pipe binding all creation given to
the Sioux by the White Buffalo Woman; its bowl representing the Earth; the
buffalo calf carving on the stone: the
four-legged creatures; the stem: wood
and growing things; the twelve feathers: the eagle and winged things; and
the seven circles on the stone: seven
rituals to be revealed
sacred space place or circle with amplified energy
sacred temple building or enclosure for
storing and generating heaven and
Earth's energy, transmitting it to the
surrounding countryside, especially the
crops, and imparting an atmosphere of
peace and harmony
Sacsayhuaman Peruvian site of a dressed
block weighing 20,000 tons of mysterious origin
Sadachbia 'good luck of the tent', third
brightest star in Aquarius, protector of
animals (Arabic)
Sadalmalik 'good luck of the king',
brightest star in Aquarius (Arabic)
Sadalsuud 'luckiest of good lucks', second brightest star in Aquarius (Arabic)
Saddharma-Pundarika Sutra Lotus of
the Wonderful Law Text (Sanskrit)
sadhana 1. spiritual discipline, practice,
self-effort, method (Sanskrit). 2. (cap.)
steamship whose engines mysteriously
failed in the Malacca Straits and which
resumed power again after George Ohsawa prayed for the suffering spirits of
soldiers killed in World War II who he
perceived had caused the power failure
sadhu holy man (Sanskrit)

sadhumati goodwill; ninth stage of the Bodhisattva path (Sanskrit)

sadhvi (sadhvistri) holy woman (Sanskrit)

Sa'di Persian Sufi mystic; *Gulistan* (Rose Garden); 1193-1291

Safawid Persian period 1502-1736

Sagarmathe 'Sacred Mother', Mt. Everest (Sanskrit)

sage someone whose heart is empty and spacious as the sky; who doesn't consider the past, worry about the future, or cling to the present (Bodhidharma)

SAGE (Senior Actualization and Growth Explorations) elderly movement emphasizing yoga, meditation, body awareness, 1974-

Sagittarius Archer; ninth sign of the zodiac; of the fiery element: ruler Jupiter: insight, restless energy

saham 'She I Am', sakta mantra (Sanskrit)

sahasrara 'thousand-spoke', crown chakra at the top of the head (Sanskrit)

sahib (pl. ashab) companion, circle of initiates. **as-Sahaba** companions of the Prophet (Arabic)

Sahn, Seung (Soen-sa-nim) Korean-born Zen master with centers in Los Angeles, New York, and Cambridge

saifun a clear noodle made from mung beans (Japanese)

St. Andrew's Cross x-shaped figure representing the union of upper and lower worlds

St. Barbe Baker, Richard environmentalist and international tree planter; *Man of the Trees*

St. Exupery, Antoine French author; *The Little Prince*; 1900-44

St. George's Farm crafts community founded by Ruskin at Sheffield, England, 1876

St. George's Hill site in Surrey, England, where the Diggers sowed parsnips, carrots, and beans

Saint-Simon (Claude Henri de Roovroy) French social utopian philosopher and social scientist; 1760-1825

Sainte-Germain, Comte de 1. European mystic, diplomat, and musician who appeared eternally young, vanished on a trip to the Himalayas in the 19th c., and has been reportedly sighted there ever since; 1710- . 2. spiritual guide in many occult traditions including that of Elizabeth Clare Prophet

Sainte-Marie, Buffy folk singer; *Universal Soldier*; 1941-

sajjada prayer rug or carpet (Arabic)

sakadagamin 'once returner', second stage of Theravada Buddhism (Pali)

sakaki sacred Shinto tree (Japanese)

sake a wine made from rice, traditionally served in small cups (Japanese)

sake lees fermented residue left from making sake used in soups or other cooking (Japanese)

Sakharov, Andrei Soviet atomic physicist, dissident; 1921-89

sakhya friendship with the divine (Sanskrit)

Sakoian, Frances astrologer; *The Astrologer's Handbook*

Sakokwenonkwas spiritual leader of the Mohawk Nation

sakura cherry blossoms or their color (Japanese)

Sakya Monastery international Tibetan Buddhist center headed by J. D. Sakya and Trinly Sakyapa in Seattle, 1974-

Sakyamuni 'Sage of the Sakyas', Mahayanist name for the Buddha (Sanskrit)

Sakyapa (Sas-kya) Tibetan Buddhist sect stressing scriptural study founded by Koncho Gyepo Khon, 11th c.-

sala tree under which Buddha passed into Parinirvana

salam (salaam) peace (Arabic)

Salam 'alaikum peace be unto you; Islamic greeting (Arabic)

Sale, Kirkpatrick author; *Dwellers in the Land*; 1937-

Salem 'peace', vegetarian children's villages in Germany, U.S., and elsewhere founded by Gottfried Mueller after World War II

salik Sufi traveler (Arabic)

Salinger, J. D. novelist; *The Catcher in the Rye*; 1919-

Salman legendary seeker and companion of Muhammad; a founder of Sufism; one of whom paradise is desirous

Salmon the totem animal of the North Pacific Rim

Salome prophetess who tutored Jesus (*Aquarian Gospel*)

salt 1. mineral compound containing sodium, chlorine, and dozens of trace elements that is essential for metabolism and health. 2. the magician, who holds the key to life (George Ohsawa). 3. the most yang nutrient and the one that most directly governs human intuition (Michio Kushi)

Salt March Gandhi's 150-mile march to

the sea to gather sea salt rather than submit to the British salt monopoly

salt pack pack or towel containing roasted sea salt applied to warm any part of the body in macrobiotic home care

salud 1. health. 2. salvation (Spanish)

Sam Bodhisattva hero of Zelazny's *The Lord of Light*

sama' 'hearing', Sufi musical festival inducing ecstasy (Arabic)

samadhana steadfast resolve and concentration (Sanskrit)

samadhi 'concentration, meditation', state of awakened mind beyond all dualist thought; eighth step of the Eightfold Path (Sanskrit)

samana 1. Buddhist or Jain ascetic. 2. vital force emanating from the solar plexus (Sanskrit)

samandow (asaman) realm between life and death (Yoruba)

Samantabhadra bodhisattva symbolizing the love-aspect of Buddha

Samarkand Central Asian city where the Spice Road to India crossed the Silk Road to China

Samayatara 'Diamond Wind', female counterpart of Amoghasiddhi (Sanskrit)

sambara destruction, evolution; third dance step of Shiva (Sanskrit)

sambhogakaya 'reward body', second of the three bodies of the Buddha, signifying fruits of meditation (Sanskrit)

sambodhi perfect enlightenment (Sanskrit and Pali)

Samech 15th Hebrew letter: hiss, S, 60

Samhain Celtic autumn festival, Oct. 31

samizdat underground newspaper (Russian)

samjna ideation; one of the five skandhas (Sanskrit)

Samkhya philosophical basis of Yoga taught in the *Bhagavad Gita*

samosa deep-fried pastry filled with vegetables (Hindi)

Samoset Pemaquid who helped the Pilgrims; 17th c.

sampaku (sanpaku) extreme whiteness of the eyes (Japanese)

samsara transmigration; life and death; suffering world (Sanskrit)

samskara innate tendency of a person; what is carried from one life to the next in karma (Sanskrit)

Samuel Biblical poet-prophet; -11th c.

samurai 1. member of the feudal Japanese military caste. 2. class of guardians in Wells's utopia (Japanese)

Samya Yoga 'union through equality', philosophy of Vinoba Bhave (Sanskrit)

Samye 'Academy for Obtaining the Heap of Unchanging Meditation', first Buddhist monastery built in Tibet after the Potala, southeast of Lhasa (Tibetan)

San Agustin site in Colombia of monolithic statuary; ancient crossroads

San Andreas Fault coastal ridge of California subject to earthquakes

San Fransisco Mime Troupe guerrilla theater company, 1967-

San Francisco Zen Center Soto group in San Francisco and Tassajara, 1961-

san-sho the Triple Heater (Japanese)

Sana'i Hakim Abu Sufi author; *The Enclosed Garden of the Truth*; 1118-52

sanae first young sprout of grain (Japanese)

sanal subcellular entity containing DNA, RNA, protein; physical basis for acupuncture (Kim Bong Han)

Sanat Kumara Lord of the World who came from Venus 80 million years ago and dwells in Shambhala (Bailey)

Sanatana Dharma 'Eternal Way', Indian term for Hinduism (Sanskrit)

Sanchi Buddhist stupa center in Western India near Bhopal

sanchita stored karma of previous lifetimes that may be cancelled for kindness and resolve (Sanskrit)

Sanctificationists women's communal society founded by Martha McWhirter in Belton, Tex., 1866-1904

sanctuary granting refuge to fugitives at a holy place; ancient and medieval practice revived in the 1960s during the Vietnam war in churches and synagogues and in the 1970s to refugees from Central and South America fleeing war and poverty

sand painting Navajo ritual drawing at which the gods appear to transmit healing energy

sandhya period when day passes into night, or night day, favorable for spiritual discipline (Sanskrit)

Sandy generous companion of Tripitika in *The Journey to the West*

Sane/Freeze network of several thousand local groups formed from the union of the National Committee for a Sane Nuclear Policy and the Nuclear Weapons Freeze Campaign, based in Washington, D.C., 1987-

sange 'contrition', sincere recognition of all that is wrong within one and acceptance of one's past karma; main gate to enlightenment (Japanese)

Sanger, Margaret founder of the birth control movement; *Woman Rebel*; 1883-1966

sangha community, order; those who follow Buddha's teaching; all those on the path; all beings (Sanskrit)

Sanghamitta daughter of Ashoka, who brought Buddhism to Ceylon

Sanhedrin treatise of the *Mishnah* that declares whoever kills one person slays the world (Hebrew)

Sanjaya charioteer of King Dhritarashtra who recited the *Bhagavad Gita* between Krishna and Arjuna

sankhara karma-formations; link in the Buddhist chain (Pali)

sankirtana group chanting, e.g. by the Hare Krishnas (Sanskrit)

sannyas life of renunciation (Sanskrit)

sannyasi (sannyasin) male ascetic (Sanskrit). **sannyasini** female ascetic (Sanskrit)

Sanskrit 'polished, perfected', classical language of India, related to Greek and Latin; rarely spoken today, though the foundation of Hindi, Bengali and other Indic tongues

Sant Mat path of the masters (Punjabi)

Santa Maria of Guadalope patroness of Mexico

Santee Eastern Sioux tribes which speak Dakota

Santeria Afro-Caribbean or Brazilian ceremony

Santiago de Compostela Spanish Cathedral over the tomb of St. James; chief medieval pilgrimage spot, 12th c.

Santiniketan 'Abode of Peace', Tagore's school near Calcutta emphasizing dance, art, and creative expression

Santorin Greek island identified as the top of sunken Atlantis

sanzen face-to-face encounter of Zen master and disciple (Japanese)

Sao Raimundo Nonato site in Brazil of cookfires and rock shelters showing evidence of human habitation dating to 47,000 B.P.

Sappho Greek lyric poetess; *Ode to Aphrodite*; ca. -7th c.

Sara heroine of the *Book of Tobit*

Saracen medieval Arab nomad, defender of the Holy Land

Sarada Devi (Saradamani Mukhopadhyaya, Holy Mother) wife of Sri Ramakrishna; 1853-1920

Sarasvati Hindu Goddess of Wisdom

Saraswati, Brahmananda (Ramamurti Mishra) Indian physician, yoga teacher, and founder of the Ananda Ashram in Monroe, N.Y.; *Fundamentals of Yoga*

Saraswati, Ma Yogashakti (Mataji) Indian spiritual teacher, founder of Sivanand International Public School in Gondia, Maharashtra; 1927-

Saraydarian, H. Near Eastern-born mystic; *Christ, Avatar of Sacrificial Love*

Sargeant Pepper explorer in the Beatles' album who originally colonized Pepperland arriving in a yellow submarine with his Lonely Hearts Club Band

sari Indian dress of six yards of cloth folded over and around the body

Sarras Mediterranean island city where Galahad transported the Grail

Sarsen Circle inner stones at Stonehenge

Sarue, Susana Latin American teacher who introduced macrobiotics to the poor in Colombia

Saruman the White corrupt wizard and ally of Sauron in *Lord of the Rings*

sarvodaya 'good of one and all', Vinoba Bhave's social movement (Sanskrit)

Sasaki, Joshu Japanese-born Zen master teaching in the Southwest; *Buddha Is the Center of Gravity*; 1907-

Sasaki, Ruth Fuller wife of Sokei-an; first American to become head of a Zen temple in Japan; *Zen Dust*; 1893-1967

Sasaki, Sadako Japanese schoolgirl who died in Hiroshima of leukemia while folding 1000 cranes for peace; 1943-55

Sasaki, Sokei-an Japanese Zen pilgrim to America in 1906, founder of the First Zen Institute of America; *Cat's Yawn*: 1882-1945

sashimi raw sliced fish (Japanese)

Sasquatch 'giant', Bigfoot being (Salish of British Columbia)

Sassanian Persian era from 226-652

Sassetta (Stefano di Giovanni) Sienese mystical artist; *Apotheosis of St. Francis*; 1392-1450

sat being, truth, that which exists eternally (Sanskrit)

sat naam name of God; Sikh greeting (Punjabi)

sat purusha 'true being', Lord of Sach Kand; Sikh teacher (Sanskrit)

satchidananda truth, consciousness, bliss; true inner nature (Sanskrit)

Satchidananda, Swami (C. K. Ramaswamy) Indian teacher, founder of the Integral Yoga Institute; 1914-

satellitium several planets in one sign

satguru (sadguru) highest spiritual teacher (Sanskrit)

Satipatthana Theravada Buddhism (Pali)

satori enlightenment; Zen awakening, illumination, usually in a flash (Japanese)

satsang 'association with truth', 1. direct contact of the spirit with God within or through a saint. 2. communion or company of devotees of a spiritual teacher. 3. spiritual discourse (Sanskrit)

Sattilaro, Anthony J. medical doctor and president of the Methodist Hospital in Philadelphia who relieved his own terminal cancer after picking up two hitchhikers who introduced him to macrobiotics; *Recalled by Life*; 1931-89

sattva goodness, harmony, rhythm; one of the three gunas. adj. **sattvic** (Sanskrit)

saturated fats fats that elevate serum cholesterol and may accumulate in and around arteries and organs, found primarily in meats, poultry, eggs, dairy, and a few vegetable oils such as coconut and palm tree oil

Saturn 1. Roman God of Time. 2. planet ruling experience, discipline, fate; limiting energy

Satya Sai Baba South Indian saint noted for materializations and psychic surgery; 1926-

Satya Yuga Golden Age of Truth and Purity (Sanskrit)

satyagraha 'truth adherence', force that is born of truth and love; nonviolence; direct action (Gandhi, *Sanskrit*)

satyagrahi male practitioner of satyagraha. f. **satyagrahini** (Sanskrit)

saucerian adj. relating to UFOS

Sauron the Dark Lord in *Lord of the Rings*

saute to fry lightly in a skillet or shallow pan

Savio, Mario leader of the Berkeley Free Speech Movement, 1963

Savitri Priya, Swami (Jessica Lynott) teacher of the Yoga Institute of Consciousness, Tiburon, Calif.; 1930

Savonarola, Girolamo fiery Italian reformer; 1452-98

Savoy, Gene founder of the International Community of Christ; *The Decoded New Testament*; 1927-

Sawyer, Tom immortal 12-year-old

Sayles, John film director; *Return of the Secaucus Seven*

scala perfectionis 'ladder of perfection', spiritual path (Latin)

scarab sacred beetle (Egyptian)

Scaramouche blustering clown of the commedia dell' arte

Schachter, Rabbi Zalman Polish-born hasidic teacher; *Fragments of a Future Scroll*

Scheherazade 1. narrator of the *Arabian Nights*. 2. orchestral by Rimski-Korsakov

Schell, Jonathan author and peace activist; *The Fate of the Earth*; 1943-

Schiller, Friedrich German romantic poet; *Thalia*; 1759-1805

Schionatulander knight-servitor of Sigune slain before their love was consummated

Schlatter, Francis faith healer, faster of the American West; d. 1896

Schlegel, Friedrich German critic, founder of comparative philology and Indology; 1772-1829

Schliemann, Heinrich German-born excavator of Troy; 1822-90

Schlovski, J. S. Soviet exobiologist; *Intelligent Life in the Universe*

schmooze v. to hang out and float through time together with maximum social pleasure

Schonberger, Martin German philosopher who discovered the correspondence of the *I Ching* and the DNA genetic code; *The Hidden Key to Life*, 1973

Schongauer, Martin German artist; *Madonna in the Rosegarden*; 1430-91

School of Esoteric Studies movement inspired by Alice Bailey

Schopenhauer, Arthur Danzig philosopher influenced by Buddhism; *The World as Will and Idea*; 1788-1860

Schubert, Franz Austrian composer; *The Lady of the Lake*; 1797-1828

Schucman, Helen channel for A Course in Miracles

Schumacher, E.F. English economist; *Small Is Beautiful*; 1911-77

Schutz, Brother Roger Swiss ecumenist, founder of Taize; 1915-

Schwaller de Lubicz, Isha novelist of ancient Egypt; *Her-Bak*

Schwaller de Lubicz, R.A. Egyptologist; *The Temple of Man*; 1887-1961

Schwartz, Jack Dutch-born spiritual teacher and author; *Human Energy Systems*; 1924-

Schweickart, Rusty Apollo 9 astronaut

who experienced satori floating outside his space craft looking at Earth

Schweitzer, Albert philosopher, theologian, organist, physician, philosopher of Reverence for Life; *The Quest of the Historical Jesus*; 1875-1965

Schwerner, Michael civil rights organizer; 1940-64

Schwimmer, Rosika Hungarian-born pacifist, feminist; 1877-1948

SCI Science of Creative Intelligence; philosophy of Maharishi Mahesh Yogi

science fiction literary genre concerned with describing life (in the future, past, or present) as it may be affected by changes in what is then conceived of as reality, extrapolated from known or inferred scientific laws

Scientology (from *scio*, 'knowing', and *logos*, 'study', *Greek*) the study and handling of the spirit in relationship to itself, universe, and other life; a route, a way, through its drills and studies one may find the truth for oneself; not expounded as something to believe but something to do; a religion founded by L. Ron Hubbard, 1952-

SCLC Southern Christian Leadership Conference; civil rights organization founded by Martin Luther King

sclerology science of diagnosing the whites of the eyes for clues to health of the whole body

score 1. number of correct hits made in an ESP test. 2. v. to obtain

Scorpio eagle or scorpion; eighth sign of the zodiac; of the watery element; ruler Pluto; keywords: originality, regenerative energy

Scot, Michael Scottish alchemist; 1175-1235

Scott, Cyril British composer and mystic; *The Voice of the Ancient*; 1879-1970

Scotch oats oats that have been coarsely cut with sharp steel blades

Scott, Sir Walter Scottish romantic novelist; *Ivanhoe*; 1771-1832

scoutcraft small UFO

Scriabin, Aleksandr Russian composer, light show pioneer; 1872-1915

script 1. life pattern or program. 2. order of service in ritual magic. 3. sample of automatic writing, speech

Scrooge (McDuck), Uncle eccentric millionaire duck who loves to play in money and spread prosperity consciousness

scrying crystal-gazing

SD Standard Deviation; theoretical root

mean square of the deviations of an ESP test

SDS Students for a Democratic Society; New Left group, 1960s

Sea Org Scientology group on Hubbard's ship

Sea People Phoenecians, Dan, or the Minoans

sea salt salt obtained from the ocean high in trace minerals and containing no chemicals, sugar, or added iodine

Sea Shepherd ecoactivist organizaton

sea vegetable an edible seaweed such as kombu, wakame, arame, hiziki, nori, or dulse

seal 1. growth on Muhammad's shoulder. 2. his epithet as final prophet of God

Sealth, Chief (Seattle) Duwamish chieftain who refused to sell his people's land; 1786-1866

seance sitting by a small group, usually with a medium

seasoning something used to flavor food such as salt, tamari soy sauce, miso, or vinegar

seaweed a plant from the sea high in minerals and vitamins; main edible varieties include kombu, wakame, hiziki, arame, nori, dulse, Irish Moss, mekabu

Second Mesa Hopi region where the Snake Dance takes place

second growth n. or adj. trees or other plants that grow in a forest after the first or old growth has been cleared

second house segment of the horoscope ruling income

second mind state of stopping one's training in Zen, becoming angry, bitter, establishing self a second time

Second Wave 1. industrial revolution (Alvin Toffler). 2. women's liberation since the late 1960s (Marsha Weinman Lear)

Secret Gospel esoteric version of *Mark* mentioned in a letter of Clement of Alexandria found in a 17th c. volume by Morton Smith in 1958 relating Jesus's magical powers, rights of initiation, and possible gayness

Seder 'order', festival meal and service of Passover during which the door is left open for Elijah to enter (Hebrew)

Sedona red rock canyon in Arizona and New Age meeting ground

seed a fertilized and ripened plant with an embryo capable of germinating

seed image archetype (Robert Bly)

Seed, John Hungarian-born deep ecologist and town crier of the Global Village

Seed Man or Woman New Age being, agent of Aquarian ideas (Rudhyar)

seed money money to set up a small business or venture, food stand, craft, or industry

seed-thought idea or suggestion that is planted and hopefully blossoms into life, especially the thought of enlightenment or peace

Seeger, Pete singer, songwriter, peace activist; *Where Have All the Flowers Gone*; 1919-

seeing 1. enlightenment; responding to the perceptual solicitations of a world outside the normative description of reality (don Juan). 2. the ability to observe, paying attention to something beyond one's own subjectivity and introspection (Robert Bly)

Sefer Yetzirah 'Book of Creation', Kabbalistic book on prophecy (Hebrew)

sei (well or spring point) point located at the ends of the fingers and toes where energy bubbles out from the meridians like water from a spring or well (Japanese)

Seicho no Ie 'House of Growth', Japanese sect combining Buddhism and Christianity founded by Taniguchi Masaharu, 1930-

Seikatsu Club a Japanese cooperative or buying club devoted to environmental protection, women's rights, and peace activism, based in Tokyo

seitan (wheat gluten, wheat meat) a high protein dynamic-tasting whole wheat product cooked in tamari soy sauce, kombu, and water (Japanese)

seiza natural right posture and natural breathing; sitting with buttocks resting on heels and back straight (Japanese)

Seka Seifu 'World Government,' George Ohsawa's newspaper in Japan after World War II

Sekai Kyusei Kyo 'World Messianity', Japanese sect devoted to creating a paradise of art and beauty on Earth founded by Okada Mokichi, 1934-

Sekhmet lion-headed Egyptian goddess

self 1. worldly mind, ego. 2. (cap.) Higher Self, divine inner spark

Self 1. One Infinity, Tao, our large mind. 2. (l.c.) delusional mind, ignorance, attachment, stagnation, arrogance; our small mind. 3. the potential controlling and organizing force of the personality; it transcends conscious and unconscious strata; dwells at the midpoint between ego and shadow; realized through the process of individuation (Jung)

self-actualization process of realizing one's full potential

self-health movement toward taking responsibility for one's own health

self-metaprogrammer ego (Lilly)

self-organizing adj. inner dynamism of the universe

self-parenting using inner conversations to love, support, and nurture oneself

self-reflection using our higher consciousness to observe, review, examine, and judge our thoughts and behavior and contemplate the larger order of nature; listening to the voice of our large self; not accusing others but realizing that I am always the cause of my own destiny and I have to change myself (Michio Kushi)

self-remembering work on oneself (Gurdjieff)

self-sufficiency capacity to function independently, especially in food and energy

Selma Alabama town, site of civil rights marches led by Dr. King, 1965

Selye, Hans Canadian neuroendocrinologist and pioneer on stress and healing; 1907-82

sema Sufi whirling dance (Arabic)

semazen Sufi whirler (Arabic)

semi-sextile planets 30 degrees or 1 house apart; minor favorable aspect

semi-square planets 45 degrees apart; major unfavorable aspect

semiotician one who interprets the meaning of signs and symbols

Semjase Pleiadian cosmonaut who conversed with Billy Meier, 1975-

semolina flour from the hardest parts of wheat which resist stone grinding

Sen, Keshab Chandra Indian reformer, founder of the Brahmo Samaj; 1838-84

sencha steeped tea Chinese-style (Japanese)

Seneca 1. New York people. 2. their Iroquoian language

Seneca Falls New York town, site of the first women's rights convention, 1848

senex archetypal old man (Marie-Louise von Franz)

sennin 'free man', sage, mountain hermit, immortal (Japanese)

Senoi Malaysian forest tribe that has

lived for centuries without violent crime, war, or mental and physical disease, attributed to group sessions of dream interpretation

sensitive medium, psychic

sensory awareness recognition of one's feelings at all levels (Charlotte Selver, 1938)

sensory deprivation ascetic method to inspire visions

sentient adj. aware, conscious

Senzaki, Nyogen Japanese-born Zen master who came to America in 1905; founder of the Los Angeles Zen Center; teacher of the precept 'keep your head cool and your feet warm'; *Zen Flesh, Zen Bones*; 1876-1958

Senzar language of Atlantis (Blavatsky)

separating aspect moving away of a planet from aspect with another

separatio state of separation; in alchemy the dismemberment of a body in which the elements lose balance and cohesion and split apart from each other (Latin)

Sephardim Jews of Spain, Portugal

Sepharial (Walter Gorn-Old) British astrologer; 1864-1929

sephiroth (sefirot) mystical hierarchy of ten creative powers emanating from the Absolute in the Kabbalah (Hebrew)

septenary group of seven elements

Septimus planet named in Cayce's readings, possibly Pluto

Septuagint 'seventy', Greek version of the Hebrew Bible, -3rd c.

Sequence of Earlier Heaven transcendental world of ideas arrangement of the *I Ching* hexagrams

sequoia 1. one of the largest and oldest living beings on Earth; member of the pine family (including redwoods) growing in the Sierra Nevada, including some 4000 years old. 2. (Lord Sequoia) King of the Trees at whose feet John Muir fasted and prayed for light

Sequoyah Cherokee chieftain, linguist; early 19th c.

seraphim cosmic powers governing love

seriality synchronistic theory developed by Kammerer

seriatim 'in succession', new forms emerging from the old (Latin)

serotonin (5-hydroxytryptamine) substance secreted by the pineal gland believed to affect consciousness; of the same chemical series as LSD, psilocybin, and the Bo tree

Serpent Mound earthworks in Adams County, Ohio made by unknown migratory people, 1254 feet long

Servadio, Emilio Italian analyst; *Unconscious and Paranormal Factors in Healing and Recovery*; 1904-

Servetus, Michael Spanish-born anatomist, mystic, and a forerunner of Unitarianism; *Resitutio Christianisma*; 1511-53

Serving Trinity Capricorn, Aquarius, Pisces

sesquiquadrate planets 135 degrees apart in a chart; major unfavorable aspect

sesshin 'to search the heart', intensive week of meditation held quarterly in Zen monasteries (Japanese)

Sesshu Toyo Japanese Zen monk and artist; *Hui-k'o Showing His Severed Arm to Bodhidharma*; 1420-1506

Sessions, George philosopher and deep ecologist; *International Ecophilosophy Newsletter*; 1938-

Seth 1. Osiris's adversary in Egyptian mythology. 2. third son of Adam and Eve. 3. parent or ancestor from whom the Gnostics saw themselves as descending. 4. discarnate entity communicating through Jane Roberts

Seton, Elizabeth Ann founder of the Sisters of Charity, first canonized American-born Catholic saint; 1774-1821

Seva Foundation 'service,' nonprofit associated with Ram Dass working in the Third World

Sevagram village in west central India, site of Gandhi's ashram

Seven Arrows 1. Cheyenne teaching symbols of an Old Man, Old Woman, Little Boy and Girl, Contrary, Spirit, Knowledgeable Fool. 2. book by Hyemeyohsts Storm

Seven Candelabra 1. golden candlesticks that the Lord specified to Moses to place in the tabernacle. 2. objects envisioned in *Revelation*, symbolizing the seven churches and gifts of the Holy Spirit

Seven Caves legendary site north of the Colorado River where a tribe (later known as Aztecs) received a message from a bird to head south, 12th c.

Seven Levels of Judgment the natural spirallic growth and development of consciousness through seven states from materialization on this Earth to union with One Infinity (George Ohsawa and Michio Kushi)

1. mechanical.....................heat and cold

2. sensory...................pleasure and pain
3. emotional.....................love and hate
4. intellectual................right and wrong
5. social..................justice and injustice
6. philosophical...............truth and error
7. supreme........................all-embracing
Seven Principles of Unity universal laws of the infinite Order of the Universe: 1. everything is a manifestation of One Infinity. 2. all antagonisms are complementary. 3. everything changes. 4. nothing is identical. 5. every front has a back. 6. the bigger the front, the bigger the back. 7. whatever has a beginning has an end (George Ohsawa and Michio Kushi)
Seven Rays lines of activity emanating from higher planes and guided by a specific master (Theosophy)
Seven Sages of the Bamboo Grove Chinese nature poets, 3rd c.
Seven Sleepers of Epheseus medieval legend of devoted soldiers who slept from 250-425 and helped convert Emperor Theodosius to Christianity
Seven Storey Mountain 1. image in Dante's *Purgatorio*. 2. autobiography of Thomas Merton
seven steps to bliss TM process
Seveners Shi'a Moslems who believe in the seventh Imam who went into concealment
Seventh Inn premier macrobiotic restaurant in Boston started by Michio and Aveline Kushi, 1971-81
seventh house segment of the horoscope ruling partnerships, law, marriage
sexism social or cultural prejudice or stereotyping of females or male. adj. **sexist** one who consciously or unconsciously practices such prejudice or stereotyping
sextile planets 60 degrees or two houses apart in a chart; favorable major aspect
sexuality 1. universal attraction, the primordial Order of the Universe, property of all living beings, as well as inorganic atoms, stars, galaxies, and universes (George Ohsawa). 2. a polarized flow of power between two people (Starhawk)
Seyfert galaxy extremely small galaxy with a bright nucleus (Carl Seyfert)
SFF Spiritual Frontiers Fellowship
sfumato 'like smoke', subtle gradation of tone from light to dark (Leonardo)
shabbat (sabbath) day of rest from sunset Friday until three stars are visible in the sky on Saturday evening (Hebrew)
Shabbethai Zevi East European Jewish

mystic, proclaimed messiah, Muslim convert; 1626-76
shabd sound, spiritual sound, sound current, audible life stream, word, music of the spheres; inner music responsible for the creation and maintenance of the universe (Sanskrit)
Shabistan, Muhammad Sufi philosopher; *The Secret Garden*; 14th c.
shadow inferior part of the personality, splinter self (Jung)
Shadowfax beautiful silver horse who served in the *Lord of the Rings*
Shah, Indries Sufi author; *The Magic Monastery*; 1924-
Shahnamah 'Epic of Kings', Persian epic by Firdausi, 1010
Shaikh-Zada Mahmud Muzahib Persian artist; *Illustrator Diwan*; 1499-1537
shaivite n. or adj. follower or disciple of Shiva
Shakers visionary movement that lived communally, nonsexistly, ascetically, led by Mother Ann, 18-19th c. adj. **Shakeresque**
shakta worshipper of the divine female energy (Sanskrit)
shakti 'energy', divine female (Sanskrit)
shaktiput psychic transferral of energy from guru to disciple (Sanskrit)
Shaku, Sokatsu Japanese Zen Buddhist who arrived in San Francisco in 1906 and organized a lay Zen movement
Shaku, Soyen Japanese master who brought Zen to the West at the World Parliament of Religions in 1893; *Sermons of a Buddhist Abbot*; 1859-1919
shakufuku (shakubuku) 'to break and subdue', zealous missionizing of Soka Gakkai and Nichiren Soshu (Japanese)
shakuhachi flute used in Zen meditation (Japanese)
Shakuntala Sanskrit drama by Kalidasa, which caused a sensation when introduced in Europe in 1789
shalom peace (Hebrew)
shaman 1. spiritual guide and healer in primitive society (Siberian). 2. a technician of the sacred. 3. a person who enters an altered state of consciousness at will to contact and utilize an ordinarily hidden reality in order to acquire knowledge, power, and to help other persons; having at least one, and usually more 'spirits' in his or her personal service (Michael Harner). v. **shamanize**

shamar Red Hat lama of the Karma Kargyudpa sect (Tibetan)

shamatha 'resting the mind in non-struggle,' sitting meditation (Sanskrit)

Shambhala 1. mythical Central Asian kindom, origin and center of the world where all spiritual energies emanate. 2. site where Buddha taught the Kalachakra Tantra. 3. heart chakra in all beings. 4. Buddha Nature, essence of all things. 5. origin and head of the mysteries on the physical plane, established 18.5 million years ago, where Sanat Kumara and his pupils dwell (Bailey). 6. American Buddhist publishing house, 1968-

shan jan holy man (Chinese)

Shang Chinese dynasty celebrated for its ritual bronzes, -1500

Shang Ti Chinese Supreme God

Shango 1. Yoruba creator. 2. Trinidad magical cult

Shangri-la utopian Tibetan community in Hilton's *Lost Horizon*

Shankara (Shankaracharya) Indian Vedantist philosopher from Malabar; *Crest Jewel of Discrimination*; 788-820

Shanker, Ravi Indian sitar player; *My Music, My Life*; 1920-

shanta awe at the Lord (Sanskrit)

shanti peace (Sanskrit)

Shanti Deva Indian Buddhist philosopher; *Bodhicaryavatara*, 691-743

shanti sena peace army; nonviolent corps (Gandhi and Vinoba Bhave, *Sanskrit*)

shanti-sainik peace soldier (Sanskrit)

Shao Yung Confucian sage whose *I Ching* diagrams fell into the hands of Leibnitz who was working on a similar binary system; 11th c.

Shaolin (Shaoling) 1. temple on the northern side of Shao-shih Mountain south of Sung Mountain in Honan, China, attributed to Emperor Hsiao Wen, 4th c.; site where Bodhidharma faced a wall for nine years and Hsuan Tsang retired to translate scriptures after his return from India. 2. shadow boxing; Chinese martial art founded by Bodhidharma, taught at the temple, and identified with the temple ever since

shareholder activism utilizing ownership of stock in a corporation to encourage management to change unjust or destructive corporate policies and practices

shareware free computer software or non-copyrighted software

shari'a path to be followed (Arabic)

Shariputra Buddhist arhat, co-speaker of the *Prajnaparamita-hridaya Sutra* whose future name as a Buddha will be Flower Light

sharira 1. solid support, frame, human body. 2. ashes of the Buddha or monk (Sanskrit)

Shariyat-ki-Sugmad 'Way of the Eternal', holy scriptures of Eckankar, which disciples study in the dream state

shashu position in which the hands are held clasped on the chest with the arms level (Japanese)

Shasta Abbey Soto Zen seminary in Mt. Shasta, Ca., founded by Abbess Rev. Jiyu Kennott Roshi, 1970-

Shasta, Mt. northern California peak sacred to the Indians

Shasta Nation bioregion encompassing northern California and part of southern Oregon from Big Sur on the south to the Rogue River on the north

Shaw, George Bernard Irish-English playwright, vegetarian; *St. Joan*; 1856-1950

Shaw, Nate (Ned Cobb) Alabama storyteller, tenant farmer, logcutter, subject of *All God's Dangers*; 1885-1973

Shawnee Prophet (Tenskwatawa) Indian spiritual leader; 18th c.

Shazam white-bearded prophet and magical name in *Captain Marvel*

She Goddess

sheathe one of various cloaks or bodies of denser vibration covering the soul; Upanishadic ones include:

annamayakosha ....physical
pranamayakosha ....vital
manomayakosha ....mental
vijnanamayakosha .... truth
anandamayakosha........................... bliss
chidmayakosha........................... divine
sadmayakosha .... reality

sheikh (shaikh) 'old man', 1. guide or master of Sufis in Sunni Islam. 2. deputy of the Pir authorized to initiate dervishes among Shi'ites. 3. title of respect (Arabic)

Shein 21st Hebrew latter: light movement, sweet sounds, Sh, 300

shekinah 'indwelling', divine spirit sharing Israel's exile (Hebrew)

shekinan wild peony tea, longevity brew drunk by Moses and the angel (Michio Kushi)

Sheldrake, Rupert biologist and theorizer of morphological resonance; *A New Science of Life*

Shelley, Percy English romantic poet, mystic, vegetarian; *Prometheus Unbound*; 1792-1822

Shelton, Herbert nutritionist, popularizer of a natural hygiene system of fasting, exercise, fresh air, sunshine; 1900-

shen spirit, power (Chinese)

Shen Hui Chinese Ch'an master, founder of the Southern School; 668-760

sheng 1. spiritual guide, high adept. 2. a sacred wind instrument used almost entirely for holy seasonal convocations, with twenty-four pipes (Chinese)

Sheol Underworld (Hebrew)

Sher-Gil, Amrita Indian Sikh expressionist artist; *The Old Storyteller*; 1912-41

Sherwood Forest English abode of Robin Hood and his merry band

shiatsu 'finger pressure', acupressure massage (Japanese)

Shibayama, Zenkai Japanese Rinzai Zen master; *Comments on the Mumonkan*; 1894-

shibui understatement, austerity by choice, naturalness; Zen quality. adj. **shibuino** (Japanese)

Shigatze monastery and seat of the Tashi Lama in Tibet

Shih K'o eccentric Chinese Ch'an artist; *Two Patriarchs Harmonizing Their Minds*; 10th c.

Shih Nai-an Chinese novelist; *All Men Are Brothers*; 14th c.

shiitake (*Lentinus edodes*) a mushroom native to the Orient used dried or fresh in cooking (Japanese)

Shi'ites (Shi'ah, Shia) followers of Islam who believe spirituality passed only through the Prophet's family, beginning with Ali, his son-in-law

shikan-taza 'just sitting', Soto Zen practice (Japanese)

shikara 1. high tower over a temple of Vishnu. 2. Kashmiri house boat (Sanskrit)

Shikasta planet in a novel by the same name by Doris Lessing, 1979

Shim Gum Do 'Way of the Mind Sword', Zen martial art founded by Chang Shik Kim, 1965- (Korean)

Shimano-roshi, Eido Tai Japanese Zen master and Abbot of the Zen Studies Society, New York

Shimoda, Donald reluctant messiah in Richard Bach's *Illusions*

shin 1. heart, mind, will, True Self, Buddha Nature. 2. the divine spirit that forms in the embryo after three months and enters with a charge causing the heart to beat and development of the chakras (Japanese)

shin chu acupoint on back about one-third down, center of governing vessel and back of heart chakra, good for moxibustion for mental tranquility (Japanese)

shin-kai the divine world, encompassing the entire universe (Japanese)

Shin Sen Do Way of the Spiritual Free Human; sennin's practice including self-mastery, longevity and health cultivation, social activity and educating others, and alchemy (Japanese)

Shin Silavamsa Burmese Buddhist monk and author; *Stories About the Way to the Other Side*; 1453-1518

Shingo Japanese village where Jesus is said to have come and lived to 112 years of age after his brother Isukiri died in his place

Shingon 'true words', Japanese tantric Buddhism brought from China by Kobo Daishi, 806-

Shinran Japanese Buddhist founder of the Jodo Shin sect; 1173-1262

Shinto 'Way of the Gods', way of life devoted to nature and ancestral spirits (Japanese)

shio kombu 'salty kombu,' pieces of kombu cooked for a long time in tamari soy sauce (Japanese)

shio nori 'salty nori,' condiment of nori and tamari soy sauce (Japanese)

shippei bamboo stick carried by a Zen master (Japanese)

Shiprock ('Tse'bit'ai) 'rock with wings', Navaho sacred summit in New Mexico

Shipwrecked Sailor Egyptian novella dealing with an island whose ruler was a bearded, talking serpent, -1750

Shire country in the northern land of Eriador where Hobbits live (Tolkien)

shirshasana yogic head stand (Sanskrit)

shiso (beefsteak leaves) leaves pickled with umeboshi plums (Japanese)

shista 'remainder', superior class left behind on a planet to serve as life seeds for the next cycle (Sanskrit)

Shiva (Siva) 'kindly', Hindu God of Illusion, Yoga, Animals, Ascetics; Lord of the Dance, who lives on Mt. Kailas, Benares, and sundry other places around the world. adj. **shaivite**

Shiva Nataraja Shiva, Lord of the Dance

Shiva Ratri spring festival devoted to

Shiva (Sanskrit)

Shivapuri Baba (Sri Govindananda Bharati) Indian pilgrim and yogi; 1826-1963

Shiwanna Cloud People of the Pueblos, spirits of the dead

Shobo 'Good Law', first period of the true law lasting a thousand years after Buddha's death when the correct teachings continued to spread; Hinyana era (Japanese)

Shobogenzo 'Treasury Eye of the True Teaching', Zen work by Dogen, 13th c. (Japanese)

shocking traditional style of cooking noodles or beans by adding some cold water to the pot each time the water comes to a boil

shofar the ram's horn, sounded in the synagogue principally on the New Year and whose blast will announce the coming of the Messiah.

shogi Japanese-style chess in which captured pieces are reincarnated

shoji sliding partition (Japanese)

shojin ryori 'cuisine for spiritual advancement', traditional vegetarian Buddhist temple cuisine (Japanese)

Shokai Reikan Japanese Zen artist; *One-Stroke Bodhidharma*; 1315-96

Shokei Japanese Zen artist; *Eight Scenic Views of the Confluence of the Hsiao and Hsiang Rivers*; 15th c.

Shoku-Yo Kai Food Cure Society; first macrobiotic society in Japan founded by students of Sagen Ishizuka, 1908

Shona main Bantu language of Zimbabwe

shonin Buddhist saint (Japanese)

shoshin beginner's mind (Japanese)

Shotoku, Empress Japanese monarch whose printing of 1 million Buddhist charms introduced printing to the world; 8th c.

Showa Japanese era from 1926-89

shoyu natural soy sauce (Japanese)

shraddha self-honesty, faith (Sanskrit)

shravaka 'one who hears', disciple (Sanskrit)

Shri Hindu Goddess Lakshmi

shri-yantra mystical diagram (Sanskrit)

Shrii Shrii Anandamurti (P. R. Sarkar) Indian teacher, founder of Ananda Marga; 1921-

shrim mantric seed-syllable of Lakshmi (Sanskrit)

shrine place to empty the mind and self-reflect and gain back the sense of One

Infinity (Michio Kushi)

shrishti overlooking, creation, evolution; Shiva's first dance step (Sanskrit)

shu gyo self-education; experiencing hunger, difficulties, travel (Japanese)

Shubun, Tensho Japanese Zen artist; *The Ten Oxherding Pictures*; 15th c.

shugyo ritual circumambulation of a mountain (Japanese)

Shuhudiyya semipantheistic Islamic school holding that the universe is a mirror of the divine (Arabic)

Shuman the Human bald truth seeker in R. Crumb's comix

Shun Chinese emperor who inspected the kingdom by testing the exact pitches of the musical notes in each region in accordance with the five tones

Shungopavi Hopi site where the Snake Dance is held in even-numbered years

Shuo Kua discussion of the trigrams in the *I Ching* (Chinese)

Shurtleff, William soyfoods educator and author; *The Book of Tofu*; 1941-

shushumna kundalini channel within the spine (Sanskrit)

shuvo turning one's face to God, repentence (Hebrew)

Shwe Dagon Golden Pagoda in Rangoon

Shwemawdaw Great Golden God pagoda in Pegu, Burma

Sibyl representation of Apollo or Artemis at the Delphic Oracle who answered questions symbolically

sickness 1. physical, mental, or spiritual disorder characterized by stagnation, blockage, heaviness, attachment, rigidity, lack of vitality, etc. 2. nature's wonderful adjustment for our selfishness and arrogance (Michio Kushi)

siddha 1. perfected male soul (Sanskrit). 2. follower of Maharishi

siddhangana perfected female soul (Sanskrit)

Siddhartha 'he who has attained his aim', 1. given name of Buddha; in usage, refers to the period before his enlightenment. 2. title and main character of Hesse's novel about a disciple of the Buddha. 3. white mustard seed (Sanskrit)

siddhi occult power (Sanskrit)

sidereal adj. stars, constellations, or apparent motion of fixed stars. **sidereal day** 23 hours, 56 minutes, 4.09 seconds. **sidereal month** 27.322 days (from Latin)

Sidgwick, Henry English educator,

founder of the Society for Psychical Research; 1838-1900

Sidpa Bardo third and last after-death stage, rebirth state (Tibetan)

Siege Perilous empty seat of the Round Table that meant death to the occupant unless he found the Grail

Siegel, Bernie surgeon and holistic healer, originator of the Exceptional Cancer Patient group; *Love, Medicine, and Miracles*; 1932-

Siegel, Mo founder of Celestial Seasons

Siegfried hero of the *Nibelungenlied*

Sierra Club environmental organization founded by John Muir, 1892-

sigil 1. signature, seal. 2. significant event in the horoscope

Sigmund hero of the *Volsunga Saga*

sign apparent location of the Sun through the zodiac each month

signature (doctrine of signatures) characteristic essence, virtue, or quality of a plant, herb, or other substance (Paracelsus)

significance ESP result equaling or surpassing chance, usually 50-1 odds

significator planet or chart factor of special significance

Sigune beloved of Schionatulander in Arthurian myth who was slain in her service

Sigurd son of Sigmund and last of the Vulsungs

Sijilmassa crossroads on the caravan routes across North Africa

Sikh 'disciple', spiritual community centered in the Punjab, emphasizing monotheism and unity, founded by Guru Nanak, 15th c.

Sikh Dharma Brotherhood of the Western Hemisphere Sikh order founded by Harbhajan Singh Yogi in Los Angeles

Sikkim tiny Himalayan kingdom absorbed into India in 1975

sila Buddhist morality, practice of the virtues (Sanskrit)

Silbury Hill site of a large megalithic mound in Ireland

silence state of total peace where one can hear all sounds in harmony

silence day July 10, observed to commemorate the day Meher Baba began his silence in 1925

Silmarils a trio of jewels holding the essential Light of the Two Trees of Valinor in Tolkien's *The Silmarillion*

Silva, Jose engineer, founder of Silva

Mind Control; 1914-

silver cord connection between the physical and astral bodies mentioned in Ecclesiastes XII:6

Simeon son of Cleophas, cousin of Jesus, Nazorean leader

Simeon ben Yochai rabbi, reputed author of the *Zohar*; 2nd c.

similimum perfect remedy for a patient in the perfect potency (homeopathy)

Simon Christlike child in Golding's *Lord of the Flies*

Simon of Cyrene man who carried Jesus's cross

Simonton, Carl holistic physician pioneering in vizualization to help relieve cancer

SIMS Students International Meditation Society

simultaneity group prose and poetry reading based on impromptu blending of sound and environment

Simurgh king of the birds in Attar's *Parliament of Birds*

Sin 1. Sumerian Moon God. 2. (l.c.) forgetting one's true self; source of ultimate suffering. 3. transgression that exists only in the mind, in dualistic consciousness (Michio Kushi)

sinanthropus (Peking Human) early human living in China ca. 350,000 B.P., excavated between 1927-37

sine wave 1. two-dimentional representation of the spiral. 2. a symbol of the spiritual journey with hell as the descending portion of the sine wave below the midline to the lowest point; purgatory the climb back up from there to the midline; paradise the rise above that midline to the highest point; and the bodhisattva's return to the world the phase coming down from there to the midline (Sherman Goldman)

sing Navajo healing ceremony

Singh 'lion', family name of male Sikhs (Sanskrit)

Singh, Darshan Urdu mystical poet, master of Surat Shabd Yoga; *Valley of Peace*; 1921-

Singh, Kirpal 1. Indian saint, founder of the Ruhani Satsang; *The Crown of Life*; 1894-1974. 2. Indian author; *The Divine Cowherd and Divine Milkmaids*; 1874-1952

Singh, T. C. Indian botanist; *On the Effect of Music and Dance on Plants*

Singh, Tara Indian-born spiritual teacher; *How to Raise a Child of God*

Singha-Nada 'Lion's Roar', Buddhist symbol of an enlightened being proclaiming truth (Sanskrit)

Singing Eagle (Juan Diego) Mexican Indian to whom the Virgin of Guadalupe (the Goddess Tonantzin) appeared on Dec. 9, 1531

singularity entry or exit point of that which is beyond space-time projecting itself into space-time

Sinhalese Indo-European language of Sri Lanka

sink v. in T'ai Chi to relax completely and concentrate all one's energy in the sole of the foot so that the ch'i will sink deeply to the intestinal center and one's movements will become light and nimble (T. T. Liang)

Sioux Plains tribe that came from the East (from a French corruption of Algonquian *Na-do-wis-sue*)

sipapu 1. hole in the floor of a Hopi or Peublo Indian kiva symbolizing the place where the ancestors came out of the underground Third World into the Fourth World of light and air. 2. alternative library journal published in Winters, Calif.

SIRD International Society of Divine Revelation

Siri Guru Granth Sahib 1. Sikh scriptures assembled by Guru Arjan from the writings of Guru Nanak and other teachers. 2. divine sound current

Siskiyou oldest mountain range west of the Rockies and national forest in Oregon; largest unprotected area of virgin forest in the continental U.S.

sister city program where municipalities from different countries adopt each other and exchange relations to build peace and understanding; initiated by President Eisenhower, 1957-

sisterhood female bonding and friendship

Sistine Chapel Vatican chapel with murals by Michelangelo, Botticelli

Sisyphus eternal stone-roller of Greek mythology

sit v. to meditate.

sit-in nonviolent tactic of physically occupying space, used to integrate shops or block military recruiters

Sita 'furrow', heroine of the *Ramayana*, wife of Rama, avatar of Shri

sitar long-necked guitar with varying number of strings (Hindi)

sitter meditator

sitting 1. session with a medium. 2. meditation

Sivananda, Swami (Kuppuswami Iyer) Indian doctor, yogi, founder of the Divine Life Society; 1887-1963

Sivananda Yoga Vedanta Centers international yoga society with headquarters in Val Morin, Quebec

Siwaliks lower Himalayas in India

Six Dynasties Chinese era from 386-581

Six Gallery San Francisco spot where Ginsberg first proclaimed *Howl*, 1955

Six Realms Buddhist realms of transmigration

sixth house segment of the horoscope ruling health, service, daily life

Sixth World coming cycle prophesied by the Mayan Calendar, starting 2011

skandha 'aggregate', one of five heaps in Buddhism into which all existence is categorized (Sanskrit)

rupa .... body
vedana ....feelings
sanjna................................. perceptions
samskara .... past impressions
vijnana .... consciousness

Skidbladnir magic ship of Frey

Skidd, Clarence King of Zing, villainous inventor of the slipperiest oil on Earth in *Plastic Man*

skillful means (upaya, *Sanskrit*) compassion, tact, subtle techniques expressing perfect wisdom, as set forth by Buddha in the parable of the burning house and three carts in the *Lotus Sutra*; seventh paramita

SKIPI (Super Knowledge Information Processing Intelligence) prototype computer program derived from cybernetics, game-theory, and psychedelic drugs developed by Timothy Leary

sky being that has room for all: sun, moon, stars, clouds, rain, snow, pure azure (Stephen Mitchell)

skyclad adj. nude

Skydancer epithet for a dakini, a female Buddha

Skywalker, Luke hero in *Star Wars*

sleep humanity's ordinary state of consciousness (Bennett)

sleepwalking the somnambulistic state of ordinary consciousness or lack of complete operational functioning (Gurdjieff)

Sleipnir supernatural horse of Odin

sloke Irish sea vegetable similar to nori

sloth torpor of the soul which, loving the good, does not pursue it energetically enough (Dante)

Slough of Despond great marsh between the City of Destruction and the Celestial City in *Pilgrim's Progress*

Small Yang one yang line atop one yin line representing Spring in the *I Ching*

Small Yin one yin line atop one yang line representing Fall in the *I Ching*

small-scale adj. energy-efficient, appropriate

Smaug great dragon in *The Hobbit*

Smith, Joseph founder of Mormonism; *The Pearl of Great Price*; 1805-44

Smith, Lillian civil rights activist, author; *Killers of the Dream*, 1897-1966

Smith, Valentine Michael hero of Heinlein's *Stranger in a Strange Land*

Smith, Wayland King of the Elves in English legend

Smith, Winston protagonist of Orwell's *1984*

Smohalla (the Preacher) visionary of the Columbia basin, founder of the Dreamers; ca. 1615-90

Smokey the Bear Sutra Buddhist discourse by Gary Snyder on Smokey, the symbol of Wilderness preservation, holding up his left paw in the Mudra of Comradely Display, 1969

smriti 'recollection', 1. Hindu sacred texts. 2. constant awareness of the present in Buddhism (Sanskrit)

smudge v. Native ritual or ceremonial practice of rubbing colors, resins, or other substances

snag large standing dead tree

snail darter tiny endangered fish for which work on dams in Tennessee was halted, 1970s-

Snake Dance traditional Hopi dance for rain and prosperity

Snake Goddess the Goddess in the form of a snake symbolizing wisdom, omniscience, and coiled life energy

SNCC Student Nonviolent Coordinating Committee, 1960s

Snoopy reflective, hedonistic puppy of *Peanuts*

Snorre first child born of European parents in North America, by Gudrid and Karlsefni in Vineland, 11th c.

Snowhill Seventh Day Baptist community in Pennsylvania, 1800-70

Snyder, Gary Beat poet, Buddhist wanderer, Earth householder; *Turtle Island*; 1930-

soba noodles made from buckwheat flour or buckwheat combined with whole wheat (Japanese)

social planetarium place to contemplate alternatives (Mead)

socialism modern industrial movement devoted to creating a society in which people work and live cooperatively on all levels

socially conscious investing (socially responsible) making investments based on social or ethical criteria, especially helping community-based projects, low-income housing, land trusts, alternative-energy companies

Society for Creative Anachronism group fostering medieval tournaments and culture

Society of Brothers (Bruderhof) Jesus community with branches in Rifton, N.Y.; Farmington, Penn.; Sussex, Eng.

Society of Psychical Research ESP group founded in London, 1882-

Society of the Mystic Animals Iroquois shamanistic healing organization

Socrates Athenian lover of wisdom; -469-399

soft adventure trip or trek featuring more creature comforts and a less physically demanding experience

Sogdiana ancient Iranian country in Uzbekistan, capital Samarkand

soil mineralization counteracting soil depletion by organic rock dust and other processes to remineralize the soil

Soka Gakkai 'Value Creating Society', Japanese lay movement of Nichiren Soshu, 1930-

Sokei-an (Shigetsu Sasaki) Japanese-born founder of the Buddhist Society of America; 1882-1945

sokushindo 'path of feet and mind', healing method based on reading the soles of the feet (Japanese)

Solar Age the future postindustrial civilization (Hazel Henderson)

solar chart horoscope with the Sun on the first house cusp in the natural degree of the native's birth

Solar Logos ruler of the solar system; personal God (Theosophy)

solar wind cloud of protons moving out from the Sun and affecting the magnetic fields of the Earth

Soleri, Paolo visionary architect; *Arcology — The City in the Image of Man*; 1919-

soli-lunar adj. Sun-Moon relationship

Solidarity Polish labor trade union that spearheaded the movement for freedom and democracy in Poland

Solo, Hans companion to Luke Skywalker in *Star Wars*

Solomon's Seal Star of David; also the seal of the Theosophical Society and a sign of Vishnu in India

Solomon's Ship vessel that bore Galahad to Sarras

Solomon's Star five-pointed star

Soloukhin, Vladimir Soviet author on ESP and plants; *Grass*; 1924-

Soloviev, Vladimir Russian mystical poet; *Winter on Lake Saimaa*; 1853-1900

solstice 'standing still', beginning of summer or winter

solunar cycle four fertile days in the monthly cycle in women measured from the angle between the Sun and Moon at the moment of a woman's birth moving counterclockwise from Sun to Moon; the day this angle recurs each month plus the past three days

soma 1. Indian plant from which an intoxicating drink was made (Sanskrit). 2. drug in Huxley's *Brave New World*

Somadeva Indian poet; *Ocean of the Streams of Story*; 11th c.

somatic n. or adj. physiological

somen very thin whole wheat or white noodles (Japanese)

Son Korean Zen Buddhism

Son of Man expression used by Jesus in reference to himself

Song of Songs (*Song of Solomon*) mystical Canaanite love poem in the Hebrew Bible

Songhay medieval West African empire

Songkran Thai Water Festival in April in which people splash water on Buddha images and each other

sonic driving drumming

Sonrin 'Honored Forest', dead sparrow companion of Zen artist Ikkyu Sojun; d. 1453

Sons of Light Essenes

Sons of the Book (Karaites) Jewish sect that accepted the *Bible* and rejected the *Talmud*, 8th c.

Sophocles Greek poet; *Oedipus Rex*; ca. -496-06

sorn scientist or intellectual in C. S. Lewis's space trilogy

sosan listening to Zen lectures in a group (Japanese)

Sotai simple natural exercise system developed by Keiji Hashimoto in Japan

sotapanna stream-enterer; first stage of Theravada Buddhism (Pali)

Sotatau Japanese Zen artist; *Gods of Wind and Thunder*; 17th c.

SOTGO Servers of the Great Ones

Sothic Calendar Egyptian calendar based on 1460-year cycles

Soto (Ta'ao-tung, *Chinese*) one of the major Zen sects brought to Japan from China by Dogen emphasizing the precepts, natural koans arising from daily life, unity of training and enlightenment, 1227-

Sotuknang first being created by Taiowa, the Hopi Creator, who then laid out the universes

souk Moroccan market

soul 1. immortal essence of all beings. 2. mediator between spirit and matter (Bailey). 3. person, especially one who is lost or suffering. 4. discarnate entity. 5. sensitivity, black roots (from Old English *saiwala*)

Soul City 1. Harlem. 2. experimental community in Warren County, N.C.

Soul Food black Southern-style cooking, especially cornbread, black-eyed peas, collard greens, and dumplings adapted by Afro-Americans from traditional Native American foodways

soul force (satyagraha, *Sanskrit*) nonviolent resistance (Gandhi)

soul garment body

soul mate one with whom an individual has had close and favorable association in more than one lifetime

Soul Travel movement of the inner consciousness through the lower states through ascent into the ecstatic state (Eckankar)

soul twin being who develops along a complementary path and joins with an individual soul in higher realms

sound current inner music, divine melody, music of the spheres (Sikh)

Sound Table 81 basic sounds manifested from the Infinite (Michio Kushi)

sourdough bread bread made with a sour starter of whole wheat flour and water or other sour food that has naturally fermenting properties

southern signs Libra through Pisces

soy milk a liquid residue from cooking tofu used as a beverage or in cooking

soybean (soyabean) versatile bean high in protein used in making tofu, miso, tamari soy sauce, and other products; available in black or yellow varieties

soyfoods products made from soybeans including miso, tofu, tempeh, natto, and tamari soy sauce

Soyfoods Center educational and technical center promoting soybean products-founded by Bill Shurtleff and Akiko Aoyagi in Lafayette, Calif., 1976-

space 1. something inside, path to one's center. 2. allowing for observation, nonjudgmental awareness (est)

space bridge televised event linking the world (Joseph Goldin)

space brother/sister extraterrestrial

space music very slow, vibrant electronic music which evokes the vast expanses of space

Space of Former Heaven Taoist term for the Third Eye (*Secret of the Golden Flower*)

space out v. to be unfocused, overly yin. adj. **spacey, spaced, spaced out**

space people beings from outer space

space shoes naturally made shoes, often with a flat heel

space therapy method of dissolving psychological space by holding a posture for a stipulated amount of time (Trungpa)

space-time four-dimensional continuum used in relativity theory to unify the traditional concepts of space and time

spaceship earth planet Earth (Buckminster Fuller)

spacetime space and time as one continuum or dimension

Spangler, David New Age author and community organizer; *Revelation, the Birth of a New Age*

species survival preserve a habitat, museum, educational center, and sanctuary for dolphins or other endangered species (Roxanne Kremer)

speciesist n. or adj. prejudiced toward human beings; anthropocentric

specific negative belief or idea that reinforces negative or destructive behavior and which surfaces in rebirthing

Spectra spacecraft stationed over Earth for the last 800 years, which first landed in Israel (Geller)

spectrobiology science of cosmic correspondences dealing with biochemical relationships of physiology and nature (Maryla de Chrapowicki)

speculum 1. light-refracting shining surface, e.g. crystal ball. 2. grid in which astrological aspects are listed

speech fast day of silence

Speedtalk language theorized by Heinlein based on a musical vocabulary

Speranza Robinson Crusoe's Island off the coast of South America

Sphinx sculpture at the base of the Pyramid at Gizeh, believed to have features of the four fixed signs: head of human (Aquarius), body of bull (Taurus), tail of lion (Leo), claws of eagle (Scorpio)

sphonduloi 'whorls', eight celestial spinning wheels or circles turning upon the cosmic spindle like a nest of bowls, fitting one inside the other (Plato, *Greek*)

sphota thought or sound that makes the mind open like a flower (Sanskrit)

spider being who shielded Muhammad by spinning a web across a cave in which he was hiding

Spielberg, Steven film director; *Close Encounters of the Third Kind*; 1947-

spin rotation of a subatomic particle about its own axis, restricted to integral multiples of a certain basic unit

spinning development of women's knowledge, both creative and destructive (Mary Daly)

Spinoza, Baruch Dutch Jewish philosopher; *Ethics*; 1632-72

spiral 1. the simple but comprehensive form that appears throughout nature, created by the collision of Heaven and Earth's forces (Michio Kushi). 2. the pulsating rhythm that infuses all life, the dance of whirling into being, and whirling out again (Starhawk). n. **spirality**. adj. **spirallic**

Spiral of Consciousness the growth and development of consciousness through seven states from autonomous, mechanical functions to sensory and emotional judgment, to intellectual and social awareness, to philosophical and universal understanding (Michio Kushi)

Spiral of Evolution the spirallically unfolding and complementary development of botanical and zoological life on Earth, culminating with human beings and cereal grains at the center of the spiral (Michio Kushi)

Spiral of History the logarithmic movement of history in which events unfold like a clock in twelve recurrent sections alternating between periods of territorial expansion and conquest and periods of universalization by idea; the current contracting spiral runs from approximately 3000 B.C. to A.D. 2030 or 2040 at which time a new, expanding spiral will begin (Michio Kushi)

Spiral of Life the spiral that arises within

the infinite universe moving inwardly through seven orbital stages (George Ohsawa and Michio Kushi)

Seventh Heaven........ One Infinity/God
Sixth Heaven.. Polarization (Yin/Yang)
Fifth Heaven........Waves and Vibration
Fourth Heaven.......Pre-atomic Particles
Third Heaven ....Elements
Second Heaven......Vegetable Kingdom
First Heaven..............Animal Kingdom including Human Beings.......................

Spiral of Physicalization (Spiral of Materialization) the inward-moving centripetal spiral that culminates in highly evolved animal species, including homo sapiens (Michio Kushi)

Spiral of Spiritualization the outward-moving centrifugal spiral leading to development of consciousness and return to One Infinity or God (Michio Kushi)

Spiral of the Northern Sky precession of the equinoxes; the great circle traced in the northern sky as the Earth's wobble causes the polar axis to constantly change position in relation to the plane of the galaxy, completing a path every 25,800 years (Michio Kushi)

spirit 'breath', 1. the divine, the holy spirit of Christinity, the Great Spirit of American Indians, the creative principle in *I Ching* hexagram #1. 2. energy with a finer, higher frequency vibration than mind or body. 3. ethereal-like phenomena. 4. distilled matter. 5. eternal part of all beings. 6. creative power behind all things. 7. indwelling agency in the hearts of all things. 8. principle of conscious life. 9. angel or demon. 10. fairy, nymph, elf. 11. discarnate essence that survives death. 12. disembodied soul that communicates with the living, especially through a medium. 13. that which is reincarnated from one life to another. 14. will to live, faith in the universe. 15. delight, existential courage, zest, enthusiasm. 16. chemical essence, distillation adj. **spiritual**. n. **spirituality** (from Latin *spiritus*)

spirit dreaming astral projection and communicating with the spirits; Native American practice

spirit keeper imaginary childhood playmate and teacher (P.M.H. Atwater)

Spirit Path the Milky Way (Sioux)

spirit people beings in the after-death realm

Spirit Pond Inscriptions three runestones found near Popham Beach, Me.,

in 1928 of possible 11th c. Viking origin

spiritism communication with those who have departed the earthplane

Spiritual Assembly governing body of a Baha'i community

spiritual channel the channel of electromagnetic energy in the body extending from the hair spiral on the back of the head through the genital region and including the chakras and meridians (Michio Kushi)

spiritual civilization the light half of the spiral of the northern sky during which the Earth receives more electromagnetic energy from the Milky Way and human society is more peaceful and harmonious; ca. 12,000-24,000 B.C. and A.D. 2100-15,000 (Michio Kushi)

spiritual constitution the energetic human structure including the spine, chakras, meridians, organs, tissues, and trillions of cells that are constantly bathed in a shower of light and radiation (Michio Kushi)

spiritual emergency a sudden shift in consciousness that may involve intense emotions, visions, and other sensory changes leading to a crisis in daily coping (Christina and Stanislav Grof)

spiritual feminism women's movement that invokes or studies the Goddess, cultural archetypes, myth, psychological symbols and tools, and use of ritual

Spiritual Frontiers Fellowship Bible-oriented ESP group with headquarters in Evanston, Ill.

spiritual hierarchy spiritual government of the world including the officers of different ranks, whether incarnated or not (Sufi Order)

spiritual journey 1. endless spiral of materialization and spiritualization; manifestation from and back to One Infinity (Michio Kushi). 2. voyage of visionary discovery and recovery of spiritual balance. 3. pilgrimage to a holy site. 4. quest for truth and understanding, health and happiness

spiritual materialism security-oriented ego-feeding spirituality (Trungpa)

spiritual practice 1. stepping out of self-deception, stopping the struggle to get hold of spiritual states, accepting and making friends with desolate and terrifying situations (Trungpa). 2. developing our spiritual energies and vibration to the maximum degree and understanding the eternal journey of life (Michio Kushi)

spiritual price the time lost at home, with family, and for meditation taken up by modern society (Gary Snyder)

spiritual push time when a space ship sends out particular powers to UFO cults on Earth below

spiritual reVision quest for an optimistic philosophy or outlook (Borysenko)

spiritual structure the underlying human constitution consisting of the spiritual channel, meridians, and chakras from which the physical body and mind develop (Michio Kushi)

Spiritualism movement teaching life-after-death and spirit communication begun by Kate and Margaretta Fox in Hydesville, N.Y., mid-19th c.-

spiritualize v. to energize, activate the chakras and consciousness

spiritus mundi world soul (Latin)

spirulina 'little spiral', green algae concentrate, harvested from Mexico's Lake Texcoco

split 1. division in the personality or consciousness. 2. v. to leave

Spock first officer and chief science adviser of the *Enterprise* in *Star Trek*

Spock, Benjamin child doctor, peace activist; *Baby and Child Care*; 1903-

Spotted Eagle (Wanbli Galeshka) highest flying of all creatures which sees everything and is a messenger of the Great Spirit (Sioux)

spotted owl (northern spotted owl) being which lives in the old-growth forests of the Pacific Northwest

Spretnak, Charlene a founder of the Greens; *The Politics of Women's Spirituality*

sprezzatura 'to scan', nonchalant brushwork of an incredibly difficult execution by a supreme art master (Italian)

sprout a bud, shoot, or young plant, often edible and tender

sprouting generation of new life from roots or stumps of plants

Sputnik first Earth satellite launched Oct. 4, 1957 (Tsiolkovsky, 1898)

Squanto (Tisquantum) Paxtuxet who befriended the Pilgrims and taught them to plant corn; d. 1622

square 1. (quadrate) planets 90 degrees or three houses apart in a chart; a major unfavorable aspect. 2. square-like mark on the palm indicating support, protection. 3. symbol of the material, the

Earth

Square Inch Field Taoist term for the Third Eye (*Secret of the Golden Flower*)

squared circle a geometic pattern of a circle and square with similar perimeter and circumferance representing the reconciliation of opposites; a common feature of temples and creation myths; reflecting the relative diameter, perimeter of Earth and Moon; e.g., Stonehenge, Plato's Atlantis, and the New Jerusalem as described in the *New Testament*

sraddha faith in the instructions of the spiritual teacher (Sanskrit)

sramanna ascetic (Sanskrit)

sravana hearing or listening to subjects with high spiritual nature (Sanskrit)

Sri (shri, shree) mister, sir; polite form of address (Sanskrit)

Srimad Bhagavatam text describing Krishna's life (Sanskrit)

Srimat (Srimad) prefix designating holy, auspicious (Sanskrit)

Srimati Ms., Miss, Mrs. (Sanskrit)

Srinagar Kashmiri capital on Jhelman River with floating gardens, lotuses, and cool air

srishti projection or gradual unfoldment of the universe from a seed state (Sanskrit)

ssu-ling four supernatural animals: Azure Dragon, White Tiger, Phoenix, Tortoise (Chinese)

stacking tool for group conversation; person saying 'stacked' is the next speaker (Storefront Classroom Collective)

stainless steel steel alloyed with chromium to resist corrosion, oxidation, or rusting, used to make quality cookware and utensils and sometimes lined with enamel

Stanchich, Lino Yugoslavian-born macrobiotic teacher and counselor; *Power Eating Program*; 1932-

Standard Macrobiotic Diet dietary principles in harmony with the environment and traditional practice modified for modern times; in temperate regions: 50-60% whole cereal grains; 5% soup (especially seasoned with miso or tamari soy sauce); 20-25% vegetables; 10% beans and bean products and seaweed; naturally fermented pickles; condiments; bancha tea or other traditional beverage; and small supplementary amounts of seeds and nuts, fruit, fish or seafood, and naturally sweetened desserts (Michio Kushi)

Standing Hollow Horn Sioux leader who received the Sacred Pipe from the White Buffalo Woman

Stanford, Ray clairvoyant working with channels called Brothers; *Fatima Prophecy*; 1938-

Stanislavsky, Konstantin Russian director, co-founder of the Moscow Art Theater; 1863-1938. **Stanislavsky method** dance school stressing spontaneity

Stanton, Elizabeth Cady co-founder of the women's rights movement; *Eighty Years and More*; 1815-1902

Stapledon, Olaf English science-fiction writer; *Last and First Men*; 1886-1950

star 1. distant luminous heavenly body. 2. a spiral of energy that is born and lives within the galactic environment (Michio Kushi). 3. starlike mark on the palm. 4. (pl.) Tarot #17, Hope

Star Country Middle Eastern or Western countries with star flags and emblems where people eat primarily bread and flour products, think analytically, and conquer others by science and technology (Michio Kushi)

Star Dust Incan name for the Milky Way

Star Festival seventh day of the seventh month when the divine Weaving Maiden and the Shepard stars are allowed by Heaven to meet across the Milky Way; traditionally celebrated in the Far East by writing poems on colored paper and hanging them on bamboo trees

Star Maker science-fiction novel by Olaf Stapledon detailing the history of the universe, culminating in the union of the Cosmic Mind with the Star Maker, 1937

star people people born on Earth but who have spent past lives on other more evolved planets and who have come to help guide us into a planetary age; may have unusual abilities and yearn for another home world

Star Trek metaphysical space adventure TV series, 1966-68, 1988-

Star Way the Apache way of knowledge

Starhawk (Miriam Simos) feminist, peace activist, high priestess; *The Spiral Dance*; 1940-

Starseed city-sized starship to be sent to the center of the galaxy to contact and exchange information with higher intelligence (Leary)

starship spaceship capable of travel between stars, usually faster than the speed of light

steady-state theory that the universe is in a state of dynamic equilibrium and does not go through a cycle of explosion and contraction

steam v. to cook by exposing to steam

Steiner, Rudolf Austrian-born founder of the Anthroposophical Society, Biodynamic Farming, and Waldorf Schools; *At the Gates of Spiritual Science*; 1861-1925

Step Pyramid structure built by Imhotep at Saqqarah, Egypt

Stephan, Karin yoga instructor and macrobiotic teacher; 1943-

steppingstone significant point of inner and outer movement along the road of an individual's life

Stevens, Henry Bailey vegetarian philosopher; *Recovery of Culture*; 1891-1976

Stevenson, Ian analyst, consciousness researcher; *Twenty Cases Suggestive of Reincarnation*; 1918-

stewardship conserving nature on behalf of the Earth and future generations

sthiti preservation, support; second dance step of Shiva (Sanskrit)

stigmata psychic appearance of wounds

Still, Andrew Taylor Virginia country doctor who founded osteopathy; 1828-1917

stir-fry v. to quickly cook food in a wok or skillet using a small amount of oil, high heat, and with continuous stirring

Stockhausen, Karlheinz; composer; *Sirius*; 1928-

stone ground adj. unrefined flour that has been ground in a stone mill that preserves the germ, bran, and other nutrients

Stone, I.F. intrepid journalist; *I.F. Stone's Weekly*; 1907-89

Stone Mother Medusa or other goddesses whose concentrated gaze turns to stone

Stone of Foundation (Ebhen Shetiyyah, *Hebrew*, Omphalos, *Greek*) huge rock created and placed by God on the Earth; navel of the Earth

Stone, Lucy women's rights organizer; 1818-93

Stone, Merlin feminist author; *When God Was a Woman*; 1931-

Stone, Randolph naturopath, founder of Polarity Therapy; 1890-

stoned adj. high, ecstatic, especially as a result of hallucinogenic drug use (Afro-American)

Stonehenge 'hanging stones', pre-Druidic observatory near Amesbury, England, ca. -2500 (Saxon)

Stonewall Summer 1969 gay riots in New York City against police repression that sparked the Gay Liberation Movement

stopping the world inducing a state of awareness in which the reality of everyday life is altered because the flow of interpretation is stopped (don Juan)

storage tank reservoir for the fluid at the bottom of a solar energy unit

Storefront Classroom Collective utopian psychology movement in San Francisco, 1971-

Storm, Hyemeyohsts Cheyenne author; *Seven Arrows*; 1935-

Stowe, Harriet Beecher abolitionist novelist; *Uncle Tom's Cabin*; 1811-96

straight n. or adj. 1. middle-class. 2. honest, truthful. 3. off drugs or a nonuser. 4. heterosexual. 5. world outside of prison (Afro-American)

Stravinsky, Igor Russian composer, *Le Sacre du Printemps*; 1882-1971

Strength Tarot #8, justice

striation a line or gradation in the aura that shows up in Kirlian photograph

Structural Integration rolfing; realigning of body structure to release tension through massage and physical manipulation

Stuart, Walking John English essayist who walked across Europe, the Middle East, and Tibet; 18th c.

Students for a Democratic Society (SDS) movement for participatory democracy, 1960-69

stupa mound usually made of earth, erected over the relics of a Buddha or saint (Sanskrit)

Stwanite 'stickman', Big Foot of the Washington mountains

Stylites, St. Simeon pillar saint who came down only to ascend to higher pillars in Antioch; 390-459

su sound of peace and harmony that may be chanted accompanied by an image of creating the universe to produce a calm, peaceful atmosphere (Michio Kushi)

Suares, Carlo esoteric Christian author; *The Cipher of Genesis*

subatomic particles a spirallic stream of energy that starts out as an electron and ends as a proton and in between appears to rest at various stops (George Ohsawa)

subconscious lower or unconscious mind that registers every perception, experience, reaction, and feeling, and sensory stimuli like a computer and makes it available to the conscious mind. 2. instinct, the Id (Freud). 3. director of the sympathetic nervous system and mechanical judgment

Subhuti disciple of Buddha who appears in scriptures as the one who really understands and practices compassion

subject person who is tested in an ESP experiment

subliminal beneath the threshold of consciousness

subliminal self subconsciousness or mind (F.W.H. Myers, 1890)

sublimation refining stage of alchemy

sublunary world the Earth and its atmosphere under the influence of the Moon

subluxation misalignment of the vertebrae that crowd the nerves which branch out from the spinal cord and reduce their ability to supply an organ/tissue with enough energy to function properly (chiropractic)

subpersonality semi-autonomous and contradictory aspect of the self (psychosynthesis)

subplane minor division within a plane of manifestation

subsoiling deep plowing for aeration

subtle body one of the nonphysical sheaths of the soul, usually the astral

Subud Javanese spiritual movement involving manifestations, shouting, leaping, weeping (from *Su*shila, *bu*ddhi, *d*harma, *Sanskrit*)

Subuh, Muhammad (Papak) Indonesian founder of Subud; 1901-

succedent houses second, fifth, eighth and eleventh houses in astrology, signifying procrastinating tendencies

success failure (Lao Tzu)

sucrose crystalline sugar found in cane, sugar beets, sorghum (from French)

Sud (Sod) 'secret', highest, spiritual level of text interpretation in the Kabbalah (Hebrew)

Suddhodana Siddartha's father

sudurjaya mastering great difficulties; fifth state of the Bodhisattva path (Sanskrit)

Sufi 'wool', follower or initiate belonging to esoteric orders that developed under the aegis of Islam, carrying over the Mazdean tradition, noted for mystical singing, dancing, and whirling (from Arabic *suf,* 'wool', referring to a person wearing garments of wool, i.e., an ascetic). adj. **sufic**

Sufi Order mystical Islamic organization founded by Hazrat Inayat Khan in San Francisco with headquarters in Suresnes, France, and New Lebanon, N.Y., 1910-

Sufism Islamic mysticism; apprehension of divine realities and the renunciation of human possessions (Ma'rufu'l-Karkhi, 9th c.)

Sufi Hierarchy

qutb	axis, pole
4 awtad (sin. wild)	supports
40 abdal (sin. badl)	substitutes
amd	pillars
70 nuiuba (sin. najib)	nobles
300 nuquba (sin. naquib)	chiefs
awliya	saints

Sufi Orders

Chishti	music and dance
Junaydiyya	sobriety
Tayfuriyya	rapture
Saqatiyya	union
Chishti	music and dance
Naqshbandi	discipline
Gurzmar	piercing body with irons
Naushahis	hanging by feet in ecstasy
Qalandars	clean-shaven wanderers
Rasul Shahis	intoxication
Malamatis	drugs, sex
Jalali	horn blowing in ecstasy
Suhagiyya	transvestism

Sufi Stages

muridi	discipleship
tariqat	potentiality
arif	knowledge
fana	annihilation
baqa	saintship

Sufi Stages of the Path
maqam, 'stations'

'ubudiyyat	service
'ishq	love
zuhd	renunciation
ma'rifat	knowledge
wajd	ecstasy
haqiqat	reality
wasl	union

Sufi States 'hal'

nasut	humanity
malakut	angels
jabarut	power
lahut	divinity

Sufism Reoriented Sufi group founded by Meher Baba in Meherabad, India, with headquarters in Walnut Creek, Calif., 1952-

suffering 1. pain, regret, remorse. 2. what brings us into the field of compassion (Joan Halifax)

Sugar character made of barley malt who accompanies the children in *The Blue Bird*

Suggestology Bulgarian technique for facilitating learning in relaxed ways

Sugimoto, Etsu Inagaki Japanese woman of letters; *A Daughter of the Samurai*; 19th c.

Sugmad formless, all-embracing, impersonal, Supreme God (Eckankar)

Sui Chinese dynasty 581-618

Sujata young woman who nourished Buddha under the Bo tree with milk and rice; his teacher and secret initiator in some schools

Sukhavati Realm of Happiness, Buddhist Pure Land obtained between incarnations by altruistic deeds and thoughts (Sanskrit)

sukiyaki a one-dish meal prepared in a large cast-iron skillet with a variety of vegetables, noodles, sea vegetables, seitan, tofu, or seafood and fish (Japanese)

Sukkah (pl. Sukkot) 'booths', tabernacles; eight-day commemoration of wandering in the desert (Hebrew)

sukr intoxication of the love of God (Arabic)

Sultan Muhammad Persian artist; *Ascension of the Prophet to the Seventh Heaven*; d. 1555

sultanu'l-adhkar 'king of dhikr', Sufi meditation to activate the lata'if through active remembrance of God (Arabic)

Sumedha name of the Buddha in a previous life when he took the vow to become enlightened upon meeting the Buddha Dipankara

Sumeru mountain at the center of the Hindu and Buddhist universe, abode of the gods

sumi-ye ink pictures (Japanese)

Summerhill progressive English school founded by A. S. Neill, 1921-

sumo (sumai) 'struggle', wrestling (Japanese)

Sun 1. Earth's star, nucleus of the solar system, source of life and energy. 2. symbol of divine illumination. 3. Tarot #19: marriage, happiness. 4. (l.c.) wind, the gentle; one of the eight *I Ching* trigrams (Chinese). 5. (l.c.) bamboo shoots (Chinese)

Sun Bear (Vincent LeDuke) Native American medicine man, founder of the Bear Tribe; *Walk in Balance*; 1929-

Sun Country Far East and Asian lands with sun flags and emblems where people eat grains and practice a healthy, peaceful Way of Life (Michio Kushi)

Sun Dance (Wiwanyag Wachipi) sacred dance of the Plains people

Sun Temple Anasazi construction in Mesa Verde used for rites and rituals

Sun, Patricia spiritual teacher and healer; *Psychological and Spiritual Blindspots*

Sung Chinese dynasty 960-1279

Sung-shan sacred mountain near Loyang, Honan Province, China

Sung-yueh-ssu 12-sided pagoda on Mt. Sung; earliest surviving in China, 520

Sunrise Ranch spiritual community founded by Lloyd Meeker in Loveland, Colo., 1945-

Suns consecutive Ages in Mayan mythology: Water Sun, Earthquake Sun, Hurricane Sun, and Fire Sun according to the nature of the catastrophe that closed each epoch

Sunray Meditation Society planetary peace society led by Dhyani Ywahoo, Bristol, Ver., 1983-

sunspot solar activity that follows a 11.5 year cycle

sunyata 'emptiness', the void, immaculacy; primary teaching of the Mahayanist Buddhist *Prajnaparamita* which stresses there is no self anywhere, nor is there anything to be attached to, and that all things are in their nature empty and immaculate (Sanskrit)

superasteroids asteroid zone postulated beyond Pluto

superconscious 'higher unconscious', realm of altruistic love, joy, intuition, inspiration, contemplative and spiritual energies (psychosynthesis)

superego conscience, controlling mechanism (Freud)

superior man sage, teacher, higher self in the *I Ching*

superior planets orbs beyond Earth

Superman 1. creative soul (Nietzsche). 2. comic strip hero created by Jerome Siegel and Joseph Shuster, 1932. 3. master yogi of the present age (Aurobindo)

supermind consciousness between Satchidananda and the lower creation, which descended and became an active force in terrestrial evolution (Aurobindo)

superpersonalization process of unity developing among individuals (Teilhard)

supersensible adj. ability to perceive directly the spiritual world (Steiner)

superspace realm of co-existing universes (Wheeler)

suppleness body condition of smooth energy flow, flexible movements, and lack of barriers between people and the environmentt

supraconscious autonomous realm from which higher impulses originate (psychosynthesis)

supradian adj. cyclic spans greater than a day

supraliminal 1. level of the psyche that responds to psychic information and data (F. W. H. Myers). 2. consciousness above the normal mental threshold, especially of artistic or musical genius

supramental n. direct self-existent truth-consciousness and the direct self-effective truth power (Sri Aurobindo) n. **supermentalization**

supraself celestial teacher, inner guide (Lilly)

supraspecies metaprogrammer celestial guide (Lilly)

Supreme Judgment 1. absolute and universal love that embraces everything and turns every antagonism into complementarism (George Ohsawa). 2. universal consciousness; natural intuition; becoming one with the infinite universe and freely playing on all other levels (Michio Kushi). 3. the art of stopping time or riding on the wave of time itself; that which stops us in our tracks, being propelled from a hurrying horizontal orientation to a vertical, timeless stance (Sherman Goldman)

Supreme Virtue giving birth and nourishing, having without possessing, acting with no expectations, leading and not trying to control (Lao Tzu)

Surabhi 'sweet-smelling', Hindu mythical cow (Sanskrit)

Surangama Sutra Mahayana Buddhist text treating obstacles arising in training, confusion, attachment (Sanskrit)

surat inner attention, inner hearing faculty of the soul (Sanskrit)

Surat Shabd Yoga (Sehaj Yoga) union of the outer expression of the soul (called attention) with the sound within; Ruhani Satsang meditation

suribachi a serrated, glazed clay bowl or

mortar for grinding and pureeing foods (Japanese)

surya Sun. adj. **saurya** (Sanskrit)

Surya Siddhanta earliest Hindu astronomical text

Susano-o-no-mikato antic Shinto God of the Wind

sushi a traditional Japanese-style dish consisting of rice served with various vegetables, sea vegetables, seafood, or pickles; in addition to spiral rounds, *nori-maki*, sushi can be prepared in several styles including deep-frying or as a salad (Japanese)

sushi mat a small bamboo mat used to roll up nori-make sushi or to cover bowls and dishes to keep food warm

sushumna main channel in the spine for unfurling kundalini (Sanskrit)

sushupti dreamless sleep (Sanskrit)

Suso, Henry German recluse, visionary Dominican; *Little Book of Eternal Wisdom*; 1295-1365

sustainable adj. agriculture, culture, or community that is renewable, recyclable, organic, stable; often lasting for thousands of years; with a rich ceremonial and ritual life

sustainable farming organic or chemical-free agriculture utilizing a variety of natural and mechanical techniques such as introducing beneficial insects and extensive and frequent crop rotations

sustainable religion spiritual development through inner growth, ecological wisdom, gender equality, and social responsibility (Charlene Spretnak)

Sutphen, Dick communicator and teacher of human potential; *Sedona: Psychic Vortex Experience*; 1937-

sutra (sutta, *Pali*) 1. thread on which jewels are strung. 2. sermon delivered by the Buddha. 3. first division of the Buddhist Tripitaka (Sanskrit)

Suzuki, Beatrice Lane Zen author; *Impressions of Mahayana Buddhism*; 1878-1939

Suzuki, Daisetz Teitaro (D.T.) Japanese-born interpreter of Zen to the West; *Mysticism, Christian and Buddhist*; 1870-1966

Suzuki-roshi, Shunryu Japanese-born Zen master and head of the San Francisco Zen Center; *Zen Mind, Beginner's Mind*; 1885-1973

svadhisthana abdominal chakra (Sanskrit)

swadeshi 'belonging to one's homeland', principle of using local, hand-crafted goods (Gandhi, *Sanskrit*)

swadharma self-reliance; doing one's own thing (Sanskrit)

Swahili (Kiswahili) East African language of Tanzania and Kenya; Bantu language influenced by Arabic

Swami lord, master, spiritual teacher; title of a monk or nun (Sanskrit)

Swamiji Maharaj (Seth Shiv Dayal Singh) founder of the Radha Soami; 1818-78

Swann, Ingo psychic artist; *To Kiss Earth Goodbye*; 1933-

Swannonoa headquarters of the Russells' University of Science and Philosophy, Waynesboro, Virginia

Swanson, Gloria actress, film star, and macrobiotic health promoter; *Swanson on Swanson*; 1899-1983

Swarga Indra's heaven

Swat beautiful Pakistani valley; former site of 1400 Buddhist monasteries

Sweat Lodge Native American steam or bath house associated with purification rites and ceremonies

Swedenborg, Emmanuel Swedish mystic and prophet; *Heaven & Hell*; 1688-1772

Swedish Massage the manipulation of body tissues by the hands for therapeutic effect

sweet rice a glutinous type of rice that is slightly sweeter to the taste than regular rice and used in a variety of regular and holiday dishes

Swift, Jonathan Irish-British satirist; *Gulliver's Travels*; 1667-1745

switchboard community crisis and counseling service, usually free with a 24-hour phone and drop-in service

Swoboda, Hermann Austrian-born co-discoverer of biorhythm; *The Year of Seven*; 1873-1963

sword 1. Buddhist symbol of Supreme Wisdom that cuts through all attachments and delusions. 2. (cap. pl.) Tarot suit symbolic of thought, adversity

sylph air sprite

symbolic style used by the psyche to communicate its messages; language of the psyche

Symeon the New Theologian Byzantine theologian, mystic; 949-1022

Symnes, Jonathan Army captain, initiator of the Hollow Earth theory in a letter to Congress in 1818

synchronicity meaningful coincidence. adj. **synchronistic** (Jung)

synchronizer gadget or machine to induce desirable states of brainwave activity

synchronous adj. changing in the same way at the same regular times

synergist healing agent that increases the effectiveness of another agent when combined with it

synergy behavior of a whole system; totality beyond knowledge of the parts or groups of parts; pioneered by Buckminster Fuller, using the tetrahedron as a model. n. **synergetics**

synesthesia transference of the data of one sense perception into the language of another, e.g. hearing colors

synocracy a society designed to optimize creativity and the joining of separate people in vital functions within society (Barbara Marx Hubbard)

synodic period time between one conjunction of two bodies and the next

synoptics *Gospels of Matthew, Mark* and *Luke*, which are parallel

syntony state of being in harmony with the environment (from Greek)

syntropy the universal energy-generating principle; complement to entropy (Buckminster Fuller)

System Dynamics way of seeing things as interconnected in complex patterns made up of stocks, flows, and feedback loops

systemmatics understanding of the laws working in life, according to the numbers 1-12 (Bennett)

syzygy 1. connection, combination, or partnership of two factors. 2. astronomical conjunction or opposition

Szasz, Thomas psychiatrist and holistic mental health reformer; *Insanity: Idea and Its Consequences*; 1920-

Szekely, Edmund Bordeaux Rumanian-born philosopher and mystic; tr. *The Essene Gospel of Peace*

Tt

T-cross opposition of two planets both squared by a third

T-group (Training group) sensitivity workshop developed by Kurt Kewin

Ta Lu advanced two-person T'ai Chi exercises

Taama legendary bearer of the coconut tree to the South Pacific

tabaqs fourteen regions created by the Name of God (Arabic)

Tabard London hostelry from which Chaucer's pilgrims left for Canterbury

table list of planetary information

table work work or therapy involving a massage table

tablets of I'sidi (Squares of Araby) Enochian system of divination; grid of 16x16 squares marked with symbols

Tabula Smaragdina 'Emerald Table', alchemy text attributed to Hermes Trismegistus, 9th c. (Latin)

tachyon postulated subatomic particle faster than the speed of light

taco a tortilla folded up and filled with beans, vegetables, or sea vegetables

tae kwon do 'kick punch way', Korean empty-handed martial art, ca. 4th c.-

tafrid annihilation or separation from the Divine (Arabic)

Tagore, Rabindranath Indian poet, mystic, and educator; *Gitanjali*; 1861-1941

tahini a thick, smooth paste made from ground sesame seeds

Taht (Thoth) Egyptian God of Wisdom

t'ai chi 1. supreme reality, the absolute. 2. (t'ai-chi ch'uan, tai ji) ancient Chinese form of classical dance for health, self-defense, and spiritual development received in a dream by Taoist sage Chang San-feng based on subtle yielding, circular movement, control of ch'i, and relaxation, 14th c.- ; major forms include solo dance, partner dance, dancing with sword, knife, and staff (Chinese)

Tai-Kyoku 'ultimate extremity,' One Infinity (Japanese)

T'ai Shan China's sacred mountain north of T'ai-an city in Shantung; pilgrimage site of Confucians, Taoists, and Buddhists; elevation 5069 feet

Tai Sung Chinese painter of water buffaloes; ca. 8th c.

Tail of the Tiger 1. image in *I Ching* hexagram #10, treading on difficulties. 2. (Karme Choling) Tibetan Buddhist meditation center in Barnet, Vermont

taishi Buddhist saint (Japanese)

Taize site in France of a New Age ecumenical center led by Brother Roger

Taj Mahal 1. beautiful monument built

in Agra, India, by Mughal emperor Shah Johan for his wife Mumtaz-i-Mahat, 1630. 2. (Ed Fredericks) musician; 1942-

tajalli (pl. tajaliiyat) divine illumination attained through awakening the five lata'if (Arabic)

Takata Reaction change in quality of blood serum correlated with sunspots (Maka Takata)

Takbir mantra *Allahu Akbar* (Arabic)

Takeuchi papers ancient documents preserved by a Japanese family of this name suggesting that Jesus visited Japan after surviving the crucifixion

Taklamakan desert west of Tunhuang, gateway to China

takuhatsu 'to get one's food in everyday life', practice of Buddhist monks and nuns begging for food. 2. humble selfless service rendered without expectation of reward or thanks (Ittoen)

takuwan a daikon pickle made with rice bran and sea salt; very strong like the legendary Buddhist monk it is named after (Japanese)

Taliesin 1. Druid member of Arthur's Court. 2. name of Frank Lloyd Wright's design center

talisman 'incantation', object charged with a specific mission (from Arabic)

Tall Trees Grove an alluvial flat of old-growth redwoods containing some of the tallest trees on Earth; surrounded on three sides by Redwook Creek in California

tamale Mexican-style salty or sweet corn patty steamed in banana leaves

tamari soy sauce traditional naturally made soy sauce as distinguised from refined, chemicaly processed soy sauce; also known as organic or natural shoyu. A stronger, wheat-free soy sauce known as real or genuine tamari, a by product of making miso, is used for special dishes, while tamari soy sauce is used for daily cooking in macrobiotics (from Japanese)

tamas ignorance, sloth, inertia; one of the three gunas (Sanskrit)

Tamil Dravidian language of South India and Sri Lanka

Tammuz (Dumuzi) resurrected vegetation deity of Mesopotamia

Tamo (P'u-t'i-ta-mo) Bodhidharma (Chinese)

Tamoe Pacific Island populated by vegetarians in Donatien Alphonse Fran-

cois's *Aline et Valcour*, 1795

tan raised platform seats in a Zen meditation hall (Japanese)

Tanaka, Jomyo N. Japanese-born Shingon priest and head of the Mandala Buddhist Center, Bristol, Vermont

tanasukh reincarnation (Arabic)

tanazzul (pl. tanazzulat) descent of the Absolute (Arabic)

tandava Shiva's world-shattering dance (Sanskrit)

tanden (hara) energy center in the intestines in the lower part of the abdomen (Japanese)

tandoor clay oven (Hindi)

Tane 1. Maori God of Vegetation. 2. life energy (Hawaiian)

T'ang Chinese dynasty 618-907

Tang T'ai-tsung (Li Shih-min) first Emperor of the T'ang, patron of pilgrim Hsuan Tsang; 627-49

Tangut people akin to the Tibetans on China's western frontier, 11-12th c.

Tanimoto, Kiyoshi Japanese minister who led a movement on behalf of Hiroshima survivers; 1912-89

Tanka (Tien-jan, *Chinese*) Ch'an master renowned for demolishing a wooden statue of the Buddha and using it for firewood; d. 824 (Japanese)

tanmatra subtle principle behind the five basic elements in Sankhya cosmology (Sanskrit)

t'ann tchong acupoint on the sternum (Chinese)

Tannhauser pilgrim of medieval ballads and Wagner's opera; 13th c.

Tano Ashanti River God

tanpura stringed instrument with a large bowl used as a drum (Sanskrit)

tantra 'action: the woof and warp', 1. set of books and methods utilizing the senses to go beyond the senses quickly. 2. meditative sexual union (the female is active, male passive, in Hindu tantra; the male active, female passive in Buddhist tantra). 3. spiritual science divided into four divisions: *Kriya,* ritual; *Carya,* conduct; *Yoga,* meditation;. *Anuttara,* wisdom. 4. series of 64 discourses delivered by Shiva to his wife Parvati (Sanskrit). adj. **tantric**

tantra, fruition discovering one's Buddha Nature (Trungpa)

tantra, ground acknowledging the potential of Buddha Nature in pain and confusion (Trungpa)

tantra, path developing an attitude of

richness and generosity, acceptance of aloneness (Trungpa)

tantri hour-glass-shaped pellet drum (Sanskrit)

tantric 1. adj. method of following opposites to their extremes in order to turn back into the middle. 2. n. a practitioner of tantra (from Sanskrit)

Tao (do, *Japanese*) (from the characters for 'moving on' and 'head', *Chinese*). 1. the way of life; the unnamable, subtle, seamless principle of the universe beyond all conception; hidden but always present, like a well used but never used up, a bellows, empty but infinitely capable, empty yet inexhaustible; the infinite, eternal process of change; that which is never born, and never dies and which does nothing and yet there is nothing left undone (Lao Tzu). 2. totality and the laws of the infinite universe; yin and yang. 3. a spiritual practice or art, e.g., the tao of archery, the tao of carpentry, the tao of writing, in which one becomes one with the work, nature, and the universe. 4. peach (Chinese)

Tao-sheng Chinese Buddhist monk who taught that Nirvana is a present reality; 360-464

Tao Te Ching (Dao De Jing) 'Classic of the Way of Life', penetrating 81-stanza poem on the infinite universe and its order and on the path to human happiness by Lao Tzu (Chinese)

T'ao t'ieh stylized dragon, tiger, or ogre face on Shang bronzes (Chinese)

Tao Tsang Taoist canon of 1120 volumes compiled over 15 centuries

Tao-yuan Chinese utopian paradise into which the Peach Blossom River flows in T'ao Ch'ien's story, 4th c.

Taoism 1. philosophy or religion associated with the teachings of Lao Tzu. 2. Chinese world view that somehow went through the sound barrier of civilization and came out the other side halfway intact—antifeudalistic, appreciative of the female principle, women's powers, intuition, nature, spontaneity, and freedom (Gary Snyder)

Taoist one who is one with the Tao

tapas austerity, purification (Sanskrit)

tape loop computer model for an independent control system in the consciousness (Lilly)

tape, positive affirmation or belief such as 'I'm responsible for everything that happens to me'

Taprobane 1. medieval name of Ceylon. 2. fanciful golden island described by Mandeville (French)

taql reason (Arabic)

Tara Tibetan Goddess, counterpart of Avalokiteshvara

Tarahumara Indians in Mexico who eat primarily corn, beans, and squash and comprise the only traditional North American community without heart disease, cancer, and other degenerative diseases; also noted for their marathon running and ball games

Tarascan Mexican people near Lake Putzcuaro noted for crafts, incense, and wood houses

target event that the subject tries to select or influence in ESP tests

tariki salvation by faith and grace (Japanese)

tariq (tariqa, pl. turuq) Sufi spiritual way, path (Arabic)

taro (albi) a potato-like tropical plant with a hairy skin and starchy, edible roots (Japanese)

taro plaster an application of grated taro that is used in macrobiotic home care to help reduce swellings and discharge toxic material, especially tumors

Tarot deck of 78 cards with archetypal symbols, 15th c. (from Italian *tarocchi*)

  0 The Fool....... choice: folly or wisdom
  1 Magician................. creative power
  2 High Priestess..... hidden influences
  3 Empress................. material wealth
  4 Emperor.......................... leadership
  5 Hierophant............... organized rule
  6 Lovers.... choice between opposites
  7 Chariot.............................. conquest
  8 Strength.............................. courage
  9 Hermit............. opening of the path
10 Wheel of Fortune................ destiny
11 Justice.............................. harmony
12 Hanged Man........ reversal, wisdom
13 Death....................... transformation
14 Temperance........................ growth
15 Devil............... bondage to material
16 Tower................. end of selfishness
17 Stars... hope
18 Moon.............................. deception
19 Sun....................................... success
20 Judgment............. spiritual renewal
21 World.................. freedom, success

Tarshish site mentioned in the Bible where Near Eastern ships sailed, possibly Sicily or Spain

Tarzs, Rebazar ageless emissary of Eckankar

Tasaday stone age people of the Philippines noted for kindness and peace

tasawwuf mysticism; Sufism (Arabic)

Tassajara Zen Mountain Center Buddhist monastic community near Carmel Valley, Calif., 1960-

tassawuri attunement to a master (Arabic)

tasseography tea-leaf reading

Tassili n'Ajjer 'plateau of rivers', site in the Sahara Desert of frescoes, -6000

Tat Tvam Asi 'That thou art', mystical identification of the self with the Absolute in the *Chandogya Upanishad* (Sanskrit)

tatami rush mat (Japanese)

Tatar 1. Mongolian state with capital at Sarai, 13-15th c. 2. language of the Vulga River region. 3. Soviet Republic, capital Kazan

Tathagatha 'thus come one', name Buddha applied to himself (Sanskrit)

tathata suchness, reality (Sanskrit)

tatsu dragon (Japanese)

tattva 1. one of the four elements. 2. Ananda Marga meeting. 3. one of 25 constituents or organs of consciousness in the *Upanishads* (Sanskrit)

Tau-Ceti nearby star postulated as a source of intelligent life

tauba turning toward God, repentance (Arabic)

Tauler, John Strassburg preacher; *The Inner Way*; 1300-61

Taurus Bull: second sign of the zodiac; of the earthy element; ruler Venus: enduring, affectionate energy

tavlas (talayots) stone monoliths of the Minorca islands

Taw 22nd and last Hebrew letter: reciprocity, Th, 400

tawa four directions of the Earth (Incan)

tawajjuh 'concentration', Sufi transmission from teacher to student (Arabic)

Taxila ancient metropolis in Punjab

Taylor, Edward English-born mystic who taught meditation to open the door between head and heart; *Preparatory Meditations*; 1642-1729

Taylor, Thomas English mystic; *The Spirit of All Religions*; 1758-1835

Tayos Equador cave site with a library of pre-Incan books on metal plates (von Daeniken)

tche inn acupoint located on the small toe useful for relieving general pain (Japanese)

te virtue, power; composed of the characters for *human, heart, straight* (Chinese)

te-ate 'hand application', healing with the hands (Japanese)

tea infusion prepared by pouring hot or boiling water over an herb and steeping; black tea is made from three dried tiny leaves at the end of the evergreen shrub Camellia, ca. -350

teach-in seminar or workshop devoted to a special topic such as war and peace or the environment; often held at a college or university over one or two days instead of regular studies

teacher 1. one who guides others to self-discovery of the Order of the Infinite Universe (Michio Kushi). 2. one who takes the students out into the woods, gives them a compass, shows them how to use it, and then loses them (Sherman Goldman). 3. whatever surfaces where I am, within the life I'm in (Gary Snyder)

Teacher of Righteousness Essene master

teaching 1. process of giving back what one has received. 2. being an agent of change. 3. helping people restore their humanity. 4. bringing out qualities in other people. 5. being a mirror and enabling others to see themselves

tech grades, self-discipline, breakthrough process (Scientology)

techno-jargon bureaucratic language and doubletalk

technosphere area of industrialization on the surface of the Earth (Barry Commoner)

Techilevsky, A. L. Soviet historian who related sunspots to historical cycles; *The Sun and Us*

Teed, Cyrus Read Hollow Earth theorist, founder of Koreshism; *The Sword of Fire*; 1839-1908

Tefnut Egyptian Goddess, twin-sister of Shu

Teilhard de Chardin, Pierre French Jesuit, geologist, mystic who worked in China; *The Phenomenon of Man*; 1881-1955

teisho Zen talk (Japanese)

tejas splendor (Sanskrit)

Tekakwitha, Kateri (Lily of the Mohawks) saintly Canadian, Indian, Christian visionary; 1656-80

tekka vegetable condiment made from lotus root, burdock, carrots, sesame oil, ginger, miso (Japanese)

tektite strange hyaline rocks in Lebanon with radioactive isotopes suggesting a nuclear origin

telegnosis form of telepathy in which a voice is heard

Telegu Dravidian language of Andhra Pradesh, India

telekinesis movement of objects without a material cause

Telemachus 1. son of Odysseus. 2. Asian monk and martyr who jumped into a Roman arena to stop the gladiators and put an end to the exhibitions permanently; 5th c.

Telemond, Jean character symbolizing Teilhard de Chardin in West's *Shoes of the Fisherman*

telenostic one who transmits a perspective of awareness through the use of extended sensory perception (Mark Probert)

teleology 'end science', theory of design or purpose to life (from Greek)

telepathist practitioner of telepathy

telepathy extrasensory awareness of the thoughts or actions of others

teleplasm substance that emanates from a medium's body and takes the form of a person

teleportation instantaneous transmission of matter from one point to another (Charles Fort, 1931). v. **teleport**

telergic adj. healing using a pendulum

telesthesia 1. sensibility to events at a distance. 2. extrasensory data perceived as heightened feeling

Tell el-Amarna Egyptian capital of Ikhnaton

Tellim cliff structures left by the medieval people of Timbuktu

tellurian an inhabitant of the Earth

telluric adj. polarized magnetic currents (Bovis)

Teltscher, Alfred Austrian engineer, discoverer of the 33-day intellectual cycle of biorhythm

temo v. to be born, to descend from heaven (Nahuatl)

tempeh a high-protein, dynamic tasting soyfood made from split soybeans, water, and a special bacteria (Indonesian)

Temperance Tarot #14: moderation

temperature differential energy derived from the thermal gradient that exists between a hot and cold reservoir

Templars, Knights medieval Christian order that protected pilgrims to the Holy Land, suppressed for heresy and magic in the 14th c.

Temple of the Sun 1. Incan shrine in Cuzco. 2. excavation at Meroe

tempura deep-fried sliced vegetables, fish, or other food usually served with a tamari-ginger dipping sauce and eaten with a little grated daikon (Portugese and Japanese)

temurah 'to change', Kabbalistic practice of substituting one letter of the Bible for another (Hebrew)

Ten Lost Tribes 27,290 Israelites deported from northern Israel in -719 by Sargon of Assyria, who settled in Halah and in Habor by the river of Gozan and in the cities of the Medes, speculated to be in Asia, Africa, or pre-Columbian America

Ten Mei Order of Heaven, the Order of the Universe; the largest current of eternal life (Japanese)

Ten Thousand Things Chinese term for the universe of multiplicity

Ten Wings seven texts and three subtexts on the *I Ching* attributed to Confucius

Ten Worlds the six material worlds plus Buddhas, Bodhisattvas, Pratyekabuddhas, and Shravakas in Mahayana Buddhism

Ten Yinfeng Chinese Ch'an master who illustrated a point to his disciples by dying while standing on his head

Tendai 'heavenly terrace', 1. Chinese mountain. 2. Japanese Buddhist sect brought from China by Saicho, with center on Mt. Hiei, emphasizing the *Lotus Sutra*, 805-

tendon a one-dish meal consisting of rice served with tempura-style vegetables and covered with a light tamari broth (Japanese)

Tendzen, Osel (Thomas Rich) Tibetan Buddhist teacher; Regent of Vajradhatu

tengetsu clear, penetrating vision (Japanese)

tenjin 'light up mind', Zen snack, refreshment (Japanese)

Tenko, Nishida (Ittoen) Japanese founder of Ittoen; *A New Road to Ancient Truth*; 1872-1968

Tennyson, Alfred English poet; *Idylls of the King*; 1809-92

Tenochtitlan Aztec capital

Tenrikyo Japanese sect stressing faith healing, unity of life, and teaching founded by Miki Nakayama, 1838-

tensegrity tensional integrity, e.g.
Earth-Moon tug, spider web amidst
branches (Buckminster Fuller)

tenth house segment of the horoscope
dealing with life's work, honor, fame,
government

tenza chief Zen cook who must be able
to reveal the Buddha Mind in a stalk of
cabbage (Japanese)

Tenzing Norkey Nepalese Sherpa, one
of the first climbers of Mt. Everest; *The
Tiger of the Snows*; 1914-86

teocallis pre-Columbian pyramids of
Mexico (Nahuatl)

Teotihuacan 'place where one becomes
a god', pre-Aztec site of the Pyramids
of Sun and Moon; Toltec capital

Tep Zepi the First Time, the Golden
Age (Egyptian)

Tepeyollotl Nahuatl God of the Heart
and of the Mountain

tequezquite leavening agent used by Indians in Mexico to enhance the flavor
and deepen the color of corn

teramanto loving earth (Esperanto)

Teresa, Mother (Agnes Gonxha Bo-
jaxhiu) Yugoslavian-born nun and saint
of the Loreto Order working in Calcutta's slums; 1910-

Teresa, St. 1. Carmelite mystic from
Avila, Spain; *Interior Castle*; 1515-82.
2. (the Little Flower) French nun;
1873-97

Terpsichore Greek Muse of the Dance

terra Earth (Latin)

Terra Incognita Australis utopia of
Gabriel de Foigny in which people
meditated and lived without a government, 1676

Terrace of Living Buddhist term for
the Third Eye

terran inhabitant of Earth

terton taker-outer of hidden books and
treasures (Tibetan)

Tertullian Carthaginian Christian theologian, pacifist, introducer of the Trinity; *The Soldier's Chaplet*; ca. 155-222

teshuvah 'turning' toward the way of
God (Hebrew)

Tet Lunar New Year's at the start of
Aquarius (Vietnamese)

Teth 9th Hebrew letter: asylum, T, 9

Tethys sea separating Laurasia and
Gondwana in Plate Tectonics

Tetractys the triangular form of the
number ten

Tetragrammaton '4 letters', YHWH;
Hebrew Name of God (Greek)

tetrahedron pyramid with three sides

Tewa 'the Dried Food People', Tanoan
people and language of New Mexico

Texapan pre-Olmec people of the Mexican highlands, ca. -9000

Texcaplipoca 'Lord of the Smoking
Mirror', Quetzalcoatl's adversary (Nahuatl)

Texcoco large Mexican lake by which
Teotihuacan was built

Texmati domestic strain of rice introduced in 1970

Thai main language of Thailand consisting of 44 consonants and 32 vowels
and 5 tones; letters separated by ideas,
not words

Thakar, Vimala author, associate of Vinoba Bhave and Krishnamurti; *Voyage
into Oneself*

Thales Greek philosopher who saw water underlying all things; -6th c.

thali metal serving tray (Hindi)

Thalia Greek Muse of Comedy

thanatology science of death, dying,
and assisting the bereaved (from
Greek)

thanatos death (Greek)

thanka wallhanging (Tibetan)

Thatcher, Becky Tom Sawyer's sweetheart

Thaur site of a cave in which Muhammad spent three nights meditating near
Mecca

THC (tetrahydrocannabinols) mind-
expanding substance in cannabis

Themistoclea Delphic priestess from
whom Pythagoras derived his ethical
doctrines

theophany divine manifestation

theophysics theistic approach to medicine emphasizing a spirit of love or
hope to heal (Bernie Siegel)

Theory of Ideas theory of a pure realm
of archetypes beyond the visible world
(Plato)

Theosophy spiritual movement founded
by Madam Blavatsky and Colonel Olcott, noted for syncretism, world cycles, cosmic initiation, secret masters,
evolution to other planets, 1875-

Theotokos Mother of God; Mary (Latin)

Thera 1. elder (Pali). 2. (Santorin) crescent-shaped island 60 miles north of
Crete postulated as the site of Atlantis
during a volcanic eruption 25,000 years
ago

Therapeutae monastic communities of

Egyptian Jews, 1st c.

Therapeutic Touch method of sending or transmitting energy through the hands (Delores Krieger)

therapy a systematic approach, method, or process designed to heal, restore health, promote general well-being; types include:

clinical theology.......... birth regression
Freudian...word association and dreams
Gestalt............................ inner dialogue
group................... analysis with a group
Jungian...............symbols and mandalas
peer-group bonding.............. screaming
Primal Therapy.......exploding outwards
rebirthing...reenactment of birth trauma
regression...................................past-life
Reichian......... overcoming body armor
Transactional Analysis.group exchange

Theravada 'Vehicle of the Elders', Buddhism of Ceylon, Thailand, Burma, Laos (Sanskrit)

Theravada Scriptures the major texts include (Pali)

Abhidhamma-pitaka............ philosophy
Dhammapada.............................. ethics
Jataka..................................... birth tales
Dipavamsa ....Ceylonese history
Vinaya-pitaka.................... community
Visuddhamagga..................... discipline
Sutta-pitaka .... dialogues

theri Theravada Buddhist nun (Pali)

thermodynamics the branch of physics dealing with time and energy and which connects living processes to the fundamental laws of nature

Theseus 1. slayer of the minotaur (Greek). 2. bridegroom in *Midsummer Night's Dream*

theta wave brain wave associated with meditation, memory and learning enhancement, vivid imagery

thetan inner person, not the body, name, or mind (Scientology)

Thich venerable; prefix for a Buddhist monk (Vietnamese)

Thien Zen Buddhism (Vietnamese)

Thimbu capital of Bhutan

think globally, act locally motto of the ecology movement, 1980s

thinking like a mountain putting oneself in nature's place beyond human needs; the perspective of deep ecology (Aldo Leopold)

Third Eye organ of intuition, located between the eyebrows; sixth chakra divided into five categories by the Tibetans: 1. *Eyes of Instinct*, supernormal range

of vision like a bird. 2. *Celestial Eyes*, taking in heaven, Earth, past and future birth. 3. *Eyes of Truth*, taking in world epochs. 4. *Divine Eyes*, taking in millions of world periods. 5. *Eyes of Wisdom of Buddhas*, taking in eternity

third house segment of the horoscope ruling siblings, short trips, studies, correspondence

Third Mesa Hopi site including Old Oraibi

Third Wave postindustrial society (Alvin Toffler)

Third World developing nations of Africa, Asia, Latin America

33-day cycle cycle of intellectual ups and downs in biorhythm

Thom, Alexander Scottish engineer, mathematician, and investigator of astroarcheology; *Megalithic Sites in Britain*; 1894-

Thomas (St. Thomas, Doubting Thomas, Didymus Jude Thomas) 'twin', one of the twelve original apostles of Jesus who converted northern Mesopotamia and India to Christianity; *Gospel of Thomas*; 1st c.

Thomas Christians Christians of Travancore and Cochin, South India, who are descended from converts of St. Thomas

Thomas, Gospel of Coptic manuscript found in 1945 near Nag Hammadi in Egypt, with 114 Logia or Sayings, comprising the earliest and most authentic teachings of Jesus

Thomas, Lewis scientist; *The Medusa and the Snail*; 1913-

Thomas, Norman socialist and peace activist; *As I See It*; 1884-1968

Thompson, William Irwin global thinker and founder of Lindisfarne; *Passages About Earth*; 1938-

Thomson, Samuel herbalist and natural health philosopher; *Botanic Family Physician*; 19th c.

Thor Scandinavian God of Thunder and Thursday

Thoreau, Henry David Concord author, dreamer, and prophet of the wilderness; *Walden*; 1817-62

Thoth Egyptian God of Wisdom

thought form 1. perfected shape floating in the air, roughly spherical, as illustrated in a book by Besant and Leadbetter. 2. mental creation that can have causal effects

thoughtography ability to project

thoughts onto photographic film

3HO Healthy, Happy, Holy Organization; Sikh Dharma Brotherhood

Three Beasts the she-wolf, lion, and leopard encountered by Dante representing the worldly sins of incontinence, violence and ambition, and fraud

Three Jewels (Three Refuges) Dharma, Buddha, Sangha in Buddhism

Three Mile Island nuclear power plant near Harrisburg, Penn., and site of a near meltdown on March 28, 1979

Three Wishes the proverbial boons given the spiritual seeker

throne cosmic power governing will

throw a successive rhythmical accretion of spirallic development or series (T.A. Cook)

Thuban ancient North Star in the constellation Draco toward which the Great Pyramid in Giza is aligned

Thule mysterious island in the Atlantic sought in medieval times

Thunder, Perfect Intellect gnostic monologue found at Nag Hamadi spoken by a female savior

Thunderbird (Wakihyan-Tanka) protector of the Sacred Pipe who cleanses and purifies the world and waters and whose symbol is the zigzagged red line forked at each end

Thurman, Howard mystic, scholar, preacher; *The Luminous Darkness*; 1900-81

Thuthu wife of Ani; co-sojourner in the *Egyptian Book of the Dead*

thwain intuition of an *I Ching* hexagram; meaning (Chinese)

thymus endocrine gland located near the heart; physical counterpart to the fourth chakra

thyroid endocrine gland in the throat; physical counterpart to the fifth chakra

Tibet high Himalayan country, with capital in Lhasa, noted for its inaccessible snow-covered mountains, dynamic Buddhist religion and way of life, vibrant arts and crafts, yaks and yetis

Tibetan 1. native of Tibet. 2. their Sino-Tibetan language. 3. Djwhal Khul; teacher of Alice Bailey

Tibetan Buddhism a form of Mahayana Buddhism known as Vajrayana that took root in Tibet, emphasizing rich metaphysical imagery, colorful ritual, and development of special powers; the four chief schools and their founders

and dates are:

Nyingmapa.... Padma Sambhava, 9th c.
Kargyudpa .... Marpa 11th c.
Sakyapa ..... Kon-chog-gyal-po, 11th c.
Gelugpa .... Je Tsong-kha-pa, 14th c.

Tibetan Buddhist Learning Center community founded by Geshe Wangyal in Washington, N.J., 1958-

Tibetan Calender time system divided into major cycles of 60 years, which is subdivided into five twelve-year cycles, each identified with an animal, bird, or reptile; the twelve years are paired with an element, alternating male and female attributes:

Male Iron Horse 1990
Female Iron Sheep 1991
Male Water Monkey 1992
Female Water Bird 1993
Male Wood Dog 1994
Female Wood Pig 1995
Male Fire Mouse........................... 1996
Female Fire Ox 1997
Male Earth Tiger 1998
Female Earth Rabbit 1999
Male Iron Dragon 2000
Female Iron Snake 2001
Male Water Horse 2002
Female Water Sheep 2003
Male Wood Monkey 2004

Tibetan Nyingmapa Meditation Center center established by Tarthang Tulku in Berkeley, 1968-

Tien 1. heaven (Chinese). 2. heavenly beings (Vietnamese)

Tien An Men Gate of Heavenly Peace in Peking

T'ien-t'ai (Tendai, *Japanese*) Chinese Buddhist school stressing compromise, tolerance, and the Middle Way. 6th c., and taken to Japan by Saicho, 9th c. (Chinese)

Tiger Lily princess who protected Peter Pan and his companions

Tikal great Maya ceremonial center in Guatemala

tilaka clay mark on the face of devotees (Sanskrit)

Tilopa 'Seseme Pounder', Indian sage whose transmissions frgm the Celestial Buddha Vajradhara inspired the Tibetan Kargyudpa line; teacher of Naropa; 988-1069

Timaeus dialogue by Plato containing the legend of Atlantis

Timbuktu medieval West African city of high wisdom, learning, and culture

time 1. the moving image of eternity

(Plato). 2. (cap.) a tall old man with a streaming beard, scythe, and hourglass who sends the children to be reborn on Earth into a galley with white and gold sails after making sure each has a gift —whether a new invention or a deadly disease—to take to their next life in *The Blue Bird*

Time of Beginnings universal First Age whose memory has influenced all subsequent human history

time travel practice of moving at will into the past or future

Time Traveler hero of Wells's *The Time Machine*

Timurid Persian period 1370-1500

Tin Man companion in *Wizard of Oz*

tincture 1. philosopher's stone or its action upon base metals. 2. solution of organic material in alcohol

ting ritual vessel with three or four straight legs, ears, and a large handle (Chinese)

Tingley, Katherine Theosophist, leader of Raj Yoga School at Point Lama, Calif.; 1852-1929

Tinker Bell fairy friend of Peter Pan

Tintagel castle in Cornwell, England, reputed birthplace of King Arthur

Tintin youthful adventurer in a Belgian comic strip; 1929-

Tintoretto (Jacopo Robusti) Venetian master; *Last Supper*; 1518-94

Tiphereth Kabbalistic Sephiroth of Beauty, Harmony (Hebrew)

Tirawa Pawnee Creator

Tiresias 1. blind seer of Thebes who aided Odysseus in returning home. 2. seeker in Eliot's *The Wasteland*

tirobhava veiling, embodiment, illusion: Shiva's fourth dance step (Sanskrit)

tirtha crossing place, ford, pilgrimage site (Sanskrit)

Tirthankara 'ford-maker', Jain world teacher (Sanskrit)

Tise Mt. Kailasa (Tibetan)

tisra til Third Eye (Sanskrit)

tissue cleansing a program of fasting and elimination designed to remove accumulated toxins from the body

Titania 1. Queen of Fairies in *A Mid-Summer Night's Dream*. 2. satellite of Uranus

Titicaca Bolivian lake; legendary birthplace of the Incas

titiksha cheerful and patient acceptance of karma (Sanskrit)

Tito Knecht's young pupil in Hesse's

The Glass Bead Game

Titurel first King of the Grail; great-grandfather of Parzival

Tjuringa Australian stone; aborigine Map of the Journeying of the Ancestors of the Dreamtime

Tlaloc Nahuatl God of Rain

Tlavath Atlantean sub-race (Steiner)

TLC Tender Loving Care

Tlillan-Tlapallan 'land of the black and red', Quetzalcoatl's paradise (Nahuatl)

Tlingit 1. people of the Alaskan panhandle. 2. their language

Tlon metaphysical planet in which the only reality is subjective (Borges)

TM Transcendental Meditation

to ho second period in Buddhism of institutionalized teaching (Japanese)

To Huu Vietnamese poet; *Emily, My Child*; 1920-

Tobias companion of Raphael and a small dog in the *Book of Tobit*

Tobiscope Soviet acupuncture device that detects acupoints

Tocharian 1. ancient Central Asian people. 2. Indo-European tongue

Todai temple with the Great Buddha in Nara (Japanese)

tofu soybean curd made from soybeans and nigari, high in protein and usually prepared in the form of cakes that may be sliced and cooked in soups, vegetable dishes, salads, sauces, dressings, and other styles (Japanese)

tofu, dried sliced tofu that has been frozen and dried with a spongy texture, light weight, and creamy beige color

together adj. centered, harmonious, organized, functional, prepared

toilet dam device that cuts the flow of water per flush for energy efficiency

tokonoma alcove with flowers and scroll (Japanese)

toku virtue, power (Japanese)

Tokugawa Japanese era of tranquillity and isolation from the West, 1614-1868

Tolkien, J. R. R. (John Ronald Reuel) South African-born fantasy writer; *Lord of the Rings*; 1892-1973

Tolstoy Farm 1. (Yasnaya Polyana, *Russian*) Tolstoy's home in Russia. 2. Gandhi's community in South Africa

Tolstoy, Leo Russian novelist, pacifist; *War and Peace*; 1828-1910

Toltec ancient Mexican culture of artisans and warriors

Tomenika Easter Island manuscript with rongo rongo script, 19th c.

Tompson, Marian founder of the La Leche League

ton life energy, divine force (Dakota)

tonal organizer of the world; guardian of being (don Juan)

tonalamatl hand-illuminated books made from the bark of the wild fig tree (Nahuatl)

tonalpoualtl Aztec calendar, account of days and destinies (Nahuatl)

Tongass national forest in southeastern Alaska, continent's greatest reservoir of old growth forest

toning use of the voice for healing, creativity, and vitality

tool 1. what is within the world of form (Lao Tzu). 2. something to be used sparingly but exactly, when and where needed, including words (Gary Snyder)

tooldom realm of whole earth systems

Top dog part of oneself in Gestalt therapy, usually the dominant part

Topocentric astrological house system permitting house cusps for some polar regions

topocosm 'place of order', the entire complex of any given locality conceived as a living organism (Theodor Gaster)

Torah 'teaching', Jewish law, especially the *Pentateuch* (Hebrew)

torii a bird perch representing a gateway to the Shinto Temple, entry to which is aided by bird song (Japanese)

tornak (pl. tornait) guardian spirit of the angakok shaman (Innuit)

torsion map pictographs cut in rocks from Chile to Canada marking early migrations by the Ancestors

torus donut-shaped universe with an infinitely small hole; model of the universe in which a part can seem separate, yet be connected with the whole. adj. **toroidal**

Toscanelli, Paolo Florentine physician and geographer whose map Columbus used in sailing West; 1397-1482

tostada tortilla served open with beans or vegetables (Spanish)

totem 'relative, clan', heraldic post, often associated with an emblem or mask of an animal or plant (Ojibway)

totora reed used for boats in Peru and Easter Island that may have made pre-Columbian voyages

tou mo governing vessel; meridian along the median dorsal line of the body (Chinese)

Touchstone wise fool in *As You Like It*

Toward the One 1. African drumbeat symbol. 2. Sufi chant

Tower Tarot #16: ruin, deception

Toynbee, Arnold British historian; *Study of History*; 1889-1975

Tozan Ryokai (Tung-shan Liang-chieh, *Chinese*) Chinese Ch'an master, principal founder of Soto Zen; *The Most Excellent Mirror-Samadhi*; 807-69 (Japanese)

TP transpersonal psychology

trace element mineral needed in small quantities by the human body

Traditionalist follower of Rene Guenon

Trager a physical therapy aimed at treating and relieving neuromuscular disorders developed by Milton Trager

Trail of Tears forced relocation of the Cherokees, Seminoles, Creeks, Choctaws, Chickasaws, 1835

trait guilt pattern entrenched in a past-life episode

Trall, Russell T. a leader of the water-cure and natural hygiene movement; 19th c.

Tran Thai Tong Vietnamese king who abdicated to meditate; *Guide for Zen, Lessons on Emptiness*; 1225-1300

trance mediumistic state of psychological dissociation in which the spirit entity takes over the person's voice or body to speak to human audiences

TRANET (Transnational Network for Appropriate/Alternative Technologies) alternative energy network, based in Rangeley, Maine

Transactional Analysis therapy based on group interaction developed by Eric Berne and Thomas Harris

transcendent function emergence from the unconscious of a higher point of view (Jung)

Transcendental Meditation spiritual movement founded by Maharishi Mahesh Yogi stressing mantra, 1959-

Transcendentalism literary and philosophical movement of Emerson, Alcotts, Lane, Fuller, Thoreau, stressing nature, Eastern thought, 1830s-50s

transformation change by which all the elements and movements of the being become ready to manifest the supramental Truth (Aurobindo)

transformer role model for someone to channel energy into a particular direction; an energy intensifier; e.g., for children, father and mother are the first transformers (Robert Bly)

transit 1. n. or v. travels of a planet leading to aspects with other heavenly bodies. 2. realm between lives (E. J. Gold)

transitionally-grown adj. produce grown without chemicals but in a field that is not yet certified organic

transmigration reincarnation from one species to another

transmission (dembo, *Japanese*) passing the Truth heart to heart from master to disciple in Zen

transmutatio alchemical change (Latin)

transnational n. or adj. international, beyond boundaries

transneptunian adj. planets beyond Neptune

Transoxiana region of Turkestan, medieval Muslim culture center, area of Bukhara, Samarkand

transpersonal n. or adj. experiences of an extension of identity beyond both individuality and personality

transpersonal psychology movement stressing full sensory, psychic, and spiritual development

transphysical n. or adj. psychic, beyond the bodily

Transpluto planet discovered by Dr. Landscheidt with a period of 680 days ruling innovation, change

transpsychic n. or adj. beyond the individual psyche; the collective unconsciousness (Jung)

transsexual person who has changed sex

transuranic elements beyond uranium in the periodic table

Trappist reformed branch of the Cistercian Christian order established at the monastery of La Trappe in Normandy, France, noted for silence, 1664-

tratak discipline of gazing at and uniting with an object (Sanskrit)

travel dramatization of life, a way of experiencing it more intensely and self-consciously, an enlightened state of consciousness, an energy exchange between the inner self and the world (Buryn)

treasures of heaven the understanding that grows greater in being shared (Dante)

tredecile planets 108 degrees apart; a minor favorable aspect

Tree of Knowledge 1. the tree whose fruit was eaten by Adam and Eve and led to their expulsion from Paradise. 2.

tree from which the cross was cut. 3. dualistic thinking that does not see the underlying unity behind all things

Tree of Life 1. plant conferring immortality in Babylonian and Hebrew mythology. 2. Kabbalistic arrangement of the ten sephiroth. 3. a type of Tarot reading. 4. human consciousness and structure growing down opposite to the energy of a tree with the roots as waves and vibrations from above, the stem in the head and back, the branches in the arms and legs, the fruit and flowers in the reproductive system, and the leaves in the cells (Michio Kushi)

tree therapy hugging a tree to increase energy

Trekkie devotee of *Star Trek*

treta yuga second Hindu world age when righteousness first declined and Rama appeared (Sanskrit)

Trevrizent brother of Anfortas, hermit; uncle and tutor to Parzival

Tri Quang, Thich Vietnamese Zen master, peace movement leader; 1923-

trial single attempt to identify a target in an ESP test

triglyceride fatty substance from animal foods

trigram three-line figure in the *I Ching*

Trigunatita, Swami (Sarada Prasanna Mitra) disciple of Sri Ramakrishna, head of the San Francisco Vedanta Society; 1865-1915

trikaya three bodies of Mahayana Buddhism: 1. *Nirmanakaya*, 'Transformation Body' used for teaching. 2. *Sambhogakaya*, 'Body of Enjoyment' used for earthly journeys, visions, divine realms. 3. *Dharmakaya*, 'Body of the Law' Buddha Mind at one with the void (Sanskrit)

trilithon freestanding megalithic archway

trilochana Third Eye (Sanskrit)

Trimurti 'three formed', Brahma, Vishnu, Shiva; trinity (Sanskrit)

trine planets 120 degrees or three houses apart in a chart; favorable major aspect

trip 1. voyage, journey, or odyssey, especially a psychological or spiritual one; an embarkation with an end, as opposed to a path or endless adventure. 2. experience, especially a heightened one. 3. LSD or other psychedelic experience. 4. peripheral or frivolous experience, journey away from home. 5. philosophy, lifestyle, or path. 6. sequence of mental events, emotional experiences, or physical movements, e.g. the breadmaking trip. 7. head space, mind set. 8. what changes put one through. n. **tripper, tripster, tripping. power trip** ambitious activity. **ego trip** self-centered activity. **guilt trip** morally intimidating activity. v. **trip out** to go off on a mental, psychological, or spiritual excursion. v. **lay a trip on** to prosyletize, preach

Triphmah planet between Earth and Mars that disintegrated (Charubel)

Tripitaka 'three baskets', 1. Theravada Buddhist scriptures consisting of the Abhidharma, Sutras, Vinaya. 2. Hsuan Tsang's name in *Monkey* (Sanskrit)

Triple Heater (cheou chao yang, *Chinese*) meridian going from the extremities of the fingers to the face regulating circulation and coordinating all bodily functions

triplicity group of three astrology signs

trishna 'longing', thirst for past experiences (Sanskrit)

Tristan (Tristam) hero of the Pictish romance *Tristan and Isolt*

Trithemius German mystic, monk, alchemist; 15th c.

triune function 1. postive, negative, neutral energy charges constituting all things. 2. energy flow from the positive pole (head), pelvis (neutral) feet (negative), back to the head (polarity balancing)

Trois Freres 'three brothers', cave in Ariege, France, with a paleolithic painting of the Dancing Sorcerer (French)

trophic adj. level of nourishment of a natural community

troubadour medieval singer (French)

truck v. to persevere, move on, especially in the face of adversity. **keep on truckin'**

True Man person of virtue in the Taoist writings of Chuang Tzu

True Man of Purple Polar Light Taoist term for the Third Eye (*Secret of the Golden Flower*)

trulli mortarless stone domes of the Adriatic coast, ca. 1600

truncatable truncated dome

Trungpa, Chogyam (Choskyi Gyamtso) Tibetan Buddhist teacher, 11th incarnation of the Trungpa Tulku, supreme abbot of Surmang monastery, founder of Vajradhatu; *Meditation in Action*; 1939-87

trusterty 'trust property', land trust

truth (from Middle English *treuthe*) 1. perfection, the highest state of being, accompanied by consciousness and bliss (Hinduism). 2. that which will make you free (Isaiah). 3. unity of thought, word, and deed (Gandhi). 4. inner guide or transcendent principle beyond the relative world, which impels one to right living. 5. only that which you know for yourself and experience consciously within yourself (Bailey). 6. suffering, that which is born of pain and confusion (Trungpa). 7. honesty, integrity, veracity

Truth, Sojourner (Isabella) abolitionist, revivalist; *A Bondswoman of Olden Times*; ca. 1797-1863

Tsaddi 18th Hebrew letter: fish hook, Tz, 90

Tsang Tibetan province, capital Tashi-lhunpho

Tsangpo (Brahmaputra, *Sanskrit*) chief river of Tibet (Tibetan)

Ts'ao Chan (Hsueh-ch'in) Chinese novelist; *The Dream of the Red Chamber*; ca. 1716-64

Ts'ao Kuo-chiu one of the Eight Immortals in China; patron of the theater

Tsefat (Safed) holy city of Jewish mysticism; home of Isaac Luria

tsing meridian (Chinese)

Tsiolokovsky, Konstantine father of Russian rocketry, psychic researcher; *Beyond the Planet Earth*; 1857-1935

Tsogyel, Yeshe enlighted Tibetan woman and Buddhist teacher; *The Life and Songs*; ca. 757-817

Tsongkapa Tibetan founder of Gelugpa Buddhism, builder of Gadan monastery; 1355-1417

tsubo one of 361 major holes or points on the meridians (Japanese). Types are:

yu................................. entering points
bo..................................gathering points
go................. meeting of energy points
gen...............................balancing points
sei........................ well or spring points

Ts'ung yellow jade earth symbol, round inside, square out (Chinese)

Tsurphu monastery and seat of the Karmapa incarnates in Tibet, founded by Gampopa, 1185-1959

Tu Fu Chinese poet; *The Army Carts*; 712-70

Tu Thuc Land of Bliss (Vietnamese)

t'uan judgment, decision of the *I Ching* (Chinese)

Tuat Underworld (Egyptian)

Tubby Little Lulu's rotund, bully boyfriend

Tubman, Harriet Underground Railway conductor; ca. 1821-1913

Tuc Trung Thuong Si Vietnamese Zen master; *Eccentric's Song*; 13th c.

Tuck, Friar vagabond monk friend of Robin Hood

t'ui lake, the joyous; one of eight trigrams in the *I Ching* (Chinese)

tui na massage or body work designed to release muscle tension (Chinese)

Tula Toltec culture center

Tulasi great devotee of Krishna in the form of a basil plant

tulku person recognized as the current incarnation of a lama (Tibetan)

Tulku, Tarthang Tibetan Buddhist master; *Time, Space, and Knowledge*

tulpa being created by thought-forms (Tibetan)

Tulsi Das Indian mystical poet; tr. *Ramayana*; 1543-1623

Tulsi Sahib Indian king turned wanderer; *Ghat Ramayana*; 1788-1848

Tum Egyptian God of Creation

tummo psychic heat (Tibetan)

tumulus Earth mound

Tun Huang Chinese Buddhist pilgrimage site of 1000 grottoes of sculptures and murals, rediscovered by Sir Aurel Stein in 1907

tune in v. to get in touch with one's deepest self or with others, to focus

Tunguska site in Siberia of an unknown explosion, possibly nuclear, June 30, 1908

tunraq spirit controlled by a shaman (Innuit)

Turanian 1. prehistoric East Asian shamanist tribe. 2. fourth sub-race of the Atlanteans who fought the Toltecs (Theosophy)

Turfan 1. Central Asian state visited by Hsuan Tsang, 7th c. 2. Chinese city at the eastern end of the Silk Road

Turin Italian city with a 15th c. cathedral, home of the Shroud

turiya 'fourth', highest state of consciousness; samadhi (Sanskrit)

Turiyananda, Swami (Harinath Chattopadhya) disciple of Sri Ramakrishna, founder of Shanti Ashrama in California in 1899; 1863-1922

turn off n. or v. bore, drag, negative experience

turn on n. or v. 1. high, ecstatic experience. 2. psychedelic voyage. 3. sexual arousal. 4. to introduce something new, exciting to someone else

turtle being who is home wherever it is

Turtle Island the old/new name for the continent, based on many creation myths of the people who have been here for millennia, and reapplied by some of them to 'North America' in recent years (Gary Snyder)

Turtle Pagoda Hanoi temple where a tortoise bore a sword to drive away the invaders

Tushita heaven from which Buddha descended for his last birth on Earth

Tuskeegee Institute Alabama educational institution founded by Booker T. Washington, 1881-

Tutankhamun (King Tut) 'Living Image of Amun', Egyptian Pharoah whose tomb was excavated by Canarvon and Carter in 1922

Tvashtri Hindu God of Arts and Crafts

Twain, Mark novelist, folklorist, saint of the Vietnamese Cao Dai; *The Adventures of Tom Sawyer*; 1835-1910

Twelfth Planet (Marduk), a large cometlike planet that comes near the Earth once every 3600 years and from which human civilization may have sprung; theorized in a book of the same name by Zecharia Sitchin

twelfth house last segment of the horoscope dealing with hidden things, karma, solitude

twelve number signifying wholeness and completion; e.g. in *Revelation* there are twelve gates, pearls, foundations, names, jewels, and angels

twelve apostles Jesus's inner circle

Twelve Laws of Change of the Infinite Universe theorems of diversity governing the relation between yin and yang formulated by George Ohsawa, Michio Kushi, and their associates: 1. One Infinity manifests itself into complementary and antagonistic tendencies, yin and yang, in its endless change. 2. Yin and yang are manifested continuously from the eternal movement of one infinite universe. 3. Yin represents centrifugality. Yang represents centripetality. Yin and yang together produce energy and all phenomena. 4. Yin attracts yang. Yang attracts yin. 5. Yin repels yin. Yang repels yang. 6. Yin and yang combined in varying proportions produce different phenomena.

The attraction and repulsion among phenomena is proportional to the difference of the yin and yang forces. 7. All phenomena are ephemeral, constantly changing their constitution of yin and yang forces; yin changes into yang, yang changes into yin. 8. Nothing is solely yin or solely yang. Everything is composed of both tendencies in varying degrees. 9. There is nothing neutral. Either yin or yang is in excess in every occurrence. 10. Large yin attracts small yin. Large yang attracts small yang. 11. Extreme yin produces yang, and extreme yang produces yin. 12. All physical manifestations are yang at the center, and yin at the surface.

Twelvers Shi'a Moslems who follow the Twelve Imams, the last of whom vanished in 878 and is expected to return in triumph

28-day cycle cycle of emotional ups and downs in biorhythm

23-day cycle cycle of physical ups and downs in biorhythm

Twin Oaks intentional cooperative community near Louisa, Virginia, 1967-

Twins celebrated pairs in world mythology include:

Amphion, Zethus .... Greece
Apollo, Artemis .... Greece
Arion, Orion .... Greece
Asvins .... India
Castor, Pollux .... Greece
Hunapu .... Maya
Isis, Osiris .... Egypt
Izanagi, Izanami .... Japan
Liber, Libera .... Rome
Mitra, Varuna .... India
Romulus, Remus .... .Rome

Twitchell, Sri Paul Eck master; d. 1971

two mirror oscillation effect hangups mutually projected by two people on each other

2001 science-fiction film by Kubrick and Clarke about the sudden awakening of cosmic consciousness, 1968

Tyberg, Judith Sanskrit scholar and founder of the East-West Center; *The Language of the Gods*

Tyl, Noel astrologer; *The Principles and Practice of Astrology*

Tyltyl woodcutter's son and seeker of happiness in *The Blue Bird*

Tyndale, William English reformer; *Parable of the Wicked Mammon*; ca. 1464-1536

Tyrker tipsy member of Leif Ericson's party who wandered off and found vines laden with grapes, source of the name *Vinland*

Tzinacan magician of the pyramid of Qaholom who attained satori by seeing the Name of God in the lines of a jaguar pacing over his jail cell (Borges)

tziruf (Chiluf) Kabbalistic practice of transposing the letters of Biblical words and making anagrams (Hebrew)

Tzolkin 'Count of Days', Mayan calendar of 260 days

tzu-jan nature (Chinese)

Uu

U Tibetan province, capital Lhasa

UAL Unidentified Aerial Lights

UCT Un-Correlated Target; flying saucer on a radar screen

udana 'breathing upwards', vital breath in yoga (Sanskrit)

udon whole wheat noodles (Japanese)

udumvara flower that blossoms only upon the birth of a Buddha; *Ficus Glomirata, Rox.* (Sanskrit)

Ueshiba, Morihei 'Abundant Peace', Japanese martial artists who founded Aikido in 1925 after a revelation of divine love; 1883-1969

Uffizi Florence art museum

UFO Unidentified Flying Object

UFOE UFO encounter

ufologist believer in UFOs

ufology study of UFOs. adj. **ufological**

ufonaut UFO traveler or visitor

Ugarit 1. ancient city found at Ras Shamra, Syria, 1928. 2. language of the Canaanites

Uhura, Lt. communications Officer on the *U.S.S. Enterprise* in *Star Trek*

uhuru freedom (Swahili)

Uigur 1. 4 million people in China and Russia, now Islamic. 2. their Turkic language

uinic 1. twenty. 2. human being (Mayan)

ukiyoye 'mirror of the passing world', floating world depicted in art prints of daily life, especially in the woodcuts of Hokusai and Hiroshige (Japanese)

Ullmann, Liv Scandinavian film actress and goodwill ambassador for world hunger organizations, 1939-

ultraconsciousness mystical awareness (Stanley Dean, 1975)

ultraego extreme point of consciousness in the individual (Teilhard)

ultrahuman advanced evolutionary stage (Teilhard)

ultrapersonalization upper limit of collective consciousness (Teilhard)

ultrapsychonization the penultimate trend toward increasing artificialization of human consciousness threatening to lead to an end of natural human beings (Michio Kushi)

ultrasonic core primal energy path in the spine (polarity balancing)

Uluru aborigine Mother Goddess

Uma Shiva's wife in gentle aspect

Umayyads caliphate with capital at Damascus under which Islam spread most widely; 661-750

ume extract concentrated umeboshi paste used for digestive disorders and other healing purposes

ume-sho-bancha macrobiotic tea of umeboshi and tamari soy sauce in bancha tea used to strengthen the blood and circulation and regulate digestion (Japanese)

umeboshi a salted pickled plum usually aged for several years with a zesty sour taste and salty flavor that figures prominently in macrobiotic cooking and home care (Japanese)

umeboshi vinegar (*ume-su*, Japanese) the liquid that umeboshi plums are aged in; used in dressings and sauces

umma community, people (Arabic)

UMMO planet and advanced civilization that has been in contact with Earth and whose symbol is three bars crossed horizontally, 1950-

Unamuno, Miguel de Spanish metaphysical author; *Every Inch a Man*; 1864-1936

Unarius Science of Life founded by Ernest Norman

uncertainty principle theory that it is impossible to know both the position and velocity of a subatomic particle with great accuracy (Heisenberg)

Uncle Remus narrator of *Brer Rabbit*

Uncle Tompa legendary Tibetan rascal; 13th c.

unconscious (unbewussten, *German*) that part of the psyche which does not, ex-

cept under unusual circumstances, intrude into awarness; in Jungian therapy, there is a personal and collective unconscious

Under Dog lower part of oneself in Gestalt therapy, usually the submissive part

underground n. or adj. avant-garde subculture spanning unconventional political, cultural, social, artistic, and sexual lifestyles

Underground Press newspapers devoted to alternative lifestyles, peace and justice, and the psychedelic culture during the late 1960s

Barb............................Berkeley
Express Times.................San Francisco
Fifth Estate....................................Detroit
Free Press.....................................Boston
Good Times......................San Francisco
Great Speckled Bird..................Atlanta
Kaleidescope.......................Milwaukee
Oracle...............................San Francisco
Old Mole.....................................Boston
Quicksilver Times.....Washington, D.C.
Rat..New York
Seed...Chicago

Underground Railroad clandestine network to free the slaves before the American Civil War

Underhill, Evelyn English poet and author; *Mysticism*; 1874-1941

underpeople beings who wage a war of love in Cordwainer Smith's *The Dead Lady of Clown Town*

Understanding, Inc. UFO cult in contact with three surviving spaceships of an annihilated Earth supercivilization which left for Mars, 1950-

underwater birthing giving birth to a baby in or under water to provide a healthy, safe environment

undine water sprite

ungrund underlying unity (Jacob Beohme)

unhappiness psychological condition resulting from a lack of modesty and faith, lack of poetic gifts, and lack of understanding of natural order in daily life, especially by poor eating and drinking leading to clouded judgment (George Ohsawa)

unicorn fabled horselike being with a single horn

Unifying Principle (Unique Principle) yin and yang; the universal compass of complementary/antagonism that explains and unifies the world of change including science, art, history, religion, philosophy, psychology, medicine, and all aspects of daily life (Michio Kushi)

unio mystica mystical union (Latin)

Union of Concerned Scientists network of scientists concerned about nuclear and other national energy policy with headquarters in Cambridge, Mass.

Unique Principle (Principe Unique, *French*) yin and yang; the nondualistic Order of the Universe that underlies all phenomena (George Ohsawa)

unisex adj. indistinguishable as to male or female; relating to both sexes

Universal Great Brotherhood Latin American spiritual movement founded by Serge Raynaud de la Ferriere combining yoga and temples, 1948-

universal ideas eternal patterns or archetypes whose memory is lost at birth but through philosophy may be recalled (Plato)

Universal Life Church Pentacostal church founded by Kirby Hensley, 1962-

Universal White Brotherhood 1. union or fraternity of higher beings in the universe. 2) cultural association founded in Bulgaria by Peter Deunov, led by his successor Omraam Mikhael Aivanhov, now based in France, 1900-

universal unconscious timeless and spaceless world of images (Cayce)

universe 1. scattered leaves of a single volume bound by Love (Dante). 2. totality of waves running in infinite space (Michio Kushi). 3. the manifestation of One Infinity alternately expanding and contracting at infinite speed (Michio Kushi). 4. beautiful multiple orchestra of trillions of spirals within trillions of spirals (Michio Kushi). 5. a single gorgeous celebratory event (Thomas Berry). 5. fluid, ever-changing energy pattern (Starhawk)

Universel unfinished Sufi temple begun by Hazrat Inayat Kahn in Suresnes, France, 1926-

University of Science and Philosophy Walter and Lao Russell's center and home-study course in universal law, natural science, and living philosophy, based in Waynesboro, Virginia, 1948-

university without walls off-campus educational movement emphasizing experiential learning

Unk 'stone', the first manifestation of the Great Mystery (Lakota)

unrefined oil vegetable oil that has been naturally processed to retain its natural color, taste, aroma, and nutrients

Unstruck Melody Name of God (Sikh)

unsui 'cloud-water', Zen novices (Japanese)

Unui, Mikao Japanese founder of Reiki

UP 1. (Uttar Pradesh) North Indian state with capital at Lucknow. 2. Unique Principle; yin and yang (George Ohsawa)

up front adj. honest, open, uninhibited

upadana 'acquiring', clinging to existence; ninth karmic link in Buddhism (Sanskrit)

upadhi instrument, vehicle, body, superimposed attribute that veils what lies beneath it (Sanskrit)

Upanishad 'near down sit (at the foot of the teacher)', Indian scripture teaching the mystical identity of Atman and Brahman; 108 in number (Sanskrit)

upaya method, skillful means (Sanskrit)

upekkha 'serenity', fourth of the Buddhist heavenly states of mind (Pali)

upper trigram top trigram in an *I Ching* hexagram

upscale adj. healthy, vital, well off

uptight adj. nervous, anxious, upset, inhibited, tense, middle-class

ur-pflanze archetypal plant (Goethe, *German*)

Ur-song (from 'original, primeval', *Greek*) melody that infants around the world sing spontaneously without having learned it from their parents or surrounding culture

Ursprache original ancestral language from which Greek, Latin, Sanskrit, and other Indo-European tongues were derived (German)

uraeus Egyptian cobra, symbolic of the Third Eye in art (Latin)

Uralic non-Indo-European language family including Finnish, Hungarian, Estonian, Mordvin, Samoyed

uranai destiny charts used with thrown sticks (Japanese)

Urania Greek Muse of Astronomy

Uranian follower of Uranian astrology

Uranian Astrology system based on eight invisible planets developed by Alfred Witte during World War I

Admetos	endurance
Apollon	peace, commerce
Vulcanus	strength
Cupido	unions, mergers
Hades	endings, salvage
Zeus	energy, force

Poseidon .... principles, knowledge
Hermes .... career

Urantia 'Earth', psychically-received teaching of the Urantia Foundation

Uranus planet associated with sudden changes, intuition, liberty, originality

Urdu language of Pakistan and Islamic India, similar to Hindi but written in Perso-Arabic script

Uriel 'light of God', archangel on the left of God's throne (Hebrew)

Urim and Thummim magic stones that enabled Joseph Smith to translate the *Book of Mormon* from Egyptian

urium element predicted by Walter Russell; later found and named Plutonium

Urizen archetypal wayward father (Blake)

urmensch primordial human (German)

urna 'wool', circle between the eyebrows; Third Eye (Sanskrit)

Uru-Keu descendents of blond-haired white-skinned gods (Polynesian)

urvernunft mystical truth (German)

urweltweisheit primordial wisdom (Steiner, *German*)

Ute Indian people originally from Mexico; first inhabitants of Colorado; Utah named after them

Utepandragun King of Britain, father of Arthur

Utgard 'outer world' between Heaven and Earth in Scandinavian mythology

Utnapishtim Sumerian flood hero from whom Gilgamesh sought the secret of immortality

Utne Reader digest of the alternative press founded by Eric Utne

Utopia 'Nowhere', Sir Thomas More's ideal island commonwealth described in his book of the same name, 1516. adj. **utopian** (Greek).

Literary Utopias
Altruria....................William D. Howell
Ata...............................Dorothy Bryant
Christianopolis........Johann V. Andreae
City of the Sun....................Campanella
Earthsea.........................Ursula LeGuin
Ecotopia....................Ernest Callenbach
Erewhon.........................Samuel Butler
Euphonia.......................Hector Berlioz
Freeland......................Theodor Hertzka
Gargardia..................................Voltaire
Herland....................Charlotte Gilman
Hygeia......... Benjamin W. Richardson
Icaria..............................Etienne Cabet
Islandia..............................A.T. Wright
Looking Backward.....Edward Bellemy

Mount Analogue..............Rene Daumal
New Atlantis...................Francis Bacon
News from Nowhere.....William Morris
Oceana......................James Harrington
Pala.............................Aldous Huxley
Reason.....................William Hodgson
The Republic...............................Plato
Shangrila..........................James Hilton
Tao-yuan Chi.....................T'ao Ch'ien
Yluana...........................Charles Searle

Utopian Communities
Apapemone.......................Henry Prince
Amana....................Christian Metz
Arcosanti.......................Paolo Soleri
Aurora...............................William Keil
Auroville.........................Sri Aurobindo
Bethel................................William Keil
Brook Farm....................George Ripley
Economy...........................George Rapp
Ephrata.......................Johann Beissel
Findhorn...............................the Caddys
Harmonie................... Rapp and Owen
Ittoen.............................Tenko Nishida
Jerusalem.....Jeremiah Wilkinson
New Harmony.............Rapp and Owen
New Lanark.....................Robert Owen
Orbiston......................Abraham Combe
Ralahine...............John Scott Vandeleur
Woman in the Wilderness.......Johannes Kelpius...
Walden II.........................B.F. Skinner
Zoar...............................Joseph Bimeler

Uxmal 'thrice rebuilt', Mayan center in the Yucatan noted for the Pyramid of the Magician and the Nuns' Quadrangle, where the *Popul Vuh* was revealed

uzait the Eye, ancient Egyptian symbol of insight and wisdom

Uzbek 1. Turkic people of Central Asia. 2. their language.

Vv

V the emblem of the Bird Goddess in ancient times, derived from the vulva; a main sign in the script of Old Europe (Marija Gimbutus)

Vagon castle near Camelot where knights of the Round Table spent the last night together before dispersing on the Grail quest

Vaikuntha Vishnu's heaven (Sanskrit)

vailxi Atlantean aircraft (Phylos)

Vainamoinen Finnish epic hero and seeker who visited the underworld

vairagya surrender, letting go, relinquishing all notions of attainment, all judgments and perceptions (Sanskrit)

Vairocana the Great Sun Buddha

vajra 'diamond, adamantine', scepter with three or five prongs, usually of copper or iron; Buddhist thunderbolt (Sanskrit)

Vajra Makut 'Black Hat' presented by the fifth Karmapa to the Chinese Emperor, the sight of which confers liberation (Sanskrit)

Vajradhatu 'the realm of the indestructible,' Tibetan Buddhist society founded by Chogyam Trungpa with headquarters in Halifax, Nova Scotia, and over 100 affiliated centers, 1970-

Vajrapani Tibetan weapon-bearing guardians (Sanskrit)

vajrasana diamond throne (Sanskrit)

Vajrasattva 'Diamond Being', 1. Akshobhya Buddha. 2. state close to enlightenment (Sanskrit)

Vajrayana 'Adamantine Vehicle', Tibetan Buddhism (Sanskrit)

Vak Goddess of Speech, Music, Language, and Intelligence (Sanskrit)

Valdez Principles a set of ten guidelines for corporate conduct with regard to environmental issues, 1990 (named after the *Exxon Valdez* oil spill in Alaska)

Valdivia site in Chile with Japanese-style pottery dated to -4000 suggesting pre-Columbian conteact

Valentine, J. Manson archaeologist, discoverer of underwater temples off a Bahamian island (identified with Atlantis) dating to -10,000

Valentinus Egyptian philosopher, developer of Gnosticism; 2nd c.

Valinor land across the western sea from Middle-Earth

Valley of the Kings ancient Egyptian burial ground near Luxor

Valley of the Shadow of Death formidable topographical obstacle in *Pilgrim's Progress*

valley spirit Chinese term for the Tao

Valmiki author of the *Ramayana*

vamachara 'left hand practice', tantra (Sanskrit)

Van Gogh, Vincent Dutch intuitive art master; *The Sunflowers*; 1853-90

vanaprastha forest-dweller (Sanskrit)

Vangelis (Vangelis Parathanassiou) New Age composer; *Chariots of Fire*

Vanity Fair carnival run by Beelzebub in *Pilgrim's Progress*

Varaha 'boar', avatar of Vishnu (Sanskrit)

Varanasi (Benares) holy city of Hinduism on the Ganges between the Varana and Asi Rivers

Varda the White Goddess in *Lord of the Rings*

Vasilyev, L. L. Soviet parapsychologist; *Manifestations of the Human Psyche*; 1891-1966

Vasubandhu Indian developer of the Yogachara school, 21st Zen Patriarch; *Abhidharma-kosa*; 4th c.

Vasudeva 1. Krishna's father. 2. ferryman in Hesse's *Siddhartha*

vatsalya parental affection toward the Lord (Sanskrit)

Vatsyayama Indian author; *Kama Sutra*; ca. 1st c.

Vaughan, Frances transpersonal psychologist; *The Inward Arc*

Vaughan, Thomas Welsh Christian mystic; *A Hermetical Banquet*; 1622-66

ve short, spontaneous poems (Vietnamese)

Veda 'knowledge', Hindu scriptures: *Atharva, Rig, Sama, Yajur*; ca. -2500

vedana feeling: seventh link in the Buddhist chain; one of the five skandhas (Sanskrit)

Vedanta Hindu philosophy derived from the *Upanishads* teaching the mystical identity of Atman and Brahman (Sanskrit)

Vedanta Societies groups affiliated with the Ramakrishna Order

Vedantist follower of Vedanta

Vega (the Weaving Maiden) ('fall', *Arabic*) a star in the constellation Lyra that was the North Star about 12,900 years ago and marked the end of the ancient scientific and spiritual world community following a partial axis shift, great flood, or other natural catastrophe (Michio Kushi)

Vega Cycle the precession of the equinoxes, reflecting a change in the North Star overhead as the Earth wobbles on its axis over the course of 25,800 years; the two poles of this great circle are the stars Vega and Polaris, whose time directly overhead signifies the end of a world age by water and fire respectively and the beginning of a new era (Michio Kushi)

vegan n. or adj. 1. diet and lifestyle that

excludes the use of animal products for food, clothing. 2. follower of this path

vegetable n. or adj. 1. any edible plant whose roots, stems, leaves, fruit, or seeds is used for food. 2. the edible part of such a plant. 3. a principal food category in the Standard Macrobiotic Diet, comprising 25-30% of daily food intake by volume; divided into groups of root, round/ground, and white/green leafy vegetables, from which at least one helping should be eaten daily (Michio Kushi)

Root Vegetables

beets, burdock, carrots, daikon, dandelion roots, jinenjo, Jerusalem artichokes, lotus root, parsnip, radish, rutabaga, taro, turnip, and others

Round/Ground Vegetables

acorn squash, broccoli, brussels sprouts, buttercup squash, butternut squash, cabbage, cauliflower, cucumber, green beans, green peas, Hubbard squash, Hokkaido pumpkin, mushrooms, onions, patty pan squash, pumpkin, red cabbage, shiitake mushrooms, snap beans, summer squash, Swiss chard, wax beans, zucchini, and others

White/Green Leafy Vegetables

bok choy, carrot tops, celery, Chinese cabbage, chives, daikon greens, dandelion greens, endive escarole, kale, leeks, lettuce, mustard greens, scallions, sprouts, turnip greens, watercress, wild grasses, and others

Tropical Vegetables

(for consumption only in hot climates) asparagus, avocado, eggplant, green pepper, plantain, potato, red pepper, spinach, sweet potato, tomato, yam

vegetable brush small hand brush made from natural ingredients used to clean vegetables without bruising the skin

vegetable kingdom organic life arising on the surface of the Earth growing and decaying according to laws of spirallic development (Michio Kushi)

vegetarian (from *vegetus*, Latin, 1842) n. or adj. 'one who is sound, whole, fresh, lively', nonmeat eater; dietary pattern and lifestyle associated with Hindusim, Buddhism, Jainism, Taoism, Zoroastrianism, Pythagoreanism, the Essenes, Trappists, Benedictines, Carthusians, Seventh Day Adventists

vegie (veggie) n. or adj. 1. vegetables. 2. vegetarian

Velikovsky, Immanuel Austrian-born psychoanalyst, historian, mythologist; *Worlds in Collision*; 1895-1979

Veni, sponsa, de Litano 'Come [with me] from Lebanon, my spouse', verse from the *Song of Solomon*; chant sung by the Heavenly Pageant as Beatrice appears and replaces Virgil as Dante's guide in the *Divine Comedy*

ventla higher plane term for spaceship (Mark-Age)

Venus 1. Roman Goddess of Love, Art, and Beauty. 2. one of the Paleolithic representations of the Goddess, usually with swelling breasts and broad hips. 3. planet associated with harmony, comfort, attractive energy

Venusian (Venerean) n. or adj. Venus

verbal pun dream symbol in which one word represents another of similar pronunciation and different spelling

veridical adj. hallucinatory vision corresponding accurately with an external source, but uncaused by it

veritas truth (Latin)

vernal equinox first day of spring

Verne, Jules science-fiction writer; *20,000 Leagues Under the Sea*; 1828-1905

Verrocchio, Andrea del Florentine sculptor, teacher of Leonardo; *Christ and the Doubting Thomas*; 1435-88

vertex Uranian astrological point signifying other people, fate

Vertical Wheel of Spinning Radiances souls in the Empyeam who in their joy at the return of Jesus and Mary to the highest heaven form into a dazzling wheel before Dante and Beatrice

Vesica Piscis (Piscine Vessel) fish shape formed by the overlapping of two equal circles; shape of the bishop's mitre, symbol of Jesus, (doubled) the Hindu temple (Latin)

Vessantara exiled prince who gave away all; Buddha in his next-to-last human incarnation

vibe general feeling picked up when entering a room, especially nonverbal expressions of thoughts or feelings; quality, aura, energy frequency. **good vibes** light, harmonious energy. **bad vibes** chaotic, heavy, or fearful feelings, sensations, or impulses

vibhuti 1. manifestation, divine glory. 2. aromatic gray ash materialized by Satya Sai Baba (Sanskrit)

vibration 1. frequency range in which something is expressing. 2. energy that manifests in the relative world as the primary field or state before and after the appearance of physical and material forms (Michio Kushi). 3. energy emitted by an individual or object

victory defeat (George Ohsawa)

videha bodiless (Sanskrit)

vidya knowledge (Sanskrit)

Viejos, los centenarians of Vilcabamba and other Andean regions of Latin America (Spanish)

vigesimal adj. number system with a base of twenty, e.g. the Mayan

vigintile planets 18 degrees apart; minor favorable aspect

vihara 'walk about', 1. Buddhist or Jain hall. 2. Buddhist heavenly state of mind (Sanskrit)

viilia soy yogurt developed from a cultured product native to Finland

vilana 1. wisdom of experience (Sanskrit). 2. pure consciousness, empirical mind; one of the five skandhas (Pali)

Vilcabamba valley in Ecuador whose people are noted for their health and longevity resulting from a simple diet, hard physical activity, large families, and no concept of retirement

village bank bank in the Third World that makes available to participating families an increasing line of credit for funding self-chosen productive investments; no collateral of any kind is required, only the borrower's word of honor

vimala free from defilement; second stage of the Bodhisattva path (Sanskrit)

Vimalakirti Mahayanist sutra about a rich learned nobleman (Sanskrit)

vimana wheels or discus weapons in the *Mahabharata* (Sanskrit)

vina stringed instrument with gourds at each end of the fingerboard (Hindi)

vinaya Buddhist monastic rules (Sanskrit)

Vinca ancient Bulgarian culture which may have yielded the earliest inscribed objects and Neolithic script

Vineta submerged city of Scandinavian legend that rises one night every hundred years

Vinland 'Wine Land', North America (Leif Erikson)

Vinland Map controversial chart with a text about Bishop Henricus's mission to Vineland in the 11th c.; ca. 1440

vinyasas the flowing sequences of move-

ments and jumping-through style of yoga (Sanskrit)

violence 1. setting yourself against something rather than flowing with it (Gary Snyder). 2. extreme behavior characteristic of those who know nothing of the structure of the infinite universe (George Ohsawa).

Violet Flame decrees missives channeled through Elizabeth Clare Prophet

Vipassana 'to see things as they really are', various forms of passive or insightful meditation aimed at heightening one's awareness, releasing previously suppressed thoughts and feelings, and developing a natural system of biofeedback (Pali)

Virabhava state of the hero; middle stage of the tantras (Sanskrit)

Viracocha 1. Incan Creator. 2. 'sea foam people', white bearded strangers who brought Incans culture

virasena heroic posture in yoga with one foot on the ground and the other on the opposite thigh (Sanskrit)

Virgil (Vergil) Latin poet and Dante's guide in the *Divine Comedy*; *Georgics*; -70-19

Virgin 1. Mary, the mother of Jesus. 2. creative cultural force (Henry Adams). 3. (l.c.) one who has not had a sexual encounter. 4. (l.c.) one who is more highly charged with ki or life energy than others and thus has more polarity or the power of attraction. 5. (l.c.) a girl or woman who is connected with the wilderness.

virgin forest community of very experienced, wise, and mature trees, birds, animals, and other living beings

Virgo Virgin, sixth sign of the zodiac; of the earthy element, ruler Mercury; keyword: service, discrimination

viriditas the property of greenness in alchemy (Latin)

virtual adj. something that exists only as an electronic representation which has no other concrete existence; referring to the electronic equivalent of organizations, groupings, settings, and even whole 'realities'

virtual reality artificial reality; instant fantasy world electronically created or computer-generated

Virtual Sanctuary a spiritually oriented computer network developed by Awakening Technology, 1980s

virtue (vrtus, *Latin,* te, *Chinese*) 1. excellence of any kind, capacity or power. 2. one of four cardinal qualities in medieval Christian philosophy: prudence, justice, fortitude, and temperance. 3. one of three theological graces in medieval Christian thought: caritas (love), faith, and hope. 4. planetary power governing form. 5. life energy in things (Lao-tzu). 6. one of five traditional values in Chinese philosophy: benevolence, righteousness, propriety, knowledge, and faith

virya 'vigor', fourth Paramita (Sanskrit)

vis viva force inherent in all substances, physical and spiritual, corresponding to Chinese ch'i (Leibniz, *Latin*)

Visakha laywoman, friend of Buddha

Visel Goddess of Wisdom who channeled the *Aquarian Gospel* to Levi

Vishnu 1. second aspect of the Hindu trinity; the Preserver. 2. protector of the dreamlike order of the delicately balanced phenomenal forms of this passing world (Joseph Campbell). adj. **Vaishnava**. n. **Vaishnavite** devotee

Vishnu-Devananda, Swami disciple of Sivananda, founder of True World Order; 1927-

vishuddha throat chakra (Sanskrit)

Vishvanath Shiva as Lord of the universe, presiding deity of Benares

Vishveshvara Shiva's Golden Temple in Benares

vision seeing without seeing (Bodhidharma)

Vision of Christ on the Cross mystic vision embedded in the Sphere of Mars, a cross in which Christ shines forth in Paradise in the *Divine Comedy*

vision quest American Indian spiritual search, especially through solitude, fasting, and dreams

VisionLink an interactive communication system to link people and projects worldwide, 1980s-

visitation UFO or other contact from another world or level of existence

visualization the process of forming positive thoughts or images, as a means of creating wellness

Visuddhimagga 'path of purification', Buddhist text by Buddhaghosa (Pali)

Vital, Hayim Kabbalist, disciple of Issac Luria; *The Tree of Life*; 1543-1620

vitamin organic substance essential in small volume to nutrition, especially as coenzymes and precursors of coenzymes in the digestive or metabolic process; available in whole natural foods and sometimes produced by the body itself

vitamin A (retinol, beta-carotene) fat-soluble vitamin that promotes the health of the eyes, skin, and inner linings; increases immunity to infection; reduces risk of tumor formation, especially lung and breast cancer; found in carrots, winter squash, rutabaga, and other yellow or orange vegetables and in broccoli, kale, and other dark green leafy vegetables; and in nori

vitamin B-1 (Thiamine) water-soluble vitamin essential to carbohydrate metabolism, nervous system function, lactation, fertility and protection against beriberi; found in whole grains, beans, vegetables, seeds and nuts, and sea vegetables

vitamin B-2 (Riboflavin) water-soluble vitamin essential to carbohydrate and protein metabolism; protects eyes, skin, and mucous membranes; facilitates antibody and red-blood cell formation; found in whole grains, beans, leafy green vegetables, nori and wakame

vitamin B-6 (Pyridoxine) water-soluble vitamin that assists in carbohydrate and protein metabolism; found in whole grains, beans, cabbage, and nuts

vitamin B-12 (Cobalamin) water-soluble vitamin that assists in red-blood cell formation and maintenace of nerve tissues and protects against pernicious anemia; found in fermented soybean products such as tempeh, natto, miso, and tamari soy sauce; in sea vegetables such as kombu, wakame, hiziki, and nori; and in fish, seafood, and other animal products

vitamin C (Ascorbic acid) water-soluble vitamin that assists in formation of connective tissue; contributes to healing of wounds and broken bones; aids in red-blood cell formation; protects against capillary wall ruptures, bruising easily, and scurvy; linked with decreased risk of stomach cancer; found in broccoli, mustard greens, kale, and other leafy green vegetables; strawberries, cantaloupe, and other fresh, seasonal, temperate-climate fruits; and in citrus fruits

vitamin D (Calciferol) fat-soluble vitamin that promotes calcium absorption essential in the formation of bones and teeth and protects against rickets; found in exposure to sunshine, fish and liver

oils

vitamin E (Tocopherol) fat-soluble vitamin that prevents oxidation of unsaturated fatty acids, vitamins A and C, and other substances in the body; lowers serum cholesterol and facilitates blood circulation; strengthens fertility and potency; inhibits tumor formation; found in green leafy vegetables, unrefined vegetable-quality oils, whole grains, beans

vitamin K fat-soluble vitamin that contributes to normal blood clotting; found in leafy green vegetables

vitarian raw foods lifestyle excluding use of fire for food, light, heat, smoke

viveka discrimination (Sanskrit)

Vivekananda, Swami (Narendranath Datta) Indian yogi and disciple of Ramakrishna who brought Vedanta to the West; 1863-1902

Vivian enchantress who foiled Merlin

VLDL very low-density lipoprotein; one of the 'bad' cholesterols

Vocations for Social Change right livelihood collective, 1960s-

voice 1. the expression of one's deepest self, one's true song; the ground of poetry, art, and literature. 2. one's own brief bubble-like body's experience of the universe (Gary Snyder). 3. the silent intention behind words (Sherman Goldman)

Volsung Teutonic hero and saga

Volsunga old Icelandic prose saga

Voluntary Poverty withdrawal from material wealth and cultivation of virtue

Voluntary Simplicity way of life that promotes personhood and self-realization

Voluspa (Sibyl's Prophecy) poem of the Eddas (Old Norse)

Vonnegut, Kurt novelist; *Breakfast of Champions*

vortex 1. astral mental construct. 2. radiant cluster, accessible to the mind (Pound)

Votan 'heart of the cities', Mayan hero identified with Quetzalcoatl

Voynich Manuscript a mysterious manuscript written in an unknown script attributed to Roger Bacon dating to at least 1586

vrata vow, act of merit (Sanskrit)

vril life energy (Lytton)

Vucab-Caquix villain of the *Popol Vuh*

Vulcan 1. Roman God of Fire and Craftsmanship. 2. planet postulated between

Mercury and the Sun. 3. planet and race of logical beings, such as Mr. Spock, in *Star Trek*, who communicate telepathically

Vulkanus seventh Uranian planet, ruling quality, magnitude, cosmic will

vulnerary agent used for promoting the healing of wounds

Vulture Peak (Grdhrakuta, *Sanskrit*) Indian peak resembling a vulture where Buddha taught the *Lotus Sutra*

vyakarana prediction of future enlightenment made to one by a Buddha (Sanskrit)

Vyasa (Krishna Dwaipayana) 'compiler', author of the *Mahabharata*

wabi 'poverty', Zen term for detachment amidst multiplicities (Japanese)

Wadi Natrun Egyptian desert where Coptic ascetics meditate

wah (pl. awliya) 'friend', saint (Arabic)

Wah-i-Guru name of God used by the Sikhs (Punjabi)

Waite, Arthur Edward British occultist, *The Holy Kabbalah*; 1857-1942

wakame a long, thin green sea vegetable used in making miso soup and other macrobiotic dishes (Japanese)

wakan life energy (Sioux)

Wakan-Tanka the Great Spirit (Lakota)

wakf deeding land to God (Arabic)

Wakonda Sioux Supreme Being

Walam Olum 'painted records', Lenni Lenape chronicle (symbols on sticks comprising five books, or 183 verses) relating the creation, migration from Asia to Alaska to the Delaware Valley, and the coming of Europeans

Walata medieval African Islamic state of learning and peace in Mali

Walden Pond site in Concord, Mass., where Thoreau lived and wrote the environmental classic *Walden*

Walden Two 1. novel by B. F. Skinner. 2. autonomous community movement inspired by this work

Waldenses Christian communalist movement of the Cottian Alps founded by French pacifist Pierre Waldo, 12th c.

Waldman, Anne poet and co-founder of the Kerouac School of Disembodied Poetics at Naropa Institute; 1945-

Waldorf schools Anthroposophical Society schools based on the teachings of Rudolf Steiner stressing art, drama, and spiritual development

Waldzell monastery-school in Hesse's *The Glass Bead Game*

Waley, Arthur Orientalist; *The No Plays of Japan*; 1889-1966

walk-in a high-minded entity from the spirit plane who is permitted under certain circumstances to take over the unwanted bodies of other human beings

walk-out someone who desperately wishes to depart or who, because of a clinical death or near-death experience, is unable to keep his/her body alive

walking 1. exercise that energizes all systems, clears the mind, and brings us closer to nature. 2. unfocused traveling consciousness (don Juan)

walking lightly on the land 1. simple, ecological way of life associated with Native Americans. 2. to be aware and alive, to be free of egotism, starting with concrete acts and the insight that we are interdependent energy fields of great potential wisdom and compassion — expressed in each person as a superb mind, a beautiful and complex body, and the almost magical capacity of language (Gary Snyder)

Walkman portable stereo radio with headphones

wall of flames the fire in which the lustful are purified, surrounding the Earthly Paradise in the *Divine Comedy*

Wampanoag 'People of the East', befrienders of the Pilgrims who taught them Thanksgiving, later massacred

Wandering Calendar ancient Egyptian calendar based on 1460-year cycles

Wandjina ancestral spirit of the Dreamtime in Australia

Wands Tarot suit denoting enterprise

wang empowerment (Tibetan)

Wang Hsia (Ink Wang) wandering Chinese artist who painted with his hands while laughing and singing; 9th c.

Wang Yang-ming Chinese writer who believed that we form one body with Heaven, Earth, and all beings; 14th c.

Wangyal, Geshe Mongolian Buddhist master and founder of the Lamaist Buddhist Monastery of America; 1901-83

Waniyetu Wowapi Dakota winter counts, picture-writing chronicle

Wanted—An Enemy science-fiction story by Fritz Leiber about a pacifist who exhorts Martians to invade Earth to effect humanity to unification, 1945

War Resisters League international pacifist organization founded by Tracy Mygatt, Frances Witherspoon, and Jessie Wallace Hughan, 1923-

war tax resistance refusing to pay taxes or portion of taxes that go toward war and war preparations

Warner, Marina feminist historian; *Alone of All Her Sex*; 1946-

warp v. to transport through a time dimension. **warp speed** faster than the speed of light

Warren, Henry Clarke Orientalist; *Buddhism in Translation*; 1854-99

warrior one devoted to the disciplined accumulation of power (don Juan)

wasabi horseradish, mustard (Japanese)

Wasteland a demythologized world, a world of mechanical existence (Joseph Campbell)

wat Buddhist temple (Thai)

Wat Phra Keo 1. Emerald Buddha Chapel in Bangkok (Thai). 2. Emerald Buddha in Vientiane, 814 (Laotian)

Wat Po Temple of the Reclining Buddha in Bangkok (Thai)

watchtower one of four cosmic planes in Enochian Magick

water 1. the highest benevolence, benefiting all beings without favor, dwelling in places which people despise, and standing close to Tao (Lao Tzu). 2. form of energy which obeys all, adapts itself to all sorts of molds, is quiet and modest, but which bears extraordinary pressure, carves a path through massive rock to regain its goal; which listens in humility to everyone, penetrates everything, crosses all obstacles, understands all, feeds all, and unifies all (George Ohsawa). 2. the infinite tendency toward modesty and a destiny full of infinite difficulties (George Ohsawa)

water baby baby born in water, an environment some mothers find safe, comfortable, and less traumatic than giving birth in the ordinary way

water purifier filtering device, usually mechanical, to cleanse municipal water from impurities and chemicals

water witching dowsing

watershed entire area of a valley that is drained by water, from the ridgetop on one side to the ridgetop on the other

watery signs Cancer, Scorpio, Pisces

Watkins, Alfred English discoverer of ley lines; *The Old Straight Track;* b. 1855

Watkins Glen site in New York of a mammoth rock festival, July 21, 1973

Watson, Dr. John H. friend, companion, and chronicler of Sherlock Holmes

Watts, Alan Episcopal theologian, Zen teacher; *This Is It*; 1915-73

wave-particle theory that subatomic matter has a dual aspect, appearing sometimes as waves, sometimes as particles

Waw sixth Hebrew letter: eye, W, 6

Way (tao, *Chinese*) the sublime path that can't be expressed in language but can be found by someone who sees his or her own nature (Bodhidharma)

Way of a Pilgrim anonymous Russian mystical classic, 19th c.

Way of the Mountain Center Taoist-like center led by ritualist Dolores LaChapelle in Silverton, Colo.

We Shall Overcome anthem of the civil rights movement, originating from a religious hymn (with the help of Zilphia Horton, Frank Hamilton, Guy Carawan and Pete Seeger)

wealth quality of being content with what one has (Lao Tzu)

weatherproofing weather-stripping windows and doors, insulation, and other measures to reduce energy consumption

Weena Eloi girl in Wells's *The Time Machine*

Wegener, Alfred German geophysicist who theorized an original single continent; 1880-1930

Wehani fragrant, deep bronze California strain of rice that is chewy and sweet

Weil, Simeon French mystic; *The Need for Roots*; 1909-43

Weilgart, Wolfgang (John) channel of *aUI, the Language of Space*

Wel (welteislehre) Horbiger's doctrine of eternal ice (German)

WELL (Whole Earth 'Lectronic Link) holistic computer network in Sausalito, Calif., 1980s-

Well at the World's End fountain of youth in William Morris's novel of the same name, 1896

well body healthy, self-healing

Welles, Orson film director; *Citizen Kane*; 1915-85

Wells, H. G. English historian; *The Time Machine*; 1866-1946

Weltanschauung world view (German)

Wen Ch'ang Chinese God of Literature

Wen, King father of the Chou Dynasty founder, compiler of the Sequence of Later Heaven in the *I Ching*; -12th c.

Wen-shu Bodhisattva Manjushri (Chinese)

Wen Yen commentary on the words of the text in the *I Ching* (Chinese)

Wentz, Walter Y. Evans California pilgrim and scholar; tr. *The Tibetan Book of the Dead*

Wesak (Vaisakha, *Sanskrit*) celebration of the birth, renunciation, enlightenment, and death of the Buddha, usually on the full moon in Taurus (Singhalese)

wesen being, essence (German)

West, Julian utopian hero of Bellamy's *Looking Backwards*

Western Wisdom Teachings Rosicrucian teachings received by Heindel

wet cell electrical apparatus mentioned in the Edgar Cayce readings

wetland a swamp, bog, marsh, or other area that is inundated or saturated by surface or ground water

Weyden, Rogier van der Flemish master; *St. Jerome in the Desert*; 1399-1464

W. H. initials of the mysterious person to whom the Shakespearean canon is dedicated

wheat cereal grass; grain of the plant from which flour is produced

wheat germ wheat embryo

wheatgrass therapy dietary regimen based on sprouts and raw foods developed by Ann Wigmore

Wheatley, Phyllis African-born poet; *Poems on Various Subjects, Religious and Moral*; ca. 1753-84

Wheel of Fortune Tarot #10: destiny

Wheel of Life (bhavachakra, *Sanskrit*) incessant wheel of karma whose twelve links are represented in Indian and Tibetan art by:

blind old lady .... ignorance
potter potting .... windings
monkey stealing fruit .... consciousness
naked man in a boat....... self-awareness
mask with eyes........ sensory awareness
kissing or ploughing .... contact
arrow in the eye .... feeling
tavern drinking .... desire
miser hoarding .... greed
pregnant woman .... becoming
child birth .... being

man carrying corpse .... death, decay

Wheeler, John A. physicist, theorizer of superspace; *Gravitation*; 1911-

Wheeler's Ranch open commune dedicated to God established by Bill Wheeler in northern California, 1967

Whirling Ecstasy Sufi dance in which members take turns whirling in the center of the circle

White Buffalo Cow Woman spiritual messenger who brought the sacred pipe to the Sioux and will appear at the end of this 'world'

white dwarf high density star of small volume and average mass

White, Ellen Harmon Adventist teacher, vegetarian reformer; *The Ministry of Healing*; 1827-1915

White Goddess Druid Supreme Being

White Horse 1. scripture-bearing animal in a dream of Chinese Emperor Ming-ti. 2. symbol in *Revelation*

White House Navajo shrine symbolizing the center of the world

White Indians North Americans of European or other descent with a grounded vision and respect for traditional Native American culture

White Knight 1. Arthurian symbol of purity and spiritual grace. 2. Kierkegaard's hero of faith. 3. being who showed Alice out of the Looking Glass Land

white light 1. mystical acid experience in which all connections are valid, all boundaries arbitrary. 2. energy that balances and restores, natural and available to all living things in Reiki

white miso a sweet, short-time fermented miso

White Rabbit hare that Alice followed

White Roots of Peace 1. symbol of the Iroquois Great Peace. 2. caravan working for Native American rights

Whitehead, Alfred North English-born philosopher; *Science and the Modern World*; 1861-1947

Whitman, Walt chanter of Adamic songs; *I Sing the Body Electric*; 1819-92

Whittier, John Greenleaf Quaker, poet, abolitionist; *Songs of Labor*; 1807-92

Who British rock group (Roger Daltry, Keith Moon, Peter Townsend, John Entwhistle); *Tommy*; 1960s-

wholcracy a synergistic democracy based on holistic understanding (David Spangler)

whole-brain adj. state in which both hemispheres of the brain can be utilized to maximum effect

whole earth n. or adj. planetary or cosmic consciousness

Whole Earth Catalog series of books promoting access to environmentally safe tools, edited by Stephen Brand, 1968-

whole foods n. or adj. foods in their natural form that have not been refined or processed such as brown rice or whole wheat berries

whole grains 1. humanity's traditional food; staff of life; most balanced and nourishing food for human life and development. 2. unrefined cereal grains to which nothing has been added or subtracted in milling except the inedible outer hull. Traditional varieties include:

brown rice	Far East
millet	China, Africa
whole wheat	India, North America
barley	Greece, Rome, Egypt, Israel
oats	Scotland, Northern Europe
buckwheat	Russia, Eastern Europe
rye	Northern Europe
corn	North, South, Central America
amaranth	Mexico
quinoa	Peru
teff	Ethiopia
sorghum	Africa

whole of wholes the universe (Plato)

whole wheat a whole cereal grain that may be prepared in whole form or made into flour or processed into noodles, seitan, fu, bulghur, couscous, and cracked wheat

wholistic (holistic) n. or adj. whole, organic, macrocosmic. **wholism**

wi-gi-e sacred songs of the Osage

Wigmore, Ann Lithuanian-born healer, founder Hippocrates Health Institute, popularizer of sprouting; 1919-

Wicca witchcraft (Old English). adj. **wiccan**

Wicked Witch of the West villainess in the *Wizard of Oz*

wickiup brush shelter, mat-covered home, sweathouse of Plains people

widdershins countersunwise

wigwam Algonquian house, circular or dome-shaped, covered with bark

Wilbur, Ken consciousness researcher; *No Boundary: Eastern and Western Approaches to Personal Growth*

wild foods edible foods that grow in the wild such as wild grains, vegetables, roots, tubers, and herbs

wild rice a wild cereal grass native to North America used primarily in holiday cooking

wild zone female space; the alter ego of patriarchal society

wilderness nature in its most pristine form; environment where where God or ultimate reality manifests itself most clearly to Siddartha, Jesus, and other spiritual seekers

Wilderness Society environmental organization founded by Aldo Leopold and others, based in Washington, D.C.

Wilhelm, Hellmut German scholar; *Change: Eight Lectures on the I Ching*; 1905-

Wilhelm, Richard German missionary in China; tr. *I Ching*; 1873-1930

Wilkins, Charles English scholar in India, first translator of the *Bhagavad Gita* into English, 1785; 1749-1836

Wilkins, John English linguist; *An Essay Toward a Real Character and a Philosophical Language*; 1614-72

will 1. essential function of being, experienced as purpose, choice, causality, ability to express or act; with three aspects: strong, skillful, good (psychosynthesis). 2. ring of magical power used by luminous beings (don Juan)

Williams, Albert Rhys radical journalist; *Through the Russian Revolution*; 1883-1962

Williams, Roger Puritan dissenter; *A Key into the Language of America*; 1603-83

Williams, William Carlos poet, inspirator of the Beats; *Paterson*; 1883-1963

Wilson, Alfred Cheyenne teacher of the Native American Church; 1877-1945

Wilson, John (Nishkuntu, Moon-Head) revealer of peyote; 19th c.

Wilson, Lt. R. Air Force pilot who disappeared over Michigan in pursuit of an UFO, Nov. 23, 1953

Wilson, Robert Anton occult investigator and author; *The Illuminatus Trilogy*

win-win view of power in which everyone benefits without limiting the development of others

wind generator device to produce electricity by wind power

Wind, Wabun teacher of the Bear Tribe; *The Feminine: Ancient Vison, Modern Wisdom*; 1945-

Windham Hill seminal New Age music record label founded by William Ackerman in Hollywood

Windstar Foundation educational center co-founded by John Denver in Snowmass, Colo., 1976-

winged sandals 1. attribute of Mercury. 2. tool Perseus used to slay Medusa

Wings additional texts to the *I Ching* attributed to Confucius

wings of perception unfolding and touching both the tonal and nagual at once without discrimination (don Juan)

Winks, Woozy sidekick of Plastic Man

Winstanley, Gerrard English Digger; *The Law of Freedom*; 1609-52

Winter, Paul musician who has composed with whales, dolphins, and other creatures; *Common Ground;* 1939-

wisdom intuitive knowledge of the mind of love and clarity that lies beneath one's ego-driven anxieties and aggressions (Gary Snyder)

witch (from *wic*, 'to bend or shape') 1. a person who bends energy and shapes consciousness (Starhawk). 2. woman who operates on the edges of language and culture (Helene Cixous)

Witch of Endor Saul's psychic

witchcraft an Earth religion

Witherspoon, Frances social activist; *The Glorious Company*; 1887-1974

withhold undisclosed contra-survival act against a Dynamic (Scientology)

witness v. 1. to observe oneself from the outside; detached, nonjudgmental technique. 2. to affirm and uphold a principle of life through nonviolent civil disobedience. **bear witness** to accept responsibility for being aware of an injustice and doing something about it (Society of Friends)

Witte, Alfred German mathematician, founder Uranian astrology; 1878-1941

wizard male witch

Wobblie member of the IWW

Wodziwob Pauite prophet, teacher of Wovoka; 19th c.

wok a deep round skillet for stir-frying and tempura (Chinese)

Wolfram von Eschenbach Bavarian knight and Grail chronicler; *Parzival*; ca. 1195-1225

Wollstonecraft, Mary English feminist; *Vindication of the Rights of Women*; 1759-97

Woman in the Wilderness Christian mystical colony in Pennsylvania led by Johannes Kelpius, 1694-1748

woman-identified woman woman who relates primarily to other women; a lesbian

Woman's Bible feminist volume of scriptures edited by Elizabeth Cady Stanton, 1895-98

womanculture activities, values, and attitudes developed from women's experience

womankind women as a whole

womanspirit feminist approach that combines women's myths, philosophy, psychology, and spiritual development

womb-door avenue of rebirth in the Tibetan bardo plane

Women's Commonwealth feminist community founded by Martha McWhirter in Benton, Tex., 1876-1906

women's liberation movement of women to attain equality, freedom from male domination and sex-role stereotypes, express their own creativity, and realize their full potential

women's studies exploration of the feminine in culture, history, art, society; the ideological wing of the feminist movement

Wonder Woman comic book heroine who serves love and peace, 1940s

Wonderland realm traversed by Alice

wood ashes residue of burnt hardwood used to soften and flavor corn, mushrooms, and other food, and as a natural cleanser

Woodhenge site on Salisbury Plain in England of an ancient ditch and earthworks with an arrangement of concentric rings set out in a series of dots, discovered 1928

Woodroffe, Sir John (Arthur Avalon) English Orientalist; *Tantra of the Great Liberation*; 1865-1936

Woodstock large rock festival held on Max Yasgur's farm near Bethel, N.Y., Aug. 15-17, 1969

Woodstock Nation the counterculture

Woolman, John English Quaker; *Journal*; 1720-72

Word (Logos, *Greek*) 1. reason, order, governing principle. 2. Jesus Christ

Wordsworth, William English nature poet; *Intimations of Immortality from Recollections of Early Childhood*; 1770-1850

Work 1. inner work, practice, spiritual discipline. 2. transformation, human perfecting (Gurdjieff and Bennett)

work brigade group that engages in saving whales, studying the rainforest, distributing seeds, or other socially re-

sponsible task during vacation or retreat

Working Assets socially responsible credit card, 1986-

working fluid medium circulating in a solar energy system, e.g. water

World Center of Birds of Prey wildlife group in Bosie, Idaho, that relocates injured and endangered falcons and other raptors

World Charter for Nature document adopted by the U.N. General Assembly with a biocentric orientation respecting all forms of life regardless of their human utility, 1982

world citizen someone who recognizes the entire world as his or her state and a world without boundaries as home; allegiance to the truth, universality of human culture

World Conference on Religion and Peace interreligious education and action body for peace and justice founded in Kyoto, 1970-

World Hunger Year organization that informs about domestic and international hunger and its causes, founded by Harry Chapin, New York, N.Y., 1975-

World Invocation Day June 4, celebrating the unity of Earth

World Parliament of Religions first East West conference on religions held in Chicago at which Vedanta and Zen were introduced to the West by Swami Vivikenanda and Abbot Soyen Shaku, 1893

World Peace University educational center in Eugene, Oregon

World Plan Maharishi's plan to spread the Science of Creative Intelligence, 1972-

world-sensorium the controlling mechanism of the psychosocial evolution of humanity (Oliver Reiser)

World Service Authority world government interim organization headed by Garry Davis, 1954-

World-soul universal spirit composed of the two opposites called the Same and the Other, with the Essence (Plato)

World Tarot #21: happiness, harmony, enlightenment

World Wildlife Fund international agency to protect endangered species

Worldly Goods friend of Everyman who declined to go with him on the final journey in *Pilgrim's Progress*

Worlds of If science-fiction genre of what would have happened historically if

worldview consciousness, scope

Worldwatch Institute organization in Washington, D.C., monitoring international resources, publisher of an annual state of the world report

wormhole hypothesized channel in modern physics connecting every part in space with every other part simultaneously (Wheeler)

Worth, Patience male control of Mrs. Curran who lived in 17th c. England and America

Wounded Knee 1. hamlet and creek on the Pine Ridge reservation in South Dakota. 2. site of a massacre of 200 Sioux by U.S. troops, Dec. 29, 1890. 3. site of the Independent Oglala Sioux Nation, Feb. 27-May 8, 1973

Woundwort, General Stalinist rabbit commander in *Watership Down*

Wovoka Paiute shepherd, founder of the Ghost Dance; 1856-1932

Wright, Frances Scottish-born feminist, abolitionist, and founder of the Nashoba community; *A Course of Popular Lectures*; 1795-1852

Wright, Frank Lloyd pioneer visionary and architect; *Experimenting with Human Lives*; 1869-1959

writer one who translates patterns of light and sound into rhythms and images into words

writing fitting words smoothly into the surrounding ebb and flow of silence according to their yin/yang qualities (Sherman Goldman)

wu 1. sudden enlightenment. 2. sorcerer (Chinese)

Wu Chen Chinese artist; *The Pagoda of the Plum-Blossom Monk*; 1280-1354

Wu Ch'eng-en Chinese novelist; *Hsi Yu Ki* (Journey to the West); 1505-80

Wu Chi the Limitless from which T'ai Chi springs; the source of motion and the mother of yin and yang (Chinese)

wu-hsin 'no mind', Bodhidharma's doctrine that the world comes from mind (Chinese)

Wu Hsing 'five agents', the five stages of transformation popularly known as wood, fire, earth, metal, and water (Chinese)

Wu Li Chinese artist, Taoist recluse who became a Jesuit priest; *The Old Snow Man on Huang Shan*; 1632-1718

Wu Tao-tzu Chinese artist who could paint a perfect circle with the sweep of a brush and whose Buddhist murals converted butchers and fishermen to vegetarianism; 8th c.

wu wei 'nondoing', Taoist concept of ceasing to strive to attain (Chinese)

Wupatki National Monument in Arizona with 800 ruins and sites inhabited by the Anasazi until the 14th c.

Xx

x chromosome chromosome in the DNA that determines sex; females have double x; males one x and one y chromosome

Xanadu city where Kubla Khan's stately pleasure dome was built

Xanga Brazilian spiritualism

Xanthyros community in Vancouver led by Robert Augustus Masters based on uncompromising honesty, 1980s-

xenoglossis speaking in tongues unknown to the speaker

Xenophanes of Colophon Greek philosopher who taught that God was an eternal sphere; -6th c.

Xhosa Bantu language and people of the Transvaal, South Africa

Xibalba underground empire mentioned in the *Popol Vuh*

Ximena heroine of *The Cid*

xioqua scientists of Atlantis (Phylos)

Xipe Totec Nahuatl God of Spring

Xochimalca flower-weavers; secret mystery cult teaching the opening of the mind like a flower (Nahuatl)

Xochipilli 'flower prince', Aztec God of Music, Dance, and Games

Xolotl Nahuatl sacred dog, companion of Quetzalcoatl

Xu-Yun Chinese Zen master; *Autobiography*; 1840-1960

Xue culture-bearer of the Chibchas, a white person in flowing robes with a beard to the waist (Bochica)

xvarnah crown of glory (Hebrew)

Yy

y chromosome partner of an x chromosome in males

y geilwad a Welsh caller or ox driver who traditionally walked backwards in front of the ox team singing to them as they worked

Y-rod dowsing rod in the shape of a forked stick or Y

ya-men 'mute gate', acupoint at the base of the skull that can help relieve deaf muteness (Chinese)

yabyum 'father-mother', symbol of skillful means and wisdom locked in loving embrace (Tibetan)

Yahgan Andean tribe noted for remaining observant while sleeping

Yahi 'the People', northern California Indian tribe of which Ishi was the last survivor; ca. -2000-1916 C.E.

Yahweh (YHVH, Jehovah) Lord of Israel; King of the Universe (Hebrew)

yajna sacrifice (Sanskrit)

Yakut 1. Soviet state in northeastern Siberia, capital Yakutsk. 2. people living there. 3. Turkic language there

Yaktayvians inhabitants inside Mt. Shasta and other secret cities around the world who use high-pitched bells to manipulate energy and to communicate

Yakushi Nyorai Gem Light Universal Spirit for Medicine; Buddha who made twelve resolutions to aid all beings (Japanese)

yalandji dolma vine leaves stuffed with rice (Greek)

Yama 1. Hindu Lord of Dharma and Death. 2. (l.c.) negative rules for moral conduct; first of Patanjali's eight steps of Raja Yoga (Sanskrit)

yama, yama yakity yak, meaningless conversation (est)

Yamagishi-Kai Association spiritual movement founded by Yamagishi Miyozo; largest commune in Japan, 1953-

yamala text-based mantra (Sanskrit)

Yamamoto, Shizuko Japanese-born shiatsu teacher; *Barefoot Shiatsu*; 1924-

yambushi mountain priests of Shugendo Buddhism (Japanese)

Yamuna 1. (Jumna) North Indian river.

2. South Indian monk-king;10th c.

yana vehicle, path (Sanskrit)   there. 3. Turkic language there

Yaktayvians inhabitants inside Mt. Shasta and other secret cities around the world who use high-pitched bells to manipulate energy and to communicate

Yakushi Nyorai Gem Light Universal Spirit for Medicine; Buddha who made twelve resolutions to aid all beings (Japanese)

yalandji dolma vine leaves stuffed with rice (Greek)

Yama 1. Hindu Lord of Dharma and Death. 2. (l.c.) negative rules for moral conduct; first of Patanjali's eight steps of Raja Yoga (Sanskrit)

Yamagishi-Kai Association spiritual movement founded by Yamagishi Miyozo; largest commune in Japan, 1953-

Yamamoto, Shizuko Japanese-born shiatsu teacher; *Barefoot Shiatsu*; 1924-

yambushi mountain priests of Shugendo Buddhism (Japanese)

Yamuna 1. (Jumna) North Indian river. 2. South Indian monk-king;10th c.

yana vehicle, path (Sanskrit)

yang n. or adj. 'sunny side of a mountain', 1. the active principle. 2. Heaven's force. 3. one of the two fundamental energies of the universe; the relative tendency of contraction, centripetality, density, heat, light, strength, and other qualities whose energy tends to go down and inward. 4. the energy of the compact seed, the germ from which new life begins 5. strong, healthy, vital, full of life. 6. (too yang) tight, rigid, forceful (Chinese). v. **yangize** to strengthen, tighten, contract, materialize. **yangization, yangizing**

Yang Fang Chinese Taoist who warned against polished rice and gourmet food during the Sung Dynasty

Yang Hsiung Chinese philosopher who rewrote the *I Ching* in the form of tetragrams; *Classic of the Great Dark*; 1st c.

Yang Lu Chan (Yang the Unsurpassable) Chinese T'ai Chi master who demonstrated ch'i power by holding a swallow on his open palm which tried but couldn't fly away; founder of the Yang Style of the martial art; 1799-1872

Yang Style T'ai Chi form developed by Yang Lu Ch'an and his family

yangie (slang) one who has eaten excessively yang foods resulting in a rigid, tense, or macho condition

yannoh a natural grain coffee made from five different grains and beans which have been roasted and ground into a fine powder (George Ohsawa)

yantra mystical diagram (Sanskrit)

Yao text of the moving lines in the *I Ching* (Chinese)

Yao-tien 'Canon of Yao', earliest Chinese astronomical document, first chapter of the *Book of History* (Chinese)

Yaquis 3000 Native Americans who live in the vicinity of Tucson, Arizona

Yaqut ibn Abdullah Greek-born Muslim geographer; *Dictionary of Learned Men*; 1179-1229

Yarmouth Stone runestone in Yarmouth Bay, Nova Scotia

Yashoda Krishna's foster-mother

Yasodhara (Gopa) 'companion to fame', Siddartha's wife, who later became a Buddhist nun

year the passage of the Earth through an octave of twelve cosmic notes or tones; based on the solar year of 365.256 days

Year of Brahma 1,555,200,000,000 years

Yeats, William Butler Irish poet, mystic, occultist; *The Vision*; 1865-1939

yehidah archetype, highest soul aspect in the Kabbalah (Hebrew)

Yellow Castle Taoist term for the Third Eye in the *Secret of the Golden Flower*

Yellow Emperor (Huang Ti) the mythical founder of the first Chinese dynasty and dynamic young monarch who is taught Far Eastern medicine and philosophy in the classics; ca. -2697-2597

Yellow Emperor's Classic of External Medicine lost ancient Chinese medical treatise that may have been found in the Ma-Wang-Tui texts in 1973

Yellow Emperor's Classic of Internal Medicine (Ni-Ching) world's oldest medical book and principal source of Chinese medicine; dating to 5000 B.P.

Yellow Hats Gelugspa Order of Tibet

yellow miso a short-time fermented miso, very mellow in flavor

Yellow Road (Hoang-tao, *Chinese*) ecliptic

Yen Hui Chinese art master; *Two Taoist Immortals*; 14th c.

yerbe mate Latin American evergreen whose leaves make a mate tea

Yerkish an artificial language designed for chimp language experiments

yeshe wisdom (Tibetan). **yeshe chowri** wise fool (Tibetan)

Yesod Kabbalistic sephiroth of form, prudence (Hebrew)

yeti (abominable snowman) mysterious being of the Himalayas

Yggdrasil world tree in Scandinavian mythology

yi 1. righteousness. 2. (cap.) (Lolo) language spoken by 3 million people in Yunnan, China (Chinese)

yidam symbolic tantric deity (Tibetan)

Yiddish Jewish language derived from German during the Middle Ages and written in Hebrew characters

yielding line yin line in the *I Ching*

yihudim spiritual unification exercises (Hebrew)

Yima first man in Avestan mythology

yin n. or adj. 'the shady side of a mountain', 1. the receptive or yielding principle. 2. Earth's force. 3. one of the two fundamental energies of the universe; the relative tendency of expansion, growth, centrifugality, diffusion, cold, darkness, and other qualities whose energy tends to go up and outward. 4. the energy of the rising seed and growing plant. 5. gentle, soft, dark, intuitive, feminine. 6. (too yin) weak, lifeless, unfocused, spaced out (Chinese). v. **yinnize** to expand, spiritualize, relax. v. **yin out** to eat desserts, sweets, and other relaxing yin foods. **yinnization, yinnizing**

yin and yang the law of universal change; the forces and tendencies that differentiate from One Infinity and manifest as centripetal and centifugal energy, space and time, and are the origin of all relative worlds (Michio Kushi)

Relative Tendencies

Yin	Yang
Expansion	Contraction
Diffusion	Fusion
Dispersion	Assimilation
Separation	Gathering
Decomposition	Organization
Passive	Active
Slower	Faster
Shorter wave	Longer wave
Higher frequency	Lower frequency
Ascent	Descent
Vertical	Horizontal
Outward	Inward
Peripheral	Central
Lighter	Heavier
Colder	Hotter
Darker	Brighter

Wetter	Drier
Thinner	Thicker
Larger	Smaller
Longer	Shorter
Softer	Harder
Electron	Proton
N,O,P,Ca, etc.	H,C,Na,As,Mg.etc.
Vibration	Air	Water	Earth
Tropical	Temperate	Polar
Vegetables	Grains	Animals
Female	Male
Hollow	Compacted
Orthosympathetic	Parasympathetic
Gentle	Harsh
Negative	Positive
Defensive	Aggressive
Universal	Specific
Future	Past
Spiritually oriented	Materially oriented
Space	Time

Yin Hsi Chinese gatekeeper who entreated Lao tzu to write the *Tao Te Ching*

Yin-t'o-lo 'Indra', Indian artist and Chinese Ch'an master; *The Monk from Tan-hsia Burning a Wooden Image of the Buddha*; 13th c.

yinnie 1. (slang) one who has eaten excessively yin foods or beverages resulting in an unfocused (yin) condition. 2. a macrobiotic sweet or dessert

yinnie syrup rice syrup

Yippies Youth International Party; politically aware hippies and young people organized by Abbie Hoffman and Jerry Rubin against the Vietnam War and Democratic Convention in Chicago, August, 1968

Yluana Zoroastrian literary utopia by Charles Searle, *The Wanderer*, 1776

Ymir first being in Norse mythology

Yod tenth Hebrew letter: power, J, 10

yodism word for being essential on all levels; dot in an infinite circle (Le Centre du Silence, from Hebrew)

yoga 'yoke', 1. union of self with the absolute or divine. 2. methods or discipline employed to obtain such union. 3. meditative practices originating in pre-Aryan India employed by Hinduism, Buddhism, Jainism, and some Moslems and Christians. 4. one of the orthodox schools of Hindu philosophy (Sanskrit). adj. **yogic**

Types of Yoga

adhyatma	self beyond
bhakti	devotion
hatha	asanas, breath
integral	supermind
japa	chanting holy name
jnana	wisdom
karma	service
kriya	shakti
kundalini	chakras
laya	inner functions
osadhi	herbs
prema	love
purna	supermind
raja	mind control
samye	equality
surat shabd (sehaj)	inner sound

Hatha Yoga Poses

tadasana	mountain pose
dhanurasana	bow pose
ustrasana	camel pose
gomukhasana	cow's head pose
matsyendrasana	fish pose
paschimottanasana	sitting forward bend
bhekasana	frog pose
salamba sirasana	headstand
salabhasan	locust pose
halasana	plough pose
salamba sarvangasana	shoulderstand
uddiyana banmdha	stomach lift
trikonasana	triangle pose

Yogachara Buddhist school developed by Asanga and Vasubandhu that taught the reality of consciousness alone (and not its objects), forerunner of Vajrayana and Tantra, 4th c.

yogamaya power of divine illusion (Sanskrit)

Yogananda, Paramahansa (Mukunda Lal Ghogh) Bengali yogi, founder of the Self-Realization Fellowship in California; *Autobiography of a Yogi*; 1893-1952

yogashakti power of divine union (Sanskrit)

yogashala yoga academy (Sanskrit)

Yogendra Mastamani Indian yogi who brought scientific yoga to America; 1897-

yogeshvara 'Lord of Yoga', title of Krishna (Sanskrit)

yogi (yogin) male practitioner of yoga (Sanskrit)

yogini female practitioner of yoga (Sanskrit)

yollotl heart (Nahuatl)

yolteoti one whose heart is rooted in God (Nahuatl)

yoni vulva; emblem of Shakti's creative power (Sanskrit)

yonimudra closing the ears, eyes, nose, and mouth with the fingers to hear the inner music (Sanskrit)

Yorick jester and childhood companion whose skull Hamlet contemplated

Yoruba 1. language of southwestern Nigeria. 2. people there

Young, Arthur helicopter designer, metaphysical author; *The Invisible Encounter*

youthing growing younger; as opposed to aging

Yril underground country in England and the galvanic force that powers its technology in Lord Lytton's *The Coming Race*, 1871

Ys vanishing city of Breton legend

Yu Chinese Emperor who expanded Fu Hsi's *I Ching* from observing the markings on the back of a giant tortoise in the Lo River; *Writing from the River Lo*; -2115-2197. 2. (l.c.) astral body. 3. (entering point) acupoint on the back where energy enters and goes toward the internal organs (Japanese)

Yu Huang Heavenly Emperor of Jade in Taoism (Chinese)

yu-kai the astral world (Japanese)

yu sen acupoint located in the planteris arch of the foot that affects the kidneys (Chinese)

yu-tai the vibrational body (Japanese)

yuan 1. sublime beginning, first cyclical movement of heaven. 2. (cap.) Chinese dynasty 1279-1368 (Chinese)

yuba soya bean protein in transparent, papery sheets that develops from heating soy milk; commonly available dried and used in many dishes, especially to simulate skin in mock duck and other vegetarian dishes (Japanese)

Yudhishthira eldest Pandu brother, seeker of truth in the *Mahabharata*

yudofu tofu simmered with other vegetables and served with a sauce (Japanese)

yuga one of four world ages in Indian philosophy which progressively decline in moral and spiritual values (Sanskrit)

satyayuga (krityayuga) .... truth
tretayuga .... three-quarters truth
dvaparayuga .... duality
kaliyuga .... dark age

Yun-men Wen-Yen Chinese Ch'an monk who attained satori when his foot was smashed in a door by his master; 864-949

Yunus, Muhammad Bengali economist who initiated microenterprise loans to the poorest people, especially women, to improve the lives of their families

and start small businesses

Yuppies young urban professionals; upwardly mobile boomers, 1980s-

yurt dome-shaped felt or woolen tent (Mongolian)

yuwipi (bundle up) ceremonies among the Lakota

Ywahoo, Dhyani Cherokee healer and director of the Sunray Meditation Society

y'zirah world of formation in the Kabbalah (Hebrew)

Zz

Z secret city of the Amazon

zabuton meditation cushion (Japanese)

Zacharias father of John the Baptist

Zachariel Angel of Administration (Hebrew)

Zachus witness of Jesus's resurrection on the road to Emmaus

zaddik 'righteous', pure ones in Hasidism (Hebrew)

Zaehner, Robert Charles English comparative religionist; *Hindu and Muslim Mysticism*; 1913-74

Zadokite militant Jewish community at Qumran, possibly Essene, named after resistance leader Zadoc, 1st c.

zafu sitting cushion used in Zen, usually made of black cloth about 6" high and 10" in diameter (Japanese)

Zagreus divine child of Orphic myth

Zain 7th Hebrew letter: whistling, Z, 7

Zain, C. C. (Elbert Benjamin) occult author; *The Brotherhood of Light Lessons*; 1882-1951

Zaitsev, Vyacheslav Soviet philologist who postulated Jesus was a cosmonaut; *Temples and Spaceships*

Zalman, Reb Shneur founder of Habad Hassidism (Lubavitch); 1745-1813

Zamenhof, Lazarus Ludwig Polish linguist, inventor of Esperanto; *An Attempt Towards an International Language*; 1859-1917

Zamna Hebrew leader of the Lost Tribes who migrated to the Yucatan and the Southwest (Cayce)

zamzum holy well in Mecca (Arabic)

Zani people of coastal East Africa

zap n. or v. blast, zoom, surprise, fixation

of attention

Zapotec pro-Columbian Mexican culture, unique in building cities on mountain tops

Zappa, Frank avant-garde musician; *The Story of the Mothers*; 1940-

Zarathustra (Zoroaster) 1. Persian prophet. 2. hero of Nietzsche's *Thus Spoke Zarathustra*; -628-551

zarch dome with an elongated center

Zardoz science-fiction film about a mystical elite defeated by primitives, 1973

Zarg sleeping dragon of the apocalypse in Thomas Bearden's *Excalibur Briefing*, 1980

Zariel astrological house system similar to the Meridian Projection

Zatara comic strip magician who spoke commands backwards and turned guns into flowers, 1940s

zawiya (pl. zawaya) 'corner', mosque, saint's tomb, small Sufi center (Arabic)

zazen 1. sitting meditation in Zen (Japanese). 2. a way to be, even when you're not sitting (Gary Snyder)

Zealot militant Jewish sect founded by Judas of Galilee which resisted Roman rule and perished at Masada, 1st c.

Zeiss, Carl optical works in Jena, East Germany, site of first geodesic dome, 1922

Zeitoun Egyptian site of miraculous appearances of Mary, 1968-71

Zelazny, Roger science-fiction writer on mythological themes; *Lord of Light*

Zen (from Zenna, *Japanese,* ch'an, *Chinese,* dhyana, *Sanskrit*) 'meditation', 1. historical Mahayana Buddhist movement introduced into China from India in the 6th c., to Japan from China in the 12th c., and from Japan to the U.S. in the 19th c., emphasizing sudden enlightenment, often through spontaneous madcap behavior, meditation upon paradoxical koans, or simplicity in daily life. 2. the way to enlightenment. 3. seeing your own nature (Bodhidharma). 4. seeing the Pole Star in the Southern sky (*The Book of Tea*)

Zen Center of Los Angeles spiritual community under the direction of Taizan Maezumi-Roshi, 1971-

Zen Patriarchs meditation teachers in direct line from the Buddha who received and transmitted the Dharma through the 7th c.: first twenty-seven were Indian, the last six Chinese:

1	Mahakasyapa
2	Ananda
3	Sanakavasa
4	Upagupta
5	Dhritaka
6	Michaka
7	Vasumitra
8	Buddhanandi
9	Buddhamitra
10	Parsva
11	Punyayasa
12	Asvaghosa
13	Kapimala
14	Nagarjuna
15	Kanadeva
16	Rahulata
17	Sanghanandi
18	Gayasata
19	Kumarata
20	Jayata
21	Vasubandhu
22	Manorhita
23	Haklenayasa
24	Simha
25	Basiasita
26	Punyamitra
27	Prajnatara
28	Bodhidharma
29	Hui K'u
30	Seng Tsan
31	Tao Hsin
32	Hung Yen
33	Hui Neng

zen-e enlightenment encounter between Zen monks or masters, usually by chance (Japanese)

Zenar Cards ESP deck of twenty-five cards with symbols of stars, circles, squares, crosses, and waves

zenbo Zen student (Japanese)

Zend father of Zoroaster, former incarnation of Jesus (Cayce)

zendo Zen meditation hall (Japanese)

zenic (zennic) adj. Zen

Zenist practitioner of Zen

zenith point directly overhead

zenji Zen master, abbot (Japanese)

zenkiga painting of Zen activity (Japanese)

Zeno of Elea Greek philosopher and maker of paradoxes; -5th c.

Zenshuji Soto Mission North American headquarters for Soto Zen Buddhism, 1927-

Zeta Reticuli star in the southern constellation Reticulus with a planet where UFOs which abducted Betty and Barney Hill are said to originate

zetetic skeptically inquiring

Zeus 1. chief Greek god. 2. third Uranian planet ruling warfare, new beings, controlled, directed energy

zhen jiu acupuncture (Chinese)

Ziggurat spiral-shaped sacred building in Mesopotamia

Zimbabwe 1. ancient stone acropolis in East Africa. 2. unknown high culture of that area. 3. African nation, formerly Rhodesia

Zimmer, Heinrich German Indologist; *Myth and Symbol in Indian Art and Civilization*; 1890-1943

zimzum contraction barrier of infinity in the Kabbalah (Hebrew)

zinjanthropus humanlike being excavated in Tanzania in 1959, 1.7 million B.P.

Zinn, Howard historian, social activist; *SNCC: The New Abolitionists*; 1922-

Zion 1. Jerusalem hill, site of the Temple of David. 2. heaven, city of God. 3. Jewish people

Zipangu medieval European name for Japan; goal of Columbus's first voyage

Ziusudra flood survivor who escaped with his family and livestock in a boat in Sumerian mythology

ziyarat pilgrimage to a shrine (Arabic)

zizal-xiu Mayan plant hailed for its immortal qualities

Zoan Egyptian mystery school where Jesus studied (Cayce)

Zoar cooperative village in Ohio led by Joseph Bimeler, 1817-98

Zobo period of the image law; Mahayana era (Japanese)

Zocolo site in Mexico of the Aztec calendar stone

zodiac twelve divisions of the sky along the ecliptic:

Aries	Mar. 21 -Apr. 20
Taurus	Apr. 21 - May 20
Gemini	May 21 - June 21
Cancer	June 22 - July 22
Leo	July 23 - Aug. 23
Virgo	Aug. 24 - Sept. 22
Libra	Sept. 23 - Oct. 22
Scorpio	Oct. 23 - Nov. 22
Sagittarius	Nov. 23 - Dec. 21
Capricorn	Dec. 22 - Jan. 20
Aquarius	Jan. 21 - Feb. 19
Pisces	Feb. 20 - Mar. 20

Zoe life, personified as a female spirit (Greek)

Zohar 'Splendor', Kabbalistic work introduced in Spain by Moses de Leon, 13th c. (Hebrew and Aramaic)

zome irregular dome invented by Steve Baer

zone therapy (reflexology) health practice based on the belief that every organ of the body is connected to a different spot on the bottom of the foot, the roof of the mouth, and the hands; invented by William H. Fitzgerald

zoni miso or clear soup made with mochi (Japanese)

zonked adj. high, intoxicated

Zonker zonked out character in *Doonesbury*

Zoques South Mexican people at the time of the Conquest

Zoroaster (Zarathustra) Persian prophet; -628-551 (Greek)

Zoroastrianism way of life based on the teachings of Zoroaster which flourished in Persia until the Arab conquest

Zosimos Greek alchemist; *Treatise on Instruments and Furnaces*; 4th c.

Zostrianos an ancient Persian seer whose mystical ascent of the soul is described in an autobiographical account by this name in the Nag Hammadi scriptures

Zozer founder of Egypt's III Dynasty, patron of Imhotep; ca. -2980-50

Zro ambrosial substance subjected to alchemical purification in Atlantis (Crowley)

Zu Caucasian tribe that invaded Egypt and set up the I Dynasty (Cayce)

zuchini long green squash

zuhd detachment from the world (Arabic)

Zukav, Gary quantum physicist; *The Dancing Wu Li Masters*; 1943-

Zuleika Potiphar's wife, beloved of Joseph

Zulu major Bantu language of South Africa

Zululand home of 4 million people in Natal, South Africa

Zuni (Spanish corruption of *A shiwi*, 'the flesh') Native people of the Southwest

Zurbaran, Francisco Spanish artist, ascetic; *St. Francis*; 1598-1664

Zurvan Persian God of Time

Zuyua language of Maya initiates

zybicolin substance in miso that helps bind and eliminate radioactive elements from the body

Resources

New Words

The editor would appreciate receiving comments and reflections on this edition of the *The New Age Dictionary*. Reviews, corrections, suggestions for new entries in future editions, and other correspondence may be sent to:

Alex Jack
Box 487
Becket, Mass. 01223

The New Age Dictionary On Line

An Unabridged New Age Data Base is being compiled, and we hope to make it available on disk for both Macintosh and IBM-compatible computers. The electronic version will contain all of the entries in this edition of *The New Age Dictionary* as well as several thousand additional terms relating to spiritual practice, holistic health, new communities, and planetary thinkers.

This software can be used in word processing, searching for correspondences and concepts (e.g., locating all the key terms of Gandhi or Alice Bailey), and creating a customized Living Dictionary with words, concepts, and biographical entries added to the dictionary from your own reading, life, and experience.

For further information, please send your name and address to New Age Data Base, c/o Kanthaka Press, Box 696, Brookline Village, Mass. 02147.

Spiritual Development Training Seminars

The Spiritual Development Program is a series of ten seminars presented by educators Michio and Aveline Kushi dealing with the development of consciousness toward infinite spiritual realization and an understanding of past and future worlds, including an introduction to the language of the ancient spiritual One World. Each 4 to 5-day session includes lectures, chanting, meditation, the use of sound and vibration for healing, the study of the teachings of Jesus, Buddha, Lao Tzu, and spiritual classics from around the world, and simple macrobiotic meals with an emphasis on thorough chewing. For further information, contact the Kushi Institute of the Berkshires, Box 7, Becket, Mass. 01223 (413) 623-5742.

One Peaceful World Network

The One Peaceful World Network is an international society of individuals, families, and organizations devoted to creating a healthy, peaceful world. Global headquarters are located at the One Peaceful World Village, a 600-acre community of friends actively pursuing personal and planetary health in Becket, Mass. Members receive invitations to conferences and special events, discounts on books and cassettes, and the quarterly *One Peaceful World Newsletter* edited by Alex Jack. For membership information, please contact One Peaceful World, Box 10, Becket, Mass. 01223.